THE CZECH MANUSCRIPTS

A volume in the NIU Series in

Slavic, East European, and Eurasian Studies

Edited by Christine D. Worobec

For a list of books in the series, visit our website at cornellpress.cornell.edu.

THE CZECH MANUSCRIPTS

FORGERY, TRANSLATION, AND NATIONAL MYTH

DAVID L. COOPER

NORTHERN ILLINOIS UNIVERSITY PRESS
AN IMPRINT OF
CORNELL UNIVERSITY PRESS
Ithaca and London

First published 2023 by Cornell University Press

Library of Congress Cataloging-in-Publication Data

Names: Cooper, David L., 1970– author.
Title: The Czech manuscripts : forgery, translation, and national myth / David L. Cooper.
Description: Ithaca : Northern Illinois University Press, an imprint of Cornell University Press, 2023. | Series: NIU series in Slavic, East European, and Eurasian studies | Includes bibliographical references and index.
Identifiers: LCCN 2022060660 (print) | LCCN 2022060661 (ebook) | ISBN 9781501771934 (hardcover) | ISBN 9781501771941 (epub) | ISBN 9781501771958 (pdf)
Subjects: LCSH: Hanka, Václav, 1791-1861. Rukopis Královédvorský. | Hanka, Václav, 1791–1861. Zelenohorský rukopis. | Czech literature—19th century. | Literary forgeries and mystifications—History—19th century. | Nationalism and literature.
Classification: LCC PG5022 .C66 2023 (print) | LCC PG5022 (ebook) | DDC 491.8/6—dc23/eng/20230302
LC record available at https://lccn.loc.gov/2022060660
LC ebook record available at https://lccn.loc.gov/2022060661

To my parents, who have always been the genuine article.

Contents

Acknowledgments

Writing this book took a whole lot of time and a little bit of money. I would like to thank the sources that freed up that time and provided the funds, in larger and smaller amounts. The University of Illinois Campus Research Board enabled initial research on this project in spring 2012 with travel funding and Humanities Released Time, and the research was generously supported by a grant from the National Council for Eurasian and East European Research, Title VIII National Research Competition. Annual university humanities/arts scholarship support funding kept the work humming from year to year, and a recent semester teaching release and semester-long sabbatical in fall 2021 enabled the completion of the manuscript. A generous Faculty Fellowship from the National Center for Supercomputing Applications (NCSA) at the University of Illinois Urbana-Champaign (UIUC) enabled a yearlong project to conduct some digital textual analysis to round out the study.

An earlier version of chapter 1 appeared as "Padělky jako romantická forma autorství: *Rukopisy královédvorský a zelenohorský* ze srovnávací perspektivy," *Česká literatura* 60, no. 1 (2012): 26–44. Many thanks to the editors for permission to reprint here.

Many colleagues have supported, encouraged, and contributed to this book over the years. My biggest debt is to Dalibor Dobiáš and Michal Charypar, along with members of the nineteenth-century group and others at the Institute for Czech Literature, Czech Academy of Sciences, in Prague, who answered my questions, assisted with publications, and always made me welcome: Michal Fránek, Martin Hrdina, Iva Krejčová, Václav Petrbok, Kateřina Piorecká, Petr Plecháč, and Michael Wögerbauer. Dalibor Dobiáš offered valuable advice and suggestions for chapters 1 and 4 in particular and translated my work for publications in Czech. Michal Charypar gave invaluable support in related projects. My thanks to the librarians of the Institute for Czech Literature's library, where I spent many pleasant and fruitful hours in 2012 and 2015. My fantastic colleagues at UIUC inspire me, support me, and generally make working there very rewarding. Thanks to Eugene Avrutin, Felix Cowan,

Maureen Marshall, Harriet Murav, John Randolph, and Daria Semenova for important opportunities, comments, and questions. Nadia Hoppe assisted in gathering critical resources as my research assistant. Thanks also to Laura Davies Brenier, Michael Finke, George Gasyna, Roman Ivashkiv, Lilya Kaganovsky, Richard Tempest, Peter Wright, Donna Buchanan, Zsuzsa Gille, Jessica Greenberg, Joe Lenkart, Olga Maslova, Judith Pintar, Valleri Robinson, Kristin Romberg, Dmitry Tartakovsky, and Maria Todorova. In the dark days of the COVID-19 pandemic, fall and winter of 2020–21, my digital project team of Michal Ondřejček and Demetry Ogoltsev were the best working and social group imaginable, keeping me sane and productive. Among the colleagues who have offered me the opportunity to give lectures or have heard and commented on my work at conferences and supported it, I would like to thank Jindřich Toman, William Nickell, Hana Waisserová, Dirk Uffelmann, Tetyana Dzyadevych, Olena Betlii, Masako Fidler, Jonathan Bolton, Christopher Harwood, Yuliya Ilchuk, and Angelina Ilieva, along with many more here unnamed.

Many thanks to Andrew Drozd and a second, anonymous reviewer for the press for very helpful comments and suggestions for revision that have made this book better and hopefully more appealing to a broader audience. Special thanks to Amy Farranto of the University of Northern Illinois Press for believing in the project, and to her colleagues there and at Cornell University Press, Ellen Labbate, Karen Laun, Alfredo Gutierrez Rios, Michelle Scott, Jane Lichty, and the entire team for turning the manuscript into a lovely book.

Last here, but first in order of importance, I want to thank my family. The pandemic, for all its real inconveniences, alienations, and tragedies, also had a small upside for our family as the rush of school and work activities came to a sudden halt and we suddenly began to quietly enjoy each other's company again. I could ask for no better companions in life. My daughters, Nika and Lana, inspire me and make me proud. And my dear wife, Valeria, is not only my closest friend but also a dedicated colleague and constant support in work and in life, and I cannot imagine doing any of this without her.

Note on Transliteration

For notes, bibliographic entries, and titles in the text I employ a simplified Library of Congress transliteration for Cyrillic and Greek text. Names in the text are also transliterated using this system, but Russian names with more established English forms, like Zhukovsky or Gilferding, are given in those standard forms. For quotations and examples in the text, I have departed from this usual system and instead employed the scholarly or scientific transliteration system for Russian Cyrillic, for two reasons: (1) this system is closer to Czech and Bosnian/Croatian/Serbian (BCS) Latin orthography and makes the parallels and borrowings between the languages far more visible in the examples, and (2) this also makes the examples more legible to Czech scholars.

Chronology

Highlights and Lowlights in the Life of the Manuscripts

1816 Josef Linda discovers, in the presence of his roommate Václav Hanka, a parchment in the binding of a book he had been using as a footrest, on which was inscribed the "Píseň na Vyšehrad" (Song to Vyšehrad).

1817 September 16, Hanka finds the Rukopis královédvorský (Queen's Court Manuscript) in the vault of the St. John the Baptist Church tower in Dvůr Králové.

1818 October, Hanka publishes the first edition of the Queen's Court Manuscript, with translations into modern Czech and German. The edition is dated 1819.

November, Count František Kolovrat receives an anonymous package with the Rukopis zelenohorský (Green Mountain Manuscript) and an accompanying letter indicating it was intended for the collection of the new National Museum. Josef Dobrovský quickly identifies it as a falsification.

1819 April, Linda's friend J. N. V. Zimmerman sends the National Museum a parchment with the "Milostná píseň Krále Václava" (Love song of King Václav), which he found in the binding of another book.

1821 Admiral Aleksandr Shishkov publishes the Green Mountain Manuscript, accompanied by a Russian translation, in the journal of the Russian Academy.

Josef Bergler, the head of the Prague Academy, on the commission of Count Kolovrat, paints *Libuše's Judgment* in a manner, based on the Green Mountain Manuscript narrative, that departs from previous treatments of the traditional theme.[1]

1822 The Green Mountain Manuscript is first published for the Czech audience in the new journal *Krok*. A German translation by Jan Ritter z Rittersberku appears as well in the Prague journal *Der Kranz*.

1823 Johann Wolfgang von Goethe publishes his version of "The Nosegay" from the Queen's Court Manuscript (a rearrangement of Václav Svoboda's German translation with several added lines).[2] This interest from one of Bohemia's literary idols is seen as a validation of the worth of the manuscript, and the aged poet's brief efforts to study Czech grammar develops into a legend traded among Czechs, which suggests these derived from his desire to read the manuscript in the original.[3]

1824 Dobrovský publishes his objections to the Green Mountain Manuscript. Svoboda replies, and Dobrovský responds. The first polemics thus take place in the German language.[4] Dobrovský does not name his suspects in the polemics, but identifies them in letters and privately names Hanka, Linda, and Josef Jungmann as the likely falsifiers.

1826 The first of the cover falsifications appears. July 14, Eberhard Gottlieb Graff, in the presence of Hanka, discovers a large number of Old Czech glosses in the National Museum's thirteenth-century manuscript copy of the *Mater verborum*, a popular Latin dictionary.

Composer Václav Jan Tomášek sets the lyric songs of the Queen's Court Manuscript to music for piano and voice (op. 82).[5]

1827 Hanka finds and publishes Old Czech translations of parts of two psalms in the museum's copy of a Latin psalter with glosses in Old Czech, known as the Glossed Psalter.

1828 Hanka finds parchment leaves, again in the binding of a book, containing fragments of a Latin Gospel of St. John with an interlineal translation into Old Czech from the eleventh century. Dobrovský, initially convinced, quickly changes his mind and declares it a forgery.

1829 Dobrovský passes on January 6.

Hanka and Svoboda publish the second edition of the Queen's Court Manuscript, including with it the Green Mountain Manuscript, "Song to Vyšehrad," and "Love Song of King Václav," a practice that will be common for many subsequent editions of the manuscript.

1832 Sir John Bowring publishes the first anthology of Czech literature in English, the *Cheskian Anthology: Being a History of the Poetical*

Literature of Bohemia, with Translated Specimens. It mentions the Green Mountain Manuscript, includes samples from the Queen's Court Manuscript, and unwittingly includes other literary mystifications from the period.

1839 At the request of František Palacký and Pavel Josef Šafařík, August Corda conducts the first chemical and microscopic analysis of the Green Mountain Manuscript and finds it "as old as possible" (*na nejvýš starý*).[6]

1840 Palacký and Šafařík publish *Die ältesten Denkmäler der böhmischen Sprache* (The oldest works of the Czech language), an edition and defense of the authenticity of the Green Mountain Manuscript and the Old Czech Gospel of St. John that became a model for subsequent defenses of the manuscripts. They respond in detail to each point of criticism by Dobrovský and include Corda's conclusions.[7]

1849 Hanka discovers and publishes seven parchment strips, found again in the binding of a book in the National Museum Library, containing "Libuše's Prophecy" in Old Czech.

1852 Albert Henry Wratislaw publishes *The Queen's Court Manuscript, with Other Ancient Bohemian Poems*, the first full edition of the manuscripts in English.

Hanka publishes *Polyglotta kralodvorského rukopisu*, a multilingual edition of the Queen's Court Manuscript (already his tenth edition), with full translations (sometimes also including the Green Mountain Manuscript, "Song to Vyšehrad," and "Love Song of King Václav") into Croatian, English, German, Italian, Polish, Russian, Serbian, and Upper Sorbian and partial translations into Bulgarian, French, Lower Sorbian, Slovenian, and Ukrainian.

1857 September 29, a fortieth anniversary celebration of the discovery of the Queen's Court Manuscript is held in Dvůr Králové. It is attended by Hanka and a few other Prague cultural figures and includes the unveiling of a statue of Záboj, an epic hero from the Queen's Court Manuscript, by František Wagner. The local commemorations, which started in 1845, begin to have national reach and clearly put the manuscript into the developing national symbolic complex.

A National Museum commission subjects the "Love Song of King Václav" and "Song to Vyšehrad" to chemical tests at the request of Julius Feifalik, who had published philological evidence that the former was a modern fake. Both are found false, but the conclusion published in the museum's journal the following year only names the "Love Song."[8]

Josef Mánes undertakes work on illustrations for the manuscripts. A partial edition (for the epic about Záboj) is published in 1860, but the full edition waits until 1886 for publication, when it must compete with editions by younger artists. The manuscripts play a key role in working out a national style in Czech visual art in the nineteenth century.[9]

1858 The Prague newspaper *Tagesbote aus Böhmen* publishes a series of articles on literary forgeries, ending with the Queen's Court Manuscript and implying that Hanka was its author. Hanka, after some hesitation, sues the publisher, David Kuh, for libel. The hearing is held August 25, 1859, and Kuh is convicted. His appeal in Prague fails, but Kuh's sentence is vacated by the Viennese High Court in April 1860.

During the trial process, which examines the evidence regarding the discovery of the manuscripts, Václav Vladivoj Tomek is able to uncover evidence that shows that the manuscript hitherto known as "Libuše's Judgment" had been found at the castle Zelená Hora u Nepomuku.

The trial is also accompanied by scholarly polemics. Feifalik and Max Büdinger both publish articles with arguments calling the authenticity of the Queen's Court Manuscript into doubt, and Palacký and Václav Nebeský reply.[10]

1861 Hanka passes on January 11. His huge funeral celebration joins together elements from the anniversary celebrations of the Queen's Court Manuscript in Dvůr Králové with aspects of other recent funerals of major Czech national figures.

1867 September 28–30, the fiftieth anniversary of the Queen's Court Manuscript is celebrated in Dvůr Králové. The event is attended by the elite of the Czech national movement and delegates from patriotic associations around the country. The desire to celebrate the sacred national symbol that the manuscripts had become mixes with protest against the new Austrian and Hungarian dual monarchy that left Bohemian state rights again unrecognized.

1872 Antonín Dvořák composes musical settings for the lyric songs of the Queen's Court Manuscript (op. 7).

1877 Antonín Baum and Adolf Patera publish their argument, in the journal of the National Museum, that most of the Old Czech glosses in the *Mater verborum* are recent additions. Patera had done the paleographic analysis over a decade earlier.

1878 Alois Vojtěch Šembera, a Moravian Czech and professor of Czech language and literature at the University of Vienna, in updates to his history of Czech literature names the Green Mountain Manuscript a fake by Linda. The reaction in the Czech press is negative and swift, even preceding the publication of Šembera's argument.[11]

1879 Antonín Vašek, also a Moravian and a secondary school teacher, publishes his argument that the Queen's Court Manuscript and the interlineal translation of the Gospel of St. John are falsifications by Hanka.[12]

1881 The National Theater, for which many small donations have been collected from the Czech people over many years, opens with the premier of Bedřich Smetana's opera *Libuše*, with a libretto by Josef Wenzig that draws liberally from the Green Mountain Manuscript for act 1, depicting Libuše's judgment.[13]

Later that year the theater is destroyed by fire. A determined effort to collect new funds and rebuild results in its reopening in 1883.

Decorations for the theater include statues on the exterior of Lumír and Záboj by Antonín Pavel Wagner and a cycle of patriotic paintings in the foyer by František Ženíšek and Mikoláš Aleš that reference the manuscripts.

1886 February, the campaign against the manuscripts begins in the journal *Athenaeum*, with Tomáš Garrigue Masaryk and the linguist Jan Gebauer in the lead. In the course of a year and a half, the polemics in major journals and newspapers would result in the publication of over 130 articles.

The Executive Council of the National Museum convenes a committee to undertake a thorough chemical and microscopic study of the Queen's Court Manuscript. The chemists Vojtěch Šafařík and Antonín Bělohoubek each conduct separate studies and conclude that the manuscript behaves in the manner expected for old manuscripts.[14]

Aleš begins publication of his illustrated edition of the manuscripts. The edition continues to 1889.[15]

1893 With an Austrian revision of school textbooks, the manuscripts disappear from the official school curriculum (until 1908). This appears to be not as a result of a consensus that they were false but instead due to their extremely controversial aspect. Both sides of the dispute want them to be included in the school curriculum, and they continue to be addressed by teachers and taught in private lessons.[16]

1899 Ladislav Dolanský claims to find a more direct piece of evidence for Hanka's involvement. He deciphers, in the red and black jumble of lines on the end of the third line from the bottom of the fourth page of the Green Mountain Manuscript, the Latin phrase "V. Hanka fecit" (V. Hanka made it). This quickly becomes a key piece of evidence for the falsification, seemingly by Hanka's own admission.[17]

1890s–1900s Continuing scholarly debates result in the consolidation of evidence and the integration of the manuscripts into the study of the early National Revival, particularly in the work of Josef Hanuš and Jan Máchal. New evidence of other forgeries by Hanka also emerges, like the coins, supposedly from the era of Rostislav of Moravia (840–71), added to the museum's collection in 1841.[18]

1911 When D. Žunkovič and B. Střemcha publish their photos of the "V. Hanka fecit" cryptogram, Dolanský's mystification regarding this direct evidence falls.

December, Josef Ladislav Píč submits the Queen's Court Manuscript to analysis by French paleographers and publishes an article in which he claims they support its authenticity. An anonymous article published the following day accuses Píč of contorting the generic conclusions of the foreign experts. One day later, Píč shoots himself in reaction to the criticism and the accusation of unauthorized mistreatment of the manuscript.[19]

December 31, a group of forty-five prominent scholars issues a statement in the national newspaper *Národní listy*, offering a summary position on the manuscripts as falsifications in an attempt to put an end to the still divisive discussion. The flurry of articles begun this year nonetheless continues into 1912.

1917 The wartime one hundredth anniversary of the discovery of the Queen's Court Manuscript is marked modestly by commemorative articles in major media outlets.

1927 Professor František Mareš, an outstanding physiologist and twice rector of Charles University, begins to publicly defend the manuscripts. The cause is taken up enthusiastically by Czech fascist political organizations but also has some broader support. Mareš's arguments place the conclusions of the natural sciences above those of the human and social sciences, whose evidentiary value he distrusts.[20]

1928 Alphonse Mucha completes his *Slavic Epic*, a series of twenty monumental canvases on Slavic historical themes begun in 1910. Absent are major themes or even discernable details derived from the manuscripts, an omission that would have been unthinkable to the previous generation of artists but that reflects the new stigma attached to the manuscripts.

1932 The Czechoslovak Manuscript Society is founded to pursue the scholarly defense of the manuscripts, keeping some distance from more political activities.

1937 The political aspect of defenses becomes increasingly strident and radical in the later 1930s. A lecture series in this year at Charles University is attended by large numbers from the fascist Vlajka organization, who manifest their disagreement with increasing intensity. The final lecture, by Zdeněk Nejedlý, has to be cut short.[21]

1952 The Czechoslovak Manuscript Society disbands. The association of the manuscript defenses in the interwar period with fascism makes their position impossible in the new socialist state.

1967 The 150th anniversary of the Queen's Court Manuscript prompts renewed scholarly activity. The journalist Miroslav Ivanov arranges for the manuscripts to again be submitted to chemical and microscopic analysis, this time by the Criminal Institute. Its work is interrupted by the Warsaw Pact invasion in 1968 and the subsequent institutional purges and is only completed in 1971. Ivanov publishes their partial results in 1969 in his book on the manuscripts, but the publication of the full protocols is delayed until 1994. In the meantime, the Criminal Institute distances itself from the study.

The results show that the Queen's Court and Green Mountain Manuscripts are palimpsests, that newer Latin texts had been scraped from the parchment and the "older" Czech texts written on top, using unusual writing instruments and preparations.[22]

1969 The Czech Academy of Sciences publishes its monumental study of the current state of knowledge of the manuscripts, *Rukopisy královédvorský a zelenohorský: Dnešní stav poznání*, edited by Mojmír Otruba.

1993 The postsocialist period sees the renewed activities of what is now known as the Czech Manuscript Society (the split of Czechoslovakia occurred January 1, 1993), preceded by the founding of its own publishing house, Neklan, in 1991.

Julius Enders publishes two studies of the manuscripts with Neklan, on the language of the texts and on their oral poetics. The latter, in its use of oral-formulaic theory, offers one of the first potentially useful innovations in methodology to come from the ranks of the defenders in many years. But there is little productive dialogue and engagement between the two sides.

Vladimír Macura publishes a number of articles and studies in this period that treat the manuscripts in the context of the play and mystification he finds characteristic of the Czech National Revival.

1996 Jiří Urban and Karel Nesměrák, members of the Czech Manuscript Society, publish *Fakta o protokolech RKZ*, disputing the protocols published by the National Museum on Ivanov and the Criminal Institute's tests.

1998 Miloš Urban, under the pseudonym Josef Urban, publishes the novel *Poslední tečka za Rukopisy (Nová literatura faktu)* (The final word on the manuscripts [A new nonfiction]). The novel marks a new manner of artistically treating the matter of the manuscripts, where the scholarly and political disputes are now the subject of artistic reinterpretation.

2004 April 16, Miroslav Pudlák's postmodern opera *Sasíci v Čechách aneb Marnost bojů proti Rukopisy* (Saxons in the Czech lands, or The futility of the battles against the manuscripts) opens and closes the same day.[23]

2008 October 28, the play *České nebe* (Czech heavens) premiers at the Theater of Jára Cimrman on the state holiday marking the founding of Czechoslovakia. In the play within the play, which stages a found manuscript supposedly authored by Cimrman, Hanka and Linda are judged unworthy of entry into the Czech heavens by a panel of distinguished historical Czech figures.

2017 The two hundredth anniversary of the manuscripts is commemorated in Prague and Dvůr Králové and at the Zelená Hora castle. Events include museum exhibits, dramatic presentations, musical performances, lectures, and radio broadcasts, extending from early September through January 2018. The National Museum exhibits the original Queen's Court and Green Mountain Manuscripts, which also are displayed for two days in October near the sites of their "discovery."

2018 The National Museum publishes the results of its most recent scientific study of the manuscripts, which, to the chagrin of the Czech Manuscript Society, does not offer any evidence to support or deny their authenticity, but instead, as planned, documents their physical condition to determine means for their preservation.

THE CZECH MANUSCRIPTS

Introduction
The Phenomenon of the Manuscripts

In the second decade of the nineteenth century, the Czech national movement was entering into a new phase. The few small circles of nationally minded Czech patriots embraced a program for the revival of the Czech language and, consequently, the Czech nation and gradually began to actively recruit new members to the national cause. The program had been outlined by Josef Jungmann (1773–1847) in 1806 in a pair of programmatic dialogues, "On the Czech Language."[1] Jungmann saw language as the primary sign reflecting national cultural identity. Language was "a great warehouse of all the arts and human knowledge . . . [and] the most superb philosophy, adapted to the particular geographic latitude, mores, ways of thinking, inclinations, and the thousands of distinctions of each nation."[2] Unfortunately, for over a century the Czech language had fallen into disuse as a language of culture, due to the particular linguistic politics of the Counter-Reformation in the Czech lands. As a result, Czech was no longer really a language of higher culture and higher learning, unlike German and French. For Jungmann, it was contradictory for Czechs to become educated, to attain to higher culture, in German or French, because the Czech language was essential to their own cultural identity. By his logic, it was imperative for any speaker of Czech to pursue the cultivation of the Czech language and to pursue their own cultivation in Czech.

Cultivating the Czech language as a means for the reestablishment of Czech culture meant, above all else, writing in Czech in all artistic and learned genres.

This was implicitly a program for the creation of a simulacrum, the invention of cultured discourse in Czech for an elite Czech-speaking audience that did not yet exist. It was explicitly aimed at winning Czechs away from the use of German, the language of education in the Czech lands, as a culture language, creating a Czech discourse that could match the refined German poetic idiom and German as a language of scholarship, both products of the renaissance of German culture that had occurred in the recent decades. Practically, the program pursued the development of a distinct Czech idiom for high literary genres and the creation of technical vocabulary for scholarship and the sciences by means of translation of foreign works and the borrowing of vocabulary from other Slavic languages. Jungmann himself showed the way in his many poetic and scholarly translations, including a translation of Milton's epic *Paradise Lost*, published in 1811, that borrowed extensively from Polish and Russian to fill perceived gaps in Czech poetic vocabulary.[3]

Václav Hanka (1791–1861), like his friends Josef Linda and Václav Svoboda, was a typical member of the generation of Jungmann's followers. When Hanka came to Prague to begin his studies at the university in 1809, he soon joined a group of fellow students who participated in a kind of friendly literary society in which they read works in Czech, made small translations from foreign works into Czech, and composed their own verse in Czech, proclaiming it at their meetings and engaging in mutual critique, activities entirely in line with Jungmann's program. He quickly became a leader among these nationally conscious students, whose activities expanded to include public lectures and amateur theater presentations.[4] But poetry was the leading literary genre of the day, and it was in the creation of a distinct language for poetry that so many new Czech patriots engaged to express their nationalist sentiments and ambitions. The turn from writing verse in German to writing in Czech was a frequent sign of the successful recruitment of a new member of the national community, like Matěj Polák, a talented poet who published his first verses in Czech in 1813 and took the markedly Czech patriotic name Milota Zdirad Polák as an additional sign of his belonging to the Czech community. The students could also attend the lectures on Czech language and literature at the university by professor Jan Nejedlý, but Hanka and some others wanted more. In 1813, Hanka and Linda joined the private seminar on Slavistics taught by Josef Dobrovský (1853–1829), who was the leading expert at the time on Slavic antiquities and Slavic philology. Hanka impressed Dobrovský quickly with his knowledge of Slavic languages (he had picked up some Serbian in his youth from soldiers camped in his hometown) and soon became his favorite student, for Hanka studied Slavistics with more enthusiasm and success than in his university studies of law.[5]

Dobrovský was interested in the discovery and publication of older Czech literary works and had a particular interest in finding genuinely old folk songs. From 1807 to 1811, he had been in correspondence with the Grimm brothers regarding the late twelfth-century Old East Slavic myth-epic *Slovo o polku Igoreve* (Igor tale). The Grimms and other German researchers were actively collecting examples of European epic poetry as foundational works for how they were reconceiving the histories of European national literatures, and in 1811 Jacob Grimm inquired if the Slavs might not have some material to compare to the Islandic Edda songs. Dobrovský replied that there may have been such material in the manuscript that contained the *Igor Tale* (a speculation that looks highly unlikely now), but that it had not been published, and instead offered a new translation of the *Igor Tale* into German by one of his students.[6] This is but one inquiry among what was likely very many, but as Dobrovský and others searched the Czech archives, they failed to find the kind of old mythic and epic poetic works that were most in demand.

In addition to what he may have learned from Dobrovský, Hanka got another lesson in the vital interest in old folk poetry from the success of his acquaintance and peer Vuk Karadžić. Hanka went to Vienna to continue his studies of law at the university there in December 1813, remaining for a year. While there, he continued to pursue his interest in Slavistics with Dobrovský's Slovenian correspondent, Jernej Kopitar, who was assisting and encouraging Karadžić with his new Serbian grammar and first publication of folk songs, the *Mala prostonarodnja slaveno-serbska pesnarica* (Little Slavo-Serbian folk songbook, 1814).[7] Hanka welcomed the volume in a small anonymous review article in the Vienna Czech periodical *Prvotiny pěkných umění* (First-fruits of the fine arts), to which he had become a regular contributor, concluding the review with a translation into Czech of a song.[8] Karadžić's songs, particularly following his second publication in 1815, would soon take Europe by storm. That collection included traditional epic songs that treated a foundational moment in Serbian national history, the late fourteenth-century Battle of Kosovo. For the Czechs' own current battle to win hearts and minds over to Czech poetry from German, Karadžić showed that the insurmountable difficulty of competing with the national idols Schiller and Goethe on the field of contemporary poetry could be avoided and that even German minds could be captivated by older Slavic epic and folk poetry.

On returning to Prague, Hanka took his place as a recognized leader in the young patriotic circles, which included appreciation for his talents as a poet. He conducted lectures in Czech language for his peers at the university starting in 1816, until forbidden in 1817.[9] He published his own collections of "original songs" (1815, 1816), which were folk song imitations, many the product of hidden translations or adaptations of published Russian folk songs, and published a volume of translations from Karadžić's songs in 1817.

And then, in September 1817, Hanka made what seemed to be the most momentous discovery. While visiting his home region in eastern Bohemia, he uncovered a small manuscript in Old Czech in the vault of the church tower in Dvůr Králové. He wrote to Dobrovský the following day announcing his discovery and giving details of its age and contents: a fragment containing the oldest Czech poems yet discovered, perhaps from the twelfth century, mostly on military matters and infused with a "truly Homeric" spirit.[10] Dobrovský, suspecting nothing, welcomed the manuscript and considered it the finest example of Old Czech poetry. But just over a year later, another manuscript appeared that aroused Dobrovský's suspicions of Hanka and his roommate Linda, though it came without any apparent connection to the two. Instead, it was sent anonymously to the highest official in the Bohemian Kingdom as a donation to the newly formed National Museum, where Dobrovský served on the board. It contained a poem in epic form whose theme was a legendary tale from the founding of the first Czech ruling dynasty and with orthography and linguistic forms that suggested it was a few centuries older than even Hanka's remarkable find. Dobrovský blocked the museum from adding it to its collections and privately suggested that he knew its authors, his students Hanka and Linda, along with Jungmann.

But the second manuscript was promoted by others, particularly by Jungmann and his brother Antonín, which eventually forced Dobrovský to publicly declare it a fraud in 1824. Svoboda was the only one brave (or foolish) enough to openly engage Dobrovský in polemics and defend his friends from the implicit charge of forgery and the old Czechs from the explicit charge that they were not culturally developed enough in the late ninth century to produce such a manuscript and the advanced forms of statehood it reflected. The controversy over the second manuscript did not yet touch Hanka's initial discovery, which he published in late 1818 and which was welcomed by domestic and foreign experts. The controversy was one of several that divided Dobrovský as a respected Czech leader from the younger generation and its nationalist pursuits, and the dispute lingered past the death of Dobrovský in 1829, with many younger nationalists determined to see the second manuscript absolved of his charges. Finally, in 1840, after many years of promising, František Palacký, author of the first history of the Czech nation, along with Pavel Josef Šafařík, the new leading expert in Slavistics, published an expert defense that responded to Dobrovský's criticisms point by point, enabling Czech nationalist patriots to finally embrace the second manuscript fully along with Hanka's discovery. The manuscripts grew in significance and reputation along with the Czech national movement in the decades to come.

The Manuscripts Phenomenon

The Czech forged manuscripts were one of the longest-lived romantic literary forgeries. They have been called "the most important Macphersonian (or Ossianic) forgery."[11] Nearly seventy years passed between their "discovery" and the definitive demonstrations of their falsehood, but their success was not just in fooling the experts for so long. They were, simply put, the biggest phenomenon in Czech letters for much of the nineteenth century, winning the acknowledgment and admiration of foreign scholars and poets, at a time when modern Czech literature was in its infancy, and providing inspiration and essential material for the development of Czech national culture across all the arts. Translations and partial translations were made into over a dozen languages by midcentury, including versions of songs by Goethe and commentary by Jacob Grimm.

The manuscripts—imitations of medieval folk epic and lyric poetry depicting the ancient Czechs successfully defending their homeland from alien invaders and thus also defending their native religion and their peaceful, democratic cultural values—played an outsize role in the Czech Revival, modeling Czech poetic practice and patriotic behavior and winning converts to the Czech national cause. It would be no exaggeration to say that one cannot imagine the Czech National Revival, as it is traditionally termed—that is, the reestablishment of Czech as a language of high culture and the articulation and mass adoption of a program of Czech national culture and politics—without the manuscripts. That is not to say that the national movement would not have succeeded without the manuscripts—that Czech would have remained a mere vernacular language, slowly disappearing alongside the closely related Sorbian and Polabian languages within the larger German cultural sphere, had it not been for the invigorating influence of the manuscripts. But they were inextricable from the National Revival as it happened and from its national mythology, which only made their necessary extraction at century's end from more accurate accounts of early Czech literary and cultural history all the more painful.

While I am using the traditional term for this period in Czech literary history, the National Revival, my understanding of the Czech national movement in the period does not at all align with the perspective that term implies, which belonged to the nineteenth-century nationalists themselves: that the nation had deep roots in the past but that, under foreign imperial rule, the Czechs had forgotten or lost elements of their national identity, necessitating their revival. Rather, like most current scholars of nationalism, I see nations and nationalism as a distinctively modern phenomenon (Benedict Anderson, Ernest Gellner, and Miroslav Hroch, among others) and nation building as a project of committed national entrepreneurs who had to overcome significant national indifference (Tara Zahra) in order to win converts to their nationalist cause and grow a mass national movement.[12] Here, insofar as I address the question, my emphasis will be on reconstructing the important roles the manuscripts played for national entrepreneurs in bringing in and committing new members to the national movement. That does not mean that many did not remain indifferent to the national appeal of the manuscripts or even that the manuscripts themselves only resonated with nationalist readings. As Dalibor Dobiáš recently reminded us, the manuscripts embody a certain tension between the crownland patriotism of the elites (which included German and Czech speakers) and the emerging ethnic nationalism, and German-speaking writers from the Czech lands continued to respond positively and creatively to the manuscripts into the second half of the century.[13]

Unfortunately, but perhaps inevitably, in the high passions of the moment when Czech cultural leaders confronted the modern origins of these supposedly medieval manuscripts, they attempted to extract them not only from their illegitimate place in accounts of early Czech history but also from their very legitimate place in recent Czech history, in the National Revival. The manuscripts were disparaged as a false foundation for the national movement, the result of a willful self-deception that had led to a false consciousness that had to be corrected. In some subsequent accounts of the history of the revival, the manuscripts were an embarrassing episode that had to be bracketed out, discussed only in order to be exorcised from the true development and rise of the Czech nation.[14] In literary history, the poetry was put into its proper place in early nineteenth-century Czech literary developments (though now seen as a largely unremarkable expression of the period's ideas and aesthetics), while the poets, the authors of some of the most influential poetry of the period, remained neglected at best, disparaged as poor poets and deceitful forgers, willful betrayers of the national trust at worst.

Corrections to this counter distortion have gradually advanced, but in general, the study of the manuscripts has been overwhelmed by questions surrounding their authenticity, which have haunted them (unevenly for different manuscripts) almost from the moment of their "discovery," and the controversy surrounding their delegitimization, which is stirred and promoted even to this day by some small circles and institutions. This has left quite a few interesting open questions and promising areas for insightful and fruitful research. In the past decade, the manuscripts have once again become an active and productive area of research, with many notable publications marking efforts to return them to their rightful, prominent place in the history of Czech literature, culture, society, and scholarship and to place the Czech experience with forgery and mystifications into the broader developments of European history. This book further advances those efforts by examining facets of the history of the manuscripts and their poetics that seemed quite important but neglected a decade ago when I began work on the topic and that still have not been adequately studied, in spite of the great volume of intervening publications and the real advance in our knowledge of the manuscripts they represent, from which this book has benefited immensely. It also poses a few questions and problems that aim to open up some new areas in the study of the manuscripts and their context.

What Are the Manuscripts?

The first manuscript to appear, in 1816, with features linking it to the main manuscripts—there had been forgeries from other sources before it—was a humble page of parchment with an unfinished fragment of a love lyric just thirty-one lines long inscribed on one side, initially dated as belonging to the thirteenth century. Known as the "Píseň na Vyšehrad" (Song to Vyšehrad), or referred to by its first line, "Ha, ty náše slunce" (Ho! you our sun), it was said to be found by Linda, in the presence of his roommate Hanka, in the binding of a book he had been resting his feet on. It was the first manuscript to be published when Hanka included it in the first volume of his new series of editions of old texts, *Starobylá skládání* (Antique writings), in 1817. It would also be, as we will see, one of the first declared false and would later be demonstrated false by an investigative commission of the Czech National Museum in 1857. Even before that, however, this humble love poem elicited only a modest response in Czech culture and largely remained on the sidelines of the main interest and controversy, though it was frequently republished, as it was usually included in editions of the main manuscripts.[15]

On September 16, 1817, Hanka, in the presence of others, found the Rukopis královédvorský (Queen's Court Manuscript) in the vault of the St. John the Baptist Church tower in the town of Dvůr Králové.[16] The date would be commemorated many times, from Hanka's inscription of his introduction to the first published edition of the manuscript on its one-year anniversary to the many events in Dvůr Králové and Prague in September 2017 marking the two hundredth anniversary of the discovery (see the conclusion for discussion of these commemorations). The manuscript was tiny, just seven parchment double leaves written on both sides, two leaves of which are incomplete with three-fourths of the page cut away. The text thus occupies four small page strips and twenty-four full pages. Each page is only about twelve centimeters high by seven to eight centimeters in width (see figure I.1).[17] What it contained was invaluable: six longer epic poems (the first, which began on the cutaway parchment strips, is incomplete), two ballads, and six lyric songs (the last of which is incomplete), a treasure of early Czech poetry whose language forms, orthography, and script suggested it had been written down in the late thirteenth to early fourteenth centuries. The manuscript was exactly what Czech patriots had been searching for: a document that gave evidence of an independent and developed Czech culture in an early period on which to found their case for the revival of Czech culture in the present. The manuscript itself and the stories around it suggested this narrative, foundational for the National Revival, of national decline and potential renewal: headings in the text marked these songs as belonging to the twenty-fifth through twenty-eighth chapters of the third book of the whole collection. There had been dozens and dozens of additional songs, it implied, a flowering Czech tradition. The legend of its discovery, together with that of the "Song to Vyšehrad," suggested that it was mere chance that these fragments had survived the decline of Czech culture and the obliteration of its artifacts. In his introduction to the first publication of the manuscript, Hanka tells readers that he chanced upon it while looking at some of the arrows stored in the vault from the time of Jan Žižka, the great Hussite warrior. What he does not say there, but circulated by other means, is that the arrows were fletched with parchment, including parchment from that very manuscript, as he told Václav Nebeský, explaining the cutaway pages.[18] This is how the later Czechs, even the Hussites, had treated valuable old manuscripts in Czech, by cutting them up to fletch arrows for a religious war or using them as scrap paper for binding newer books. "Little has escaped the rage of overwhelming zeal," Hanka intoned to readers, likely implicating the Counter-Reformation along with the Hussite Wars in the destruction of Czech manuscript collections.[19]

Modern Czechs with a new sensibility could rescue this treasure from oblivion. Hanka donated the manuscript to the newly founded National Museum and published it just over a year after his discovery, in October 1818 (though it is dated 1819), in a volume that included translations into modern Czech and German. The discovery was welcomed not only in the small circles of Czech patriots at the time but also by local German speakers along with scholars and

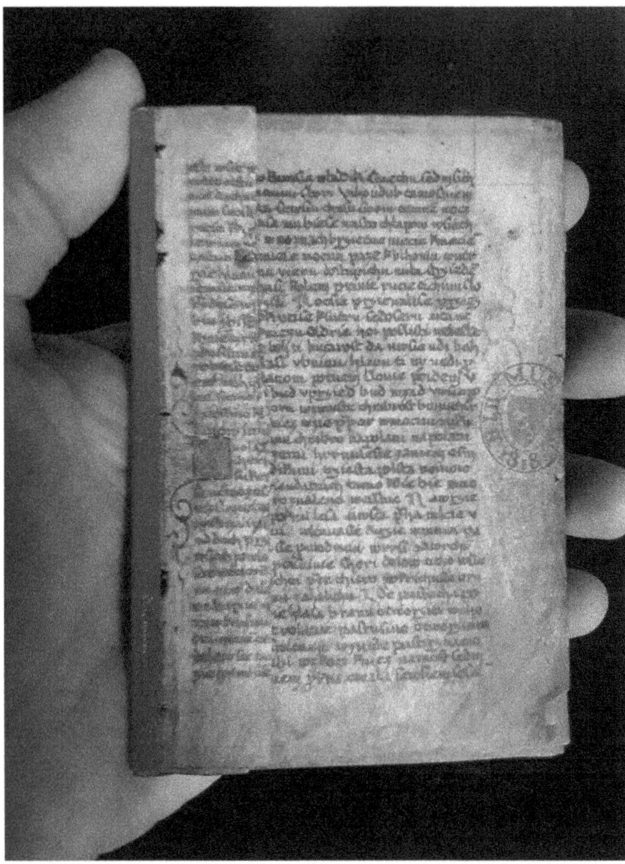

Figure I.1. Author holding full-size facsimile edition of the Queen's Court Manuscript (Rukopis královédvorský), published by the Slavoj Library in Dvůr Králové nad Labem in 2017. *Rukopis královédvorský* (Městská knihovna Slavoj ve Dvoře Králové nad Labem ve spolupráci s Městským muzeem, 2017). Based on the Czech National Museum Library manuscript Rukopis královédvorský, 1 A b 6. Author photo.

experts abroad. The Queen's Court Manuscript was the most important and influential of the fabrications, inciting very few doubters until very late and meanwhile playing a prominent role in Czech society and the arts and the development of the national movement.

Its counterpart, the Rukopis zelenohorský (Green Mountain Manuscript, figure I.2), provoked skepticism from the very moment of its appearance, and in part due to the manner of its appearance.[20] It consists of just two damaged parchment double leaves of somewhat larger size, about sixteen centimeters high by twenty-two centimeters wide (for two pages), and thus only eight pages of written text.[21] A fragment of an epic poem on the first page is followed

FIGURE I.2. Green Mountain Manuscript (Rukopis zelenohorský), pages 4 and 5. Collection of the National Museum, National Museum Library, Prague, Czech Republic, 1 A b 1, fol. 02v–03r.

by an epic poem usually titled "Libušin soud" (Libuše's judgment). The fragment, when published as a separate poem, was given the title "Sněm" (Assembly), but it serves entirely organically as the ending to the "Libuše's Judgment" narrative. Its language forms, script, and contents suggest it was produced in the late ninth to early tenth centuries. It was sent anonymously in November 1818 to Count František Kolovrat, the highest burgrave of the Bohemian Kingdom, as a donation to the collections of the National Museum. A later investigation showed it had been found by the revenue officer at the castle Zelená Hora around the same time as the discovery of the Queen's Court Manuscript but was only sent over a year later. In a note to accompany the manuscript, the anonymous sender wrote in part:

> I discovered the enclosed pieces of parchment in a dusty corner of our archive, where they had clearly been forgotten about. They have likely been there for centuries. But, familiar as I am with the high-minded patriotism of my master, a veritable German Michel, and his feelings toward the national museum, I know that he would rather see such a

> specimen rot or burn than relinquish it to the hands of such an institution—which is why I came upon the idea to send these pages to Your Excellence anonymously. Were my name to appear, I would risk losing my position, and I would therefore ask that, when they are displayed in your venerable institution, the documents be credited to an unnamed but true patriot.[22]

For Dobrovský, the intrigue of this story was too much, especially when used as cover for a manuscript that looked quite doubtful based on his years of research into early Czech history. It would move the date for the beginning of Czech writing back several centuries and suggested a well-formed Czech state with its own written legal tradition in that very early period.

Dobrovský used his position to prevent the manuscript from being added to the museum's collections and made his doubts, which now included the "Song to Vyšehrad" as well, and his suspects known privately.[23] The manuscript's advocates, though, promoted it abroad and managed to get it published in a Polish study dedicated to Slavic law traditions by Ignacy Benedykt Rakowiecki in 1820 and in the journal of the Russian Academy with a translation by Admiral Aleksandr Shishkov in 1821.[24] This provided sufficient legitimation and cover for Antonín and Josef Jungmann to then publish it in the new Czech scholarly journal *Krok* in 1822. That, together with the fact that Count Kolovrat commissioned a new painting titled *Libuše's Judgment* (1821) by Prague Academy head Josef Bergler that significantly altered, based on the manuscript's narrative, how Libuše was depicted from prior works, pushed Dobrovský to publicly declare it a fraud.[25] Only Hanka's friend Svoboda dared to respond, initiating the first polemics on the manuscript (see chapter 4 on their exchange).

Dobrovský's suspects, whom he refrained from naming publicly, though word got around Prague soon enough, were, as we have seen, his students in Slavistics, Hanka and Linda, along with Josef Jungmann. No incontrovertible direct evidence has appeared in the intervening two hundred years, and this list remains nearly complete for the most likely participants. Hanka's involvement is almost certain, based on the manuscripts and published sources that the manuscripts drew from and that he, and in some cases only he, had timely access to, and which he sometimes drew on in work published under his own name. He further implicated himself with a series of other falsifications, some easily detected and others that took careful study to uncover, that can only be realistically assigned to him. The case has been made periodically for Linda's participation in the composition particularly of the epic poems, although for several poems the case for Hanka as the author seems stronger and there remain doubts in some quarters.[26] Dobrovský's suspicion of Jungmann did not really stick to this acknowledged leader and spiritual father of Hanka's generation of Czech national activists. The respect he had earned largely kept him above suspicion until more recently, when his name has again begun to turn up in the list of those most likely at least initiated into the conspiracy, though I am not aware of any detailed arguments to support his authorship.[27] Svoboda was also probably in on the scheme, though most doubt his participation in authoring the poems. The list of most probable coconspirators can be finalized with the name of one of the witnesses at Hanka's wedding, the painter and art restorer František Horčička, suspected in the preparation of the physical manuscripts (figures I.2 and I.3).

The last of the early manuscripts is another parchment that remained more marginal, like the "Song to Vyšehrad." It also resembled that manuscript in consisting of a single sheet of parchment that had allegedly been found in the binding of a book, this time by Linda's friend J. N. V. Zimmermann, with additional sheets supposedly lost when drying. The "Milostná píseň Krále Václava" (Love song of King Václav) was sent to the museum by Zimmermann in April 1819. The twenty-four-line poem fragment appeared to be an earlier Czech version of a love song attributed to King Václav from a collection of German-language minnesinger songs. Dobrovský dated it to the thirteenth century.[28] Just as importantly, on the reverse there was a full copy of the ballad "The Stag" from the Queen's Court Manuscript that appeared to be a few decades older than that manuscript, thus corroborating the wider circulation of those songs. Hanka published the love song in the fifth volume of his *Starobylá skládání* in 1823. Dobrovský doubted that the Czech version was prior to a German version, deflating the implied story that an early Czech ruler had preferred to sing in Czech over German, and Julius Feifalik demonstrated, in 1857, that the Czech version had been translated from a late German edition that included textual errors. The museum commission thus declared the manuscript false that same year alongside the "Song to Vyšehrad."[29]

Cover Falsifications

Following Dobrovský's more detailed arguments against the Green Mountain Manuscript, a series of other falsifications appeared that seemed to provide corroborating evidence for the questionable linguistic and cultural details of the manuscripts, the so-called *krycí falza* (cover falsifications; see chapter 3 for additional discussion). Following his donation of the Queen's Court Manuscript to the new National Museum, Hanka received an appointment in the

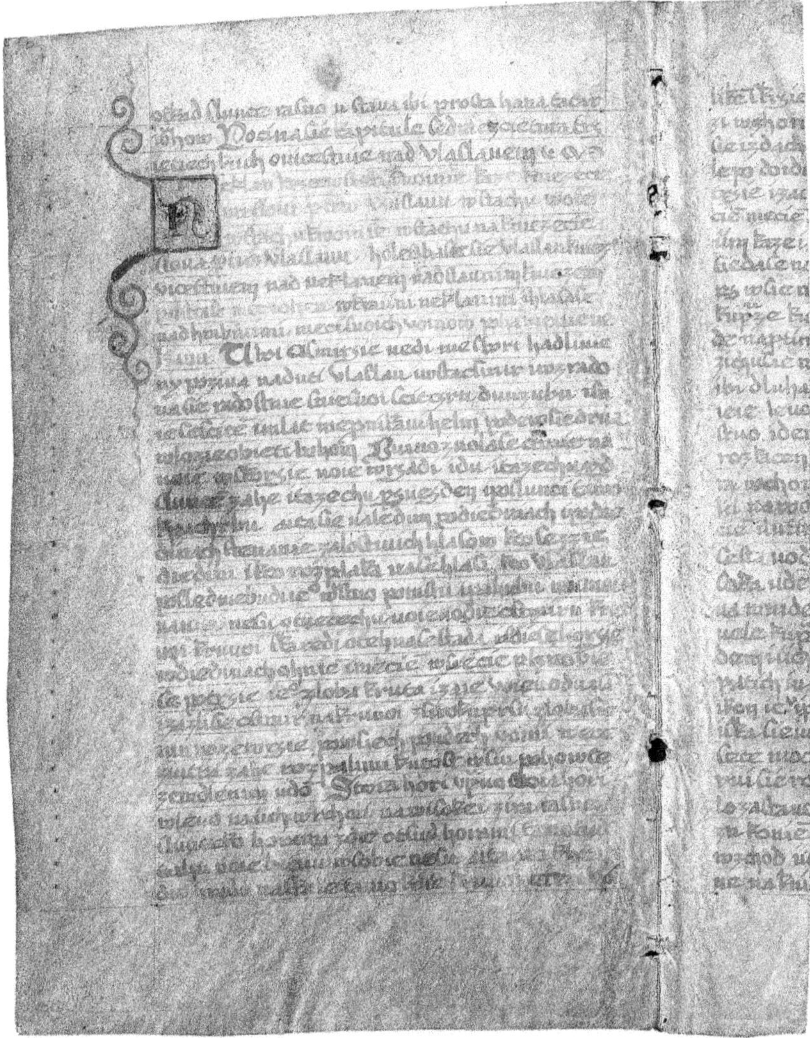

FIGURE I.3. Queen's Court Manuscript (Rukopis královédvorský), page 14 and partial page 3. Collection of the National Museum, National Museum Library, Prague, Czech Republic, 1 A b 6, fol. 07v.

museum, soon becoming its librarian. In that position, he helped to bring to light a number of important older Czech manuscripts, but he also apparently used his access to strategically alter and enhance a number of genuine manuscripts.

The first of these cover falsifications to be discovered involved the museum's copy, made around 1240, of a popular Latin dictionary, the *Mater verborum*, which explained Latin and a few Hebrew and Greek words. To the genuine glosses of terms in Latin, German, and Old Czech (339 of these) in this illuminated manuscript were added an additional 950 glosses in Old Czech that reflected the mythology and pagan religion of the Czechs and their close linguistic relationship to other Slavs, providing crucial support to some doubtful usages in the manuscripts. These glosses were discovered by the linguist Eberhard Gottlieb Graff in the presence of Hanka on July 14, 1826. Dobrovský recognized them as authentic and even defended them to his Slovene correspondent, Kopitar, in 1828 when the latter suggested that the number of glosses had somehow increased since the moment of their discovery. The revelation that the majority of the glosses were recent additions, made by Antonín Baum and Adolf Patera in an article in the museum's journal in 1877, marked the beginning of the end for the manuscripts.[30]

In 1827, Hanka himself found, and quickly published, Old Czech translations of Psalm 109 and the beginning of Psalm 145 that had been inscribed interlineally in another authentic museum Latin manuscript, the so-called Glossed Psalter from the late thirteenth to the early fourteenth century, which contained genuine interlineal glosses in Czech. These short texts corroborated the orthography and grammar, as well as the Russified vocabulary, of the manuscripts, but largely avoided the attention given to the other discoveries. Patera and Antonín Vašek both separately argued the translations were falsifications in 1879, and this was confirmed by another museum commission in 1886.[31]

The final manuscript fragment combines the kind of discovery legend of the first finds with the typical content of the later cover falsifications: the two parchment leaves, supposedly found by Hanka in March 1828 in the binding of a book from 1595, contained fragments of a Latin Gospel of St. John from the tenth to the eleventh century with an interlineal Old Czech translation that appeared to belong to the eleventh century. The language forms again supported doubtful aspects of the main manuscripts (see chapter 3). Dobrovský initially deemed the translation authentic, but quickly changed his mind and forbade Hanka, whom he recognized as the author, to publish it. Hanka only refrained until after Dobrovský's passing and published it in 1829. Vašek and Alois Vojtěch Šembera each made the case it was another falsification in 1879 and 1878, respectively, and this was supported by the museum commission in 1886.[32]

There was yet another manuscript, but it might better be called a revealing, rather than a cover, falsification. Hanka was again the discoverer, this time of seven parchment strips that "happily remained together" in the binding of another museum manuscript, titled *De arte moriendi*, that contained "Libuše's Prophecy."[33] The Green Mountain Manuscript had contained only the beginning of the full legend of Libuše. This text had the end (without the middle: her sending for Přemysl the plowman to become her husband and found the ruling dynasty). It corresponded to a Latin text of the prophecy that had been found a few years earlier, both apparently dating from the fourteenth century, and Hanka had them both published in the museum's journal in 1849, having announced his discovery to the museum's historical section on June 28, 1849. It was met with an embarrassed silence until, a decade later when Hanka was under public attack as the probable author of the Queen's Court Manuscript, it was closely examined by the museum's experts and found false (unlike the Latin text). As Nebeský paraphrased the consternation of Max Büdinger, "It's a strange thing with that Mr. Hanka! In 1817 as a young man, he had begun so gloriously that half of Europe was in wonder. Then he waited thirty years and came up with the wretched malformation that is Libuše's Prophecy."[34]

A Phenomenon of Their Time

The manuscripts were not the first Czech forgery in the period, nor would they be the last. Chapter 1 examines the social and literary conditions that seemed both to prescribe forgery as a method and to set uncertain limits beyond which it was proscribed. If we expand from forged documents and manuscripts to include other kinds of hoaxes, *supercheries*, counterfeits, and various forms of "fakelit," all of which Czech scholars discuss under the heading of mystifications, we will find with Vladimír Macura, the top interpreter of the semiotics of the period in Czech culture, that in the first half of the nineteenth century these appeared "quite often" and "one can even reasonably presume that a number of them have remained undisclosed to this day, while we know very little about others."[35]

The manuscripts were not even the first Macphersonian mystification in Czech, offering epic poetry with famous Czech heroes. That distinction belongs to a composition by the Slovak Samuel Rožnay, who sometime around 1810 offered to his teacher Juraj Palkovič his own text as the beginning of an old epic poem. (Slovak protestants at this time used Czech as a literary language.) "Žižka anebo Historie o činech Jana Žižky, udatného vůdce husitů v Čechách" (Žižka, or The story of the deeds of Jan Žižka, brave leader of the Hussites in the Czech Lands) was not published or circulated more broadly, and Rožnay admitted his mystification several years later.[36] Nor were they the last: one of the heroes of the Queen's Court Manuscript would later come into doubt as a result of the appearance of other historical documents, themselves mystifications. The official archivist of the Moravian part of the Czech kingdom, Antonín Boček, inserted some false documents into a publication of official records, the *Codex diplomaticus et epistolaris Moraviae* (Codex of diplomatic documents and correspondence from Moravia), to tilt a dispute between Moravian and Bohemian historians over some of the details of the battle against the Mongols at Olomouc depicted in the epic "Jaroslav," including the name of the hero from the house of Sternberg, whom the Moravians claimed was Zdislav, not Jaroslav. The Moravian scholar Šembera (whom I have already mentioned as a later critic of the authenticity of the manuscripts) soon enough discovered the ruse and communicated it to his opponent in the dispute, František Palacký, about a decade later in 1851. Ironically, Palacký, who had used Boček's sources in his magisterial 1836 history of the Czech nation, refused to believe it and warned Šembera against going public with the accusation. As with Hanka and the manuscripts, of which he had become one of the most prominent defenders, Palacký could not believe that Boček had the skills to pull off the deception.[37]

The wider sphere to which Ossianic epic poetry belongs, collections of oral literature or folklore, was rife with practices that today we would not hesitate to call falsification. To be fair and a little less historically biased, we should admit that what the first collectors of folklore sought was not authentic oral traditions in the way we understand those today. Rather, they sought an ideal of folk poetry as an alternative to contemporary literary poetry and as a model for a more nationally oriented literature. They found a source for that ideal in the voices of the people in songs, but also much else that did not meet that ideal and needed to be edited out or ignored entirely. They also found that ideal in some pieces composed by their literary friends or by themselves. Thus Johann Gottfried Herder, in his *Stimmen der Völker in Liedern* (Voices of the people in songs), could include, among other things, a ballad by Goethe. The earliest editors of Czech folk song collections acted in keeping with these period norms by including translations from other languages and their own compositions, normalizing the language and editing variants to produce a favored version, and ignoring in particular the sexual- or scatological-themed material.[38] The reconstructed epics and folk songs of the ancient Czechs in the manuscripts do not look anomalous against this continuum of practices.

Another interesting and productive area for mystifications in Czech literature was in the field of women's poetry. At a time early in the century when women did not have the same access to education, particularly in Czech, the leisure time, or entrance to the social circles where Czech male patriots cultivated poetry, the lack of a female voice was clearly felt, and there were several instances of publication of poems by male authors under female pseudonyms.[39]

František Ladislav Čelakovský, who would become one of the leading poets of the period, published a few poems in 1821–23 under the name Žofie Jandová that were met by admiring responses from other poets. While some were in on the secret, he led his closest friend and confidant, Josef Vlastimil Kamarýt, with whom he conducted a "daily practice" of mystifications, deeper into the deception with hints of news about sightings of the author in various places and by serving as an intermediary for communication with her, only lifting the veil in February 1824. Čelakovský ultimately planned to publish a book of twelve poetic idylls by Jandová, but the manuscript, already submitted to the censor, had to be withdrawn when the secret became more widely known.[40]

Sir John Bowring's *Cheskian Anthology: Being a History of the Poetical Literature of Bohemia, with Translated Specimens* (1832), begun in the early 1820s, offers a telling snapshot of a representative selection of Czech poetry from the period, including mystifications of all these types. Bowring opens the anthology with information on the oldest Czech documents, discusses the Green Mountain Manuscript without providing the text (and noting Dobrovský's reservations), and provides translations of the "Song to Vyšehrad" (without noting Dobrovský's doubts), a robust selection from the Queen's Court Manuscript, and the "Love Song of King Václav."[41] The forged manuscripts and their companions, as representative works held by most to be genuine, had to be included in an anthology claiming to be a historical survey. A further selection of songs from Čelakovský's collection of Slavic folk songs also included some of the falsifications that were peppered through that collection.[42] Finally, the selection of the poems of a number of living poets included all the major poets of the period, but also a single poem by "Sophia Jandowa" that was headed by this note: "Of this lady I have been able to obtain no other particulars than that she is the daughter of a bohemian schoolmaster, and is married in Moravia. She has published only two or three pieces of poetry, which I have found in the periodicals."[43] He might well have learned more from Čelakovský, who was his intermediary in the undertaking and from whom he had requested information on Jandová in correspondence in 1827, long after the hoax had been revealed. But instead, Čelakovský provided minimal information and allowed Bowring to go ahead and insert the mystification into a new context, giving it new life.[44]

Bowring's anthology thus, in the estimation of Macura, "reflected the reality that in Czech revival culture the border between the mystifying and 'genuine' constituents of creative work is invisible and hardly fixable at all." He further suggests that, in spite of Hanka's documented character flaws, his mystifying behavior and participation in a variety of forgeries, from the manuscripts to publishing others' poems as his own to his numismatic forgeries of coins from the Great Moravian Empire, "are nothing extraordinary in the period. Probably it would be more precise to interpret these as derived from the state of Czech Revival culture than from pathology of character."[45] This is an important insight that altered the approach to the manuscripts and their likely authors in the postsocialist period, but Macura's interpretation, with its analytical lens focused closely on the particular nature of the Czech National Revival culture, tended to suggest it was unique or unusual, or perhaps deviant. More recent work has done much to put the Czech Revival culture and the manuscripts into their broader regional and European context.

To take just one list of analogous phenomena from the region in the period—this one, to be precise, from a recent article by Dalibor Dobiáš—the manuscripts can be compared to the so-called *Ramschak Chronicle* that recorded the history of Jewish life in Prague, created by the secretary of the tax office of the Prague Jewish community, Marcus Fischer, in the early 1820s;[46] the *Chronicon slavosarmaticum Procosii* propagated by the Polish writer Pryzbysław Dyjamentowski in the mid-eighteenth century, first published in 1825, which documented the myth of Polish Sarmatian origins in the tenth century; the "Wooden Book of Túróc," a birch bark piece with fragments of Hungarian runes supporting Hungarian Scythian origins, produced by Samuel Literati Nemes; the questionable ethno-national designations of the "Serbian" songs collected by Karadžić or the "Finnish" *Kalevala* as forms of nationalist falsification; the Bulgarian *Veda Slovena*, a collection of folk songs of the Muslim Bulgarians with references to Slavic mythology, a likely mystification by their collector Ivan Gologanov, and so on.[47] A Hungarian-Scythian forgery that is perhaps even closer to the manuscripts is the *Csíki Székely krónika* (Székely chronicle of Csík), a Latin chronicle manuscript that appeared with a Hungarian translation in 1796 and supported the privileges of the Hungarian Székely noble clans because they directly descended from the Scythian Huns of Attila. For much of the nineteenth century it was considered authentic but was later shown to have been forged by Sigismund Sándor, who had "discovered" it in his family castle.[48] Few of these documents can match the manuscripts, though, for significance. The *Kalevala* and Karadžić's songs had and continue to have undeniable reach, even beyond their own cultures, but they are not really of the same order of falsification as the manuscripts, which do indeed stand out, as Donald Rayfield suggested, as "the most important Macphersonian (or Ossianic) forgery," one of the very few worthy of comparison to James Macpherson's reconstructions of Scottish epics that resounded across Europe for a solid century and a half.

The Significance of the Manuscripts

Any literary forgery is worthy of study. Forgeries are very instructive as to reigning literary norms and fashions, the boundaries of what is possible and not possible within a particular literary culture, the nexus of readers' desires and writers' possibilities. As Julia Abramson's clever book title suggests, there is much that we can learn from lying.[49] This is true for the manuscripts as well, and these lessons are all the more emphatic for the fact that the deception was successful for so long. But the significance of the manuscripts goes beyond that, because they represent not merely a very successful forgery; rather, by many indexes they are by far the most important literary artifact in Czech culture for much of the nineteenth century. By 1886, the manuscripts had been published in book form thirty-three times, which is three times more often than the national poet Karel Hynek Mácha's masterful poem "Máj" (May) and six times more often than Božena Němcová's foundational Czech novel *Babička* (Granny).[50] In the 1860s and 1870s, they came out in new editions nearly every year, not counting their constant partial republication in school readers at the time.[51] Such a rate of publication goes beyond what we might imagine to have been a demand for the manuscripts for reading purposes and reflects instead their status as cult objects. In this, they also exceeded other available texts and artifacts, like the Prague Bible, one of the earliest full translations of the Bible into European vernacular languages, an unrealized potential locus of national cultural veneration.[52]

How did the manuscripts come to function as cult objects? That was ultimately the result of a developing line of interpretation of the manuscripts by nationalist-minded Czech scholars that was embraced by the growing Czech national movement.[53] But the manuscripts were in many ways well designed to take on such interpretations and functions. The stories that the epic poems of the manuscripts told—of the battle to throw off cultural domination by the Frankish empire imposing its foreign (Christian!) religion on the still pagan Czechs; of the battles to drive out Polish and Saxon invaders; of the turning back of the Mongol hordes near Olomouc by Jaroslav of Sternberg, thus saving Christian Europe—these stories from the infancy of the Czech nation confirmed certain traits of Czech national identity: that the Czechs were a peace-loving Slavic nation with democratic inclinations but stalwart in battle in the defense of their faith and homeland from outside aggression. The manuscripts supported and were incorporated into the national mythology. Their truthfulness as authentic manuscripts thus became the foundation for even greater truths, those of the sacred national narrative (to take one definition of myth).[54]

We can see the beginning of this process in one of the first and most influential reviews of the Queen's Court Manuscript, published in German by the recently retired professor of aesthetics from the University of Prague Joseph Georg Meinert. He wrote that the epic songs are,

> without question, the important part of the manuscript. These texts are utterly unique among their kind, for not only do they display true, seemingly innate, poetic magnificence and the purest love of country, but they are based on highly significant events and deeds that can be traced with considerable accuracy—including accuracy of location—back into the ninth century and to the not-so-bloodless conversion of the Czechs. These pieces are a trove of ancient beliefs, morals, and customs, and, to a certain extent, documentation of their existence—a key to the entire history of the Czechs.[55]

In Meinert's interpretation, the epic songs are documentation for and evidence of key aspects of the Czech national character in its infancy.

This type of interpretation belongs to what Joep Leerssen terms the "literary historicism" of the period, a conception of European national literary histories that he reads as one of the important legacies of Macpherson's Ossianic translations and the theories surrounding them.[56] Literary historicism arises together with cultural nationalism, and oral epic poems play a fundamental role, which is why they are collected, published, and produced in such quantity in the period. This historicism is built on several related presumptions: "a) that European literature is naturally divided into different traditions, each individually characterized by its separate language; b) that each of these 'national literatures' follows a parallel, stadial progression of development, from primitive national origin towards latter-day cosmopolitan refinement; c) that the primitive origin of each literature lies in an epic whose *topic* describes a formative episode in the nation's collective experience, and whose *form* is closely linked to the nation's anonymous, oral-collective traditions."[57] We should note that this conception is a kind of scholarly myth, a master narrative of European national literary traditions regarded as true—today we no longer believe these underlying presumptions and the national literary historical narratives built on them. The mythological aspect here extends to the role assigned to primitive epic, which by virtue of its orality and its time setting (in the period of formation of the nation) stands as a sign of the mythical origin of the nation and its literature. Here we touch on another way of defining myth: by its time setting in the period when the world (here, the world divided into nations) is forming.[58] From the perspective of this conception, the epics of the manuscripts were destined for a role in the Czech national mythology.

The establishment of the manuscripts as essential to the national myth still required the work of mythmaking interpretations and their acceptance by the public, a process that Mojmír Otruba has traced.[59] The significance of the manuscripts grew together with the Czech national movement. Initially the manuscripts fed the poetic program of the small circles of intellectuals in the second decade of the nineteenth century, inspiring some new poetry, some musical settings composed for the songs, and contributing to discussions of national forms.[60] As examples of fine Czech poetry, the manuscripts also helped these early nationalist entrepreneurs to recruit new members to their slowly growing movement. The manuscripts remained available as the movement began to articulate a national myth, particularly following the cleansing of the Green Mountain Manuscript by Palacký and Šafařík in 1840, which contributed to and was followed by a number of new interpretations in the mythic vein. The national movement also began to broaden beyond the intellectual class with other forms of expression than literature, including formal balls at which Czech was spoken, "patriotic excursions," and attempts at national fashion.[61] As inspiration for the arts, the influence of the manuscripts also broadened with the development of the Czech visual arts, which began to work out the stylistic possibilities and ideas about national art using the manuscripts, along with some early operas.[62] When the Czech national program took on the character of a growing mass movement, leading up to and particularly following the revolutionary year 1848, the manuscripts were quickly becoming intertwined in Czech cultural expressions and the national mythology.[63]

By the 1850s, the mythological interpretation is established as the primary interpretation, within Czech national circles, of the manuscripts. References to the manuscripts as the Czech "Palladium" became frequent, linking the manuscripts to the protective statue of Pallas Athena in Troy and suggesting that the manuscripts had a similar cultural protective function for the Czech nation. This is the period of the high functioning of the manuscripts as sacred texts, objects of cult veneration that could support a rapid turnover of new publications as everyone in the growing Czech cultural public sought to own a copy of the text. Otruba explains the circular process by which the manuscripts establish themselves as myth. At first they (and really, primarily the Queen's Court Manuscript) are but one in a series of documents that function as signs of the myth, motivating its formation, but they come to serve as the primary sign of the myth and guarantee its truth. The fact that they served as motivating evidence is gradually pushed aside so that they can later be read as a symptom of it, as corroborating evidence, if perhaps the most important and frequently invoked evidence of its truth.[64] This is how the manuscripts became, if you will, truer than true, the foundation of truth, in the culture of the Czech National Revival.

Doubts about the authenticity of the manuscripts, then, do not have implications merely for their documentary value as historical sources. They impinge on the truthfulness of the Czech national mythology. As Otruba notes, this affects the defenses of the manuscripts' authenticity in a fundamental way, because the defenses operate primarily within the mythological interpretation, using the myth to defend the manuscripts and thereby to support the entire structure of manuscripts and myth. Any effective criticism of the manuscripts, then, had to also take on the national myth.[65] For a long time, there was little incentive within the Czech national movement to take up such a critique, for attacks on the manuscripts were perceived as coming from outside and the defenses followed the mythological model from the manuscripts' narratives, in which the Czechs were fated to forever defend their homeland from outside attack.

But the successful growth of the national movement and the diversification of Czech politics would eventually open enough internal division to make the reconsideration of the manuscripts a possibility. The revolution of 1848 introduced the possibility of a constitutional reform to the Habsburg monarchy and started the Czechs down the path of nationalist politics.[66] The realization of a more liberal order waited, though, for Austrian defeats in wars with Sardinia and France in 1859 and with Prussia in 1866 that forced genuine administrative compromises.[67] Czech national political parties emerged and grew with these changes. One division that existed from early on was between the Bohemian and Moravian Czechs, as the National Revival started later in the Moravian part of the Czech lands and the political interests did not always align between the two separately administered crownlands.[68] For the Bohemian Czechs, a single national party sufficed for the first while, but a new party of Young Czechs emerged in the late 1860s and established itself in the mid-1870s.[69]

As more and more cover falsifications failed to hold up to scrutiny, the time became ripe for a reconsideration of the main manuscripts, and it was a pair of Moravian scholars who made the first arguments from within the Czech national community that these, too, were falsifications. Šembera made his case against the Green Mountain Manuscript in 1878, and Vašek took on the Queen's Court Manuscript as well in 1879. Their arguments were vigorously disputed by Bohemian Czechs, and it would be several more years before the case would be taken up there. Ironically, it came from the institution that represented one of the greatest successes of Czech political and cultural striving: the Czech faculty of the Charles-Ferdinand University in Prague, which had been split into Czech and German faculties in 1882, making full university instruction in Czech available for the first time.[70] New, younger Czech faculty members were eager to establish their credentials and the latest methodologies and standards of scholarship. Not that the decision to make the case against the authenticity of the manuscripts was at all an easy one (see chapter 4), but scholarly scruples, combined with a new vision of what Czech national identity could mean, encouraged the linguist Jan Gebauer and the sociologist Tomáš Garrigue Masaryk to lead a campaign in Masaryk's journal *Athenaeum* starting in 1886, harnessing arguments from multiple fields of scholarship and publishing nearly sixty articles over the course of a year and a half, to prove the modern origins of the manuscripts.

Otruba sees the meaning and the root of the effectiveness of this campaign to dislodge the manuscripts from their seemingly unassailable position in the fact that it took on the national myth along with the manuscripts.[71] But the myth, and its adherents, did not surrender easily. The polemics over the authenticity of the manuscripts quickly turned vicious, with the critics ostracized in Czech society, labeled as national traitors, hounded and even spat on. The disputes of young men in cafés even led to occasional fistfights.[72] Jaroslav Goll, a historian and one of the manuscripts' critics, looked back on the manuscript battles twenty-five years later and wrote: "[Today] we can more easily understand the pain and perhaps even the wrongful anger of the defenders, from whom we took a piece of their national faith. We can explain to ourselves why it even came to fanatical cruelty here; heretics were always burned, so long as there were plenty of believers."[73]

The Czechs were forced into an early, painful confrontation with the false aspects of their national mythology and history because these had been based in part on a pair of false manuscripts. This outsize significance of the Czech manuscripts within Czech Revival culture, their status as cult objects and, as part of the national mythology, as texts that were the foundation of truth, embodies what makes the manuscripts unique and most worthy of study. I am not aware of any other literary forgeries that reached such heights of significance and forced such an early and fundamental confrontation with the artificial and falsifying aspects of national cultural history.[74]

Recent Scholarship

The past decade has seen a resurgence in studies dedicated to the manuscripts. Many scholars in the Czech Republic and abroad have contributed important new studies in which the manuscripts are seen not as an aberration but as a quite normal expression of the needs and tendencies of the time in Czech culture and in European culture more broadly, the authors of the manuscripts are given credit for the contribution their work made to the progress of Czech culture in the period and their impact abroad as well, and the manuscripts themselves are opened up to new lines of interpretation and new understandings of their form and nature. I will not attempt to survey this rich literature here, but I would like to highlight a couple of the more ambitious and important volumes.

In 2010, the publisher Host released a new edition of the Queen's Court and Green Mountain Manuscripts in its Czech Library series, which brings new editions of important older texts to the Czech reading public.[75] The volume, edited by Dobiáš, offered an attractive entryway for new readers with the modern Czech translation from 1961 by Kamil Bednář, supported by a helpful glossary of terms, followed by a transcription and transliteration into modern Czech orthography of the original text of the manuscripts faced by Hanka's translation from 1818 for more ambitious readers. The 120-page "Commentary" by Dobiáš that rounds out the volume also makes it a valuable modern critical edition of the manuscripts. It includes a brief history of the manuscripts' publication, thorough analysis of their language and of the language of both Hanka's and Bednář's translations, a detailed discussion of editorial decisions for the volume, an extensive history of the two-hundred-year life and reception of the manuscripts, and detailed commentary on each poem. The systematic assessment of the state of knowledge of the manuscripts offered there by Dobiáš, in a volume that made the texts widely available again to readers, certainly laid an important foundation for much of the work that has followed.

Dobiáš was joined by his colleagues at the Institute for Czech Literature, Czech Academy of Sciences, including Michal Fránek, Martin Hrdina, Iva Krejčová, and Kateřina Piorecká, in a project to reassess the reception of the manuscripts and their impact on the Czech human and social sciences from the moment of their discovery until just before the manuscript wars and the campaign to prove them false. The resulting study, published by Academia in 2014, runs to nearly one thousand pages, with one quarter of the volume dedicated to articles by the authors tracing the history of the manuscripts in Czech scholarship and the remainder to an extensive anthology of important reviews and studies of the manuscripts from that period (several translated from German to Czech for the first time), with detailed commentary and annotations.[76] This fascinating and detailed history of the manuscripts' reception in the period when they were largely considered to be genuine offers many new historical details and interpretations and expands our contexts for understanding this reception. Importantly, this new narrative of the development of Czech scholarship belies what had been asserted by the manuscripts' late nineteenth-century opponents—that the attachment to the manuscripts had hindered the development of Czech scholarship. Vašek, for example, complained, "The manuscripts were considered to be a pure source of history, culture, and the Czech language. That is why so much time and effort was devoted to them, rather than to any other monuments of Old Czech literature. This caused irreparable damage to Czech linguistics and history."[77] The authors of this volume demonstrate, though, that the manuscripts in many ways propelled the development of the Czech scholarly disciplines, demanding new methods of study and the development of new areas of expertise (paleography, folkloristics), at least until the 1860s, when, as we have seen, the mythological interpretation came to dominate the increasingly ritualized defenses of the manuscripts, at which point their opponents began to do more to advance scholarly methods.

The most recent undertaking is also the most ambitious of all. Dobiáš again edited and coordinated the work, this time of dozens of Czech and international scholars across multiple disciplines, to assess the impact of the manuscripts in culture and the arts in two volumes numbering 1,750 pages. The collection, published by Academia in 2019, examines how the manuscripts were received and reflected in Czech society and in culture both high and low from the time of their discovery to the present.[78] Building on the work of the previous decade, these forty-four articles together offer a thorough reassessment of the significance of the manuscripts in Czech culture and their impact abroad as well. Articles examine the reflections of the manuscripts in Czech literature, including lyric and epic poetry, drama, and prose, in the work of individual authors (Jan Neruda, Jaroslav Vrchlický, Julius Zeyer), and in the treatment of popular themes (Libuše, Jaroslav of Sternberg); the impact of the manuscripts on the fine arts, from music and opera to painting and sculpture; their reflections in memoirs and public celebrations, their incorporation into school curricula, and their use as sources in history; and their reception abroad, from France, Italy, and Germany to Finland, Hungary, and Sweden, and in many Slavic cultures.

These volumes constitute a thorough reassessment of the manuscripts around the 200th anniversary of their discovery and stand as worthy successors to the assessment of the state of knowledge assembled at the 150th anniversary, edited by Otruba, which had been the go-to volume of reference for a long time.[79]

This Book

No single-author book can undertake an agenda as broad and ambitious as the multiauthor volumes just discussed. Nonetheless, when I first conceived of this book over a decade ago, I saw quite a few areas where I thought I could contribute important chapters to our understanding of the manuscripts. The work of my colleagues in the meantime has obviated the need for at least one of the chapters I had conceived (a survey of the scholarship on the manuscripts in the nineteenth century), and the many new insights their work has brought have enabled me to reach much farther on shared topics. But some significant questions have still not been addressed, and the development of new areas of scholarship, like the recent emergence of translation studies as a distinct discipline, has opened up new perspectives and possibilities for understanding the manuscripts, how they were formed and how they proved so successful.

The chapters that follow aim to advance our knowledge of the manuscripts in a few different areas, furthering research on established topics but also asking some new questions and opening up new areas for further research.

Chapter 1 puts the productive vein of scholarship on forgery in English literature into dialogue with the Czech manuscripts and investigates the impact that the changes the new romantic paradigm brought to the notion of authorship may have had in promoting the creation of the manuscripts. The theoretical discussions of forgery and authorial intention in particular can offer new ways of seeing the probable authors of the manuscripts not as transgressors but as creative agents in the context of period demands and emerging romantic values. The comparative perspective also offers a new way of understanding the romantic values of originality and authenticity as a form of performance involving romantic irony as well, which gave room for expressions that later would come to be censored as forgery when the irony was lost in a more positivist age.

Chapter 2 examines the epic poems, the most valued and significant poems for the reception of the manuscripts and their integration into the national myth. Their aesthetic qualities sufficiently spoke for their authenticity for many nineteenth-century observers. I examine their poetics, drawing on the oral-formulaic theory of US scholars Milman Parry and Albert Lord and their followers (John Miles Foley in particular) and its comprehensive description of South Slavic oral epic poetry and related traditions like the Russian byliny. One of the more prolific recent defenders of the authenticity of the manuscripts, Julius Enders, published a book in 1993 that argued that the manuscripts were authentic oral-formulaic poetry, citing the work of Lord and Parry, but this argument has been ignored by serious students of the manuscripts.[80] I reopen the question, going much farther than Enders in exploring the formulaic aspect of the poems not just at the level of phraseology, to which I also apply new techniques of digital analysis, but also at the levels of formulaic scenes and plots.[81] I come to a conclusion that contradicts Enders, but also those opponents of the manuscripts, like Masaryk, who argued that the manuscripts were incompetent imitations of genuine folk poetry and therefore even the poetic hacks Hanka and Linda could have written them; I find that the epic poems in the manuscripts are, in fact, surprisingly good, though not perfect, imitations of their foreign folk models, from which they shamelessly appropriate formulaic structures.

Chapter 3 takes up a topic that has received far too little study: the role that translation played in the composition of the manuscripts and their reception. The lack of connection between translation studies and work on mystifications and forgeries is not unique to the Czech manuscripts, though, and this chapter tries to bring the small literature on pseudotranslation—an important technique of mystifications—that has developed in translation studies into contact with the much larger literature on forgery. Translation theory illuminates the conditions that make pseudotranslations (originals disguised as translations) possible and why reigning conceptions of translation make this an attractive and effective technique for forgeries. For the manuscripts, I show that certain romantic translation practices, some akin to pseudotranslation, shape them in fundamental ways, including the deliberate grammatical distortion of Old Czech that would eventually lead to their unmasking as forgeries.

I return in chapter 4, the final chapter, to the cult of the manuscripts and their implication in Czech national mythology to examine the rituals surrounding the manuscripts and the roles they played in Czech society in the period while they functioned as genuine and even sacred texts. Reactions to the campaign to demonstrate the manuscripts' falsification at the end of the century are violent and vehement, exposing the deep personal attachment many Czech patriots had to the manuscripts and to the faith they had in their authenticity. This chapter explores some of the ways in which that attachment grew in the practices around the manuscripts in Czech patriotic society. The quasi-religious rituals and practices that developed around the manuscripts raise the important question of the role of religion in the Czech national movement, which unlike some of its neighbors, where religion became an important marker of national identity (Catholicism in Poland, Orthodoxy in Russia, and so forth), remained ecumenical in regard to religious identity. Could the manuscripts have offered, with their depiction of the pagan Czechs prior to their conversion and division by foreign religious powers, a functional alternative to institutionalized religion for the Czech national movement?

Chapter 1

Forgery as a Romantic Form of Authorship

The Manuscripts in Comparative Perspective

Following the manuscript battles of the 1880s, Czech literary studies adapted fairly rapidly to the fact of the nineteenth-century origins of the Queen's Court and Green Mountain Manuscripts and the poetry they contained and began to interpret them in histories of Czech poetry, studies of Czech prosody, and discussions of Czech literature as a part of the literary production of their time.[1] In this sense, the Czech forged manuscripts have had a better fate than some other forged literature, like James Macpherson's Ossianic poems or Thomas Chatterton's Rowley poems, which until recently remained mostly outside the purview of legitimate English literary history.[2] On the other hand, the purported authors of the manuscripts, Václav Hanka and Josef Linda in particular, have been relegated to the margins of the literary canon, and their other works have been studied, when at all, largely only for the indirect (if often damning) evidence they provide of the authors' participation in the forgeries.[3] Thus it would seem that Czech literary scholarship, until very recently, managed to sever the manuscripts from their authors in order to treat the poetry as literature while still treating the authors as damned forgers. One of the ways this has been accomplished is by treating the poetry of the manuscripts primarily only in other contexts: their verse forms in relation to the prosodic and metrical experimentation of the time; their mythic picture of Czech nationhood in connection with the developing ideology of the Czech National Revival. Questions of authorship have remained largely neglected. Dalibor Dobiáš recently noted that while the likely participants in the creation of the manuscripts have been identified, the details of the particular contributions of each author to specific poems has not been resolved, so that the authorship of the poems remains an open question.[4] This neglect of the question of authorship is not by chance but follows from the nature of the manuscripts themselves as they present their implicit authorship. As I will argue below, by the time the Queen's Court Manuscript came into question, the possibility of attribution of the poems to *any* individual author was a powerful argument in the inauthentication of the manuscripts, and detailed analysis and allocation of responsibility was unnecessary to the economy of such arguments. The stigma attached to "forgery" in the dominant moral framework has also largely inhibited the possibility of the reexamination of the activities of Hanka and company in connection to larger theoretical questions of authorship as a cultural institution, in particular the rapidly changing notions of authorial creativity, authorial identity, and author-reader relationships, among others, connected to the emerging romantic paradigm.

This chapter puts the Czech forgeries into dialogue with the scholarly literature that appeared in the past few decades around English literary forgeries, to bring a new perspective to the Czech case and to see what the Czech case can contribute to the larger comparative and theoretical discussion. Of particular interest are the attempts in that literature to theorize literary forgery in a way that gets beyond legal or moral discourse and sees forgery as a regular part of the literary process, maybe even as essential to literature. For this chapter, I would like to examine some theoretical questions and hypotheses regarding the connections between forgery and romanticism, and in particular the question of romantic authorship. Clearly, the author-forger remains problematic in Czech literary studies in ways that the forged text does not. I suspect that this has to do in the first place with the troubling intentions ascribed to the authors: the intent to deceive, to deliberately falsify history, and so on.[5] But to what degree, in any particular case, are such intentions really present? And even if they are present, how important are they in the overall matrix of forces of intent, motivation, and pressure that produce the forged document? Formalist criticism has reminded us how inaccessible an author's intent is to the reader, and thus how unimportant it must be to the judging of an artistic work (William K. Wimsatt and Monroe C. Beardsley's "intentional fallacy").[6] But however irrelevant to the work's meaning or its artistic value, intention remains an aspect of readers' construction of the author, and so I would like to investigate those intentions a bit further, to see if there are not other, perhaps more important, intentions and forces acting in this case of forgery as well, and less reprehensible authors as a result. I would also like to develop other frames for viewing the authorial creativity of the forgers, to see forgery as an aspect of romantic creativity and literary practice, which means also to explore such notions as authenticity, originality, and simulation.

The Intent to Deceive

Nick Groom in *The Forger's Shadow: How Forgery Changed the Course of Literature*, one of the more ambitious recent attempts to theorize forgery, regards authorial intention as "wholly irrelevant," noting, "It is a common defense by art forgers that they never *intended* to deceive: they merely painted; the signatures were added later by dealers or restorers or other forgers, the forgery that arose was not a deliberate act."[7] Working with the concept of "fraudulence" rather than forgery, Scott Carpenter comes to some conclusions similar to Groom's about the intimate relationship between forgery / fraudulence and literature, but authorial intent is definitional to his main term: "Fraudulence does not exist without a motive, and it cannot occur by accident. Without intent, deception becomes merely a mistake, stupidity. . . . [Fraudulence] is thus a deliberate attempt to deceive."[8] The choice of terms here is crucial, and I prefer the approach of Groom to Carpenter's, decentralizing the importance of authorial intent under the rubric of "forgery."[9] This opens a wider field for investigation as well. While fraudulence cannot occur by accident, it is possible for something to be taken as a forgery by accident, through misappropriation, misreading, mistake. In fact, the two most prominent recent skeptics regarding the twelfth-century origins of the Old East Slavic *Slovo o polku Igoreve* (Igor tale), Andrei Zimin and Edward J. Keenan, ultimately suggest that the text was composed by their candidate authors as a kind of exercise in stylistic imitation, which was later misused and passed off as ancient by other parties.[10] That we are, in this case, in fact dealing with a genuine medieval manuscript (Andrei Zalizniak's weighing of the linguistic evidence and the arguments on both sides is, it seems to me, incontrovertible) should not deter us. Regardless of the actual ontological status of the contested object (which is not always knowable), the disputed and ever-shifting ground of the realm of forgery includes the possibility of such inadvertent cases.

Groom goes on to illustrate the multiplicity of artists' intentions in cases of forgery, and how even those intentions are often subordinate to other factors, including the economic motivations of other involved parties. In cases when artists are creating in response to particular demands, whether of their paying patrons or of an expectant audience or market, their intentions are often overridden or altered, deflected into new paths and shaped by the demands placed on them. Susan Stewart, in the seminal *Crimes of Writing*, relates the situation of George Psalmanazar, who "from 1702 to 1708 . . . presented himself to British society as a Formosan [Taiwanese] pagan converted to Christianity."[11] Much of Psalmanazar's creativity in inventing ethnographic information came as a direct response to the demands of his interlocutors for information. "Alas, for me," he wrote in his memoirs, "my fancy was but too fertile and ready for all such things, . . . and when any question has been started on a sudden, about matters I was ever so unprepared for, I seldom found myself at a loss for a quick answer, which, if satisfactory, I stored up in my retentive memory." Stewart notes, "There is no supply of answers here without the demanding questions."[12] Note also that what is saved of the fictionalizing is that which is "satisfactory" to its receptive audience—Psalmanazar was able to test the credibility of his inventions on a live audience and adjust to their expectations. When he wrote his entirely fictive *Historical and Geographical Description of Formosa*, public imposture was translated into ethnographic forgery and his audience could not wait to be deceived. He later recalled, "All this while, both [my patron, Dr. William Innes] and the booksellers were so earnest for my dispatching it out of hand, whilst the town was hot in expectation of it, that I was scarcely allowed two months to write the whole."[13] Whatever Psalmanazar's initial intentions when coming to London, his impersonation and forgery were strongly shaped by the willing audience he found there.[14] Groom observes, "Sceptics made a crucial contribution to Psalmanazar's incessant performance of otherness purely by being sceptical: they themselves were performing scepticism much as Psalmanazar was performing Formosan, while his believers performed belief."[15] In other words, Londoners had as much a hand in shaping Psalmanazar's Formosa as Psalmanazar (whatever his real name) himself.

A similar dynamic of demand and reward shaped the creative translations/adaptations undertaken by Macpherson of Scottish folk songs into prose-poem epics in English. Macpherson had to overcome an initial reluctance to do the first translations of "fragments" of ancient Scottish poems, but these highly mediated attempts produced an overwhelmingly enthusiastic reaction and garnered and promised rewards on multiple levels, from personal contacts with the Edinburgh literary elite to renewed cultural prestige for a dying Highlands culture. He very soon faced insistent demands from Scottish intellectuals that he find and translate a complete Scottish epic. His patrons, including David Hume and Hugh Blair, continually pushed him to do more and financed his travels through the Scottish Highlands in search of epic material.[16] The intent of audience and patrons to have the material here seems to be the fundamental force, and any authorial intent to produce a Scottish epic is itself already a product of that demand.

In the case of Hanka, Linda, and Josef Jungmann, we do not, so far as I know, have evidence of such immediate personal pressures from patrons or audience.[17] But the demand for Czech epic poetry and the expectation of its discovery were very prominent at the time. One source of the demand was German researchers like the Grimms and the Schlegels who were collecting European epic materials in this period for their histories of European literary traditions. To be unable to supply meant quite literally having nothing to contribute to the new grand narratives of European "romantic" literary history. In the reigning historical understanding of the day, all national literatures progressed through a stadial development proceeding from origins in epic.[18] Czech patriots certainly believed that they had a national literary tradition, and therefore there must be an epic origin in their past.[19] These expectations, and the delight at their fulfillment by Hanka's discoveries, are eloquently expressed by František Palacký in a Czech literary history written for the *Wiener Jahrbücher der Literatur* in 1822:

> The Czechs too had their history sung to them in old heroic and love songs: but the period seemed to have safeguarded nothing of itself for us; for the rhymed legends . . . and the romances of the fourteenth century had no national import. . . . One began to think that it had all been irretrievably lost, until Mr. Hanka had the luck . . . to discover in Dvůr Králové in Bohemia the remains of a Czech codex. . . . Only six longer heroic songs and eight delightful shorter songs did destiny grant us: but let us be thankful to the spirit of the Czechs even for this![20]

Palacký nicely illustrates the way in which the historical theories shaped perceptions of reality: he has no doubts that the Czechs had heroic epic. The lack of such material in preserved manuscripts does not cast doubt on this assumption but is attributed to losses in the manuscript collections.

I would suggest that the demand for a Czech epic in the context of the theoretical understanding of the day, according to which a Czech epic *must have* existed, allows us to frame Hanka and his collaborators' work as an attempt not to falsify history, but to rescue and resurrect history, to reconstruct the Czech epic in its most probable form, to fill a lacuna in Czech manuscript collections that could easily have been caused by the destruction wrought on Old Czech manuscripts by the Hussite Wars and the Counter-Reformation. We might then see their Czech epics as reflecting the kind of drive to reconstruct origins that also motivated the contemporaneous efforts to reconstruct the Proto-Indo-European language, which in the end also revealed itself as a theoretical fabrication, if perhaps to a lesser degree.[21] The idea that the Czechs must have had an epic tradition was only shown to be false by comparative Slavic literary studies in the later nineteenth century.[22]

In this perspective, Hanka and his collaborators' reconstructions form a regular part of the methodology of romantic science. Roman Jakobson made precisely this argument in an article dedicated to Hanka's memory in 1931 that seems to have had little effect on Hanka's reception in Czech literary studies:

> Scholars of the Romantic period painted the national past in bright strokes. In "restoring" the picture of the ancient way of life, its customs and beliefs, they gave their fantasy free reign. A Middle Ages without bards or epic poetry seemed to them a contradiction in terms. If no epos had come down to us, it could mean only that the following centuries had wiped away all traces of it: the oral tradition had died out, the manuscripts had been destroyed. But one could reconstruct the hypothetical content and artistic form of such works by using the comparative method, and the plausibility of such reconstructions was not so inferior to the authenticity of the grammatical forms established by the Romantic linguists of the time. From the point of view of the scientific Weltanschauung of the period, it would be a grave error to conclude from the lack of preserved monuments that they simply did not exist: would it not be better to try to reconstruct these treasures that were lost by chance? Thus the line separating the quasi-scientific dreams and literary mystifications of the Romantics became obliterated in principle.[23]

How different are the false foundations laid for Czech literature by Hanka and Linda and company from the contemporary refounding of national literary traditions in other parts of Europe on long lost and forgotten "national" epic poems like *Beowulf*, *The Song of Roland*, or even the *Nibelungenlied*? In addition to the serious problems in national patrimony for some of these (the canonical Roland, for example, survives in a single manuscript in a British library, and one that is written in an Anglo-Norman dialect), treating them, in analogy with Homer, as the foundation of the national literary tradition ignores how marginal they had become and creates a fictive genealogy as a basis for modern literary practice.[24]

Still, such national literary myths are often profoundly effective moments of culture-creation, and no less so in the case of the Czech manuscripts. If I were to ask, who were the most influential and important poets of Jungmann's generation, would we not be far more likely to cite František Ladislav Čelakovský and Jan Kollár than Hanka and Linda (or Jungmann, whose poetic translations are valued over his original poetry)? That may be wrong, and at least is debatable. Just one example of how Hanka and company were more successful poetically and programmatically can be found in their successful Slavicizing of the Czech language. Kollár's experiments with mixing Czech and Slovak into a new literary idiom in the 1820s and 1830s were rejected, though they appealed to the popular values of Slavic nationality, a shared Slavic literary language, and *libozvučnost* (euphony).[25] Hanka and company, on the other hand, were able to successfully introduce dozens of Russian and Serbian elements into the manuscripts and have the resulting macaronic idiom accepted as genuine Old Czech language, which helped to prepare the way for Čelakovský's later echoes of Russian folk songs. This intervention both justified and contributed to Jungmann's Slavicizing modernization of Czech by demonstrating the shared language basis in the deepest past and thus the common national ground. Some of these Slavic elements eventually became primary evidence of the forgery: the use of short adjectives in the attributive function, of *i* instead of *a* as the primary copulative conjunction, adverbs ending in *-o* instead of *-e*, and so forth, all of which did not correspond, in frequency and function, to other Old Czech documents. I would argue that the manuscripts were not meant to correspond, that these are not mistakes but deliberate distortions (the misuse of the aorist and imperfect past tenses are mistakes, on the other hand), and they have their source not only in Jungmann's programmatic borrowing from Slavic languages (see the detailed argument in chapter 3). The other source is Homeric epic, which also represents an unusual mixture of Greek dialects. I would suggest that Hanka and company are here creating (or re-creating) a Czech epic language on the model of the Greek, with its mixing of dialects—as Vladimír Macura and others have observed, the Greek dialects were a particularly influential model for the Czechs in thinking about the relationship between the various Slavic "dialects," as they called them.[26]

While the careful covering up of any direct evidence of the production of the manuscripts leaves little doubt about an intention to deceive on the part of its producers, when we reconsider the larger complex of motivations, intentions, and pressures that converged in the production of the Czech forged manuscripts, deception is mitigated by a number of much more positive motivations and intentions, and by a reconstructive methodology that is very much in line with the best contemporary scholarly practice. I believe, then, that there is good reason to stop treating Hanka, Linda, and their other possible collaborators as damned forgers and to fully recognize them as the authors of the most successful Czech poetry of the day, poetry that inspired and in many cases literally made Czech patriots (in the quasi-religious idiom of the day, "converted" readers to the Czech cause) and contributed greatly to the success of the Czech national movement.

Forgery and Romanticism

Hanka and his collaborators' fictions belong very much to a romantic context, responding to Romantic theories of national literatures and epic. Some more recent work by Czech scholars on the manuscripts is finally discussing them in connection to romanticism, instead of pre-romanticism, which had been the standard periodization term covering Czech literature from 1800 to 1830.[27] But what exactly is the relationship between forgery and romanticism? Is forgery, as the chapter title might suggest, an especially romantic form of authorship? How does forgery contribute or respond to the development of the romantic ideology of authorship?

Literary forgery of course predates romanticism—there are medieval forgeries, early modern forgeries, forgeries in every period. Historically speaking, literary forgery is practically coeval with literature. The theme is even readable in Homer's *Odyssey*, in the explicit question of the possibility of lying narrative and in the juxtaposition of incomplete and therefore inadequate narratives to the authoritative narrative of the *Odyssey* itself. Laura M. Slatkin analyzes the moment in book 11 where Odysseus's narrative of his adventures to the Phaeacians breaks off and he is encouraged to continue by Alkinoos:

> Odysseus, we as we look upon you do not imagine
> that you are a deceptive or thievish man, the sort that the black earth
> breeds in great numbers, people who wander widely, making up
> lying stories, from which no one could learn anything. You have
> a grace upon your words, and there is sound sense within them,
> and expertly, as a singer would do, you have told the story
> of the dismal sorrows befallen yourself and all of the Argives.[28]

As the audience knows, however, Odysseus is a very deceptive man, a master of disguise, of half-truth, of misleading answers, of narrative shaped to achieve his purposes with his audience. Alkinoos alludes to his mistrust of the fantastic tales Odysseus has sung so far and, as Slatkin observes, asks for a confirmation of their truthfulness by an appeal to epic singers and their narratives. He compares Odysseus to such singers and asks him to continue by relating the heroic exploits of his companions at Troy. "Alkinoos' reminder to Odysseus of the *topoi* of the Trojan heroes both acknowledges a conventional hierarchy of subjects within epic and reverts to it as a touchstone of poetic truth. . . . Recounting stories of the heroes at Troy will authenticate, for Alkinoos and the Phaeacians, Odysseus' claims about himself—and, by extension, his unprecedented adventures outside the Trojan sphere (that is, outside the realm of common human history)."[29] But Odysseus's easy transition into that narrative, his ability once again to adapt his narrative to his audience, calls into question that conventional standard of truthfulness, of historicity. Moreover, Odysseus's own narratives are often incomplete, and while he can narrate his experiences, at crucial moments he is unable to account for them, while the larger narrative provides its audience that perspective. Thus the *Odyssey* works to establish a standard of narrative authority, completeness, authenticity, and truthfulness, which it opposes to the conventions of epic-historical narrative and the unreliable eyewitness account (thereby calling into question the conventional ground of "authenticity" in bodily experience).[30]

This example from the *Odyssey* reminds us that literature has always been invested in distinguishing between authoritative, truthful, authentic narrative and narrative that is inadequate to that standard. I think some of the best attempts to rethink forgery place it in this broadest of literary-historical contexts and interrogate the relationship between forgery and literature. Stewart and Groom both suggest that literature in part creates the legitimacy of its inventions by using forgery to mark a boundary to invention and exorcise forged works as illegitimate invention. In that sense, forgery as the Other to literature helps to constitute literature as a legitimate practice. K. K. Ruthven goes on to perform the Derridean deconstruction of this binary opposition (genuine literature / forgery), arguing that genuine literature is haunted by its expulsion of the spurious and that, in fact, spuriousness is the common ground of literature and forgery.[31] Literature and literary forgery, then, are not merely coeval, they are consubstantial. Groom discusses forgers as makers, as practitioners, that is, of poesis in its most basic sense. "In a sense," he writes, "the literary forger is a shadow, forging what is already itself a fabrication, and thereby showing that literature, that most monumental fabrication, is no less forged than any shadowy literary forgery."[32]

If forgery has always haunted literature, why does forgery seem to flourish in particular periods? How to account for the flowering of literary forgery in the later eighteenth and early nineteenth centuries, the period of the rise of romanticism? I would suggest that *in part* this is the effect of romanticism's fundamental redefinition of literature, its redefinition of creativity, of the author and reader relationship, of the nature and continuity of tradition, and so on. The drive to expose forgery is a part of the setting up of new boundaries and protecting new categories. It is not so much, then, that more people intended to forge literature (this intent is, as we have discussed, not necessary) but that more forgeries are identified as a way of reconstituting literature. Formerly legitimate practices of copying, imitation, and variation become newly illegitimate, and thus more forgeries are identified (hence the rising concern with plagiarism as well, which may have less to do with new copyright laws and more to do with the romantic transformation of literature).

Ruthven notes that the 1760s were the decade of both Macpherson and Chatterton, as well as of the emergence of the category of "original genius."[33] In fact, Chatterton's and Macpherson's creations seem designed to illustrate precisely that category. If Homer is the model "original genius" of literature, then Macpherson's Ossian stands at a similar place for the origin of Scottish literature, and Chatterton' s Thomas Rowley—purportedly a fifteenth-century monk who "composes Pindaric Odes two centuries before Cowley, anticipates Surrey in his experiments with blank verse, writes a tragedy whose plot foretells *Othello*, and, most notably, invents several variations on" what is known as the Spenserian stanza, three centuries before Spenser—is a medieval monk poetic genius who originates the forms and themes of modern English poetry.[34] These are founders of traditions, poets whose creativity opens up new practices rather than following old ones. They are creative fictions that respond to the displacement of the classicist method of agonistic *imitatio* by the new romantic value placed on originality.[35] But they are rejected as illegitimate approaches and claims to this new value, even as they continue to stand as ideal models for what is sought. Here we see exemplified the complex role of forgery in defining new boundaries, even as it is censored according to them. Cases of "forgery" would seem to be ideal sites for exploring historically changing notions of what literature is, what authors are, and so on.

Another value that gains prominence under romanticism is "authenticity." The authentic is a category that aims to address a perceived lack in modern subjectivity, like the romantic nostalgia for a lost organic wholeness. One scholar who has addressed forgery's relationship to this in a helpful way is Margaret Russett in *Fictions and Fakes: Forging Romantic Authenticity, 1760–1845*. She argues that "spectacular fakes participated in defining the 'fictional identity' bequeathed to the modern subject by Romantic culture." Her thesis offers a subtle perspective on authenticity, fictionality, forgery, and modern subjectivity:

> Poetic identity, even and especially in the honorific mode called "authenticity," is a *fictional* construction, but this does not make it false. Indeed, I will ultimately suggest that the acknowledgment of subjectivity *as* fiction is an ethical condition of authenticity in its fully Romantic sense. My thesis, then, is that modern subjectivity should be understood as a subset and, to some extent, as a precipitate of the representational practices the Romantics called "romance" but which, in their derogated forms, also go by such names as "imposture," "forgery," "plagiarism," and "delusion."[36]

That authenticity is a fictional construction sounds like a very modern idea, but in fact it accords very well with the perspective of Homer's *Odyssey* on truthful and authentic narration, which requires great artistry and is itself an artifice.

Another scholar who has explored romantic identity in its artificial aspect is Melissa Frazier, in the context of a study of one of the most problematic authors of Russian romanticism: Osip Ivanovich Senkovskii. Born Józef-Julian Sękowski into a minor Polish noble family and trained as an orientalist, Senkovskii came eventually to serve as the editor of the highly successful journal *Biblioteka dlia chteniia* (Library for reading), a position he used to torment Aleksandr Pushkin and his allies, making him a figure of scorn and disdain in Russian literary history. Senkovskii was not only the editor but also the author of much of the journal's content, and as a critic he practiced a strange brand of criticism: a highly personal criticism performed in the masks of author-personas of his own invention, including Tiutiun'dzhiu-Oglu, O. O. . . . O!, and his most prolific, Baron Brambeus. Thus Senkovskii presents a figure of dramatic insincerity and inauthenticity and could be taken as anything but romantic, but Frazier shows that, in fact, his extremism reveals an underlying romantic tendency: "While few are as brazen as Senkovskii, there are a great many Romantic writers who deliberately construct inauthentic, insincere, or fragmentary selves and in fact, as we will see, despite their reputations even Rousseau and Wordsworth partake of a certain bent in this direction."[37] For Frazier, Senkovskii's artifices of identity help to reveal the place of irony in the formation of the romantic subject, which fundamentally changes how we understand the romantic categories of authenticity and originality. "Just as Romanticism understands a national literature as the original and unique expression of its people, so does it see a given text as the original and unique expression of its creator. Along with a new concept of authorship, Romanticism also offers an emphasis on authenticity that seemingly grounds the text in the real experiences of a real person. . . . [But] to take the Romantic concept of originality without a good dose of Romantic irony is to ignore the extent to which Romanticism is not about originality nor even imitation, but rather simulation."[38]

Frazier's invocation of Jean Baudrillard's notion of the simulacrum here will remind Czech scholars of Macura's interpretation of the Czech National Revival's strong tendency toward the creation of simulacra, in an analysis that includes the forged manuscripts.[39] Macura follows Baudrillard in opposing the simulacrum to a more "natural" or "organic" relationship to signification—for Macura, the Czech Revival cultural type is contrasted to a more natural cultural type, where cultural products meet specific cultural needs and audiences, rather than creating the illusion of the existence of such a culture and audience. Frazier's reading of Senkovskii suggests another way of interpreting this: seeing the Czech case not as different but rather as an extreme that reveals an underlying artificial tendency in romantic "national cultures."[40] For the study of forgery and fakes, Ruthven suggests we follow Gilles Deleuze and reject the Platonic denigration of simulacra: "This redemptive manoeuvre puts a positive spin on the much despised simulacrum by redefining it as the site of creativity rather than the absence of reality."[41]

While their terms are different, both Frazier and Russett point to a fictional or artificial moment that structures romantic categories in counterintuitive ways, and perhaps to a greater comfort with that fact among the romantics than among those of us who have inherited their categories. I would suggest that forgery, broadly conceived, is incorporated in a fundamental way in romantic literary practice, even as the new romantic categories set the stage for the later expulsion of many of these works as forgeries.

To sum up, then, the connections between romanticism and the flowering of forgery are manifold and intricate. First, it would seem that the redrawing of literature's borders through terms like *originality* and *authenticity* places some formerly legitimate practices outside the new bounds, and these practices get labeled forgery, plagiarism, and so forth. This happens even when these practices help to constitute the new categories and boundaries. In fact, this contamination of the new categories by their nominal opposites seems to be unavoidable, because romantic identity, whether individual or national, is founded on a moment of fictive play or ironic performance, a creative forging of identity. But there are limits drawn to this creative aspect as well, and some actors are found to have transgressed those limits, not necessarily because they are acting more cynically or with a more explicit understanding of the fictive roots of identity (I want to avoid here reintroducing the problem of potentially censurable authorial intent at another level). Romantic identity thus both *prescribes* forgery as a method and *proscribes* that activity beyond a certain vaguely defined limit.

Author and Authority in the Manuscripts

I move now from these theoretical considerations back to the Czech manuscripts and the relationship between the author figure and authority that they construct. Scholars have noted the central role that Macpherson's Ossianic poetry played in advancing the concept of "oral tradition."[42] The Czech manuscripts also gesture strongly toward oral traditions, but in a very different manner. For Macpherson, the past survives in the voice of the bard as still reflected in living Scottish song traditions. There is a continuity of tradition that keeps alive the voice of the bard, and thus continues to speak a living witness to ancient.[43] The figure of the bard thus mediates between the romantic "original genius" and the elevation of the oral tradition as its carrier. There is little demand, at first, to see the material sources for Macpherson's translations because they nominally derive not from manuscripts but from the still living oral tradition that keeps alive the authoritative and original voice of the bard.

In contrast, while the Czechs had a living folk song tradition, it did not include any considerable epic material. The continuity of the oral tradition was, presumably, broken. What they needed, then, was material evidence from a much older period, before the continuity had been broken. Hence the forging of medieval manuscripts, which had to represent a kind of fragmentary writing down of a much larger oral epic tradition and, at the same time, be a sign of Czech *writing* traditions in a much earlier period than hitherto attested (in order that the Czechs be able to compete with the Germans in civilizational development). This introduces a profound tension in the manuscripts between oral and written forms, because the authority of the manuscripts to speak to ancient history and poetic traditions had to be grounded not merely in the representation of the oral tradition, but also in the representation of the writing tradition.[44] It is not surprising to find, then, that the figure of the bard in the Czech manuscripts, the singer Záboj (with mere mention as well of Lumír), is much more marginal. The Czech songs are not Záboj's songs, but the songs of the Czech people. This is exemplified primarily in the manifold ways that the manuscripts make use of oral poetic figures, syntax, and narrational devices, and thus present themselves as belonging to the anonymous and collective patrimony of folklore.[45] The Czech manuscripts represent a later conception of authorship in relation to the oral tradition than Macpherson's Ossianic poems: original genius is ascribed not to an individual but to the national collective, the people, the carriers of the tradition as its creators.[46]

I would also argue that this anonymity of collective authorship and authority is reflected profoundly in the epic battle scenes of the Czech manuscripts. As so often in epic, many of the battles at their climax are decided in the single combat of the leaders of the opposing sides. But in the battles that precede these final showdowns, where many oral epic traditions describe numerous other individual encounters between powerful warriors individualized and given by name (the *aristeia* of each hero—see the analysis in chapter 2 of such scenes), the Czech epics primarily represent the warriors in synecdoche by their arms and represent battle almost exclusively in storm similes (amusingly, in a kind of realization of the simile, the decisive battle against the invading Mongols is turned, in the poem "Jaroslav," by an actual storm).[47] Ultimately, it is the force of the Czech people as a whole that is elevated over the exploits of individual warriors—they speak with one voice; they fight like an elemental force of nature. Unified Czech nationhood is represented above all else. The voice of the Czech people in its oral traditional form, tenuously captured in the forms of an early writing tradition, this is what constitutes the performance of a fictive authenticating basis for modern arguments for Czech membership in the family of nations. This is national mythopoesis at its best, if perhaps also in its most transgressive mode.

The authority and authenticity of the manuscripts derived from this collective anonymity of authorship. In such a case, any evidence that can be taken to demonstrate a unitary authorial consciousness behind the manuscripts, a single author, becomes a powerful argument against the authority of the manuscripts. The existence of an author is equivalent to the inauthentication of the manuscripts. The Moravian Germanist Julius Feifalik was the first to present evidence, in 1860, that the poems of the Queen's Court Manuscript were not folk poems but had the characteristics of the work of a single, educated author.[48] Others later contributed to this line of argument, and for many, as for the great literary historian Jaroslav Vlček, this evidence remained decisive.[49] As I have already noted, in the economy of this argument it was not necessary to work out the disagreements and contradictory attributions of the poems to various authors proposed by different investigators. Whether there was one author or a small group and whether the author of a particular poem was Hanka, Linda, Jungmann, or some combination of them together did not matter. Authors and the manuscripts did not go together. This logic has continued to shape the study of the Czech manuscripts to this day, and the question of the authorship of the manuscripts, both in its specifics of attribution and in its theoretical and contextual aspects, remains open to investigation.

Conclusion

When a version of this chapter was published in 2011, I concluded by suggesting that the case of the Czech manuscripts offers a wonderful site for exploring the manifold connections between romanticism and forgery in more depth and investigating whether, as the theory advanced here suggests, the assignment of the work to the category of forgery is a part of a larger process of the reorganization of literature as an institution, including new understandings of authorship, and the subsequent reinterpretation of these new romantic values. The initial unquestioned legitimacy of the manuscripts in patriotic circles, with notable exceptions, followed by a long and slow-developing process that eventually leads to their labeling as forgeries, offers rich material for analysis that can contribute greatly to the international theoretical discussion of forgeries and their place in literature. The detailed history of the manuscripts' reception in Czech scholarship by Dobiáš, Fránek, Hrdina, Krejčová, and Piorecká, published in 2014, offers a number of insights that support the thesis that it was later reinterpretations of romantic categories that narrowed them and led to the labeling of more works as forgeries.[50] There is also a telling parallel between the falling popularity of Ossian in the later nineteenth century and the rise of critical voices directed at the Czech manuscripts. Vlček observes, "Toward the end of the [18]50s, with the decline of the romantic perspective in scholarship and poetry, after the fall of Ossian and other analogical phenomena . . . a new sobering occurs that affects Libuše's Judgment along with other supposed Old Czech monuments, including the Queen's Court Manuscript."[51] This parallel suggests a tolerance for forgeries among romantics that begins to disappear with the rise of a new literary ethos. Václav Svoboda's oft-cited statement from his early polemics with Dobrovský, "We would value highly a second Chatterton, if we had him among us, and we would not place particular weight on the historical authenticity of his work," should not be read as representative of a cynical ahistoricism among the Czech romantic generation.[52] It accords very well with what scholars have observed in the reception of the Ossianic poems in the early nineteenth century, when readers were already aware of the problems surrounding the provenance of the poems but still valued them for the authentic literary value they presented.[53] In fact, there were more editions of Ossian from 1800 to 1835 than there were in the first thirty-five years following Macpherson's publication.[54] Here too we see a tolerance for artifice, simulation, and invention in the creation of works that appeal to the romantic values of originality and authenticity, a tolerance that would disappear as those values came to be defined more strictly. The attacks on the manuscripts beginning in the late 1870s parallel the sharpening debates in Scottish Gaelic studies in the 1870s concerning authenticity.[55] Forgery as a romantic form of authorship came eventually to be seen as an illegitimate and nonliterary practice, and certain authors and their forged works were expunged from the canon of literature.

The Czech case offers one of the more explosive confrontations between opposing perspectives on the same values of originality and authenticity, when the matter of the manuscripts, which had been embraced by Czech nationalists as part of the sacred text of their national mythology, came into contact with the antimatter of stricter scholarly investigations and notions of truth. It has taken a long time to recover from the intense stigmatization of the forgers and their work and to begin to restore them to their rightful and even honorable place in their romantic Czech context.

Chapter 2

Successful Forgeries

Oral Traditional Epic Poetics in the Czech Manuscripts

A number of factors converged to make the Queen's Court and Green Mountain Manuscripts the successful forgeries they were, able to meet the demand of an eager public with their convincing simulation of ancient Slavic poetry. Not least among these factors was the skillful imitation of oral poetic forms the songs of the manuscripts represented. As we shall see, while the first responses and early defenses of the authenticity of the manuscripts gestured vaguely toward their ancient aura, as the arguments on both sides developed, the specification of their oral poetic features became an important aspect in arguments for their authenticity. In making the definitive case, in the mid-1880s, that the manuscripts were forgeries, the realist critics in Tomáš Garrigue Masaryk's circle thus had to denigrate the supposedly folk features of the poems, and their reputation on that front has never really recovered. But just how good are the manuscript songs as imitations of folk poetry? Can they stand up to the later, highly valued, and canonical *Ohlas písní ruských* (Echo of Russian songs, 1829) by František Ladislav Čelakovský? In what ways do they resemble oral poetry, and how deep is that resemblance?

The question of how the *epic poems* of the Queen's Court and Green Mountain Manuscripts are structured and work poetically might best be answered through comparison to their clearest poetic models, the South Slavic oral epic songs collected and published by Vuk Karadžić, and to related oral epic traditions. Karadžić's songs very quickly became a huge hit in a Europe that was all too eager for examples of native epic poetry. Václav Hanka was among those at the very forefront of that enthusiastic reception.

Hanka went to Vienna in 1813 to continue his studies of law at the university there. He arrived with a letter of recommendation from Josef Dobrovský, who had just taken on Hanka as a private student in Slavistics, introducing him to Jernej Kopitar, Dobrovský's Slovenian colleague, with whom Hanka began to study and collaborate. That same autumn, Karadžić also arrived in Vienna and quickly made an impression on Kopitar. With Kopitar's collaboration and encouragement, Karadžić published in 1814 both his new grammar of the Serbian language, based on the popular spoken language, and his first collection of folk songs, the *Mala prostonarodnja slaveno-serbska pesnarica*.[1] Hanka responded to this collection with a small article published anonymously in 1814 in *Prvotiny pěkných umění*, notable for being the first call for the Czechs to begin to collect their own folk songs. "It would be highly desirable if some gentleman patriot would make the effort to collect for us our lovely folk songs, so that the Czechs might be led back to Slavic song, from which, alas! we have strayed so far with harsh sounds and the imitation of German songs. . . . Even the Serbs outdid us this year in this, having published their folk songs in Vienna." The article was followed by one song from the collection, "Oj devojko dušo moja," and Hanka's translation of it.[2] That volume included only a handful of shorter epic songs.

Karadžić's second volume, the *Narodna srbska pjesnarica* published in Vienna in 1815, was the first to contain a significant selection of heroic epic songs alongside lyrics and other song types. These were the relatively compact epic narratives sung in the shorter ten-syllable epic line, the *deseterac*, about the Battle of Kosovo and Marko Kraljević.[3] Kopitar reviewed the volume in 1816 in *Wiener allgemeine Literaturzeitung* and included translations of five songs into German. Hanka translated these same five into Czech, adding two additional lyrics from the volume and one from the first collection, and published it in 1817 as *Prostonárodní srbská muza, do Čech převedená* (The Serbian folk muse, led over into Bohemia).[4] Of the eight songs Hanka translated, three were in the deseterac form of traditional epic.[5] Hanka, following Kopitar, thus preceded with his translation the later and more substantial efforts by the brothers Grimm (1818) and Sir John Bowring (1827).[6]

Even if we did not know of Hanka's engagement with Karadžić's epic songs or did not believe Hanka to be the forger of the manuscripts' epics (or even that they are forged), it would be clear that the South Slavic epics are the key model (or analogue, or genetic relative) for the poetic form of the songs. Five of the seven epic songs in the two manuscripts are entirely, or at least partially, in ten-syllable lines; moreover, in their similar length, and in features that we will explore further in this chapter of their phraseology and narrative techniques, they best resemble the South Slavic epics.[7] Other oral epic traditions also served as models and occasional sources of particular phrasing and features, including Homeric epic, Russian byliny, and Gaelic epic in the highly mediated and multiply translated form in which the authors encountered Macpherson's Ossianic songs (which nonetheless sometimes preserved original features).[8] The twelfth-century East Slavic *Slovo o polku Igoreve* (Igor tale) provided a properly medieval Slavic model with a number of features that recalled oral epic traditions. But the prose form of the *Igor Tale*, like the Ossianic prose translations, encouraged an association of the earliest oral traditions with looser poetic forms, which, as we will see, causes a number of problems of poetic form in the manuscripts.[9] Finally, among the probable models for the epic poems, we can move beyond those closer to oral traditions and include European literary epic sources, which could be tapped as models for scenes and imagery in compositions that, on the whole, pursued folkloric as opposed to literary form, especially insofar as those literary epic traditions traced their lineage back through Virgil to Homer and maintained some traditional features, particularly in battle scenes. In the analysis that follows, we will have occasion to note the contributions of each of these sources to the language and poetics of the manuscripts.

For our primary point of comparison, though, we are fortunate to have a tradition that has been subject to intensive study as to its form and nature over the past century. Milman Parry recognized the value of the living oral epic traditions among the South Slavs for understanding epic composition, and in a series of studies, based on his collecting fieldwork among Bosnian and Montenegrin Muslim singers, he fundamentally recast the dogged question of Homeric authorship. Parry and his local collaborators, along with his student Albert Bates Lord, conducted experiments, testing how a singer would sing the same song on a second occasion, distant in time from the first recording, and whether a singer could learn a song that had not been in their repertoire and sing it after hearing another singer perform it.[10] It became clear that the singers did not in any way memorize their lengthy songs, but instead that every performance was a new improvisation of the song, composing it anew. As Lord put it, "Singing, performing, and composing are facets of the same act."[11] They developed the oral-formulaic theory to account for how singers were able to compose narratives in verse form with the speed necessary for performance, showing that certain features of epic poetic language such as fixed epithets, commonplace actions and phrasings, and traditional plot elements all served as part of a repertoire of devices that enabled a skilled singer to renarrate the traditional tales in a dynamic performance.[12] Their research initiated a period of intensive study of oral epic traditions in the second half of the twentieth century, which included not only Slavic and Greek epic but also Old English literature, Germanic epic, biblical literature, and African epic traditions, among many others. These studies tested their definitions of the characteristic features of oral epic across many different language traditions and sparked controversy about whether one could determine if a text had been composed orally and then written down or if writing had played a role in the composition; whether a text's density of formulaic language or its thrift in its phrasings were adequate tests of oral origin; what the essential differences were between oral and written composition and where they might overlap; whether the formulaic nature of the language did not reduce how we might interpret the epics, diminishing their aesthetic qualities, and so on. In the wake of this broad research, John Miles Foley offered a revision of oral-formulaic theory in two studies, focused on the South Slavic, Homeric, and Old English epic traditions, that broadened Parry's and Lord's definitions of the formula and theme in order to better address comparisons across languages and traditions (*Traditional Oral Epic* [1990] and *Immanent Art* [1991]). His account of the nature of the South Slavic epic will serve as the basis for my comparison with the Czech manuscripts.

Although it potentially offers important revisions to some of the arguments both in support of and against the authenticity of the Czech manuscripts, as well as insight into their form and nature, oral-formulaic theory has not been applied systematically to their study. The single example I am aware of is the study by Julius Enders, *Rukopis Zelenohorský a Královédvorský: Vznik, styl a básnická hodnota staročeské orální poesie* (The Green Mountain and Queen's Court Manuscript: Origin, style, and poetic value of Old Czech oral poetry; 1993). While this is a very problematic volume for a number of reasons, it only received a couple of dismissive reviews that failed to engage, or even mention, its argument regarding the oral-formulaic nature of the poetry of the manuscripts.[13] The curt dismissal by the experts is probably understandable in its context: in the early postsocialist period, such a work, defending the authenticity of the manuscripts, probably represented an unwelcome return, with the arrival of a newly open publishing industry, to an argument that official discourse and scholarship under the socialist regime had managed to suppress. Enders, a linguist, had been penning samizdat articles in defense of the manuscripts since 1970, shortly after the definitive summation of the scholarship on the manuscripts and the decisive arguments for their fabrication published by scholars of the Czech Academy of Sciences in 1969.[14] While the oral-formulaic theory is key to Enders's argument, with the density of formulaic phrasing in the manuscripts touted as definitive evidence of their authentic, oral origins, the examination of this evidence makes up but a small part of the work, which is otherwise dedicated to highly detailed traditional stylistic analysis that takes no account of the supposed oral nature of the songs and the specificity of oral stylistics.[15] The examination of oral formulas comes only in chapter 17.7 and occupies just sixteen pages. Nonetheless, I shall have occasion in the course of my own account to return to Enders's work and his arguments.

The analysis below examines the epic poems of the Queen's Court and Green Mountain Manuscripts that are composed entirely in ten-syllable lines or that make use of the ten-syllable line along with lines of other length in a more flexible form. This respects the genre specificity of comparison, as urged by Foley, and the fundamental link between the verbal formula and the metrical form as defined by Parry, in comparing to the South Slavic epic poems in the deseterac line. This includes the poems "Oldřich and Boleslav," "Jaroslav," and "Libuše's Judgment" entirely in ten-syllable form; "Čestmír and Vlaslav," in which 84 of the 229 lines of the poem are in ten-syllable form (counting only segments with more than 2 lines consecutively in the form), primarily in the battle sections describing the taking of Kruvoj's keep and the defeat of Vlaslav's army; and "Záboj, Slavoj, and Luděk," in which 21 of the 255 lines of the poem are in ten-syllable form (again counting only segments with more than 2 lines consecutively), in the 11 opening lines and a few small sections after. When the following analysis moves beyond formulas in the stricter sense, tied to meter, to other levels of phraseology and repetitions, story elements, and whole plots, evidence and examples from the remainder of these two poems and from the other epics, ballads, and lyrics of the manuscripts will also be brought in where relevant. The analysis will examine the elements similar to and different from oral epic compositions and the probable sources of some of these elements.

Traditional Oral Epic: Formula, Theme, Song

For Parry and Lord, oral-formulaic epics of the type that they were studying were formulaic on multiple levels. While the term *formula* itself was reserved for the typical phraseology of the oral epic, with its repeated and repeatable words, phrases, and whole poetic lines, the epics also demonstrated repeated and repeatable phrasing and structures on higher levels. They called *theme* the commonplace story-building elements that are deployed successively by the singers to build the larger plots of the tales—elements such as the arming of the hero, his departure from a city, or the gathering for a feast. The *songs* as a whole also revealed common and repeated plot structures, such as the plot of what Lord named the Return Song, embodied in its classical variant by the *Odyssey* and studied by Foley alongside multiple South Slavic variants in *Traditional Oral Epic*. In this section and the following, we will examine the Czech manuscripts' epics in relation to oral epic traditions at each of these levels.

The classic definition of a formula, made by Parry and repeated by Lord, is "a group of words which is regularly employed under the same metrical conditions to express a given essential idea."[16] The archetypal example, analyzed extensively and rigorously by Parry, is the traditional epithets used to name characters, like swift-footed Achilleus, divine Achilleus, man-slaying Hektor, divine Hektor. The Homeric singer, in order to evoke the essential idea of "Achilleus," had at his disposal a repertoire of epithet-noun combinations that were suitable to evoke the character and that fulfilled different metrical conditions, so that if he were beginning a hexameter line by naming the character, one adjective would be used, and if he were ending the line, another would fit. Parry was also able to show that the Homeric diction was characterized by a remarkable thrift: under given metrical conditions, there was usually only *one* epithet that would be used to name a particular character.[17] A formula, then, was defined rather narrowly as a phrase that was repeated and repeatable regularly to make up a particular part of the metrical line and fill it with an essential idea. But Parry also considered other types of formulaic language, such as substitutional syntactic systems combining subjects and verbs or prepositions and objects, where some parts of the phrase would be repeated while other parts were subject to regular and limited substitution.[18] In such cases, the repetition of words is only partial and the essential idea of the phrase could be hard to distill, but the utility to the singer in the forming of metrically sound phrases was no less. This pointed suggestively to the formulaic nature of the whole of Homeric diction as a spectrum of phraseology, without providing "a comprehensive theory of formulaic structure."[19]

Lord continued in this direction in his discussion of South Slavic epic diction, defining formulaic units as lines and half lines that "follow the basic patterns of rhythm and syntax and have at least one word in the same position in the line in common with other lines and half lines."[20] These constitute the kind of formulaic substitutional systems also explored by Parry and form a part of the basic "poetic grammar" that enabled the singer who mastered it to sing the traditional songs. The move into a different language tradition already required Lord to alter some of Parry's key observations regarding Homeric diction. For one, epithets applied to characters were far less common, because in the short deseterac line, name and title or patronymic were usually sufficient to present a character.[21] Furthermore, the thrift that characterized the

Homeric diction was not so marked in the South Slavic tradition. In comparing the songs of singers from different areas, it became clear that the phraseology was relatively flexible, and while an individual singer might use a thriftier repertoire of phrasings under identical metrical conditions, the larger tradition was richer and more variable. "A singer's thriftiness is significant; that of a district or tradition less so (if it exists) for our purposes."[22]

If Lord's comparative analysis gave reason to doubt the cross-cultural value of the principle of thrift, his analysis of the pervasiveness of formulaic language suggested a standard of formulaic density that came to be used, also across linguistic and cultural lines, however dubiously, as a test to determine whether texts had their origins in oral composition.[23] He examined a sample section of fourteen lines in relation to a total of twelve thousand lines by the singer Salih Ugljanin from the Parry and Lord collections, eleven different songs, and subjected it to analysis as to the formulaic basis of its lines. He concluded,

> Even within the limited number of lines used in the experiment, that is, 12,000, one quarter of the whole lines in the [14-line] sample and one half of the half lines are formulas. It is most significant that there is no line or part of a line that did not fit into some formulaic pattern. . . .
>
> Had we gone beyond 12,000 lines, the number of formulas would have continued to mount, and had we included material from other singers it would have increased still further, until it became clear that almost all, if not all, the lines in the sample passage were formulas and that they consisted of half lines which were also formulas. . . . There is nothing in the poem that is not formulaic.[24]

Formulas, strictly speaking, make up 25–50 percent of the phrasing, and 100 percent of the language belongs to formulaic systems in his sample. This showed that the language of his singer was pervasively formulaic and set a relatively high bar for the formulaic density expected of material from other traditions.

In his revision of Parry's and Lord's work, Foley, who had the benefit of the results of years of cross-tradition research, insisted on the specificity of each linguistic tradition in the particulars of its manifestation of features. For Foley, who aimed at a more rigorous and comprehensive theory of formulaic structure, one had to begin with an analysis of the prosody of the particular poetic tradition in order to respect the unity of content and meter that the formula represents. And since the notion of formula itself proved to be difficult to define, as it covered a spectrum of phenomena—"classically defined formulas, substitution systems, collocations, sound-patterns, and even purely metrical dispensations"—it might have to be put aside in the process of better defining the formation of epic diction.[25] Foley's solution was to work from a description of the epic prosody in the particular language tradition toward a series of "traditional rules" that "governed the symbiosis of prosody and phraseology and were thus responsible for the creation and maintenance of all structures from classical formulas to metrical dispensations." These rules implicitly govern how well-formed epic phraseology is generated in a given tradition and amount to a kind of formalization of what Lord called its grammar. Each tradition would thus have its own particular set of rules that was "highly idiosyncratic; while certain tendencies proved common to some traditions and genres, often because of similar evolution from Indo-European metrical prototypes, no single set of rules could account for all traditions and genres."[26] Foley's terminology changes to mark this development in the theory of oral epic: he largely avoids the descriptor "oral-formulaic" and instead titles his volume that develops the traditional rules for Greek, Serbo-Croatian, and Old English epic *Traditional Oral Epic*.

Before we turn to the rules for Bosnian-Croatian-Serbian epic, let us return briefly to Enders's study of the formulaic aspect of the Czech manuscripts in light of the theory just discussed. While Enders's study was published after Foley's revisions, his manuscript may have been largely completed by 1988 and waited several years before its publication was possible.[27] Even without accounting for Foley's studies, though, Enders takes a rather too straightforward approach to the oral-formulaic aspect of the manuscripts' poems that does not take into account the many controversies and developments that preceded Foley's revisions. In fact, his understanding of the main principles and reasons for oral-formulaic theory is often lacking. The main problem in Enders's account of the formulaic aspect of the manuscripts' songs is that it misses the critical metrical aspect of the definition of the formula, the "under the same metrical conditions" of Parry's definition. His analysis of fixed epithets (adjective-noun combinations) thus lists repeated combinations of various sorts and suggests they are "formulové výrazy" (formulaic expressions), but does not at all account for their placement in the poetic line.[28] His list of true formulas, which he defines as any combination of two or more words that is repeated in the manuscripts, also does not differentiate at all for placement in the verse line.[29] At the end of this list, he excuses his lack of attention to the verse line by arguing that the ten-syllable verse line of the manuscripts is "rozmanitější a volnější" (freer and more various) than the deseterac.[30] This perhaps connects to his prejudice regarding verse forms, one encouraged by the freer forms of the songs of the Queen's Court Manuscript set in pagan times: "It's understood that neither Homer's heroes nor the figures mentioned in the Queen's Court Manuscript sang in hexameters or deseterac lines. Clearly the form of their songs was free or seemingly free verse, as we find in 'The Stag,' 'Záboj,' and 'Čestmír.'"[31] Nothing in oral-formulaic theory would support this notion, and one wonders what use formulaic language would be to singers using free verse forms. Perhaps it is only an aesthetic means, which is how Enders also interprets the notion of thrift: "snahou pěvců bývalo být 'thrifty,' tedy 'úsporný'" (the singers endeavored to be thrifty) with their poetic means.[32] Thrift is not for him a means to enable the rapid composition, in performance, of a narrative sung in a complicated metrical line, but merely a part of oral style.

And yet, a lack of differentiation between oral-formulaic traditions and any other type of oral poetry underlies Enders's entire argument. The formula is, he says, "the characteristic mark of our genre, realized among all nations in all times, until written literature took precedence."[33] Just how inconsistent oral-formulaic poetry was across languages and cultures, though, was being shown by the expanding research on the topic at the time, particularly in regard to the density of formulas in constituting the verse, making it dubious at best as a test for the oral provenance of the verse.[34] Enders nonetheless declares, without citation, that "authorities insist that about forty lines of verse from a previously unknown author are sufficient to determine their oral or literary provenance."[35] Despite the very small corpus the manuscripts represent, then (and even though he once admits that this is a problem for determining the formulaic aspect of repetitive expressions), this principle underlies his conclusion that the manuscripts are undeniably of oral origin.[36] This indifferentiation regarding types of oral poetry, meter, and genre gives him a somewhat larger corpus to work with, as he includes not only the epic poems in ten-syllable verse but all the epic, lyric, and ballad/romance poems of the manuscripts in his analysis of formulas. But of course, ballads and lyrics are short genres that are reproduced from memory, not recomposed each time through the grammar of a formulaic tradition. He chooses a segment of the short romance "Zbyhoň" as his text for a formulaic analysis à la Lord, and in a number of cases it is the lyric songs that are given as evidence for the formulaic nature of the expressions, all of which ignores entirely the genre-specific aspect of formulas.[37] Finally, the other levels of formulaic composition—theme and song—are not considered at all by Enders, except insofar as he notes in passing in his discussion of the epic genre (based primarily on the traditions of *literary* epic analysis) that the descriptions of palaces, arms, and feasts are very modest in the manuscripts.[38] Given these serious faults, one need not take at all seriously Enders's claim to have proved the oral authenticity of the manuscripts' texts, even while allowing him precedence in demonstrating the potential insights oral-formulaic theory can add to the discussion of the manuscripts, recognizing the value of his carefully compiled lists of fixed epithets and other formulaic expressions and systems (even including some grammatical figures), and thus still taking seriously his contribution to the scholarly discussion.

Prosody and Traditional Rules in BCS Epic and Their Czech Imitation

As we delve in this section into what will necessarily be a complex and technical versological analysis of the South Slavic epics and their Czech imitations, readers are encouraged to engage it as far as their interest takes them and to skim as necessary for the insights and conclusions that result. I have attempted to define all my terms and explain the import of the analysis in as accessible a manner as possible.

The ten-syllable deseterac epic line, according to Foley's description, has a number of features that relate it to its likely Indo-European prototype. These include its very stable syllable count and an even more stable caesura (or institutionalized word boundary) after the fourth syllable, which divides the ten-syllable line into uneven halves, the four- and six-syllable cola. (A colon is a basic metrical unit, like a foot but longer.) It also includes features that derive from the principle of right justification, or the tendency of the verse to be more rhythmically organized (to have a more regular succession of quantities or stresses) toward the end of the line or colon. Thus, each colon ends with a strong long-short, or stressed-unstressed, pattern; stressed monosyllables tend toward the cola openings to further mark these line and cola boundaries, so that the primary ictus (metrical stress) placements are on syllables 1, 3, 5, and 9.[39] The second colon in general is more stable and organized than the first, and longer, which also reflects the principle of right justification. The second colon is also governed by a shorter-before-longer rule for word placement, with a possible exception for initially accented disyllables, which can supersede this rule and take the line final position in order to mark the ictus in the ninth syllable with the word accent. Most commonly, then, the second colon is formed by words of 2 + 4 syllables, followed by a much less common 4 + 2 and then 3 + 3.[40] In the case of two trisyllables, if one is medially accented, it will take the line-final position (like the disyllable, again to mark the ictus with the accented syllable in the ninth syllable). In the freer first colon, initially accented disyllables also move to colon-final position, but there is no real shorter-before-longer rule in play and the most common word length pattern is 2 + 2. These principles constitute the fundamental inner metric of the verse, according to Foley.[41]

Foley's "traditional rules" are essentially these same prosodic principles restated as a set of rules for the shaping of the phraseology of the epic. He takes the ten-syllable line length and caesura as obvious and formulates the remainder of the rules that are the result of right justification as follows:

1. an initial four-syllable colon followed by a six-syllable colon, the more extensive unit following the less extensive one;
2. preference for ictus at positions 3 and 9, then 1 and 5;
3. shorter-before-longer words and accentual groupings (SBL) in both cola;
4. initially accented disyllables (IAD) favored at positions 3–4 and 9–10;
5. medially accented trisyllables (MAT) favored at position 8–10;
6. a generally greater flexibility in colon 1 . . . and, correspondingly, a generally greater fixity in colon 2.[42]

In essence, then, the "grammar" of oral poetry is a prosodic grammar—these are the implicit rules that all formulas and formulaic systems in the diction follow and that, further, allow the singer to generate well-formed sung narrative verse even in those instances when no fixed formulas or flexible formulaic systems provide a clear support, or when they offer so much variety and flexibility that it would be possible to stumble. If for Lord "the poetic grammar of oral epic is and must be based on the formula," that is, on the seemingly premade repeated phrases that combine and recombine to make up the verse, for Foley the formula follows the more fundamental rules of the prosaic grammar, which give it its metrical shape long before it takes on the more fixed aspect of repeated phrase and also shape all those other repeating elements that are not strictly speaking formulaic (involving no essential idea, for example).[43]

Foley performs a formulaic analysis of a short passage à la Lord, finding a similar pervasiveness of formulaic diction, but further examines a number of the lines and cola in their formulaic aspect, demonstrating that elements marked as classic formulas may rather or additionally participate in formulaic systems involving full lines or multiples of lines, that many participate in multiple systems, and that some do not really qualify as formulas because they fail to embody a distillable idea.[44] In all of these cases, he shows that the traditional rules remain in effect in shaping the diction. He concludes, "We have seen, in short, that all elements of phraseology . . . are not equal. The wide spectrum of diction includes some units that are always repeated exactly, some that undergo only morphological change, some that admit regular substitution and can be meaningfully described as formulaic systems, and some 'non-formulaic' cola and lines that are best viewed as the inevitable issue of fundamental traditional rules." Thus, "while formulas and systems explain the poetic idiom inexactly as a dictionary of quantitatively equivalent but qualitatively different paradigms, traditional rules account for the entire spectrum of traditional phraseology—every line of every song-text."[45]

Formulas and formulaic systems do have a role in shaping the diction, nonetheless, but it is secondary, serving as a second-level focusing. Any actual verse line must be shaped by the traditional rules and, subsequently, may be shaped as well by formulas. In a hierarchy of gradually diminishing frequency, in terms of the number of lines affected, other second-level focusing processes include sound patterning (among them leonine or end-colon rhyme, colon-initial rhyme, alliteration, assonance, and consonance), syntactic patterns of terracing and parallelism (syntactic balance), and, finally, thematic focus (as multiline units transition toward thematic storytelling units).[46] Any actual verse line can be shaped by one or more of these in addition to its fundamental prosodic shape derived from the traditional rules.[47] For Foley, this analysis "re-complicates" poetic composition, removing the stigma of formulaic composition that it somehow implies inflexibility and a mechanical stringing together of premade material, opening the door to an aesthetic appreciation of the singer's art and the singer as a practitioner of *poiesis*.[48]

These rules result in certain observable tendencies in the shaping of the verse lines. Epithets as more fixed formulaic elements tend to appear in the more stable second colon, which also harbors the less variable formulaic systems in general. The more flexible first colon is the realm of verbs and syntactic determinations. In other words, the first colon's open formulaic structure is often focused by the more stable second colon, or, in the reverse perspective, the stable formula of the second colon is shaped to the particular context by the first.[49]

These rules and tendencies of the South Slavic deseterac epic verse tradition offer a sound basis from which to compare their imitation in the Czech manuscripts. In regard to the ten-syllable poetic line, it finds its counterpart in three epic songs that are entirely in ten-syllable form and in two others with some significant passages in the form. The syllable count is quite consistent, although in some instances the published versions have undergone editorial emendation (from their first publisher, Hanka, forward) to correct a few hypometric (nine-syllable) verses from the manuscripts. (One might also extend some of the passages of ten-syllable lines in the other poems by a line or two, here or there, with similar emendations.[50]) When we come to the other "obvious" feature, the caesura after the fourth syllable, we encounter a problem. While the majority of the verses conform, a significant percentage of lines (that varies from poem to poem) do not. Given the caesura's status as a very stable traditional element of the South Slavic epic line that derives from its likely Indo-European precedent and which Foley finds reflections of in both Old English and Homeric verse, its absence in the supposedly most ancient Czech verse stands out as anomalous and, potentially, as another piece of evidence that these songs are not authentic. Before we examine the details of this deviation, let us consider some of the possible reasons for it. First, if we suppose the nineteenth-century composition of the songs, we see evidence of a strange conviction among the authors (shared by Enders, as noted earlier, and perhaps influenced by the Old East Slavic *Igor Tale* and Ossianic epics) that the oldest epic verse forms were looser and did not follow strict metrical schemata—that is clear from the form of the two epic songs set in the pre-Christian pagan period from the Queen's Court Manuscript that only use sections of ten-syllable lines and lines of variable length elsewhere. This, however, is sharply contradicted by the Green Mountain Manuscript, for the song about Libuše's judgment falls in between the other two in the time-setting of its plot and supposedly long before them in terms of its recording in a manuscript, yet it adheres strictly to the ten-syllable line. Second, even if the authors recognized the significance of the caesura, they may have opted for a less strict adherence because the Czech tradition would have been related, but not identical, to the South Slavic one; this might have been further suggested by the more mobile caesura in Latin epic and in Greek. Third, if we allow for the possible medieval origin of the songs, it may indeed be the case that the caesura in Czech tradition became more mobile, in which case we ought to be able to articulate rules regarding its variation in the songs of the manuscripts.

What is the nature of the variation of the caesura? In the Green Mountain Manuscript, that is, in the epic poem "Libuše's Judgment," in the vast majority of the lines the caesura does fall after the fourth syllable, as in the South Slavic deseterac, but in 7.4 percent of the lines (9 of 121 total lines, by my count), it falls instead after the sixth syllable, dividing the line into reversed 6 + 4 cola. Given that this is the "oldest" manuscript, as judged by its paleographic signs, we might attempt to explain this as a closely related analogue to the South Slavic line that has developed some additional flexibility. When we look to the epics in the "later" Queen's Court Manuscript, the variation grows and becomes more complicated. In "Oldřich and Boleslav," already 16.7 percent of the lines do not have a caesura after the fourth syllable (10 of 60 full lines).[51] The longest epic, "Jaroslav," has an alternative caesura in 19.0 percent of its lines (55 of 289). In both cases, the alternate caesura after the sixth syllable is the most common (9 and 45 instances, respectively), but they also add another possibility, two half lines of 5 + 5 syllables (1 and 7 instances).[52]

Again, these cases are similar enough that we might imagine a gradually developing epic line in the Czech tradition. The greatest variation is found, though, in the poems that treat the oldest historical events and also suggest their great age through their noncanonical poetic form, "Čestmír and Vlaslav" and "Záboj, Slavoj, and Luděk." Both are set in the pre-Christian period, and if their age is also to be suggested by their poetic form, we might expect it to be closest to the older "Libuše" epic. Instead, these are the least regular in form and deviate the farthest from any clear relation to the South Slavic epic form. Both use the ten-syllable line for isolated lines and couplets as well as for occasional runs of as few as 3 lines to as many as 33 lines amid lines that otherwise freely shift in length, and while the caesura after the fourth syllable is still the most common, these vary more frequently from that basis. In "Záboj," 33.3 percent of the ten-syllable lines (7 of 21, out of a total of 255 lines) have an alternate caesura, with the 6 + 4 division only slightly more common than 5 + 5 (4 and 3 instances, respectively). In "Čestmír," 23.3 percent of the ten-syllable lines vary (20 of 86, out of a total of 229 lines), and here the 5 + 5 division greatly outnumbers 6 + 4, with whole runs of lines together in that shape (13 versus 7 instances).[53] It is very difficult to see how one might put this variation into an ordered narrative of the historical development of Czech oral epic verse form, particularly if one considers, from a contemporary perspective, what we know about the highly conservative and traditional nature of such verse forms and the role they play in generating and preserving the traditional diction, with the knowledge of ancient customs and realia that it fossilizes. This kind of variation, in which the songs supposedly from the oldest period represent the extremes from strictest conformity to a fixed caesura to wildest deviation while the later songs offer multiple forms of moderate deviation, looks nothing like the relatively stable verse forms we know from other oral epic traditions, like the South Slavic one.

For the nineteenth-century defenders of the manuscripts' authenticity, the limited variation in the Green Mountain Manuscript (that is, in "Libuše's Judgment") proved to be more attractive and explicable. Josef and Hermenegild Jireček, in the section on verse forms from their 1862 study defending the Queen's Court Manuscript, claim that the ten-syllable verse form has a caesura after either the fourth or sixth syllable, which fails to fully describe any of the epics in that manuscript and implicitly takes "Libuše's Judgment" as the norm.[54] Jaroslav Goll examined Czech ten-syllable verse in his first published scholarly study in 1871, before he later joined the organized campaign against the manuscripts' authenticity.[55] While he acknowledges the verses with a caesura after the fifth syllable and finds analogues in Czech folk songs, he explicitly takes "Libuše's Judgment" as the best and the model that better allows for the formulation of abstract rules regarding the verse form.[56] It is worth noting that his comparison to other folk songs involves different genres, although he does at least make his comparisons to the shorter narrative forms like ballads. There were no other oral epic songs to which one could make a comparison.

Modern verse studies that address the manuscripts have largely proceeded from the expert consensus that they have been demonstrated to be falsifications. As a result, they do not attempt to formulate the laws of the Czech ten-syllable epic line (a difficult task in any case, given the variation just examined), but rather examine it (insofar as they do at all) as an imitation of the South Slavic deseterac that may have also been influenced by some native Czech poetry in ten-syllable lines, whether of medieval or modern provenance.[57] The question that they have debated instead is what effect the syllabic poems of the manuscripts had in the developing Czech poetic tradition, appearing as they did in a moment when it was polemically occupied by competing syllabotonic and quantitative models of prosody.[58]

Interestingly, for Roman Jakobson, the fact that the ten-syllable line in the manuscripts followed the South Slavic deseterac produced an unexpected but clear effect on the verse form that also served as a kind of signature, marking those poems as belonging to Hanka's circle. The different development of word stress and quantity in Czech, as opposed to Bosnian/Croatian/Serbian (BCS), changes the metrical properties. In Czech, word stress is always on the first syllable and is definitive for verse ictus, while quantity (Czech has long and short vowels) plays only a supplementary metrical role; there could be no laws for Czech decasyllable, then, like Foley's laws that promote special treatment of the classes of initially accented disyllables or medially accented trisyllables. In Czech, *all* two-syllable words are initially accented, and *no* three-syllable words can have an accent on the middle syllable. When following the shape of the deseterac line in Czech, then, the words cannot be moved around in the same way to maintain the metrical scheme, and, as a result, the metrical properties change significantly. Jakobson found that in Hanka's translation of Karadžić's epic "O knížeti Lazaru" (Tsar Lazar and Tsaritsa Milica), stress (word beginning) fell on the seventh syllable in 60 percent of the lines, while on the ninth syllable just 33 percent of the time (a 27-point difference).[59] Given what we know about the importance of the ictus on the ninth syllable in the deseterac, related to the general right justification of Indo-European verse (the greater quantitative organization of the verse at its end), this is a striking change. Jakobson finds a similar organization of the ten-syllable line in the poetry of Hanka's friends, Josef Linda and Václav Svoboda, with 23-point and 15-point higher incidence of stress in the seventh compared to the ninth syllable. The statistics for the manuscript poems entirely in ten-syllable lines are less extreme but represent the same tendency: "Jaroslav," 6 points higher on the seventh; "Oldřich," 3 points higher; "Libuše," 7 points higher. In contrast, the typical shape for native Czech ten-syllable poetry, from medieval syllabic traditions to modern trochaic pentameter, while the rates vary, always includes a higher incidence of stress on the penultimate ninth syllable (16 points higher for the fourteenth-century "Ot božieho těla," 26 points higher for late nineteenth-century poet Jaroslav Vrchlický, and just 2 points higher for their contemporary, and also minor suspect in the conspiracy, Josef Jungmann). For Jakobson, this marks the manuscript poems as sharing the orientation toward the deseterac with Hanka and his friends and serves as additional confirming evidence of their authorship and falsification.[60] We should note as well that it is an orientation toward translation of a foreign verse shape that marks this shift in verse form. Further, using Foley's terms, we might note that we should expect native Czech verse, as an Indo-European-derived verse tradition, to exhibit right justification. The fact that the ten-syllable epic line in the manuscripts does not can also be seen, then, along with the chaos around the caesura, as a sign of this verse's inauthenticity.

It is now clear that the Czech ten-syllable epic line in the manuscripts is not a proper traditional oral epic line, and the formulation of traditional rules that governed its diction would not be possible or appropriate. The change in language, with different prosodic and stress characteristics, already changes the metrical shape of the line. As it is an imitation of the deseterac line, though, we can nonetheless make a fruitful comparison and see in which characteristics it is able to imitate the traditional oral epic line with its broadly formulaic diction and other shaping characteristics (sound patterning, syntactic patterning, and thematic focus) along with the resulting characteristics of the line (epithets and other more fixed formulaic language in the second colon with a more flexible first colon).

Formulas

If we begin with Parry's classic example of the formula, *character epithets*, we find that in the Czech manuscripts, as in the South Slavic tradition as noted by Lord, these are not that common (with the notable exception of one poem). Frequently, the character's name alone, or name and title, are sufficient to fill a colon. Given the fact that no character's name appears in more than one song in the Czech manuscripts, and without any other corpus against which to search for the repetition that is definitive of a classic formula, aside from a few cases of repetition within a single song, we cannot really speak of formulaic naming in the Czech songs. Nonetheless, the naming very much resembles the formulaic naming in the South Slavic tradition, using similar means and in many cases the same adjectives.

Name and title are the means used to name Kublai Khan in the poem "Jaroslav": "Kublaj, chám taterský" (Kublai, the Tartar khan; l. 36).[61] This fills the entire second colon of the line, which has the deseterac 4 + 6 division, placing it where such names most frequently occur in the deseterac line as well. His son and daughter are only named in the poem through their patronymic forms: the son, Kublajevica, in line 276, when it comes to the final single combat with Jaroslav; here, too, the name, together with a proclitic pronoun, occupies the entire second colon ("na Kublajevica" [at Kublai's son]).[62] The daughter is introduced via epithet and simile in line 15: "lepá Kublajevna jako luna" (Kublai's daughter, lovely as the moon). The patronymic with its epithet here occupies the longer six-syllable colon, which is, in this case, the first colon, a situation impossible in traditional deseterac. But the entire line is marked by Slavic borrowings: the adjective *lepý* existed in Old Czech in the senses of both "good" and "beautiful" (the comparative and superlative forms of it are still standard for "better" and "best"), but, as Julius Dolanský observes, "it appears numberless times in South Slavic folk songs . . . , because it is precisely at home in Serbo-Croatian in the sense of 'beautiful.'"[63] To this we can add that it is also an archaic adjective in that sense in Russian, and this Slavism is repeated multiple times in the manuscript songs. Finally, the term for the moon is also here a Russianism. In imitating the oral poetic device of fixed epithets, then, the authors of the Czech manuscripts often resorted to borrowing the formulaic adjectives from other Slavic folk traditions, as we shall see repeatedly further.

The song fragment "Oldřich and Boleslav" offers a single example of a character named by title, Prince Oldřich (knězu Oldře, line 15, in the dative case), but in this case, the title-name quasi-formula is embedded in a longer two-line quasi-formula that introduces the speech of one character to another: "aj ta vece Výhoň knězu Oldře: / 'Hoj, poslyš, ty veleslavný kněže!'" (Then Výhoň spoke to Prince Oldřich, / "Hark you now, o glorious prince!"). Václav Flajšhans already noted the echoes in the second line of the speech taglines from the oral-formulaic bylina songs ("Oj ty, goj esi, dobryj molodec" [Hail to you, good youth]) and the interjection *oj* followed by the vocative in Karadžić's collection.[64] The author has constructed an Old Czech quasi-formulaic speech tagline modeled once again on formulaic Russian and BCS models. Another example of the inclusion of a character epithet phrase in a multiline expression can be seen in what is also the only example of an adjectival character epithet in "Jaroslav": "slavný Vneslav" (glorious Vneslav). First, we should note that the adjective here is almost tautological for the name, repeating almost all of the sounds of the name—an example of the secondary shaping by sound patterning typical of oral diction. At the moment of Vneslav's death, this epithet-name combination is also shaped by syntactic terracing: "Pro bóh—aj, nastojte! slavný Vneslav, / slavný Vneslav sražem s násep šípem!" (My Lord, alas, glorious Vneslav! / Glorious Vneslav felled from the walls by an arrow!; ll. 178–79).[65] In both lines the adjective-name combination occupies the shorter four-syllable colon (the lines are 6 + 4 and 4 + 6), so that these lines also form a type of structural chiasmus that is impossible for terracing in the South Slavic deseterac (which cannot alter the caesura). Also in this case, the repetition of the adjective and name is more than a syntactic device for emphasis, as it forms part of the emotional expressiveness of the lines, surrounded as it is by conventional formulaic (in the common language sense) interjections of grief.[66] The rich texture of sound repetitions in the second line draws out further the tautological repetition of the adjective-name combination for even greater effect. The author(s) of "Jaroslav" have here done remarkably well in creating the illusion of a traditional oral epic diction, with all of the aesthetic effects that diction makes possible (and some it does not), without the benefit of actually having such a tradition.

Before examining the very interesting and complex cases of character epithets in "Libuše's Judgment," the other epic entirely in ten-syllable form, we should also note what is happening in the other epics of the Queen's Court Manuscript that use the ten-syllable line partially, "Čestmír and Vlaslav" and "Záboj, Slavoj, and Luděk." There is just one case in each poem of the use of an epithet with a character name within a section of ten-syllable verse, and in both instances the same epithet is used. Line 2 of the opening of "Záboj" introduces the character with an epithet at the end of the line, "silný Záboj" (strong Záboj)—the phrase occupies the end of the line, as we would expect in BCS epic, except this line has the caesura after the sixth syllable, so it occupies the smaller, four-syllable part of the line. As we will see, in the Czech manuscripts noun-epithet quasi-formulas tend toward the end of the poetic line, whether the second colon is longer or not. Line 218 of "Čestmír" begins the death scene for the enemy leader Vlaslav: "Kypieše krev ze silna Vlaslava" (Blood frothed from strong Vlaslav). Here the epithet is in a prepositional phrase that occupies the entire six-syllable second colon, as one would expect to see also in the South Slavic tradition. Outside of the ten-syllable line sections, however, there are quite a few instances of characters named by title or with epithets, so that the quasi-formulaic naming extends beyond the formal boundaries of the ten-syllable lines, drawing the lines of varying length into the same oral poetic orbit.[67] "Čestmír" gives us several instances of naming by title: "Vlaslav kněz" (Prince Vlaslav, l. 7), "vojevodě Čstmíru" (commander Čestmír, dative case, l. 36), and "Neklan[a] kněz[e]" (Prince Neklan, accusative case endings added by editors, l. 37); it gives a similar number of cases of naming by epithet: "nadutý Vlaslav" (haughty Vlaslav, l. 17), "Kruvoj škaredý" (Kruvoj the foul, l. 37), and "udatna Čstmíra" (valiant Čestmír, genitive case, l. 72). "Záboj" furnishes a single instance, "hbitý Luděk" (nimble Luděk, l. 151).

The character naming in "Libuše's Judgment," the epic with the most named characters, could have been analyzed by Foley to demonstrate the complexity of formulaic diction and the insufficiency of the standard counting of line and half-line formulas. Character names and epithets function in colon and whole-line quasi-formulas that may also extend over multiple lines, and they are shaped by sound patterning, syntactic patterning, and thematic patterning as the multiline systems grow toward theme-level units. As we shall see, some of this structuring comes from the imitation of oral or orally derived texts from Slavic traditions.

The brothers whose quarrel Libuše will be called to judge are introduced in an extended passage of naming (ll. 10–17):

Vadita sě kruto mezu sobú,	They quarreled cruelly between themselves,
lútý Chrudoš na Otavě krivě,	Fierce Chrudoš on the crooked Otava,
na Otavě krivě zlatonosně,	The Otava, crooked and gold-laden;
Staglav chraber na Radbuze chladně,	Staglav the brave on the cold Radbuza.
oba bratry, oba Klenovica,	Both brothers, both sons of Klen,
roda stara Tetvy Popelova,	From the old house of Popel's Tetva
jenže pride s plky s Čechovými	Who came along with Čech's hosts
v sěže žírne vlasti pres tri rěky.	Across three rivers to this fertile land.

The brothers are here named, the elder first over two lines and the younger second in one, identified again as brothers and by their patronymic, and then named by their ancient clan, which participated in the migration and settlement of the current homeland. Each brother is named with an epithet that occupies the full first four-syllable colon of the line, but they are also each named by the river on which they are currently settled in the second, six-syllable colon, so that each half-line quasi-formula also participates in a full line unit (line 11 does actually repeat, with grammatical adjustment, at line 91 when Chrudoš rises to contest the judgment: "Vstanu Chrudoš od Otavy krivy" [Chrudoš from the crooked Otava arose]).[68] There is some noteworthy sound patterning in the epithets applied to the younger brother and his river: *chraber* and *chladně*, so that the river and its resident are described harmoniously.[69] The whole-line units mirror each other as well with parallel syntax.

The whole-line unit of the elder brother's naming continues to a second line through terracing repetition that extends the epithet phrase attached to the river (in this case, the caesura is still maintained after the fourth syllable, as it is in all of these lines).

The brothers' naming by patronymic and clan functions as a multiline formula within the poem, repeating, with small adjustment to the first line, when Radovan addresses them with the decision of the assembly (ll. 85–88), "Oba rodna bratry Klenovica . . ." (Both you brothers, sons of Klen). This repetition has a different function than the first instance, serving to remind the quarreling brothers that they belong to a larger tribe whose customs and laws form the basis of the judgment they are about to hear. And it is that connection that has allowed editors to reconstruct the final line where the manuscript breaks off: "u nás pravda po zákonu svatu, / juže prinesechu otci náši / v sěže [žirné vlasti pres tri reky]" (we have justice by the holy law / that was brought here by our fathers / to this [fertile land across three rivers]; ll. 110–12). The beginning of the final line is enough to invoke the final line of the naming of the brothers by clan to complete it in its fullness as a whole-line formula.

Another extended passage of naming follows, when Libuše calls the Czech elders and leaders to an assembly to help judge the case (ll. 30–43):

Káže kněžna vypraviti posly	The princess ordered heralds sent
po Svatoslav ot Lubice bielé,	For Svatoslav from white Lubice
iděže sú dúbraviny unie,	There where the oak groves are fair;
po Lutobor z Dobroslavska chlmca,	For Lutobor from Dobroslav's fastness
iděže Orlicu Labe pije,	There where the Elbe drinks the Orlice;
po Ratibor ot gor Krkonoší,	For Ratibor from the Krkonoše mountains
iděže Trut pogubi saň lútu,	Where Trut once killed the fierce worm;
po Radovan ot Kamena mosta,	For Radovan from the stone-built bridge,
po Jarožir ot Brd vletorečných,	For Jarožir from Brdy, Vltava-washed,
po Strezibor ot Sázavy ladny,	For Strezibor from lovely Sázava,
po Samorod se Mže strebronosné,	For Samorod from the silver-laden Mže,
po vsě kmety, lechy I vládyky,	For all the elders, chiefs, and lords,
i po Chrudoš i po Staglav bratry	And for Chrudoš and Staglav, brothers
rozvaděma o dědiny otně.	At odds over their father's estate.

This passage parallels a number of features of the earlier one naming the brothers, who are invoked again at the end of this epic list: the first three guests are named in two-line units and the next four in whole-line units; the second colon, following the name in the first colon, introduces their place of residence, nearly always involving a noun-epithet phrase (and with rivers reappearing at the end of the list), so that the syntactical parallelism here is fundamental; sound patterning is also evident ("Ratibor ot gor"; "Trut . . . lútu"); the two-line units are also all syntactically parallel, with the second line further qualifying the place of residence. Furthermore, several of the whole-line units repeat as characters are invoked to take part in the activity of the assembly, and when they repeat, they participate in another two-line unit that introduces their speech or activity. Thus, lines 73–74, "Vsta Lubotor s Dobroslavska chlmca, / je sě tako slovo govoriti" (Lutobor from Dobroslav's fastness arose / And began to speak these words); lines 81–82, "Vsta Radovan ot Kamena mosta, / je sě glasy číslem preglédati" (Radovan from the stone-built bridge arose / And undertook to tally the votes); and lines 107–8, "Vsta Ratibor ot gor Krkonoší, / je sě tako slovo govoriti" (Ratibor from the Krkonoše mountains arose / And began to speak these words). Note that these all form a kind of formulaic unit with the repetition of the older brother's introduction, cited earlier.

In addition to the shaping by noun-epithet and name-epithet formulas, by sound patterning and syntactic parallelism, these lines are also thematically shaped as together they make up one of the classic *themes* of traditional oral epic, the sending of a messenger and the calling of guests to a feast or assembly. The authors could have found their model for such a theme in the feasts and assemblies in South Slavic tradition, but Dolanský found only two similar lists in Karadžić's collections. The first is a list of names of Serbian lords that the speaker is threatening to kill, and the second is a list of Turkish dead following the battle on Mišar in 1806.[70] Rather, Dolanský demonstrated, a more convincing model can be found in the list of wedding guests for the wedding of Stipan Kristić from Andrija Kačić Miošić's *Razgovor ugodni naroda slovinskoga*, which constructs a lengthy list with some similar techniques of naming and syntax.[71] This book, which Hanka is very likely to have encountered either in Prague studying with Dobrovský or in Vienna, where Kopitar had suggested that Karadžić republish it in his new orthography, represents a literary reworking of South Slavic epic traditions in deseterac form by the author, a Franciscan monk (1704–1760) from Dalmatia who styled himself a *guslar* (that is, a traditional singer of epics, the accompaniment to which was played by the singer on the *gusle*, a single-stringed, bowed instrument).[72] Where Karadžić instead collected oral traditions, it may be that Hanka took the book as an occasional model for his own imitation of South Slavic epic traditions, and perhaps particularly as a model for typical scenes or themes.[73]

Finally, one ought not to end an account of naming in this poem without a glance at the title character. Libuše is almost never named directly in the song. Her name is used in the possessive to name the place of the assembly, Vyšehrad, but otherwise she is evoked through her title, princess. The fact that her name is three syllables long seems to have made the adjective-name combination difficult, as these so often cover four syllables for characters with two-syllable names in the manuscripts. Just once she is named directly, in a variation on the formula for beginning to speak that we examined earlier (ll. 99–100): "[V]sta Lubuša s otňa zlata stola, / vece: 'Kmeté, lesi i vládyky!'" (Libuše arose from her father's gold throne / And quoth, "Elders, chiefs, and lords!"). Another earlier speech is introduced similarly, but through her title (ll. 55–56): "Poče kněžna s otňa zlata stola: / 'Moji kmeté, lesi i vládyky!'" (The princess began from her father's gold throne: / "You my elders, chiefs, and lords!"). The two-syllable verb here demands the shorter two-syllable title, rather than her name. When she is addressed directly by Lutobor in the assembly, an epithet is attached to her title (l. 75): "Slavná kněžno s otňa zlata stola!" (Great princess on her father's gold throne!). Like the quarreling brothers and the elders and lords, Libuše has a whole-line formula that is used repeatedly to name her based on her royal residence, the site of her father's gold throne. This second colon formula has its own existence (with a slight variation) outside of naming the princess, in a quasi-formula that names the place (ll. 21–22). The messenger swallow arrives "v Lubušině otně zlatě siedle, / siedle otně, světě Vyšegradě" (in the golden seat of Libuše's fathers, / the fathers' seat, holy Vyšehrad). This second colon formula that echoes repeatedly through the poem has a recognizable Slavic ring to it, for those who were familiar with the hits of Slavic epic poetry. Dobrovský knew its source well and named it in the article in which he gave his evidence that the Green Mountain Manuscript was a fraud: "So how did our clever impersonator even come up with *oteň*, a word otherwise never used in the Czech language? From the Russian poem 'Igor,' where the entirety of the phrase 'otna zlata stola' appears multiple times."[74]

In fact, the phrase appears twice in the late twelfth-century *Igor Tale*, once in a striking passage that tempted the authors of the Czech manuscripts to borrow more than one resounding and potentially formulaic phrase. The passage describes Igor's younger brother, Vsevolod, in glorious battle:

> Jar" Turu Vsevolodě! Stoiši na boroni, pryščeši na voi strělami, gremleši o šelomy meči xaralužnymi. Kamo, Tur", poskočjaše, svoim" zlatym"

> šelomom" posvěčivaja,—tamo ležat' poganyja golovy Poloveckyja. Poskepany sabljami kalenymi šelomy Ovar'skyja ot" tebe, Jar" Ture Vsevolode! Kaja rany, doroga bratie, zabyv" čti i života, i grada Čr"nigova *otnja zlata stola*, i svoja milyja xoti, krasnyja Glěbovna, svyčaja i obyčaja![75]

> Fierce Bull Vsevolod! / You stand your ground / you spurt arrows at warriors, / you clang on helmets / with swords of steel. Wherever the Bull bounds, / darting light from his golden helmet, / there lie pagan Kuman heads: / cleft with tempered sabers / are [their] Avar helmets—/ by you, Fierce Bull Vsevolod! / What wound, brothers, / can matter to one / who has forgotten / honors and life, / and the town of Chernigov—/ *golden throne of his fathers*—/ and of his dear beloved, / Gleb's fair daughter, / the wonts and ways![76]

In addition to the fathers' golden throne, the comparison to a fierce bull and even the syntax-forming correlative adverbs *kamo-tamo* (wherever-there) proved enticing and useful to the authors of the manuscripts, as we shall see later.[77]

As the foregoing analysis of character epithets has shown, while they are not very numerous, they participate in phraseology in the Czech manuscripts that behaves remarkably similarly to the complex traditional diction of the South Slavic epics, forming quasi-formulas of colon and whole-line lengths that are shaped by sound, syntax, terracing, and thematic units and that participate in multiline quasi-formulaic phraseology. In this aspect of the imitation of traditional oral epic, we can conclude that the authors of the Czech epics were observant and successful in their mimicking of important characteristics.

The use of *fixed epithets with nouns* (aside from character names) is a related characteristic of oral epic, and one that extends as well to other oral poetry genres. It is also a striking and easily imitated feature, so one would expect the authors of the Czech epics to be successful here as well. Within the ten-syllable epics and parts of epics, there are approximately 140 distinct adjective-noun combinations that could potentially repeat or function as fixed epithets.[78] How does their placement compare with the South Slavic models? The vast majority of these fall in the longer second colon of the line, which is where, on the model of the deseterac, we would expect the more fixed formulaic material to appear. In 114 instances, the adjective and noun fall in the six-syllable second colon (additionally three times in a three-syllable second colon). In nine additional instances, where there is no caesura after the fourth syllable, so the line divides 6 + 4, the adjective and noun fall in the second, shorter colon.[79] The adjective and noun appear in the first colon just twenty-five times (of which five are in inverted-line six-syllable first cola)—and four of these are cases of terracing, where the combination repeats from the end of the previous line. In other words, in lines with an equal or longer second colon, 85 percent of the time the noun-epithet phrase appears in the longer second colon. In inverted 6 + 4 lines, just 36 percent of the time the noun-epithet phrase appears in the longer colon, suggesting a stronger pull toward the end of the line than to the longer colon.

There are nineteen additional instances where the adjective and noun are split across the caesura, occurring in the songs "Jaroslav," "Čestmír," and "Libuše's Judgment" (nine, one, and nine instances, respectively). This was an initially unexpected result. Sometimes the caesura falls directly between the two elements, and sometimes they are further split by an additional word in between. Thus, in "Jaroslav" (ll. 80, 248, 272): "že je jak *zveř* | *plachý* rozprnuchu" (that they scattered them like a *timid animal*), "i by *pótka* | *kruta* posledněјé" (and the final *cruel battle* occurred), and "když mu *teplú* | *krev* sě udá zřieti" (when it chances to see *warm blood*); and in "Libuše" (ll. 3, 17): "Za tě *lútá* | rozvlajáše *búra*" (Did the *savage storm* disturb you) and "v sěže *žírne* | *vlasti* pres tri rěky" (to this *fertile land* across three rivers). If we initially analyze for formulas by colon as Parry and Lord did, it would seem odd to have a formulaic fixed noun-epithet phrase broken across cola. This would be mitigated in cases of whole-line formulas, as in the last example from "Libuše," which repeats as a whole line in the song. On the other hand, there is no reason for formulaic combinations to be limited to a single colon, even outside of whole-line repetition. If we recall Foley's observation that the shorter first colon, while it sets up the syntax and context of the line, is often incomplete and needs the focusing of the more formulaic second colon to complete it, then traditional noun-epithet combinations can be a part of that focusing.[80] In fact, if we return to the model formulaic analysis of Lord, even in the small sample of twenty-four lines we see just such a split of traditional adjective and noun (and of verb parts as well) across the caesura: "*Đogatu* se | *konju* zamoljila" (She implored the *white horse*).[81] The caesura is a word boundary, not necessarily a syntactic or semantic boundary, and it is clearly not an insurmountable boundary for formulaic phrases, either. We can still conclude, then, that adjective-noun combinations in the Czech manuscripts predominate in the longer and more formulaic part of the line, as in South Slavic tradition.

How many of these noun-epithet combinations are truly formulaic, though? Allowing for contextual morphological variation, there are just nine that repeat across songs in the ten-syllable portions.[82] An additional sixteen combinations repeat within a single song; these often are thematic repetitions, and we have seen several already (like "s otňa *zlata stola*" [from her father's *gold throne*]) in our analysis of character epithets above.[83] That is a respectable number of formulas, just under 18 percent of the unique adjective-noun combinations here assessed, given the very limited material available. If we include the additional parts of "Čestmír" and "Záboj" not in ten-syllable lines for comparison (not to add new combinations), we can confirm four more phrases.[84] If we extend our corpus for comparison to the entirety of the manuscripts (two additional epics, two ballads, and six lyric songs), we can enrich our stock of traditional noun-epithet phrases by nine more.[85] That would give us an even more satisfying result, with 27 percent, over a quarter, of the combinations found in the ten-syllable lines confirmed as quasi-traditional in our comparative corpus.[86] The impression from reading the manuscripts would suggest a higher proportion of traditional combinations. This impression may be suggested by what we might call a formulaic epithet system: the repeated use of a limited set of adjectives with multiple nouns and combinations where the adjectives or nouns do not repeat but are replaced by synonyms. We will look at examples from several of these categories in context below.

The Queen's Court Manuscript opens with the ending fragment of the epic "Oldřich and Boleslav," and the fragmentary end of the first line contains the first epithet-noun quasi-formula we will discuss (here examining only those that repeat across songs): ". . . sě v *črn les*" (. . . into the *black forest*). The single repetition, with morphological change, also occurs at the very beginning of another song, "Záboj, Slavoj, and Luděk": "S črna lesa vystupuje skála" (From the black forest a rock juts forth). This quasi-formula operates as an opening formula that joins several other elements linking these two epics thematically, with their opening conspiracy in a black forest to drive out a foreign occupation.[87] Even this short phrase, then, is not without its thematic aspect.

What is notable about several of the other quasi-formulas is that they are derived from traditional Russian epithet-noun phrases. Their repetition in the manuscripts, then, also echoed their repetition in Russian sources, for those that were familiar with them, confirming their traditional status and suggesting again their antiquity from a shared Slavic heroic past. One appears in the address to Prince Oldřich by Výhoň Dub early in that epic, urging him on to the fight (ll. 16–22):

"Hoj, poslyš, ty veleslavný kněže!	"Hark you now, o glorious prince!
Bóh ti bujarost da u vsě údy,	God gave you vim in all your limbs,
bóh ti da věhlasy v *bujnú hlavu*;	God gave you wit in your *brash head*.
ty ny vedi proti zlým Polanóm!	Lead us now against the evil Polans!
Po tvém slově pójdem v pravo, v levo,	By your word we'll go right or left,

buď v před, buď v zad, u vše pótky lúté.	Forward or backward in all fierce battles.
Vzhóru! Vzmušte chrabrost bujných srdec!"	Arise! Wake valor in vigorous hearts!"

The brash or reckless head is a commonplace in Russian traditional oral epic. A typical example, which also includes a formula of address similar to the one here, can be found in the epic "Ilya Muromets and Kalin Tsar," recorded by Aleksandr Gilferding from the singer T. G. Riabinin: "'Aj že ty, Vladimir-knjaz da stol′nokievskij! / Ne srubi-tko mne da *bujnoj golovy*'" ("Hail to you, Vladimir, Prince of Capital Kiev! / Don't cut off my reckless head!").[88] It was not, however, traditional in Old Czech poetry, although the adjective existed both in the sense of "vigorous" and "unruly." It is embedded here, though, in a speech that abounds in traditional and quasi-formulaic phraseology. It ends a pair of lines formed by parallel syntax (*bóh ti da* X *v* / *u* Y) that also feature significant sound repetition (*bujarost—bujnú hlavu*). In this case we also have the repetition of the adjective in a compound neologism, combining the sense of *bujný* with *jarý* (an epithet that we will examine shortly). The adjective repeats again in the final line, in a combination that does not reoccur in the manuscripts. The repetitions in this passage already begin to establish the traditional, quasi-formulaic nature of the epithet even before it repeats in "Jaroslav." Another quasi-formula appears in the passage as well, *pótky lúté* (fierce battles), which repeats in "Jaroslav" (l. 277), and the phrase *veleslavný kněže* (glorious prince) is echoed in eight-syllable lines in the epic "Ludiše and Lubor" (l. 4). Finally, the everyday formulaic language of right or left, forward or backward, rounds out the traditional and quasi-traditional phraseology of this passage.

This epithet-noun phrase reoccurs in a similarly densely quasi-formulaic passage in "Jaroslav," in which the Christian armies are described as they prepare to turn the tide of the battle (ll. 240–43):

Těžcí meči po bocéch jim visá,	Heavy swords hang at their sides,
plní túli na plecech jim řechcú,	Full quivers clatter on their shoulders,
jasní helmi jim na *bujných hlavách*	Bright helms on their *brash heads*
i pod nimi ručí koni skáčú.	And beneath them leap swift steeds.

Here, too, the phrase finds its place in a series of lines formed by parallel syntax (with a small inversion in the final line that maintains the caesura after the fourth syllable, to offset the addition of the conjunction at the beginning of the line) and sound repetitions (*plní túli*; *plecech—řechcú*; *jasní helmi jim*). Surprisingly, the epithet-noun phrases relating to their arms (heavy swords, full quivers, bright helms) do not reoccur in the manuscripts, although they sound entirely traditional in this context.

"Swift steeds" (*ručí koni*), on the other hand, is the single most recurrent epithet-noun phrase in the manuscripts. This phrase first appears early in the epic "Jaroslav," in a passage describing the departure of Kublai's daughter with her retinue (ll. 22–23): "i vsedachu vsi na *ručie koně,* / i brachu sě, kamo slunce spěje" (and mounted their *swift steeds,* / and headed where the sun speeds). The phrase repeats, with occasional morphological adjustment, a third time in "Jaroslav," twice in "Čestmír" within the ten-syllable sections and once outside them, once in "Záboj" outside the ten-syllable sections, and once in "Ludiše." Flajšhans points to the source of this phrase, once again, in a passage from the *Igor Tale* that is worth citing at length.[89] In this scene, Igor has just met up with Vsevolod, who urges his brother to prepare to join him in the fight:

> sědljai, brate, svoi *br″zyi komoni,* a moi ti gotovy, osědlani u Kur′ska naperedi. A moi ti Kurjani svědomy k″meti: pod″ trubami poviti, pod″ šelomy v″zlelějany, konec′ kopija v″skr″mleni, puti im″ vědomi, jarugy im″ znaemi, luci u nix″ naprjaženi, tuli otvoreni, sabli iz″ostreni.[90]

> Saddle, brother, your *swift steeds.* / As to mine, they are ready, / saddled ahead, near Kursk; / as to my Kurskers, they are famous knights—/ swaddled under war-horns, / nursed under helmets, / fed from the point of a lance; / to them the trails are familiar, / to them the ravines are known, / the bows they have are strung tight, / the quivers, unclosed, / the sabers, sharpened.[91]

In this case, the authors translate the Old East Slavic epithet (contemporary Russian: *borzyj*) with a suitable Old Czech adjective and update the noun as well (with one exception). This passage with its more colorful listing of arms parallels the earlier passage from "Jaroslav," which also treated the preparations for battle, in a number of elements of that list besides the horses. And the saddling here also suggests the mounting in the second passage from "Jaroslav."

Mounting the war horse is again the context for all three of the repetitions of the phrase in the epic "Čestmír," suggesting a strong thematic context for the epithet-noun phrase. Čestmír encourages the liberated Vojmír to put aside his desire to sacrifice to the gods in thanks and join the battle (ll. 138–9): "a nynie nám na vrahy pospěti. / Nynie vsedni ty na *ručie koně*" (But now we must hasten after our enemies. / Sit now on your *swift steed*). The second line is repeated nearly verbatim when Vojmír carries out this order. The third occurrence follows Vojmír's sacrifice, when he once again joins the war column (l. 170): "vzkoči Vojmír na svój *rúčí komoň*" (Vojmír leapt onto his swift stallion).[92] Strikingly, this time the authors deploy the Old East Slavic term for horse from the model phrase in the *Igor Tale,* the only instance of its use in the manuscripts. They thus gesture rather dramatically, to those who would recognize it, toward common phraseology with the prestigious Old East Slavic epic poem in the repeated thematic usage of their own quasi-formulaic phrase.[93]

The other notable epithet-noun phrase borrowing from the *Igor Tale* is better characterized by its use to delineate a contrasting theme from how it appears in its source. Vsevolod is twice addressed as *Jar" Ture Vsevolode* (Fierce / Wild Bull Vsevolod) in the passage first cited earlier, which depicts him in his apotheosis as a warrior. A number of features here recall the Scandinavian tradition of the *bersirkir* (bearskin) warrior: the mythological transformation into the wild animal with an accompanying change in behavior. Like his brother Igor, who transforms into a wolf in his rapid escape homeward, Vsevolod here can be seen as transformed into an aurochs (tur), with an accompanying berserker-like ability to ignore his wounds and leave behind human values ("What wound, brothers, / can matter to one / who has forgotten / honors and life, / and the town of Chernigov—/ golden throne of his fathers—/ and of his dear beloved, / Gleb's fair daughter, / the wonts and ways!").

This type of mythological, supernatural poetics is beyond the bounds for the authors of the Czech manuscripts, who favored a more rational, poetic use of animal comparisons. They were also hindered by an established stereotype about the peaceful Slavic character, in contrast to the German. This conception had a number of sources, not least among them Herder's description of the Slavic character. In fact, in 1815, just two years before the Queen's Court Manuscript was discovered, Dominik František Kinský explained the absence of an ancient Czech heroic epic on the basis of the distinct character of the Slavs, who "being partial to peaceful activities, like plowing and trade, perhaps preferred tavern songs to war songs to sweeten their spare time."[94] The newly discovered ancient epic songs in the manuscript, although they drew heavily from the imagery and poetic apparatus of traditional heroic epic, nonetheless managed to cleverly leave that contrast intact.

In the Czech manuscripts, then, the comparison to a wild bull is applied mostly negatively to enemy warriors and to Czech characters when they forget their Czech cultural and behavioral norms. The latter is exemplified in "Libuše's Judgment," where the comparison is applied to the older brother, Chrudoš, when he rises to contest the ruling of Libuše and the assembly and demand his (German) rights as the firstborn, insulting Libuše in the process (ll. 91–98):

Vstanu Chrudoš od Otavy krivy,	Chrudoš from the crooked Otava arose,
žlč sě jemu rozli po útrobě,	Bile spreading in his bowels,
trasechu sě lútosť'ú vsi údi,	All his limbs shaking with fury,
máchnu rukú, zarve *jarým turem*:	Waved and shouted like a *wild bull*:
"Gore ptencém, k nimže zmija vnori,	"Woe to the birds that a viper stalks;
gore mužém, imže žena vlade:	Woe to men who are ruled by a woman:
mužu vlásti mužem zapodobno,	It is proper for men to rule men,
prvencu dědinu dáti pravda."	And to give the estate to the firstborn."

Chrudoš is like a wild bull, then, not in battle, but in a legal dispute when he is demanding rights that are not appropriate or sanctioned by Czech law and tradition, as he will be further instructed by the assembly's leaders. The antithesis of Czech and German is maintained.

The enemy leader is described metaphorically as a wild-headed bull in "Čestmír and Vlaslav." Čestmír is discussing a strategy for defeating Vlaslav's army with its superior numbers and suggests that wit can outmaneuver brute strength (ll. 185–86): "Čemu čelo protiv skále vzpřieci? / Liška oblúdí tur jarohlavý" (Why set your forehead against a rock? / A fox will trick the wild-headed bull). In this case, as in others, the Czech war leaders are fox-like in their clever war strategies, which enables their defeat of the more violent enemy warriors.[95] During the earlier storming of the keep of Vlaslav's deputy Kruvoj, the latter is also compared to a bull, although by means of a synonymous Czech term (ll. 81–84):

Řváše na hradě Kruvoj řvániem *býka*,	In the castle Kruvoj roared the roar of a *bull*,
řváše chrabrost v svoje ludi	Roaring valor into his people,
i meč jeho padáše v Pražany	And his sword fell on the Praguers
jako drvo se skály;	Like a tree from the bluff.

This is the closest we have to the transformation of a warrior in battle into an animal form, and in this case the authors did *not* use their favored epithet-noun phrase from the *Igor Tale*, although that would have created thematic ties as well to the image of Vsevolod in battle.

Only once is the phrase used positively to characterize a Czech hero, in the epic "Jaroslav." There, the main hero's potentially speaking Slavic name oversees a minor theme around the epithet *jarý*, which in Old Czech was used only to describe things with a relation to spring (*jaro*) but, with the addition of the Russian quasi-formulaic phrase in the epic, broadens to include violent passion. The adjective first appears in a description of the standoff in the first battle between the Christian and Tartar forces (ll. 71–72): "Obě straně *jarobujnú* silú / druha druzě postúpati bráni" (Both sides with *vigorous* strength / barred the progress of the other). Here we have the inversion of the components of the term seen earlier, *bujarost*. As there, it here can suggest a fullness with life force characteristic of the spring, but within the military context, it also takes on some of the implications of violent passion in the Russian term.

When Jaroslav appears late in the epic to finish off the enemy, he is introduced with a couple of animal comparisons. The wild bull, though, is not among them, although the *jarý* theme is present (ll. 266–73):

Aj ta Jaroslav jak orel letě!	Lo! Jaroslav flew in like an eagle!
tvrdú ocel na mohúcech prsech,	Firm steel on his powerful breast,
pod ocelí chrabrost, udatenstvie,	Beneath the steel: bravery, valor,
pod helmicú velebyster věhlas,	Beneath his helm swiftest insight,
jarota mu z žhavú zrakú pláše.	*Fervor* flashing from his burning eyes.
Rozkacen hna, jako lev drážlivý,	He charged angrily, like an enraged lion
když mu teplú krev sě udá zřieti,	When it chances to see fresh blood,
kehdy nastřelen za lovcem žene;	And when struck, it turns on the hunter.

Jarota is a substantive clearly derived from the adjective *jarý* in its Russian sense; it did not exist in Old Czech. And while Jaroslav is characterized by this passionate violence, he is compared not to a bull, but to an eagle and a lion. These are traditional royal and imperial symbols, appropriate to the historical noble personage of Jaroslav of Sternberg and to a warrior. The lion simile, though, has another, Homeric, source as well, to which we will return later in our discussion of epic similes.

The Czech warrior who is compared positively to a wild bull is a passing hero in the epic. After the leader of the initial battles, Vneslav, has fallen and the Christian army is suffering from thirst on top of Hostýn, the unsteady Vestoň suggests that dying of thirst is worse than by the sword and proposes surrender and capture. Vratislav appears to confront this treacherous proposal and then leads the warriors to the chapel to pray to Mother Mary for rain, a prayer that is answered and turns the tide of the battle (ll. 202–5):

Tu Vratislav jak *tur jarý* skoči,	Then Vratislav leapt like a *wild bull*,
Vestoňa za silně paži chváti,	Seized Vestoň by his strong arm,
die: "Prorado, škvrno křesťan věčná!	Said, "Traitor, eternal stain to Christians!
V záhubu chceš vrci dobré ludi?"	You wish to cast good folk to their doom?"

Vratislav is indeed acting heroically in his capacity as a warrior here, only not in battle, but rather as a leader in a struggle to persuade the warriors to continue to fight for the Christian cause. Vratislav is a wild bull only in a verbal argument in the midst of the battle. Like Chrudoš, he fights with words. But he is compared to a wild animal precisely in the moment when he is reminding the Czech warriors of their culture and Christian faith that differentiates them from the "savage Tartars." Vratislav, unlike Chrudoš, is firmly on the side of civilization and may only resemble the bull in his anger and perhaps the speed of his response. Even this positive use of the comparison, then, reconfirms that, as a whole, the wild bull epithet-noun phrase is deployed by the authors of the manuscripts in a manner that is contrary to its thematic use in their source to describe a Slavic hero in berserker mode.

Among the *epithet-noun phrases* from the ten-syllable sections *that do not repeat* in the corpus of the manuscripts, there are several that derive from sources in traditional epic poetry or are formed in a characteristic manner, which gives them a traditional aura in spite of their uniqueness in the manuscripts. *kalené střely* (tempered arrows) of line 250 of "Jaroslav," like some of the quasi-formulas examined earlier, repeats a fixed phrase from Russian byliny for which the adjective existed in Old Czech only in a different sense (like *jarý*). The adjective may also have been familiar from the *Igor Tale*, where it modifies *sabers* instead.[96] A different sort of echo is represented by the tautological phrase *sila silna* (forceful force) ("Jaroslav," l. 130), which is formed on the same root like many phrases in South Slavic epic.[97] These phrases, then, even though they do not repeat within the manuscripts, echo traditional epic phraseology in productive ways that reinforce the impression produced by the oral epic quasi-formulas.

Antonín Vašek, one of the first Czech scholars to argue that the Queen's Court Manuscript was a forgery, pointed to the Homeric source of two epithet-noun phrases in that manuscript: "The figure . . . *věkožízní bohové* [age-lived/

eternal gods] is Homer's *theoi aien eontes* [the everlasting gods].—Line 50 [57–58] of 'Záboj,' 'pěvce [*sic!*] dobra milujú bozi; pěj tobě ot nich dáno' [A *good singer* is loved by the gods. Sing, you have it in your heart] reminds us of Homer's Odyssey XVII 518, VIII 479, and *theios aoidos* [divine singer]."[98] Hanka himself began his introduction to the first edition of the manuscript by drawing the parallel with Homeric and other Greek sources, so his readers would be listening for such echoes: "Just as the Greeks, the Argonauts, the heroes of Troy, and the seven against Thebes—just as they found their Homer, Aeschylus, and Orpheus, so our Lumírs and Zábojs sang the glorious feats of ancient heroes, the wars of the princes, the bloody skirmishes of the earls, the pleasures and sorrows of love, and other similar adventures."[99] The echoes of commonplaces of Homeric phraseology also add prestige and an ancient pedigree to the manuscript. And in fact, Vašek's first example represents another notable aspect of the manuscripts' phraseology: the use of compound adjectives, which were very uncommon in Old Czech, and which we might attribute to an attempt to imitate Homeric compounds and their echoes down through the epic tradition.[100] Such compounds are not uniformly distributed through the epic poems. They abound in "Libuše's Judgment," that is, in the supposedly older manuscript, with nine examples; but in "Záboj," which narrates a story at least as old and uses a noncanonical verse form to further mark its age, there is only one. The other pagan-era epic, "Čestmír," has four (three of which occur in ten-syllable lines), while "Jaroslav" has three and "Oldřich" one.[101] Within the manuscripts, there are partial repetitions (one half of the compound) of two, and only one (*jarobujný*) repeats as a compound. Nonetheless, their echoing of Homeric diction also contributes to an ancient and traditional aura.

There is further a kind of *formulaic system* at work within the manuscripts that reinforces the repetition of epithet-noun phrases through the deployment of a limited arsenal of adjectives and nouns (some of which also belong to quasi-formulaic phrases) that continually combine with each other, without exact repetition. The adjective *lútý* (fierce) combines (with morphological adjustment for gender and number, and sometimes with the intensifying prefix *vele-*) with the nouns *potka* (battle, as seen earlier), *boj* (fight), *Tataři* (Tartars, as seen earlier), *vrah* (enemy; a Russianism), *buřa* (storm), *dav* (throng), *seč* (slaughter, as seen earlier), and *saň* (dragon).[102] The similar adjective *krutý* (cruel) combines with the nouns *hněv* (anger), *žel* (sorrow), *žizn* (thirst, as seen earlier), *Tataři* (Tartars), and *potka* (battle). A small subsystem is formed between these two adjectives for modifying a few synonyms for battles (*potka*, *boj*, *seč*) that is highly repetitive, despite its variation. A number of other adjectives form smaller systems (which could be expanded by including the whole corpus of epic poems, or the manuscripts as a whole). *Črn(ý)* (black) modifies *mrak* (cloud), *les* (forest, as seen earlier), *noc* (night), and *ščít* (shield). *(Pře-)udatný* (brave) modifies *sbory* (companies), *vojni* (warriors), *sěč* (slaughter), and *lev* (lion). *(Vele-)slavný* (glorious) modifies *sněm* (assembly), *pověst* (story), and *kněz* (prince, as seen earlier). And *bujný* (vigorous or brash) modifies *srdce* (heart), *kravice* (cow), and *hlava* (head, as seen earlier).

There are also a number of cases where the same noun is modified by synonymous adjectives. Thus *paže* (arms, as in the human limbs) is modified once by *mocná* (powerful) and twice by *silná* (strong). *Noc* (night) can be *temná* (dark) in addition to *črná* (black), and *les* (forest) adds to those synonymous descriptors yet another, *tmavý* (dark). One *děva* (maiden) is described as *lepá* and another as *krásná*, which both mean "beautiful." The enemy *Tataři* (Tartars), in addition to being cruel and quasi-formulaically fierce, are also described once as *zlostiví* (furious) and later as *svěřepí* (savage). The repetition through synonymy here adds to the formulaic impression of the verse. A final notable case is in the phrases *tichými slovesy hovořili* (spoke with quiet words; "Oldřich," l. 12) and *vetchými slovesy nad sím vzpěchu* (they chanted over it ancient words; "Jaroslav," l. 58), as both echo (through the non-Czech noun form) the memorable beginning of the *Igor Tale*, where the narrator suggests that one might rather "begin with old words" (*načjati starymi slovesy*), like the older singer Bojan.[103] Both phrases manage, with different modifiers and in different contexts, to once again invoke this model for medieval Slavic epic narrative.

As we have seen, epithet-noun phrases are, like character epithets, embedded in a complex phraseology that mimics the traditional diction of the South Slavic epics. While the percentage of repeating phrases is small when measured against the total number of adjective-noun combinations, the impression of traditional oral repetition is magnified by the use of traditional fixed epithets from other oral epic traditions (particularly Russian, but also Greek and South Slavic), by the repeated use of a small repertoire of adjectives to modify nouns and by repetition through synonymy of nouns and adjectives. Some of the repeated quasi-formulas recur in particular thematic contexts (for example, preparation for battle) in a manner that also mimics traditional oral epic (even as others are deployed in a manner *counter to* their thematic use in other oral epic traditions).[104]

When we move from the rich field of formulaic epithets to other types of formulas, we find that there is a distinct decline in formula frequency in the Czech manuscripts. Lord observed, "The most stable formulas will be those for the most common ideas of the poetry. They will express the names of the actors, the main actions, time, and place."[105] We have, of course, already examined character names along with other epithets. We have also, along the way, noted a couple of *action-related formulas*: speech introduction tags, while examining character epithets, and a formula for mounting a horse in connection with the fixed epithet *ručí koni* (swift steeds). To these we can add a small number of additional action quasi-formulas. One of the more common actions across epics in the manuscripts is the gathering of a group, whether for an assembly, a tournament, or battle preparation. Many of these gatherings share aspects of their verbal expression:

. . . sě v črn les	. . . into the black forest
tamo, kam[o] sě vládyky sněchu	To the place where the lords had assembled
("Oldřich," ll. 1–2)	
sněchu sě mužie sěmo v les črn.	The men assembled in the black forest.
("Záboj," l. 15)	
Kda sě sněchu lesi i vládyky	When the chiefs and lords had assembled
v Vyšegradě [v Lubušině siedle]	At Vyšehrad [at Libuše's seat]
("Libuše," ll. 44–45)	
I kdaž bě den ustavený,	And when the chosen day arrived,
sněchu sě sem vsici páni	All the lords assembled here
("Ludiše," ll. 18–19)	

All share the same verb, two share the "black forest" location, and two others share the title used (*vládyky*) for those assembling. While only two of these appear in ten-syllable verse (the first and third) and can thus be said to constitute a kind of quasi-formula (by our criteria), there is a more broadly shared verbal patterning across verse forms that we can see here within the manuscripts.

A more exact verbal repetition between verse lines of different lengths is visible under the assembly theme as well, expressing the seating of the assembly in "Libuše" and "Ludiše" (our third and fourth examples above): the next line (l. 46) of the former is "prokní stúpi rozeňá dle svégo" (each took a place according to his birth), and a few lines farther down in the latter (ll. 26–27) we read, "Za předlúhé stoly sedú, / prokní rozenie dle svého" (They sat at lengthy tables, / Each according to his birth). This verbal repetition (allowing for [simulated] historical morphological changes and a single word that differentiates the ten-syllable from the eight-syllable line) became one of the key pieces of evidence linking the two manuscripts, so that when the doubts about the Green Mountain Manuscript became unavoidable, the Queen's Court Manuscript, which for most had been beyond doubt for so long, had to be reconsidered as well. And yet, if one were operating under the thesis that these are traditional epic poems, such a verbal repetition is no evidence at all of shared authorship, only of shared oral tradition. Only other evidence against such a perspective allows us to designate this, rather, as an effective imitation of such oral epic traditions.

A final assembly quasi-formula involves one of the epithet-noun phrases we have already seen, describing the verbal discussions in the assembly. Thus in "Oldřich" (l. 12): "tichými slovesy hovořili" (took their council with quiet words); and in "Libuše" (ll. 70–71): "i počechu ticho govoriti, / govoriti ticho mezu sobú" (And began to quietly confer, / To confer quietly among themselves). Both of these translate phonologically the commonplace phrase from South Slavic epic, *tiho govoriti*.[106] And in fact, this is a phrase that Hanka translated similarly in his edition of Serbian songs, in the song about Tsar Lazar from Karadžić's collection, where *poče tiho govoriti* is rendered *počne ticho hovořiti*.[107] This is, again, an effective imitation of a South Slavic verbal formula that gives an antiquated Slavic ring to the simulated oral diction of the manuscripts.[108]

Another sphere of action with potential for quasi-formulaic repetition is in the battle scenes across the epics in the manuscripts. Enders includes about ten phrases from battle scenes in his list of formulas, but none of them really add up to a formula under more strict criteria.[109] Only one repeats within the ten-syllable epics or sections, and most repeat minimally and with significant changes in order or morphology. They involve verbal descriptions of actions that are formulaic in an everyday language sense: warriors charging, swinging or striking with swords, covering with shields, and retreating; similar verbal repetitions could be found in chronicle accounts of battles. In my opinion, these phrases do not reflect a systematic imitation of the kind of repetition found in oral epic traditions or add to the impression of the orality of the texts. There are some other phrases, though, related to warriors' deaths, that echo other epic traditions and that should be considered as a part of such imitation. When the enemy Vlaslav perishes in single combat against Čestmír, the departure of his soul is described as follows (ll. 218–22):

Kypieše krev ze silna Vlaslava,	Blood frothed from strong Vlaslav
po zeleně trávě v syrú zem'u teče.	Over the green grass into the bleak earth it flows.
Aj a vyjde duša z řvúcej huby,	Lo! His soul leaves his wailing lips,
vyletě na drvo a po drvech	Flies to a tree and from tree to tree
sěmo tamo, doniž mrtev nezžen.	Will flit here and there till the dead one is burnt.

This scene shares a number of verbal features with the death of the young warrior in the ballad "Jelen" (The stag) (ll. 18–23):

vyrazi z junoše dušu, dušicu.	His soul, sweet soul, departed the youth.
Sě vyletě pěkným, táhlým hrdlem,	It flies along his fine thin throat,
z hrdla krásnýma rtoma.	Leaves his throat by his red lips!
Aj tu leže, teplá krev	Ah, here he lies. The warm blood flows
za dušicú teče za otletlú,	Out behind the soul that fled.
syrá země vřelú krev pije.	The bleak earth drinks the ardent blood.

These scenes share the departure of the soul through the mouth and the detail of the flowing of blood into the "bleak earth." Both gesture toward pagan beliefs about death and in particular toward Russian sources for the reconstruction of such beliefs. The epithet-noun phrase *syrá země* (bleak earth) is another phonological translation (the Czech adjective has a different meaning than the Russian one) of a Russian phrase that encapsulates a resonant figure in folk beliefs: *mat' syra zemlja* (mother damp earth).[110] The detail of the departure of the soul through the throat seems to echo, once again, the *Igor Tale* as it describes the death of a warrior from the older generation, Iziaslav: "edin" že izroni žemčjužnu dušu iz" xrabra těla čres' zlato ožerelie" (thus all alone / you let your pearly soul drop / out of your brave body / through your golden gorget).[111] These two deaths are linked by verbal and thematic repetition of Russian sources, even if these barely amount to a theme or have sufficient repetition to constitute quasi-formulas. The death of another enemy warrior, Kublai's son, invokes rather a Homeric formula, once again as noted by Vašek: "The verse 'zarachoce nad ním túlec s lukem' [his quiver and bow fell with a rattle; "Jaroslav," l. 284] is imitated from Homer's *arabēse de teuche' ep' autō* [his armor clattered upon him]."[112] Even without repetition within the manuscripts, such phrases resound with traditional associations to informed readers.

Formulas for time and place are even less common than those for actions in the manuscripts. One time marker that does have a minimal core of repetition is the beginning of a new day, dawn. As Foley has noted, in South Slavic tradition dawn marker formulas, which can range from one line to several in length, not only announce a new day, but they also mark the beginning of a new narrative segment and thus serve as an initiatory narrative signal, a function that he observes is also performed by Homer's "rosy-fingered dawn" phrase.[113] In the manuscripts, not every mention of a new morning serves as such a narrative transition, but several do. In "Oldřich and Boleslav," the morning marks the transition from the nighttime gathering in the black forest to the action to drive the Poles from Prague, initiated by Výhoň Dub's exhortation of Oldřich (ll. 13–15): "Noc sě převalíše přes pólnoci, / pokročíše k jutru šedošeru; / aj ta vece Výhoň knězu Oldře" (The night flew on till well past midnight / And hastened toward the gray-dark morn. / Then Výhoň spoke to Prince Oldřich). A similar transition is marked by similar language in "Jaroslav" (ll. 183–85): "Večer tich tu projde na noc chladnu, / noc sě proměníše v jutro šero, / i v táboře Tatar klidno bieše" (Quiet evening became cold night, / Night changed into gray morn, / And in the Tartar camp it was quiet). The transformation of the night here operates as a line-initial quasi-formulaic system in six-syllable cola ("Noc sě převalíše"; "noc sě proměníše"), and an epithet-noun quasi-formula names the result of the transformation, morning, once in a six-syllable second colon, once in a four-syllable ("k jutru šedošeru"; "v jutro šero"). In the second case the transition is not to another day of fighting, as we might have expected, but to the exposition of the suffering of the Christian soldiers from thirst while trapped for another day on top of Hostýn, which leads to the entry of the new hero Vratislav. Interestingly, in the poem "Záboj, Slavoj, and Luděk," the approach of dawn marks the end, rather than the beginning, of a narrative segment as the night meeting in the forest comes to an end and the young men disperse. They will commence their action to drive out the foreign occupier only with the arrival of the third night (rather than morning) later (ll. 80–84): "I přicházéše noc před jutro, / aj vystúpichu z úvala rózno, / vezdě ke všěm dřevóm, / ke všěm stranám brachu sě lesem" (And as night approached the morn, / They each left the vale separately, / In every direction among the trees, / To all sides they moved in the forest). The first line here also echoes the quasi-formulaic lines of the dawn marker, but it is a nine-syllable line and thus outside an analysis of the imitation of the deseterac.

A similar function as a narrative initiatory signal is performed by the interjection *ajta* or *aj ta* in the manuscripts. It combines with the dawn marker in the first example above as a redundant signal (within the first twenty lines of the Queen's Court Manuscript, thus connecting the two in their function and shaping readers' expectations). And it repeats a few lines later, as Oldřich responds to Výhoň's encouragement and takes up the banner, thus taking up the heroic role: "Ajta kněz vzě prápor v mocnú ruku: / 'Za mnú, za mnú, chrabro na Polany, / na Polany, vrahy našich zemí!'" (Lo, the prince seized the standard: / "Follow me, follow me, bravely at the Polans, / At the Polans, the enemies of our lands!"). In "Jaroslav" the interjection marks three important transitions. After the first two days of fighting at Olomouc, the Tartars gain the upper hand and force the Christian armies to retreat up Hostýn (ll. 120–21): "Ajta rozmnožie sě Tatar mnostvie, / jak sě množie večerní tma v jeseň" (Lo! Now the Tartar multitude increased / Like the evening dark increases in autumn). The tide of the battle turns back the other way following the soldiers' prayers to Mother Mary to end their thirst (ll. 232–36): "Aj hle! na vznoj[e]ném nebi mráček! / Vzdujú větři, zahuče hrom strašný, / chmúráše sě tuča po všěm nebi, / blsky ráz ráz bijú v stany Tatar: / hojný přieval pramen chlumský zživi" (Behold! A cloud in the scorching heavens! / Winds blew, thunder roared, / Storm clouds darkened the entire sky, / Lightning tore at the Tartar tents. / A torrent renewed the spring on the hill). Finally, Jaroslav himself unexpectedly appears to join the fray and bring the battle to its successful conclusion (l. 266, cited at greater length earlier): "Aj ta Jaroslav jak orel letě!" (Lo! Jaroslav flew in like an eagle!).

Dolanský noted the stylistic and functional similarity between this interjection and the interjection *eto* in South Slavic epic, which "always appears at the beginning of a sentence and introduces an important, surprising or unexpected reality."[114] We should also consider Foley's commentary on a Bosnian song's beginning: "*Line-initial expletives* such as *Oj!* and *Ej!* are common signals that mark the onset of performance in South Slavic oral epic, and, more rarely, important narrative junctures within performances. They function rhetorically as attention-getting devices and idiomatically as announcements of significant beginnings, whether of the song as a whole or an important section within the song."[115] *Ajta* in the Czech manuscripts thus functions as a parallel to these important stylistic and functional narrative markers in the South Slavic oral epic tradition, and thus as an effective imitation of that tradition.[116]

A contrasting case involves another important functional marker in South Slavic epic, where the manuscripts make use of the formula, but only in its literal meaning and without its traditional functional sense. In "Jaroslav," when Kublai's daughter determines to go to see the lands in the West, a retinue prepares to join her (ll. 19–20): "Na nohy tu skočí junóv desět / i dvě děvě, ku próvodu jejé" (Ten young men leapt to their feet, / And two maids, to attend to her). Dolanský observes that the first line here "repeats with a small change one of the most beloved verses of South Slavic folk epic," and he notes that both the detail of jumping to feet and the fact that it is ten *junóv* point to the South Slavic origins of the line.[117] In South Slavic epic, *junak* is the term for the hero, and its meaning connects it to the good youth, the corresponding Russian epic hero, or *molodec*. Foley examines this particular commonplace in Bosnian epic as an example of how certain established phrases invoke traditional meanings from the immanent tradition of epic beyond their literal sense and can even be used in situations where their literal sense may be out of place.

The line appears when a character is faced by a crisis or threat and responds by beginning to take action to counter the threat—the line thus marks the beginning of heroic counteraction in epic narrative.[118] The ten young Tartar men leaping to their feet here are undertaking a quest with Kublai's daughter, but not a heroic one and not in response to a threat, though they will be slaughtered along with her soon enough. This resonant line from South Slavic epic does not here carry its traditional, functional sense—these young men are not the epic heroes undertaking the heroic task. The fact that two young women also leap to their feet does not, on the other hand, necessarily contradict the South Slavic usage: Foley examines the use of the phrase in relation to a female character as well, who leaps to her feet to respond to a knock at the gate, where she will receive a message about the imprisonment of her betrothed and subsequently undertake counter action to free him.[119] But this aspect of heroic counteraction is absent for the maidens in "Jaroslav" as well.

It is worth noting that the very possibility that Foley explores in *Immanent Art* of metonymic reference to the whole of the existing oral tradition through resonant signals in the formulaic language and themes of epic poems was not available to the authors of the Czech manuscripts: this is not an aspect of the epic tradition that they likely recognized or could have imitated if they did. When they make use of some of the traditional language from the South Slavic tradition that is invested with such metonymic meanings, those meanings mostly disappear, as they have in this case. Their own artificial epic language, however appropriately they could apply epithets to characters and nouns or imitate formulaic epic language to describe actions, had to operate without the resonant and aesthetically enriching background that an oral tradition supplies. The lack of examples of formulaic phrases in the Czech manuscripts where the denotative meaning does not exactly fit the context, but the phrase still works in its functional meaning, is thus a kind of negative evidence that these are not, in fact, oral traditional epics.

Two other scenes from the manuscripts, however, suggest that some of the functional sense of the verb for leaping (without the detail of leaping to feet) may have nonetheless remained attached to the verb as it was deployed by the authors of the manuscripts. In "Jaroslav," as we have already seen, Vratislav enters the epic as a hero to counter the traitorous suggestion by Vestoň to surrender and hope for water in captivity (ll. 202–3): "Tu Vratislav jak tur jarý skoči, / Vestoňa za silně paži chváti" (Then Vratislav leapt like a wild bull, / Seized Vestoň by his strong arm). He is leaping like a wild bull, in a simile that draws on a Russian source, but he is also leaping up like a hero in a crisis to begin counteraction that will turn the battle. Vratislav's entry as a hero thus has South Slavic along with Russian epic overtones. The same verb is at work in "Záboj" when the gathering of young men, having heard Záboj's song about their plight and allegory about their preparation and future victory, arise to undertake the offered counteraction (ll. 76–79): "Aj, skočichu vsici v dól k Záboju / i tiščechu jej v přesilna paži / i s prsú na prsi vsi kladechu ruce, / věhlasno dávachu slova k slovóm" (Lo! Then all sprang down to Záboj / And pressed him in their strong arms. / And with breast to breast they laid on hands, / Sagely putting words with words). The repetition of the same verb from the formulaic phrasing in South Slavic tradition in these cases suggests that the authors of the manuscripts may, at times, have understood, at least implicitly, more than they were able to fully imitate.

To conclude this section on the formula, and more broadly on the richly textured poetic discourse that the South Slavic oral epics and their Czech imitations embody, it is worth examining a few more examples of passages where the Czech manuscripts demonstrate the characteristic texture of their models. The opening and closing lines of the first song in the Queen's Court Manuscript, "Oldřich and Boleslav," establish the mode well (ll. 1–9):[120]

. . . sě v črn les	. . . into the dark forest
tamo, kam[o] sě vládyky sněchu,	To the place where the lords had assembled,
sedm sich vládyk s udatnými sbory.	Seven such lords with stalwart companies.
Výhoň Dub tamo s niem [s] snahú chváta	Výhoň Dub speeds there eagerly
se vsjú chasú svojú temnem nočniem.	With his entire band in the dark of night,
Sě chasa mu bieše na sto chlapóv,	A band of about a hundred men,
všěch sto jmieše v nožnách břietné meče,	All hundred had a sharp sword sheathed,
k mečém všěch sto jmieše mocná paže,	And a strong arm each one for the sword,
k Výhořu v útrobách statnú vieru.	And stout faith in Výhoň in their guts.

Two-thirds of the lines (1, 3, 5, 7, 8, 9) end in adjective-noun combinations that could easily be formulaic (several are quasi-formulaic in the manuscripts). The *črn les* (dark forest) of the first line is, as we have seen, part of a thematic focusing for a gathering in a dark forest to conspire against an illegitimate or foreign power. Many of the remainder relate to a thematic focus in this opening that fleshes out the accoutrements of the *udatní sbory* (stalwart companies), with their *břietné meče, mocná paže*, and *statnú vieru* (sharp swords, strong arms, and stout faith). The passage is also characterized by repetitions occurring at multiple levels from assonance and alliteration and other sound patterning (*tamo-kamo, sněchu-snahú-statnú, chváta-chasa-chlapóv, bieše-jmieše-meče-paže, nožnách-útrobách*) to preposition repetitions (*s*, "with," in the fourth line, with the second instance added as necessary by the editors), word repetitions, sometimes repeated through grammatical changes (*tamo, sto, chasú-chasa, meče-mečém*), and syntactical forms.[121] The final three lines of the passage all repeat the same syntactical units in a kind of parataxis, even if they are slightly rearranged in order: if A = *všěch sto jmieše* (all hundred had), B = *v nožnách* (in sheaths or other containers), C = *břietné meče* (sharp swords or other adjective-noun), D = *k mečém* (for the sword or for some other dative object). These lines are then of the form ABC, DAC, DBC. The variation in the line openings is reduced to strict parallels in the end, which we expect from the principled right justification of the verse.

More straightforward parataxis characterizes the ending of the epic, with frequent anaphora and terracing (ll. 49–61):

Strach uderi u vsě u Polany:	Fear and panic struck all of the Polans.
aj, Polené oružie chvátajú,	Hey! The Polans seize their weapons,
aj, vládyky sěčne rány sekú!	Hey! The lords mow them down,
Polené tu skáčú sěmo tamo,	The Poles then flee hither and thither,
davem trčú ku bráně přiekopy	A throng rushes to the moat gate
dále, dále před udatnú sěčú.	Then further and further from the gallant slaughter.
Aj, vícestvie jesti bohem dáno!	Lo! God has granted victory!
Vstane jedno slunce po vsěm nebi,	One sun will ascend in all the heavens,
vstane Jarmír nad vsju zem'u opět.	Jarmír will ascend again in the land.
Roznosi sě radost po vsiej Praze,	Joy spread through all of Prague,
roznosi sě radost kolkol Prahy,	Joy spread throughout Prague,
rozlétnu sě radost po vsiej zemi,	Joy flew through all the land,
po vsiej zemi od radostnej Prahy.	Throughout the land from joyful Prague!

The parallel second and third lines here contrast the two fighting sides, and the final four lines again offer a more strictly parallel syntax, with repetition of the line opening in the first two lines, varied only by a changed but similar verb in the opening of the third line, and altered in the final line by terracing, with the repetition of the end of the third line, while still returning to the line-final prepositional phrase to close the series. The parallelism of the eighth and ninth lines here serves to liken Jarmír to the sun, a comparison that links the end of this song once again to the Old East Slavic *Igor Tale* and the ending of that myth epic, as Hanka himself noted in the introductory materials to his translation of that work.[122] Much of the sound and word repetition here happens in the syntactically parallel lines, but we can note another preposition repetition in the first line and some additional sound patterning (*sěčne-sekú-sěčú-skáčú-trčú*).

The opening of "Záboj, Slavoj, and Luděk" is linked to the opening of "Oldřich" through formulaic repetition, its verse form, and many of the same poetic figures of repetition (ll. 1–10):

S črna lesa vystupuje skála,	From the forest blackness a rock juts forth,
na skálu vystúpi silný Záboj,	Out on the rock stepped strong Záboj,
obzíra krajiny na vsě strany;	Looked out over the lands all around.
zamúti sě ot krajin ote všěch	They saddened him, all of them,
i zastena pláčem holubiným.	And he wept with the tears of a dove.
Sědě dlúho i dlúho sě mútě,	Long he sat and long he grieved,
i vzchopi sě vzhóru jako jelen,	Then gathered himself and stood like a stag,
dolóv lesem, lesem dlúhopustým,	Down through the forest, the desolate forest,
bystro spěcháše ot muže k mužu,	He hurried quickly from man to man,
ot silna k silnu po vsickéj vlasti.	From mighty to mighty, throughout the homeland.

The quasi-formulaic black forest in the first line links this opening to the first song and suggests the theme of the conspiracy of rebels. At the same time, the parallel syntax with a shared verb of the first two lines serves to compare "strong Záboj" to the firm rock on which he stands. The parataxis in the following three lines characterizes him further by his actions. The final two lines are linked by a kind of syntactical terracing, *ot muže k mužu / ot silna k silnu*, where the adjectives in the second phrase modify the nouns in the first. These word repetitions, with grammatical variation, are matched by others without such variation (*dlúho, lesem*). We even have another instance of preposition repetition, with grammatical variation, in the fourth line.

Having opened in this characteristic way, though, "Záboj" almost immediately departs from the deseterac form. This is the longest passage in this lengthy poem (it extends one line further in fact) that uses the South Slavic epic verse form. Nonetheless, much of the remainder of the poem is also characterized by similar repetitions and sound and syntactical figures. The texture of the poetic discourse largely extends throughout the manuscripts and is not limited to the ten-syllable epics. If, as Foley has suggested, for the South Slavic tradition, sound patterning, syntactic parallelism, and terracing are second-level processes in forming the verse, subordinate to the traditional rules that shape them as well as the formulas, for the Czech manuscripts I would argue that these are the primary forming processes. As I argued earlier, there are not and cannot be traditional rules for the Czech epics and they cannot follow the traditional rules of the South Slavic epics, because the differences between the languages negate certain possibilities (Czech has no medially accented trisyllables) and reshape the verse in new ways (reduced stress in the important ninth syllable).

This highly repetitive poetic texture, including quasi-formulaic phrases, parataxis, terracing, and sound patterning, is the means by which the Czech forged manuscripts quite successfully imitated their South Slavic primary (and Russian secondary) models, even if those models were shaped more fundamentally by other traditional rules and an oral tradition unavailable to the Czech imitators.

It was quite a convincing performance for many contemporary experts and remained so for decades. Dobrovský seems not to have doubted the Queen's Court Manuscript at all, until the other forgeries began to cast vague shadows of doubt on it. In his first recorded reaction, in a late addition to his 1818 history of Old Czech language and literature, he called it "a collection of lyrical-epic unrhymed folk songs, which surpass any of the old songs previously discovered."[123] Jungmann reviewed the reactions of Bohemian German, Polish, Russian, and Czech experts in an article on the Queen's Court Manuscript in 1822. Many connected the strength and simplicity of its poetic language, which stood in sharp contrast to contemporary norms of literary poetry, to its presumed age.[124] František Palacký connected the ten-syllable epics explicitly to Slavic epic forms in 1829, and the lack of rhyme was an important authenticating factor for him as well.[125] The critic Václav Nebeský declared, in an extended discussion of the manuscript, that "every line of the Queen's Court Manuscript is certainly also a witness to its authenticity" and cited the recognizability of the poems to Serbs, Russians, and other Slavs as corroborating evidence.[126] It was not until 1862, in the defense of the authenticity of the manuscript by the brothers Josef and Hermenegild Jireček, that the specifics of poetic form and language became explicitly analyzed as evidence in favor of the age of the manuscript. They connected the freer-form epics to Russian byliny and the *Igor Tale* and the stricter decasyllable epics to South Slavic examples. They also examined as clear evidence of the folkloric aspect of the verse such characteristics as alliteration and assonance, word repetitions, tautological adjective-noun combinations (formed on the same root), preposition repetitions, terracing, repetition of whole verses and verse parts sometimes with variation, and parataxis.[127] The initial impressionistic responses to the ancient aspect of the poems becomes more explicit, as the study of the manuscripts advances driven by questions of their authenticity, in the enumeration of their oral poetic qualities and similarities to other Slavic epic traditions, which served as key evidence for supporters of their ancient origin. To this point, early in the second half of the nineteenth century, the imitation remained convincing for many expert critics.[128]

Digital Analysis

Having just explored the many ways in which the manuscripts successfully recreate and simulate the oral-formulaic discourse of South Slavic oral epic traditions, it is worth asking whether that discursive texture is as pervasive in the manuscripts as it is in the South Slavic or Russian traditions. Impressionistically, while the features we have examined in particular passages are very much akin to oral-formulaic poetry, there are also many places in the manuscripts where the discourse does not present these features as prominently. I think most readers would recognize that the Russian byliny are far more repetitive in their phraseology than the manuscripts. And would a passage from the manuscripts, analyzed by Parry's and Lord's methods, have a similar formulaic density to the passage of South Slavic epic analyzed by Lord, with up to 50 percent of the phrases being formulaic and 100 percent belonging to formulaic systems? The question called for some digital analysis of the texts in comparison with South Slavic and Russian oral-formulaic epics as well as with literary epic and lyric poetry of the period to see where the manuscripts fit. With my colleague from the University of Illinois's National Center for Supercomputing Applications (NCSA), Michal Ondřejček, we received Faculty Fellowship funding from NCSA to pursue this analysis.[129]

Calculations of formulaic density became commonplace after the publication of Lord's *The Singer of Tales* and were often used to try to determine whether a text or set of texts were of oral provenance. There were also attempts to get beyond the problem of using a sample passage, employing digital analysis to calculate the formulaic density for a whole text or corpus of texts.[130] David E. Bynum criticized the uses to which calculations of formulaic density were being put, noting that Parry's and Lord's calculations had been done on texts whose formulaic aspect had already been well established and that the point was to demonstrate the pervasiveness of formula, not to establish a baseline to determine oral provenance. He particularly criticized the simplistic conception of formula that underlay such calculations, reducing formula to any phrase that repeats in the text or corpus without any consideration of whether such repetition was formulaic or not—since all poetic texts use repetition for a variety of purposes.[131] The digital methods were subject to the same problems, with more complex conceptions of formula being ruled out as impossible to calculate, so they defaulted to verbatim repetition of two or more words.[132] Vaira Vikis-Freibergs and Imants Freibergs further applied their calculation to a corpus of texts, Lithuanian lyric sun songs, for which a formulaic phraseology would not be necessary or expected. Foley criticized the practices of calculating formulaic density in the context of insisting on genre- and tradition-dependence for the analysis of formulas.

Given this fundamental critique of calculations of formulaic density and our desire to compare the Czech manuscripts not just to oral-formulaic traditions but also to contemporaneous literary poetic traditions, which were certainly not formulaic, we elected not to try any calculation of formulaic density. Rather, we tested a number of whole-text measures from natural language processing and informatics that could be applied to any text and looked promising to differentiate oral-formulaic texts from other types of texts. We hypothesized that the repetitiveness that characterizes formulaic texts would make them stand out in calculations of the lexical diversity of texts (type-token ratio, or TTR) and in calculations of textual entropy, including word or unigram entropy, word-pair or bigram entropy, and conditional entropy. Entropy is a basic probabilistic measure of uncertainty in informatics that calculates the amount of information a text presents, which can be calculated by letters or by words or word pairs. The notion of conditional entropy can be used to calculate the remaining uncertainty for successive pairs of words if the first word in each pair is known. Highly repetitive texts should have low TTR and low entropy by these various measures.

We assembled corpora of texts for comparison to the Czech manuscripts, including oral epics from Karadžić's and Kirsha Danilov's collections that Hanka and his collaborators knew; larger collections of Russian byliny and South Slavic oral epics from both Christian and Muslim singers; folk ballads in Czech, BCS, and Russian; and large corpora of literary epic and lyric poetry in all three languages from the early nineteenth century or as close to it as possible. All the texts had to be lemmatized, to eliminate morphological variation across repetition of words and phrases so the computer could recognize all lexical repetition. Further, because all of these measures are dependent on the length of the texts (longer text = more information) and we were comparing texts and corpora of highly divergent sizes (from the 3,093 words of the ten-syllable portions of the manuscripts to corpora of literary epics and lyrics of over half a million words), we needed a way to compare texts of different sizes. Our calculations were conducted by breaking the texts up into smaller segments (chunks) of the same size and calculating the average and standard deviation of each measure for all segments. We gradually increased the size of the segment, and texts fell out of the calculation when the chunk size exceeded the length of the text. The texts could then be compared for any measure at the same chunk size, with the most reliable data at the largest chunk size available for both texts.

While conditional entropy did not prove diagnostic for the differences between literary poetry and oral poetry, bigram entropy, unigram entropy, and TTR did, with the clearest distinction visible in the basic measure of TTR. Figure 2.1 represents the TTR results for all texts, with genre represented by color (blue = literary epic, red = literary lyric, green = oral epic and ballads, black = manuscripts) and language by shape. Within each language tradition there was a clear distinction between oral poetry and literary poetry, but as the graph shows, these Slavic traditions are close enough that the distinction is clear even across languages. The manuscripts, along with František Ladislav Čelakovský's later highly praised imitations of Russian folk songs, fall in between the oral-formulaic texts and literary texts, but closer to the formulaic texts.

By these measures, then, we were able to conclude that the manuscripts clearly distinguished themselves from their contemporary Czech literary poetic practices, moving far in the direction of the oral texts, but not, in the end, quite as far in the direction of reduced and repetitive or ritualized lexicon.[133]

Another means to quantify the reduced frequency of repeated or quasi-formulaic language in the manuscripts in comparison with genuine oral-formulaic texts came with our use of the Natural Language Toolkit (NLTK) to search for lexical collocations as a means of identifying potential formulas in the manuscripts. Here we created small corpora of texts of very close to the same size as the ten-syllable portions of the manuscripts, meaning just two to four byliny or South Slavic epics, and compared the number of potential two-word collocations for each set of texts. Table 2.1 shows the results.[134]

The manuscripts present a significantly smaller number of potential collocations of pairs of words for a similar number of poetic lines. Collocations

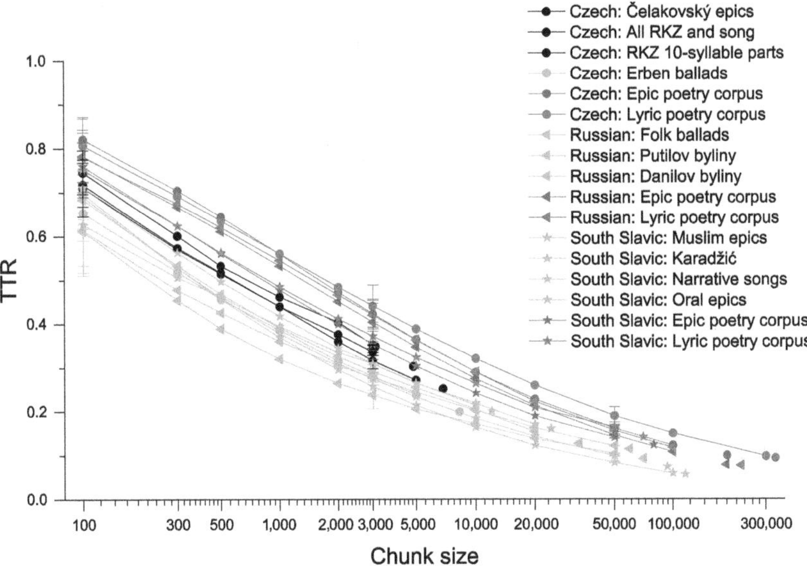

FIGURE 2.1. Graph of average type-token ratio (TTR) plotted across different chunk sizes on a logarithmic scale for study texts and corpora.

Table 2.1 Potential collocations from comparable size selection of texts

TEXT	NO. OF POTENTIAL COLLOCATIONS (NO MIN. WORD LENGTH)	NO. OF POTENTIAL COLLOCATIONS (MIN. WORD LENGTH OF 3 LETTERS)
Manuscripts, 10-syllable parts	142	75
Karadžić epics	300	200
Danilov byliny	234	153
Putilov byliny	381	201

are not formulas, though they share certain characteristics, like the specific meanings that can attach to the combination of the words. The calculation at least shows that these word pairs appear together significantly more often, statistically, than other pairs of words. Here too, then, the manuscripts appear to be less pervasively formulaic, using a proxy measure for formulas, than their models.

Themes

How do our imitators fare when we examine the next level of the formulaic aspect of traditional epic poetics, the theme? Any attentive reader of oral epics will notice the repetition of certain types of scenes across songs, sometimes even across traditions: the arming of the hero, saddling of the warhorse, sending of emissaries, and so forth. But how essential such commonplaces of narration are to the traditional narrative structures only became clear in the course of the intensive study of these traditions that occurred following the work of Parry and Lord.

Lord writes, "Following Parry, I have called the groups of ideas regularly used in telling a tale in the formulaic style of traditional song the 'themes' of the poetry."[135] The focus here is on the narrative idea, rather than the verbal form, although Lord always sought a kernel of verbal identity as well in identifying such units.[136] Foley found no consensus among researchers regarding the "internal structure" of the theme, "specifically on the questions of its phraseological texture, the significance of the order of its constituent parts, and the exact relationship among various occurrences."[137] To address such questions, he analyzed the common theme of "Shouting in Prison" from the large Return Song repertoire of the South Slavic singers. Here the hero of the song, who has been held for a long time in captivity, begins shouting so loudly and for so long that it disturbs his captor's wife and children, so that the captor is forced to negotiate for the hero's release. Foley examines this theme in the songs of a single singer (at the level of the singer's idiolect, in Lord's terms), of two singers from the same place (the dialect), and, finally, a singer from a distant location (the language of the tradition). He breaks the theme down into a series of smaller motifs, which individually also embody some idea or perform a function in the larger theme and which vary in length from a single line to several lines in length.

Even within the occurrences of the theme in the songs of a single singer, Foley finds the theme to be a malleable multiform. While some motifs are quite set in phrasing, others are entirely distinct, and there is flexibility in the order in which motifs occur (often in response to the different storyline as the theme is deployed in different songs).[138] In moving to the dialectal level, he already finds little to no identity in formulaic phraseology, and the motif structure of the theme becomes even more variable, with different sequences and omitted or added elements. At the level of the traditional language, while the general idea of the theme is still recognizable, with a core of motif elements still present, there is no real verbal correspondence between singers.[139] Like formulaic phraseology, then, the theme is a complex and variable structural instrument not reduceable to verbatim repetition of phrase.

This complicates our attempt to analyze the Czech forgeries for any use of traditional narrative themes in building the epic narratives of the manuscripts, as the identification of traditional themes cannot rely only on verbal echoes between songs or from their likely sources. We have already seen examples where the quasi-formulaic language of the manuscripts *does* echo traditional sources in connection to thematic structures: the jumping (to feet) when the hero undertakes the heroic task and the "swift steed" formula in connection to mounting the warhorse. But we should also try to identify traditional themes that lack such verbal echoes or any repetition within the manuscripts, yet have similar structures or motifs. Further, we will have to ask the question of what role these traditional themes play in the Czech songs' narrative structures and how they compare to the pervasive structuring by theme of their South Slavic, Russian, and other traditional models.

Our examination of themes will necessarily lead to a discussion of the traditional plots or song structures that the succession of themes ultimately creates. When that occasion arises, then, I will elaborate on the multiform nature of traditional story patterns in the Muslim South Slavic tradition studied by Parry and Lord, but will also have to note the particular aspect of the Christian South Slavic tradition in relation to story patterns, as elaborated by Foley.

We can start with the first epic of the Queen's Court Manuscript, "Oldřich and Boleslav," which presents itself as the ending fragment, just sixty-one lines, of a longer song in the ten-syllable epic line. It begins, as so many traditional songs do, with an *assembly* or meeting of the military leaders. We have already examined this theme in relation to some verbal quasi-formulas associated with it here and in other songs of the manuscripts, with the shared setting of a dark forest ("Záboj") and the verb for gathering. The song continues with a descriptive theme, *characterizing the assembling forces* connected to the hero Výhoň Dub, followed by *speech in the assembly*, here presented as a general discussion, marked by the quasi-formula of "quiet words" here as in "Libuše." A *dawn time-marker* quasi-formula marks the transition to the next theme, in which there is *direct address* of the prince by the hero, *exhorting* him to take counter action against the Polish occupying forces in Prague. Prince Oldřich responds by literally taking up the banner as a signal of his *taking up the heroic task*. The next few lines mark another narrative transition between themes with a *change of place*, followed by a descriptive or ornamental theme, *describing the place of battle*, in this case a lyrical portrait of Prague in the morning fog. The very common traditional theme of *disguise* follows, though not in the usual way with the disguise of the returning hero preparing for a later recognition, but here with the disguise of the soldiers as a part of a clever plan to sneak into the city walls and begin the decisive battle (a less common usage, perhaps, but with a notable classical antecedent in the Trojan horse episode). The final theme of the *battle* can be broken down into several motifs: *commencement with drums and horns*, the *striking by fear* of the opposing side, *chaotic battle* with wounding and chaotic movement to and fro, and, finally, *victory and expressions of joy*.

We will examine a couple of these themes more closely, but it is worth noting here that, at least at this level of description, this progression of themes looks quite similar to the what one would find in traditional oral epics and South Slavic epics in particular. Themes that are common in traditional epics are linked together with traditional transitional markers to build a larger tale, and, in fact, although this epic is presented as a fragment and is short, it tells a whole story, from the traditional opening in an assembly to the hero taking up the task to its completion in the final battle. We will come back to the question of whether the plot here created is recognizable as belonging to the repertoire of traditional songs.

The theme of *characterizing the assembling forces* occurs in "Oldřich" (ll. 4–9), "Jaroslav" (ll. 237–43), and "Záboj" (ll. 86–92, not in decasyllable lines):

Výhoň Dub tamo s niem [s] snahú chváta	Výhoň Dub speeds there eagerly
se vsjú chasú svojú temnem nočniem.	With his entire band in the dark of night,
Sě chasa mu bieše na sto chlapóv,	A band of about a hundred men,
všěch sto jmieše v nožnách břietné meče,	All hundred had a sharp sword sheathed,
k mečém všěch sto jmieše mocná paže,	And a strong arm each one for the sword,
k Výhoňu v útrobách statnú vieru.	And stout faith in Výhoň in their guts.

Minu búřa.—Voje v řady hrnú;	The storm passed. Warriors joined in ranks
ze všěch vlastí, ze všěch krajin země	From all realms, from all parts of the land,
k Olomúcu choruhvy jich věјú.	To Olomouc, their standards waving.
Těžcí meči po bocéch jim visá,	Heavy swords hang at their sides,
plní túli na plecech jim řechcú,	Full quivers clatter on their shoulders,
jasní helmi jim na bujných hlavách	Bright helms on their brash heads
i pod nimi ručí koni skáčú.	And beneath them leap swift steeds.

bra sě Záboj v les,	Záboj took to the forest,
lesem za Zábojem sbory;	And the company through the forest after him;
i bra sě Slavoj v les,	And Slavoj took to the forest,
lesem za Slavojem sbory.	And the company through the forest after him.
Vsjak jmě vieru k vojevodě,	Each one with faith in the captain,
vsjak srdce úporno králu,	Each with a heart opposed to the king,
vsjak zbraň bystru na král[e].	Each with a weapon swift for the king.

These three passages are quite similar in their construction, even if there is very little verbal repetition (the "faith" in the captain in the first and third passages along with the verb "to have" [*jmieše, jmě*] being the sole example). The arrival of the troops transitions to a description of their attributes that is built on parallel syntax and rife with adjective-noun quasi-formulas or combinations that at least sound traditional in this context. The lack of verbal repetition here would not negate this as an example of a repeated theme, if this were traditional oral epic, but is similar to the kind of variation Foley found in the South Slavic tradition between singers. In fact, this short theme has fairly stable syntactical and motif structures.

The *battle* theme is much more complex in structure and will allow us to examine in greater depth the variations in themes and their possible sources in the Czech manuscripts. Battles occur in all of the epic songs, in deseterac form or not, with the exception of "Libuše's Judgment." The final battle in "Jaroslav" has the most complete motif structure of the battles in the ten-syllable epics, so we can use it as our nominal model and add additional motifs as we examine other battle scenes. Motif 1 (following the model of Foley and numbering motifs) is *commencement with drums and horns*, as in "Oldřich." *Chaotic battle*, motif 2, here emphasizes sound over movement. This is followed by a *description of battle victims*, motif 3. Motif 4, *retreat of the hero's army*, is cut short by motif 5, *the arrival and characterization of the hero. Single combat*, motif 6, naturally follows, to be succeeded by motif 7, *retreat of the enemy army*, and motif 8, *victory*. This complex theme immediately follows the *characterizing the assembling forces* theme just examined and brings the epic to its conclusion ("Jaroslav," ll. 244–89):

1 Vzezvučaly hlasy rohóv lesních,	The forest horns sounded their voices,
uderily zvuky bubnóv břeskných.	The sharp drums beat out sounds.

2 Nalit srážajevě straně obě.	Suddenly both sides met in battle.
Podvihaje sě mhla ote pracha,	A haze of dust rose up from the ground,
i by pótka kruta poslednějé.	And the final cruel battle occurred.
Vznide chrest i drnket ostrých mečév,	The din and clang of sharp swords rang,
vznide siket kalených střel strašný,	The terrible hiss of tempered arrows,
lom oščepóv, rachet kopí bystrých.	The breaking of spears and thunder of lances.
I by klánie i by porubánie	There were fights and there was slaughter,
i by lkánie i by radovánie.	There were cries and there was laughter.
3 Krev sě valé jak bystriny dščevy,	Blood flowed like streams after rain,
mrch tu ležéše jak v lese dřievie.	Corpses lay like logs in the forest.
Sěmu hlava na dvé rozcepena,	This one's head split in two,
sěmu srubeně stě ruce obě,	That one with both arms chopped off,
sěn sě kotie s oře pře[s] druhého	One falls on another from his warhorse,
i sěn zeřivý své vrahy mláti,	Yet another hammers his enemies madly
jak po skalách lútá búřa dreva,	Like a wild storm the trees on a cliff.
sěmu v srdce po jilce meč vtasi	This one got a sword in his heart to its hilt,
i sěmu Tatarín ucho střieže.	That one his ear slashed by a Tartar.
4 Uh, by ryk, stenánie žalostivo!	Oh, there was screeching, bitter moaning!
křestěné počechu utiekati,	The Christians then began to run,
Tateré je lútým davem hnáti.	The Tartars in fierce hoards to chase.
5 Aj ta Jaroslav jak orel letě!	Lo! Jaroslav flew in like an eagle!
tvrdú ocel na mohúcech prsech,	Firm steel on his powerful breast,
pod ocelí chrabrost, udatenstvie,	Beneath the steel: bravery, valor,
pod helmicú velebyster věhlas,	Beneath his helm swiftest insight,
jarota mu z žhavú zrakú pláše.	Fervor flashing from his burning eyes.
Rozkacen hna, jako lev drážlivý,	He charged angrily, like an enraged lion

když mu teplú krev sě udá zřieti,	When it chances to see fresh blood,
kehdy nastřelen za lovcem žene;	And when struck, it turns on the hunter.
tako zlúti sě, vz Tatary trči.	Likewise provoked, he targeted the Tartars,
Češie za niem jako krupobitie.	And the Czechs came after like a hailstorm.
6 Vrazi kruto na Kublajevica,	He struck fiercely at Kublai's son,
i by pótka ovsěm velelúta.	And their combat was certainly savage.
Srazista [sě] oba oščepoma,	They clashed together with their spears
zlomista je oba velím praskem.	And broke them both with a colossal crack.
Jaroslav ves ve krvi s ořem sbrocen	Jaroslav, all splattered with blood like his steed,
mečem Kublajevica zachváti,	Struck down Kublai's son with his sword,
ot ramene šúrem [k] kyčlu protče,	Cutting slantwise from shoulder to hip,
takož spade bezduch mezi mrchy.	So he fell lifeless among the corpses.
Zarachoce nad niem túlec s lukem.	His quiver and bow fell with a rattle.
7 Uleče sě ves lud Tatar lútých,	All the fierce Tartar folk took fright,
otmetáše dřevce séhodlúhé,	Threw down their lances a fathom long,
palováše tu, kto téci može,	And then fled, who was able,
tamo, otkad slunce jasno vstává.	To whence the sun brightly rises.
8 I by prosta Hana Tatar vrahóv.	And Haná was free of the Tartar foes.

These motifs cover the majority of the action and description in all the other battle scenes in the epics of the manuscripts, including earlier battles in "Jaroslav," though we will have to add a few more motifs in a few instances.

Motif 1 also appears, as we observed earlier, in the final battle of "Oldřich" (ll. 45–48): "Uderichu rány bubny hromné, / vyrazichu zvuky trúby hlučné. / Choróhvy tu sbory na most vraz'ú, / ves most otřása sě pod jich davem" (They beat blows on the thundering drums, / They blew sounds from loud horns. / The companies and banners dashed onto the bridge / So the whole bridge shook under their weight). There is a minimal verbal repetition here, in the verb and noun for striking drums, but not as a quasi-formula. None of the other battles in the manuscripts commence in this way. In a couple of cases, we might explain the absence by the fact that horns and drums are the attributes of a formal army, and the Czech side in those instances is not such a force ("Beneš, Son of Herman" and "Záboj, Slavoj, and Luděk"). In "Čestmír and Vlaslav," the final battle commences with a deceitful maneuver by the Czech forces, who march their armies nine times around a hill to magnify the size of their forces and instill fear in the enemy—the same effect as the horns and drums in "Oldřich." And here it is worth noting that the motif of *striking by fear* does not follow in "Jaroslav." While in "Oldřich" the horns and drums are part of a surprise attack and magnify the effect of surprise, in "Jaroslav" they rather function to announce the arrival and joining of the battle by reinforcing Christian armies. This flexibility in the use of motifs and in the larger theme to include or exclude them is similar to the variation in oral traditional epics.

Any reader of the Czech manuscripts is likely to recall the sounding of quite a few more horns and drums. The eight-syllable epic "Ludiše and Lubor" includes a whole-line formula that repeats seven times in that 136-line poem: "Zevzně hlahol trub i kotlóv" (The horns and drums sounded peals).[140] It marks not the beginning of a military battle but the end of each round of sparring in the knightly tournament being hosted by Ludiše's father, as well as marking a transition between narrative parts in at least one instance and the end of the poem. This narrative motif thus has additional uses outside the theme of battle, strictly speaking.

Chaotic battle, motif 2, can be described in a number of different ways. The example above from "Jaroslav" is a wonderfully poetic passage that paints the battle chaos in sound, including the remarkable final two lines with their parataxis and leonine (end-colon) rhyme across both lines: "I by klánie i by porubánie / i by lkánie i by radovánie" (There were fights and there was slaughter, / There were cries and there was laughter). A number of other passages describing the chaos of battle also use sound, and a thin thread of repetition ties them together and to the passage above ("Jaroslav," ll. 67–70; "Beneš," ll. 49–60; "Čestmír," ll. 208–10):

Tu sě prvý boj v hromadu srazi;	Now the first battle was joined in mass:
střely dščichu jako přieval s mrakóv,	Arrows rained down like a torrent from the clouds,
oščepóv lom jako rachot hroma,	The breaking of spears like the rumble of thunder,
blsket mečév jako oheň búře.	The flash of swords like a storm's fire.

Srazistě tu obě straně,	The sides then met and clashed as though
jakž by les v les sě valil;	A forest fell on a forest.
jak blesk hroma po nebi,	Like the flash of thunder in the heavens
tako blesk mečév.	Was the flash of swords.
Vzezvuče skřek hrózonosný,	A terrifying shout rang out
poplaši ves zveř leský,	That frightened the forest beasts,
vsě nebeská letadla	And all the heaven-flyers
až po třetí vrch.	Three peaks away.
Rozléha sě po úvalech	Now the strike of club, now sword,
ot skalnatých [. . .] hor	Like the felling of ancient trees,
tu ráz kyjév, tu mečév,	Reverberated in the valleys
jak kot vetchých dřev.	From rocky hills.
Aj, řiče les řváníem iz úvala,	Ho! The forest and the valley roared,
jak by hory s horami válely,	As though mountain warred with mountain
i vsě drva v sebe rozlámaly.	And all the trees broke on each other.

The first battle in "Jaroslav" here prefigures the chaos of the final battle cited above, listing three of the same weapons in its description (arrows, swords, and spears). While in the final battle it is the sound of the weapons themselves that provide the imagery, though, here simile links both visual and aural characteristics of the weapons to storms. Nonetheless, the single sound here is precisely the same sound, in the same first colon verbal formula (with altered word order) as later, and evokes the same sound in the second colon as well: "lom oščepóv, rachet kopí bystrých" (the breaking of spears and the rumble [thunder] of quick lances). The longer passage from "Beneš" repeats some of the same imagery and words (*blsket* = *blesk*) in its simile. Finally, the last passage here from "Čestmír" picks up other parts of the description from "Beneš."[141] In some Czech dialects, *hora* (mountain) can also mean *les* (forest), so a mountain warring with a mountain is more or less the same simile as a forest with a forest, particularly as the breaking of trees is emphasized.[142]

This storm and nature imagery to describe battles and the elemental nature of the military forces and their clashes appears in battle scenes across multiple epics in the manuscripts, but is most prominent in "Jaroslav." This is appropriate thematically to that epic in particular because the Christian forces, suffering from thirst on the top of Hostýn, are rescued initially by an actual storm that appears following their supplicatory prayers to Mary. This storm was prefigured in some of the battle imagery, as we have seen, but also in the characterization of the opposing Tartar forces ("Jaroslav," ll. 93–96):

Tateré sě hnuchu v pravú stranu.	The Tartars charged to the right-hand side.
Jak mrak č[r]ný, kehdy ledem hrozí	Like a black cloud that threatens to pound
posúti úrody tučných polí:	The crops in the fertile fields with hail,
tako by roj slyšán ot daleka.	So was the swarm heard from afar.

In "Záboj" it is the Czech forces that are likened to a hailstorm (ll. 135–36): "I vyrazi Záboj v před jako krupobitie, / i vyrazi Slavoj v bok jim jako krupobitie" (And Záboj charged straight on like a hailstorm, / And Slavoj charged their flank like a hailstorm).

What conclusions can we draw regarding the motif of *chaotic battle*? While there are some continuities in phraseology and, perhaps more so, in imagery, there is also considerable variety. It is hard to say if this is similar to the kind of variation one finds for theme motifs in an oral epic tradition. Given what Foley calls "the protean reality of thematic structure," it would be foolhardy to positively affirm or to deny any resemblance of an example like this one to oral tradition.[143] The evidence here is ambiguous, and we will have to examine additional motifs and themes and their use in structuring narrative in the manuscripts.

Retreat of the enemy army, motif 7, offers another fine example of a quasi-formulaic phrase that links together multiple instances of the motif. This does not include, however, the longer variant of the motif in the final battle of "Jaroslav" cited above. The passages are the following ("Beneš," ll. 73–76; "Záboj," ll. 192–96; "Jaroslav," ll. 160–63):

Ide pótka s chluma v rovňu;	The battle moved from the hill to the plain.
i by Němcém úpěti,	The Germans were made to groan,
i by Němcém prnúti,	And the Germans had to flee,
i pobitie jim!	And they were slaughtered!
Aj ta otvrže Záboj ščit	Ho! Now Záboj threw down his shield,
i v ruce mlatem i v druhéj mečem,	And hammer in one hand and sword in the other,

tako i v přieč proráže dráhy u vrazéch.	This way and that cut a path through the enemy.
I by úpěti vrahóm i by ustúpati vrahóm.	The enemy groaned and the enemy retreated.
Třas je hnáše z bojiště.	Třas drove them from the battleground.
Napínachu ruče tuhy luky	They swiftly bent their taut bows
i máchachu silno ostré meče;	And powerfully swung their sharp swords;
i by Tatarovóm ústupati.	And the Tartars had to retreat.

The closing four lines of "Beneš, Son of Herman" compress together the enemy retreat and final defeat; the lines from "Záboj, Slavoj, and Luděk" follow upon Záboj's victory in single combat, but also compress together multiple motifs into a few lines—the opening of Záboj's apotheosis as a hero (to which we shall return), the enemy's retreat, and the operation of fear (personified here as a pagan god of trembling fear); the lines from "Jaroslav" occur in the midst of a back-and-forth battle between the Christian and Tartar forces and thus mark only a temporary retreat of the latter. What they all share, though, is a formulaic system of phrasing with a formulaic line or colon beginning; a verb in the infinitive that varies between three verbs, two of which repeat; and a variable dative object (functionally the subject of the phrase): "I by [dative object] [verb: *úpěti, ustúpati, prnúti*]" (The [enemy] was forced to groan / retreat / flee). This quasi-formulaic phrase (only in "Jaroslav" does it occur in a ten-syllable line) constitutes the motif of the enemy's retreat in battle, then, for all instances in the manuscripts except the final battle in "Jaroslav" and in a very attenuated retreat at the end of "Oldřich."

Motif 5, *the arrival and characterization of the hero*, is another flexible motif that varies considerably in length and placement in the epics. The aspect of arrival is really only present for Jaroslav as a hero, who comes late to the tale, while the other heroes are largely present from the beginning of the other narratives. Thus Výhoň Dub, the nominal hero of "Oldřich," is described at the beginning of that narrative fragment through the characterization of the forces he leads (in a passage we examined earlier). Beneš, son of Herman, leads the Czechs' uprising against their Saxon occupiers but only really moves to the center of attention in a few lines of the final battle when he stands on a height and directs his forces to the right and left with his sword. Čestmír, on the other hand, is the only hero in the Czech manuscripts to get that most iconic heroic treatment through the theme of the *arming of the hero* (ll. 18–23):

I vsta Čsmír i vzradova sě,	And Čestmír rose and rejoiced,
radostně sně svój ščít črn	Gladly took his black shield,
dvú zubú, i sně se ščítem	two-toothed, and with the shield
i mlat i nepronikavý helm.	His hammer and invincible helm.
Pode vsě drva	Under every tree he offered
vložie oběti bohóm.	Sacrifices to the gods.

Čestmír here takes up the heroic task offered by his Prince Neklan (by rising, not by jumping to his feet) and takes up his armor and weapons as well. He is also characterized through his pagan piety in offering the required sacrifices before battle. This is a compact treatment of one of the most common epic themes, but it is unique within the epics of the Czech manuscripts.

The characterizations of Jaroslav and Záboj are more complex and interesting. I will cite again here the motif from "Jaroslav" (ll. 266–75):

Aj ta Jaroslav jak orel letě!	Lo! Jaroslav flew in like an eagle!
tvrdú ocel na mohúcech prsech,	Firm steel on his powerful breast,
pod ocelí chrabrost, udatenstvie,	Beneath the steel: bravery, valor,
pod helmicú velebyster věhlas,	Beneath his helm swiftest insight,
jarota mu z žhavú zrakú pláše.	Fervor flashing from his burning eyes.
Rozkacen hna, jako lev drážlivý,	He charged angrily, like an enraged lion
když mu teplú krev sě udá zřieti,	When it chances to see fresh blood,
kehdy nastřelen za lovcem žene;	And when struck, it turns on the hunter.
tako zlúti sě, vz Tatary trči.	Likewise provoked, he targeted the Tartars,
Češie za niem jako krupobitie.	And the Czechs came after like a hailstorm.

I have already commented earlier on the prominence of the adjective *jarý* in its Russian sense in connection to Jaroslav, which appears here in a substantivized form as *jarota* (fervor). This inventive characterization looks beyond the surface of the warrior's armor to the character traits that lie beneath and allows his impassioned soul to shine out through his eyes. For a nobleman like Jaroslav of Sternberg, the royal symbols of eagle and lion were also not inappropriate, but the lion simile has a particularly notable antecedent. In book 5 of the *Iliad*, Diomedes, having been struck by an arrow, returns to the fighting at the urging of Athena:

> now the strong rage tripled took hold of him, as of a lion
> whom the shepherd among his fleecy flocks in the wild lands
> grazed as he leapt the fence of the fold, but has not killed him,
> but only stirred up the lion's strength, and can no more fight him
> off, but hides in the steading, and the frightened sheep are forsaken,
> and these are piled pell-mell on each other in heaps, while the lion
> raging still leaps out again over the fence of the deep yard;
> such was the rage of strong Diomedes as he closed with the Trojans.[144]

The Czech epic in repeating the Homeric simile does not imitate that particularly Homeric aspect, in which the vehicle expands into a mini narrative of its own. There are no Homeric similes of that type in the manuscripts. Here, too, the grounding motivation of the simile is missing. Diomedes has, like the lion, been wounded. But Jaroslav has only just appeared, not having taken part in the battle at all until its close. His comparison to a wounded lion is unmotivated, as is his appearance in the poem in general. Still, the use of the extended simile is clearly a notable descriptive thematic element in the Czech epic as it is in the oral-formulaic Homeric one.[145]

The comparison of Diomedes to a lion is part of a longer formulaic narrative sequence that begins in book 5 of the *Iliad*, the *aristeia* of Diomedes. As Seth L. Schein explains, "*Aristeia* is a word used in later Greek for 'excellence' or 'prowess,' including, in particular, the excellence or prowess of a Homeric warrior when he is on a victorious rampage, irresistibly sweeping all before him, killing whomever of the enemy he can catch or whoever stands against him." Scholars like Schein apply the term as well to an elaborate theme in Homeric epic:

> In the *Iliad* the *aristeia* is the main compositional unit of battle narrative. One can distinguish five sections of a normal *aristeia*. First there is a description of the hero arming himself, including an especially detailed description of his triumphantly gleaming armor. Next the hero turns the tide of a deadlocked battle by killing an opponent who stands against him. Thirdly, the hero breaks into the grouped ranks of the enemy and wreaks havoc among them. Thereafter the hero is himself wounded (which causes a temporary setback for his side), but he prays to a god, is healed or strengthened, and reenters the battle to kill an important enemy. Finally, there is a fierce battle over the corpse of this enemy, until

> it is taken (often with divine aid) from the clutches of the hero. Although not every *aristeia* in the poem has all these sections in identical sequence and form, the normal *aristeia* would have been present in the minds of both poet and audience, since it was a major element of the oral poetic tradition.[146]

The authors of the Czech manuscripts once again did not have such an oral tradition operating as a resonant background adding meaning and context to their expressions and scenes, but they did have their classical educations and European literary epic traditions derived from Homer, with their oblique reflections of these narrative commonplaces.

For our own examination of the battle theme in the manuscripts, the Greek *aristeia* model is most illuminating for "Záboj." The eponymous hero is characterized extensively in the epic, not through his arming, but through his melancholy reflection in the poem's opening that turns to decisive action, calling an assembly of the men in the forest; through two allegorical songs he sings there, the first of which tells the history of their subjugation with suppression of their pagan religion, while the second offers a model for their military training and uprising; and, finally, through his clever preparation for and leading of the battle. Záboj engages Luděk in an extensive and detailed single combat in which Záboj finally ends the deadlock by throwing his heavy hammer through Luděk's shield and into his chest.

It is here, when Záboj breaks the deadlocked battle and in his subsequent rampage through the retreating enemy army, that the narrative resembles the Greek *aristeia* (ll. 190–207):

"Zá[b]oji bratře, ty udatý lve;	"Záboj, brother, you bold lion!
neupúščej búřit u vrahy!"	Don't neglect to harry the enemy!"
Aj ta otvrže Záboj ščit	Ho! Now Záboj threw down his shield,
i v ruce mlatem i v druhéj mečem,	And hammer in one hand and sword in the other,
tako i v přieč proráže dráhy u vrazéch.	This way and that cut a path through the enemy.
I by úpěti vrahóm i by ustúpati vrahóm.	The enemy groaned and the enemy retreated.
Třas je hnáše z bojiště.	Třas drove them from the battleground.
Strach z hrdl jich vyráže skřeky.	Fear drove shrieks from their throats.

Koni řechce vešken [. . .] les.	The entire forest with horses neighed.
"Vzhóru na koně, s koni za vrahy	"Mount your steeds and after the foe
přese vsě vlasti!	Throughout the entire land!
Ručí konie neste	Swift steeds carry our cruelty
v patách za nimi nášu krutost!"	Hot on their heels!"
I vzkočichu hluci vz ručie koně,	And the ranks mounted their swift steeds,
i skok na skok po vrazéch sě hnachu,	And chased the enemy in leaps and bounds,
ránu na ránu soptichu krutú krutost.	Wound on wound they spewed cruel cruelty.
I míjechu rovně i hory i lesy,	They passed plains, and hills, and forests,
v pravo i v levo vsě ubieha vzad.	To the right and left, everything flew by.

Záboj penetrates the enemy ranks and creates havoc like a Greek hero. The detail of his casting aside his shield is also telling for its oblique suggestion of the Islandic skaldic tradition of the animal warrior. There the terms *bersirkir* (bearskin) and *ulfheðnar* (wolfskin) are used for warriors who give off wild war shrieks and can endure pain in a superhuman manner. A common motif of the berserker warrior is the shedding of clothing and armor before entering the battle, which not only demonstrates the bravery of the hero but also symbolizes the change from human to animal skin.[147] Although Slavoj addresses Záboj as "bold lion" immediately preceding this moment, typically for the Czech manuscripts, there is no suggestion here of a mythological transformation into animal guise, and the epithet remains a metaphor. Nonetheless, this is the closest any Czech warrior in the manuscripts gets to "wild bull" Vsevolod in his battle frenzy, which we examined above in connection to that epithet. This is also, then, the single exception to the typical portrait of Czech warriors in the manuscripts as stalwart in defense of their land, but peace loving and more cultured than their animal-like enemies (though here, too, it is part of a complex portrait of Záboj that begins with his melancholy and bardic role).[148]

We might wish to add the motif of *pursuit* to follow *retreat of the enemy army* to our motif structure for the larger *battle* theme, given this example in "Záboj." We should note as well, given the richness of quasi-formulaic language in this passage ("swift steeds" and the retreat formula), that only five lines of the passage are decasyllable, and with the exception of one connected pair (ll. 203–4), all are isolated among lines of varying length. This *pursuit* motif is quite extensive in "Záboj" and continues nearly to the end of the poem. The passage immediately following is notable both as the single example of the verbatim repetition of a longer passage in the manuscripts and for the possible model for the passage in Achilleus's pursuit of the retreating Trojan warriors (ll. 208–30):

Hučie divá řeka,	A wild river rumbled,
vlna za vlnu sě válé;	Wave washed over wave.
hučechu vsi vojí, skok na skok	The armies rumbled, leap by leap
vsě sě hnáše přes búřúcú řeku.	Everything rushed across the raging river.
Vody uchvátichu mnostvie cuzích	The water ensnared many strangers,
i přenesechu své zvěsty na druhý břech.	But brought its familiars to the far bank.
I po krajinach vezdě v šíř i v šíř	And wider and wider throughout the lands
lútý ostřiež [r]ozepě svoje křiedle dlúzě,	The fierce falcon spread its great wings
bystro léta za ptactvem.	And quickly pursued the birds.
Zábojevi vojí rozehnachu sě v šíř,	Záboj's warriors scattered wide,
vezdě po vlastech	Everywhere throughout the lands
hnachu lúto po vrazéch;	Fiercely chasing the enemies,
vezdě srážechu je i stúpachu koni.	Attacking and trampling them at each turn.
Nocú pod lunú za nimi lúto,	At night by the moon after them fiercely,
dnem pod sluncem za nimi lúto,	By day by the sun after them fiercely,
i opěty temnú nocú	And again in the dark night,
i po noci šedým jutrem.	And then in the gray dawn.
Hučie divá řeka,	A wild river rumbled,
vlnu za vlnu sě válé;	Wave washed over wave.
hučechu vsi vojí, skok na skok	The armies rumbled, leap by leap
vsě sě hnáše přes búřúcú řeku.	Everything rushed across the raging river.
Vody uchvátichu mnostvie cuzích,	The water ensnared many strangers,
i přenesechu své zvěsty na druhý břech.	But brought its familiars to the far bank.

Verbatim repetition of a passage is something not uncommon in oral-formulaic epic and is often found in thematic units, as, for example, when a leader dictates a message to an emissary, who then repeats the message verbatim to its recipient. Here, a passage in the *pursuit* motif, involving the assistance of a river, is repeated. The repetition is divided by a wonderful poetic image of Záboj's warriors as a falcon hunting—incidentally, probably the closest the manuscripts come to imitating the device of Slavic antithesis (or negative analogy), lacking only the negation of the vehicle, the image of the falcon. This encounter of a river in pursuit of the enemy recalls the extended *aristeia* of Achilleus, who at the end of book 20 is wreaking havoc among the Trojan forces, while book 21 opens with the encounter with the Xanthos river:

> But when they came to the crossing place of the fair-running river
> of whirling Xanthos, a stream whose father was Zeus the immortal,
> there Achilleus split them and chased some back over the flat land
> toward the city. . . .
>
> . . . Meanwhile the other half
> were crowded into the silvery whirls of the deep-running river
> and tumbled into it in huge clamour, and the steep-running water
> sounded, and the banks echoed hugely about them, as they out-crying
> tried to swim this way and that, spun about in the eddies.[149]

Whether or not the authors of "Záboj" were imitating the *Iliad*, the coincidence of motif structures in larger *battle* themes here suggests that they had a good sense of traditional epic narrative structure.

To conclude the examination of the *battle* theme, let us consider motif 6, *single combat*. "Záboj" provides an extended example, while "Čestmír" and "Jaroslav" treat this decisive moment in battle more succinctly. Here one also must consider "Ludiše and Lubor," which narrates a knightly tournament, but, as a number of commentators have observed, the violent encounters between participant warriors therein resemble single combat far more than the playful and competitive exchanges of a tourney.[150] This resemblance is also observable at the level of the quasi-formulaic language of these encounters ("Jaroslav," ll. 276–84; "Čestmír," ll. 211–19; "Ludiše," ll. 69–79, 87–95; "Záboj," ll. 141–67):[151]

Vrazi kruto na Kublajevica, i by *pótka ovsěm velelúta.*	He *struck* fiercely at Kublai's son, And their *combat* was certainly *savage.*
Srazista [sě] oba oščepoma,	*They clashed together with their spears*

zlomista je oba velím praskem.
Jaroslav *ves ve krvi* s ořem sbrocen
mečem Kublajevica zachváti,
ot ramene šúrem [k] kyčlu protče,
takož spade bezduch mezi mrchy.
Zarachoce nad niem túlec s lukem.

And broke them both with a colossal crack.
Jaroslav, all splattered *with blood* like his steed,
Struck down Kublai's son with his sword,
Cutting slantwise from shoulder to hip,
So he fell lifeless among the corpses.
His quiver and bow fell with a rattle.

I vyskoči Vlaslav protiv Čsmíru
i *vyrazi* Čsmír proti[v] Vlaslavu,
v *lútú sěč*; [a] *ránu, opět ránu*—
srazi Vlaslav[a] dolóv.
Vlaslav strašno po zemi sě koti,
i v bok i v zad, vstáti nemožéše;
Morena jej sypáše v noc črnu.
Kypieše krev ze silna Vlaslava,
po zeleně trávě v *syrú zem'u* teče.

Now Vlaslav sprang out against Čestmír,
And Čestmír *charged* straight at Vlaslav
In *fierce battle*. A *blow, and a second*
Knocks Vlaslav down.
Vlaslav writhes terribly on the ground,
On his side and his back, but cannot get up.
Morena cast him into a black night.
Blood frothed from strong Vlaslav
Over the green grass into the *bleak earth* it flows.

Srpoš Spytibora zývá.
Vsedasta oba na koně,
vzesta dřevce ostrú hrotú.
I hna Srpoš v Spytibora,
vysadi jej z tvrda sědla.
Sám sě s koně ruče vrže.
Oba dobysta tu m[e]čí,
ráz po ráze v črná ščíty,
jiskry vzprchú z črnú ščítú.

Srpoš called out Spytibor.
Both then mounted on their horses,
Took their lances with sharp points,
And Srpoš charged at Spytibor,
Unseated him from his firm saddle.
He himself dismounted quickly.
Both now reached down for their swords,
Blow for blow on the black shields,
So sparks flew from the black shields.

Spytibor Srpoše seče,
Srpoš v *chladnu zem'u* pade;

Lubor Bolemíra zývá.
Vsedasta oba na koně,

vzesta dřevce ostrú hrotú,

ruče v ohradu sě hnasta
protiv sobě zaměřista,
srazista sě oščepoma.
Bolemír sě s koně koti,
ščít mu daleko zaletě,
otnesú jej chlapi z dráhy.

Aj prudkost *vyrazi* Ludĕkem
z četných vrahóv protiv Záboju.
I vyrazi Záboj. Hořúciema očima v Luděk
zlobivo mieři. Dub protiv dubu

zřieti ze vsěho lesa:
Záboj hna protiv Luděku
nade vsě voje.
Luděk uderi silným mečem,
přetě třie kóže v ščítě.

I uderi Záboj mlatem,
otskoči hbitý Luděk,
v dřevo vrazi mlat
i skoti sě dřevo na voj
i třiedeset jich otide k otcém.
I zlúti sě Luděk:
"Aj, ty zhovadilý,
ty veliká potvoro hadóv,
mečem sě potýkaj se mnú!"
I máše Záboj mečem,
kus ščíta vrahu otrazi.

Spytibor struck Srpoš a blow,
And Srpoš fell to *the cold earth.*

Lubor called out Bolemír.
Both then mounted on their horses,
Took their lances with sharp points,
Quickly charged onto the field
Taking aim at one another.
They met sharply with their spears.
Bolemír tumbled from his horse
And his shield flew far away,
The bondmen took him from the lists.

Lo! Luděk *charged* Záboj fiercely
From among the numerous foe.
Záboj also *charged.* He angrily measured
Luděk with hot eyes. Just as oak to oak
One can see across a forest,
So Záboj charged Luděk
Across all the companies.
Luděk struck with a strong sword,
Cut through three skins on the shield.

And Záboj struck with the hammer.
Nimble Luděk jumped aside
And the hammer struck a tree;
The tree fell on the army
And thirty went to their fathers.
Luděk became enraged:
"Ho! You swine!
You great slithering beast,
Engage me with the sword!"
And Záboj swung his sword,
Struck off a piece of his enemy's shield.

I tasi Luděk [meč], meč sě smeče po koženě ščítě.	And Luděk slashed, The sword glanced off the leather shield.
I zapolesta sě oba *k ranám*, *ranami* vsě po sobě stesasta, i vsě kolem *zbrocesta krv'ú*, i *krv'ú zbrocechu* je mužie kolkol jejú vezdě v *přelútéj sěči*.	Both grew hot for *blows*, Striking *wounds* all over each other, *Spraying blood* all around, And men *sprayed them with blood* All around them in that *cruel slaughter*.

A number of verbal repetitions mark these passages. Blows/wounds (*rána* in Czech has both meanings) and blood, along with verbs for charging or attacking, frequently appear, though not in a quasi-formulaic manner. Closer to quasi-formulas are the "bleak/cold earth" phrases in the second and third passages, which as I noted earlier, derive from the Russian formula for mother damp earth, along with repetition through synonymy of phrases meaning "fierce battle" (*velelúta pótka, lútá sěč, přelútá sěč*). The only new quasi-formula here is the repetition of the line from "Jaroslav," "Srazista [sě] oba oščepoma" (They clashed together with their spears) in "Ludiše" without the word "oba" (both) to adjust to the eight-syllable line. This phrase is particularly apt as a formula for single combat in the manuscripts, as it also exhibits a grammatical feature that runs through all of these scenes: the use of the dual number. Past-tense (aorist) verb endings in *-ista*, *-ysta*, *-asta*, and *-esta* and nouns in *-oma*, *-ama*, and *-ima* (dative and instrumental cases) or in *-ú* (genitive and locative cases) mark actions undertaken by both combatants and objects in pairs that give these scenes a unique verbal texture in Old Czech. The dual number is a strong verbal formulaic marker for single combat in the manuscripts.

We have now explored a few themes from "Oldřich and Boleslav," examining parallels in other epics from the Czech manuscripts and possible sources for several of them. We have also investigated the complex and prevalent *battle* theme and its motifs in the manuscripts. In traditional oral epic poetry, theme is a highly flexible multiform, and, in many cases, the themes in the manuscripts vary in their structure and verbal expression in ways similar to such poetry. There is nothing really in the themes that we have examined that would rule them out as traditional.

Songs

The progression of themes in "Oldřich," which also uses traditional formulas to transition between themes, results in a satisfyingly complete story, in spite of the clear signs in the manuscript, with its fragmentary pages of text preceding this one, that the original song was perhaps four times as long. Here we move from the level of themes to that of *song or story pattern*, the next level of formulaic ordering in traditional epic. As Foley writes, "By marshaling thematic content, story-pattern gives both life and direction to the song; within a context of multiple possibilities, it provides parameters and determines the overall shape of the text. This kind of variation characterizes the largest and most abstract of traditional multiforms, making possible formularity at the level of narrative sequence."[152] For the Return Song pattern Foley examines in detail, the story pattern has five elements: absence, devastation, return, retribution, and wedding, each of which is composed of several varying themes.[153] The Return Song was a favorite of Parry and Lord because it linked the South Slavic songs to Homeric epic, the *Odyssey* in particular. Other common patterns in their collections and the South Slavic tradition include wedding songs, rescues, and captures of cities.[154] As always, though, these are malleable patterns, and Lord argues that, in some sense, all of these belong to the same larger song pattern, as all involve reconfigurations of the same complex of "disguise, journey, deceptive story, recognition, games or tests, [and] wedding."[155] The *Iliad* as well belongs to the larger song pattern of the *Odyssey*, with its withdrawal, devastation, return series focused on Achilleus.[156]

At first glance, "Oldřich and Boleslav" does not seem to belong to this larger pattern. The song fragment relates Oldřich's liberation of Prague from its occupation by the Polish duke Bolesław the Brave and the restoration of his brother Jaromír (abbreviated as Jarmír in the poem) to the throne. Dolanský has suggested two possible story-pattern antecedents in James Macpherson's *The Songs of Ossian* for the recurrent plot in the Czech manuscripts of the driving out of foreign occupiers: "Carric-Thura" and "Lathmon."[157] In the first, the palace of Cathulla, king of Inistore, is besieged by Frothal, king of Sora. In the second, the British prince Lathmon is advancing on the royal residence Selma. However, in both cases the danger is connected to the absence of Fingal, and it is the returning Fingal who turns aside the danger / devastation, engaging Frothal in single combat and capturing him in the first song, and forcing Lathmon's retreat in the second, enabling Ossian and Gaul to capture him.[158] Macpherson's adaptive translations from traditional materials still operate with recognizable traditional story patterns.

It is appropriate to ask again here what the fragmentary opening of "Oldřich" may have included, particularly as the analogous songs in the manuscripts *do* narrate the withdrawal of a community leader and describe the devastation that ensues. "Beneš, Son of Herman" opens with the absence of the prince and warriors, which has enabled the Saxons to invade, plundering and burning the villages. In "Záboj, Slavoj, and Luděk," Záboj makes vague reference in his first song to an absent or deceased "father" and the subsequent arrival of a foreign ruler who is forcing them to adapt new customs and destroying their sacred pagan sites. Notably, though, in neither case is it the *return* of the absent leaders that leads to liberation. Rather, Beneš and Záboj step in to drive out the foreign occupier. Perhaps the opening of "Oldřich," if it ever existed as a complete poem, included an account of the withdrawal of the prince (Jaromír or Oldřich perhaps) and the subsequent attack by Bolesław. The fragments of text that occupy the first two cut-away pages of the Queen's Court Manuscript are too incomplete to enable a reconstruction at the level of plot, though it is clear that the poem begins with Bolesław calling out ("Zvola B[oleslav]," l. 1) and includes the night and day maneuvering of armies, battles, and perhaps even single combats (". . . ne v krva / . . . sta oba před"—blood and the dual number, ll. 42–43) in Prague and at glorious Vyšehrad ("[k Vy]šehradu k sl[avnu]," l. 26); the actions of a wild youth ("Jarý junoše," l. 30); and Veleslav, a character who disappears before the fragments give way to whole text.[159] It is perhaps worth noting that the names Jaromír and Oldřich do not seem to occur in the fragments, while the latter is already appealed to by Výhoň Dub (whose name is in the fragments) in the fifteenth line of the whole text—which could suggest a return. For "Oldřich," then, the traditional pattern still remains implicitly in play.

For "Beneš" and "Záboj," the aspect of *return* is missing, and the traditional pattern is altered for a more "democratic" response to devastation, as the heroes lead the people against their occupiers. Another model, also suggested by Dolanský in connection to "Oldřich," should be considered here: the song "The Beginning of the Revolt against the *Dahijas*" published by Karadžić in his 1815 collection.[160] As that song relates, "The Serb chieftains, they did not wish to fight, / nor did the Turks, the Turkish exploiters. / But the *raja*, they were more than eager, / The poor *raja* could pay the tax no more, / no longer bear the Turkish oppression" (ll. 5–7).[161] In fact, what that song represents is the remarkable adaptation of the traditional epic idiom to the narration of recent history. The singer, Filip Višnjić, had himself witnessed the battles of the insurrection in 1809. He narrated those events to Karadžić less than a decade later as an accomplished professional singer, connecting recent history and the beginning of the liberation of the Serbs to the period of their subjugation through the traditional epic idiom and song forms that had kept memory of that history alive.[162]

Such a song must have been highly suggestive to the authors of the manuscripts of the adaptability of the traditional song medium to new contents, including the stories of the Czechs' own liberation they could find in their chronicles, or invent in prehistory. Tradition and innovation meet, for example, in the assembly of the *dahijas* to discuss their plan of action, a traditional theme, that takes place in a "large coffee house." The introduction of a new epithet-noun formula into the traditional diction here is seamless: "all seven *dahijas* / sad and worried, set out on a short walk, / . . . / and then went on to a large coffee house. / There they sat down in the large coffee house. / They sat down there one beside another" (ll. 75–80). For a singer like Višnjić, fluent in the traditional narration, the narration of recent events can be accomplished through deployment of the same narrative patterns, scenes, and language.[163] The authors of the manuscripts were similarly adapting a Slavic epic tradition, which they conceived of as native to themselves, to more distant historical events and, at least in part, another language. Even their deviation from traditional story patterns, then (like the uprising of the people rather than the return of the absent hero) can find its justification in the tradition they followed most closely.

The single song in the Green Mountain Manuscript, "Libuše's Judgment," stands out from the epics of the Queen's Court Manuscript in a number of ways, including the absence of any battle narration. Instead, it draws on the legends around the founding of the Czech Přemyslid ruling house and narrates a judgment by "princess" Libuše in a dispute between two men over the inheritance of their father's estate. Once again, Dolanský has suggested an apt possible model from Karadžić's 1815 publication, "The Division of the Jakšićes."[164] The general narrative situation is similar: there as well two brothers quarrel over the division of their father's estate. Interestingly, though, the principles at stake in the two poems are somewhat at odds: in the South Slavic poem, the brothers have divided the estate against the principle that feudal estates were not to be divided. They quarrel over just two items: a jet-black horse and a gray falcon—small items in relation to a large estate and yet symbolically important as the attributes of a warrior. The Czech poem, by contrast, offers the options, within the proper Slavic inheritance tradition, of division of the estate or joint rule (and the assembly decides for the latter), while the elder brother wants the Germanic principle of primogeniture to apply, giving him the entire estate.

In addition to the quarrel over inheritance, the Czech poem resembles the South Slavic one in its lyrical or mythological opening. The South Slavic song opens with the Moon addressing a question to the Day Star, asking where she has wasted the past three days. The Day Star replies that she spent them over Belgrade, where she saw a wonder and relates the quarrel of the brothers. Similarly, in the Czech song an unknown interlocutor addresses a question to the Vltava river, asking why she has troubled her waters. The Vltava replies that the troubling derives from the quarrel of the two brothers, which she introduces.

Even if the particular model for the address of a river with clouded water may have come from other Slavic lyric folk songs, the Jakšić epic authorized this type of lyrical opening.[165]

The resolution of the quarrel in each song, however, is quite different. In Karadžić's song (and it is his: he recorded it from his recollection of his father's singing), the resolution is both heroic and tragic.[166] The elder brother steals the horse and falcon and tells his wife to poison his brother. Instead, she goes and offers the younger brother wine from a gold chalice and in a suppliant manner asks for the horse and falcon as a gift, which he gives. Meanwhile, the elder brother in his hunting expedition has a pair of accidents leading to the breaking of the falcon's wing and the horse's forelegs, fatal injuries for each. He hurries home with regrets to check on his brother, and his wife informs him that rather than poisoning him, she has made peace between them.

The Czech song instead adapts the common theme of assembly to the purposes of a national court, with Libuše as judge. The speeches in the assembly here turn on the point of inheritance law, with Libuše offering two alternatives for her decision to the assembled nobles, both of which would conform to the traditional laws: either they manage the estate jointly or they should divide it between them. The nobles vote by secret ballot (definitely an anachronism), and Radovan announces the verdict: they should administer the estate jointly.[167] At this point, the elder brother, Chrudoš, rises and speaks in the assembly (ll. 91–98):

<table>
<tr><td>Vstanu Chrudoš od Otavy krivy,</td><td>Chrudoš from the crooked Otava arose,</td></tr>
<tr><td>žlč sě jemu rozli po útrobě,</td><td>Bile spreading in his bowels,</td></tr>
<tr><td>trasechu sě lútost'ú vsi údi,</td><td>All his limbs shaking with fury,</td></tr>
<tr><td>máchnu rukú, zarve jarým turem:</td><td>Waved and shouted like a wild bull:</td></tr>
<tr><td>"Gore ptencém, k nimže zmija vnori,</td><td>"Woe to the birds that a viper stalks;</td></tr>
<tr><td>gore mužém, imže žena vlade:</td><td>Woe to men who are ruled by a woman:</td></tr>
<tr><td>mužu vlásti mužem zapodobno,</td><td>It is proper for men to rule men,</td></tr>
<tr><td>prvencu dědinu dáti pravda."</td><td>And to give the estate to the firstborn."</td></tr>
</table>

This insulting speech with its defiance of the stated principles of law in some ways recalls the visits in several songs of the great South Slavic hero Marko Kraljević to the court of the sultan, his nominal sovereign, with his trampling of court decorum, insubordination, and thinly veiled threats of violence. It also recalls the common theme of bragging at a feast, when one of the assembled brags excessively of his wealth or exploits, insulting the others in the assembly, who then arrest the braggart or put the boast to the test.[168] In this case, though, Libuše offers to withdraw as judge even as Ratibor rises to restate the principles of their law and governance that support the justice of the judgment offered. The song ends without any consequences of the decision being realized, though those who know the old legends know that Libuše will now arrange to be taken to Přemysl the plowman, whom she will take as her husband and who will rule over the Czechs. The adaptation of the theme of boasting in the assembly or perhaps insubordination at court here proves to be an effective means of relating the founding legend of the Přemyslid dynasty in traditional epic form.

This adaptation of traditional epic themes to new narrative situations is, as we have already noted, also something that can be found within living epic traditions.[169] To give another example, Foley subjects another song by Višnjić, "The Death of Kraljević Marko," to an extended analysis, including Marko's final act of killing his companion horse Šarac and destroying his weapons as he prepares to die. Foley shows that this scene gains its power through the inversion of the typical themes of the hero saddling his warhorse and arming, as he takes his leave of his heroic role.[170] In fact, though, the songs of the Christian South Slavic tradition collected by Karadžić present a distinct aspect when compared with the songs sung by Muslim singers that were the focus of the collection activities of Parry and Lord and that served as the basis for articulating oral-formulaic theory. While sung in the same language and using the same formulaic diction, the Christian songs were shorter and, Foley suggests, more "textual" in their composition than the Muslim traditional songs. This textual aspect has to do with how they make use of traditional themes and story patterns: in Foley's reading, the songs are much less reliant on formulaic story patterns and instead articulate a number of unique plots in connection with particular heroes. Multiformity, then, is reflected in variants of a specific song, not of a common story pattern, even if they sometimes follow more general patterns. Themes in these songs have the traditional referentiality, so that each case of the hero arming evokes the act of arming across heroes and songs, but they also have a more textual referentiality similar to literary allusion, so the theme of arming evokes as well the cycle of songs related to the particular hero. The stories and their meanings derive additional depth from connection to a particular hero who has a unique set of associated myths and legends. The hero-centric aspect of the Christian epic tradition alters in some specific ways the nature of the formulaic aspect of those songs.[171]

The Czech imitations of this tradition also adapt and alter traditional themes and story patterns, but not exactly in the same way. If anything, the epics reflect a distinct *lack* of a set of useful legendary material about heroic warriors, so that, with the possible exception of Záboj, none of the heroes seems particularly central to the action or is fully developed as a character.[172] Here again, the authors found it difficult to imitate products of an oral tradition without actually having a pertinent oral tradition to draw on. In "Libuše's Judgment" we do see an adaptation of theme and story toward legend and myth, but outside of a heroic tradition. The eight-syllable epic "Ludiše and Lubor" offers another example of adaptation. The initial situation suggests unambiguously to readers of traditional epics the expected story pattern: a king with a beautiful daughter invites all the local nobles to a feast. Here we have the plot entanglement of a typical wedding song.[173] But instead of the hero having to complete a series of impossible tasks or defeat a great adversary (in "The Wedding of Tsar Dušan," the first of the heroic songs in Karadžić's 1815 publication, both are required), here various attendees are called out to fight in games that more resemble dangerous single combat. In the end, the victor Lubor receives not the hand of Ludiše, but a laurel of oak leaves from her hand. Such a wreath, in the context of a wedding song, would clearly function as a maiden wreath, given to the future husband, but the wreath here lacks that traditional symbolic resonance. Given that this plot does not have a clear antecedent in Czech chronicles, it is unclear why the authors chose to deviate from the traditional wedding song pattern in this instance.

In the case of "Jaroslav," it is precisely the combination of various materials from the chronicles that produces the deviation from traditional story patterns. "Jaroslav" is the longest epic in decasyllable form in the manuscripts and perhaps most resembles what we expect from a national epic, with its multiple battles and named heroes and with a decisive historical episode: here the Czechs can claim to have turned back the Tartar invasion, saving Christian Europe. This made it a favorite among Czech nationalists. With the late arrival of Jaroslav, who defeats the enemy captain in single combat to secure the final victory, it is also highly suggestive of the story pattern of the *Iliad* or of Macpherson's epic "Fingal." While "Fingal" and the *Iliad* share the traditional withdrawal-devastation-return pattern, though, Jaroslav's arrival at the end of his epic is entirely unanticipated within the text of the song. While all are likely familiar with Achilleus's quarrel with Agamemnon that leads to his withdrawal from the battle at Troy, it is probably worth detailing the plot of "Fingal": informed of the landing of the invading armies of Swaran in Ireland, Cuthullin convenes a council of chiefs in which he decides to engage Swaran immediately, rather than wait for Fingal, "king of those Caledonians who inhabited the north-west coast of Scotland, whose aid had been previously solicited."[174] Cuthullin is defeated and forced into a dangerous retreat that is only halted by Fingal's landing. Fingal's armies then engage Swaran, and eventually the two meet in single combat, with Swaran being defeated and taken captive.

Jaroslav's arrival with his army similarly turns the tide of a battle that had once again turned in the direction of retreat for the Christian side; however, he appears, as it were, out of nowhere. His name has not previously been mentioned, and even as the Christian armies gather while the Tartars move closer and closer to Olomouc, conquering Kiev, Novgorod, and Hungary as they come, there is no indication of any armies that are missing or awaited. This was an opportunity missed by the authors to make this epic resemble even more its traditional models.

Research into the historical sources for the plot of "Jaroslav" offers some explanation for this lack. The plot of "Jaroslav" in fact combines the material from three distinct groups of historical legends found in Czech chronicles. The first is a set of legends that explains the Tartar invasion as revenge for the murder of the Tartar princess; the second, a set of accounts of the siege of Christian forces on top of Hostýn; and the third, legends regarding a battle with the Tartars at Olomouc under the leadership of Jaroslav of Sternberg. While some later Czech chronicle accounts did connect the final two episodes, it is only in the Queen's Court Manuscript that all three are combined into a single narrative arc.[175] And the seams are showing, in the fact that Hostýn is too distant from Olomouc for the battles to connect as they do in the song, but also in the fact that Jaroslav, the eponymous hero of the epic, appears only in the third part, when the legendary material that was connected to his name enters the plot. The authors of "Jaroslav" were unable to distance themselves enough from the chronicle accounts to adapt them into a properly coherent traditional epic plot.[176]

Conclusion

This failure stands in contrast to what we have found in general to be the case: that the authors of the epics of the Czech manuscripts were able imitators of oral-formulaic or traditional epic, perhaps most successfully at the level of the formulaic phraseology, but quite effectively as well in their building of plot through progressions of elements that very much resemble formulaic themes and resulting in plots that often have a recognizable relationship to traditional story patterns. Judging qualitatively on the basis of what is there, we would have to conclude that the authors of the epics of the manuscripts were more than capable imitators of traditional epic. Our quantitative methods suggested that the manuscripts were not as pervasively formulaic as their models, but still much closer to those models than to contemporaneous literary poetry in degree of lexical repetitiveness.

In their shaping of the simulacrum of a traditional epic medium, though, while the story patterns and themes they use are close to their traditional models or adapt them in similar ways, the authors of the Czech manuscripts neglected some of the most common patterns. One of the most common themes across multiple heroic traditions is the arming of the hero, a theme that appears but once in the manuscripts.[177] Other very common themes, particularly from their South Slavic models, are absent or severely diminished: saddling the warhorse, sending emissaries, writing letters, shouting in prison, becoming blood brothers, to take but a few.[178] And significant song patterns—wedding songs, rescue songs, capture of cities—are not represented. Even the very effective imitation of the phraseology of the oral epics produces quasi-formulas that lack any of the layered traditional meanings, derived from a larger oral tradition, that exceed context of their use in particular instances. These absences, probably more than anything that is present in the manuscripts' language and narrations, mark the songs of the manuscripts as an imperfect reconstruction of the Czechs' own, presumed lost, national epic traditions.

In many ways, imperfection was unavoidable. In the face of the lack of their own formulaic epic tradition, the forgers struggled to simulate its existence. They wavered between the stricter form of the South Slavic epics and the looser forms of their Russian models and Ossianic prose poems, failing in the end to represent a coherent epic poetic form. And while they could imbue their language with traditional overtones through the borrowing and imitation of formulaic language from South Slavic, Russian, and Greek traditions, the absence of the resonant background of a multitude of stories and heroes in their own tradition meant their language lacked the more intense referentiality that elevates the aesthetic functioning of the formulaic language in living traditions. Given such barriers, the forgers did a remarkable job in imitating salient features of oral-formulaic discourse and story building, including many that the long-term, international, collaborative study of oral epics took years to identify and define. They were clearly skilled readers and imitators of their models. Even the mixing of elements from different traditions (Serbian, Russian, Greek) cannot be labeled a misstep, given the many features shared across oral-formulaic traditions. But, as we shall see in the next chapter, their deliberate bending of the Old Czech language in the direction of their Slavic models, their creation of a kind of inter-Slavic Old Czech epic idiom, would in the end prove decisive in uncovering their simulation.

Chapter 3

Translation, Pseudotranslation, and the Manuscripts

The Czech manuscripts, like much of the literature produced in the first few decades of the nineteenth century in the reviving Czech literary culture, were profoundly influenced by the practice of translation. At all levels, from the grammatical forms of the language and vocabulary to syntax and formal poetic features to genre models and preferences, foreign models and translation practices shape the new national mode of literary production.[1] One might say, in a play on words that seems to fly in the face of romantic notions of national originality, that the national is forged upon translation of the foreign. The dual meaning of the verb *forged* here, implying both "making" and "faking" (explored in chapter 1 along with the challenges it poses to our understanding of romantic literary values), also raises the question of the role of translation in literary mystifications and forgeries. In spite of the fact that pseudotranslation is a favorite device of literary mystifications and forgeries, there has not been an adequate exchange between the extensive recent scholarship on fakelit and the developing literature in translation studies on pseudotranslation. This chapter aims to open the door to that exchange. Although the Czech manuscripts are not a pseudotranslation in the usual sense (that is, a text that presents itself as a translation but is in fact an original text, not translated from another text), exploration of that phenomenon will facilitate our examination of how translation aids in their forgery and lead us into a deeper exploration of how the manuscripts are shaped, and misshaped, by translation.

Since Gideon Toury's 1995 book *Descriptive Translation Studies and Beyond*, with its short section on the phenomenon of pseudotranslation, a small literature on the topic has developed in which it has been recognized that pseudotranslation is a far from uncommon practice that, as a particular form of translational activity, offers a neglected site for analysis within translation studies, one that has the potential to bring theoretical and historical insight into the nature of translation more broadly.[2] In general, this literature is still in its formative stages, and pseudotranslation has not yet found its major theoretical exponents, with the bulk of the work focused on the pragmatic functions pseudotranslations perform in the target language literature and culture.[3] Moreover, as we will see, it mostly remains scandalized by the fakery involved and the illicit shadow that pseudotranslation seems to cast on translation in general. On the other side of the coin, pseudotranslation is also a particular and common form of the larger practice of literary mystification or forgery, a phenomenon that over the past two decades has seen an explosion of critical activity, including major theoretical expositions and analyses and serious reflection on terminology.[4] When the writers on pseudotranslation and those on forgery analyze the same texts, as they often do, the forgery specialists mostly win hands down for depth of analysis and theoretical sophistication. The literature on fakelit has challenged legal and moralistic approaches to literary forgery and demonstrated that mystification and forgery are forms that offer theoretical and historical insight into the nature of literary creativity in general (see chapter 1), helping to move beyond the stigma and scandal of forgery. But for all their discussion of terminology (*fake, hoax, mystification, forgery, supercherie, counterfeit*, and so on), they do not discuss pseudotranslation, and they have not raised the question of why forgeries resort to pseudotranslation as a form so often. These two literatures have not connected and not enriched each other in any way that I can see. My modest proposal, which I will essay here, is to bridge that divide and bring together the analysis of mystifications and pseudotranslations, to try to show that the analysis of pseudotranslation as a form of mystification can address central concerns of translation theory and that translation theory can contribute to our understanding of a common method of literary forgery. This means examining what mystification and translation have in common, how they are alike.

Pseudotranslation and Forgery

Pseudotranslations, to borrow the definition of Thomas O. Beebee, "are texts that exhibit manifest signs that they are translations, even though there is no 'original' text from which they come."[5] They are, in other words, original texts that pretend to be secondary texts, derivative texts, translations. In the history of literary mystifications and forgeries, pseudotranslations are fairly common. James Macpherson's *The Poems of Ossian*, the work that in many ways set off the whole series of romantic forgeries of national epic poetry, is an excellent example of a pseudotranslation, even if, as study of the case has made clear, he was not making up the poems from whole cloth but drawing from manuscripts and the oral tradition. To the public, though, Macpherson's translations were presented as literal translations from some "original." Both Hugh Blair in the introduction to the first publication in 1760 and Macpherson in his dissertation on "Fingal" insist on this literalness and point to the evidence of it in the English. "All that can be said about the translation," Macpherson writes, "is, that it is literal, and that the simplicity is studied. The arrangement of the words in the original is imitated, and the inversions of the style observed."[6] In fact, though, all that can be said about the translations is that they were anything but literal. Nonetheless, the English texts are thoroughly suffused with linguistic and literary features that suggest that they are derived from Gaelic originals. This deployment of "translatorese" is a technique of pseudotranslation. Macpherson himself highlighted syntactical inversions as reflecting the original, and Howard Gaskill observes that Macpherson found ways of introducing the verb-subject-object word order of Celtic into the English prose.[7] Elsewhere Gaskill cites a whole list of related features: that the prose poem form itself comes from Gaelic sources; episodic qualities and abrupt narration, requiring the reader (or listener) to fill in (characteristic of oral narration); abundant similes that point to the traditional stock; the use of short lines with parataxis; and the musical qualities of the prose, with internal rhyme, assonance, and alliteration.[8] All of these features, along with others that stood out strongly against the conventions of contemporary English poetry, suggested powerfully to readers the relationship of the English text to Gaelic originals that gave voice to a vanished heroic age.[9]

But were there any such originals? Walter Scott speculated that Macpherson composed his poems, at least in his mind, first in Gaelic, and Gaskill has substantiated this speculation, presenting the evidence that exists which suggests that Gaelic originals of some form were being composed by Macpherson, not just in his mind but on paper, at a fairly early stage in his publication of his translations, in particular for the epic "Fingal," and that, while others may have also had a hand in creating these, Macpherson was in some sense translating himself.[10] But why did Macpherson take such an indirect route? Having been asked for translations of Scottish Highlander poems, why neglect the manuscripts he had so painstakingly collected and the oral versions he had heard? Macpherson was initially quite reluctant to translate because he was concerned not to subject Highlander culture to further derision, and perhaps also because he himself found the existing tradition to be altered, debased, inadequate to how he imagined the third-century originals.[11] For the protection of Scottish pride, the straight translation of even the more substantial ballads was ruled out.[12] Macpherson instead opted for a form of cultural translation: "Macpherson's 'translations' involved acts of interpretation not only between Gaelic and English, but also between the oral culture of the depressed rural communities of the Scottish Highlands, and the prosperous urban centres of Lowland Britain, where the printed word was increasingly predominant."[13] At the same time, these translations aimed to restore the tradition to its original purity, to re-create a lost ancient heroic tradition.[14] The techniques of pseudotranslation in this case are deceptive in the narrow sense, insofar as there were no extant ancient originals from which the "literal translation" was derived—and few would have accepted the Gaelic originals being composed by Macpherson and others as the same thing, as shown by the reception of the one published in 1807. This is the level at which the entire Ossian controversy functions. But in another sense, pseudotranslation here is in the service of a higher truth, the representation of a more authentic, original, ancient heroic tradition (such as it was understood at the time), a creative restoration of inaccessible originals through a literal translation of their imagined, idealized forms.[15]

One could similarly examine other examples of mystifications and forgeries that present themselves as translations when there are no originals in the usual sense, from Prosper Mérimée's *La guzla* (1827), presented as a translation of South Slavic folk poems, to Pierre Louÿs's *Les chansons de Bilitis* (1894), supposedly a translation from the ancient Greek of the poems of a female contemporary of Sappho. And in each case we would find different configurations of the impetus and motivations for the production of the pseudotranslation, from the playful to the very serious, and different techniques for suggesting a relationship to the nonexistent original text.[16] But within all of these diverse techniques and goals, what is shared, what makes pseudotranslation such an attractive form for literary fakery?

Let us take a closer look at pseudotranslation. For Douglas Robinson, "The concept of pseudotranslation is interesting [for translation studies—this is for an entry in the *Routledge Encyclopedia of Translation Studies*] in large part because it calls into question some of our most cherished beliefs, especially the belief in the absolute difference between a translation and an original work."[17] Can something be a translation if there is no original? The *pseudo-* of the term tries to reassert the difference: it pretends to be a translation, but it is not, it is an original work. But the phenomenon of pseudotranslation calls precisely this asserted difference into question, suggesting that the original work is always already a translation, and a translation is always an original work. Robinson correspondingly widens the definition of pseudotranslations to include texts that are in fact translations but that are "frequently taken to be an original work." He suggests that "generally speaking . . . a pseudotranslation might be defined as a work whose status as 'original' or 'derivative' is, for whatever social or textual reason, problematic."[18] This broadening of the definition will allow us to soon consider the Czech manuscripts as pseudotranslations, or perhaps as pseudo-originals.

This vacillation in the boundary between original and translation, this foundational undecidability in categories, seems to me to be fundamental and part of the key to the attraction of pseudotranslation for the placement of false originals (disguised as translations). We know from the history of translation that translations are often taken for original works. Bible translations, like St. Jerome's Vulgate, and the authority given to their texts are an oft-cited example. What the phenomenon of pseudotranslation helps us to see, I would argue, is that such "mistakes" in taking translations for originals are not accidental to translation. Rather, they are inherent to a certain conception of and practice of translation, a natural consequence of the drive of translation to replace the original text, to supplant it with its "equivalent" in another language, to let the translation fully and transparently function in place of the original text. "Translations that read like originals"—that is the advertising slogan of a professional translator who is a frequent contributor to a Slavic-language Listserv that I subscribe to. It is posed as an ideal. Pseudotranslation exposes, by relying on, this supplanting intention of translation, trusting that we will not go back to see the original because the translation is sufficient representation of it. I would suggest that forgeries and mystifications have had such frequent recourse to the method of pseudotranslation in part because translation (at least a particular, institutionalized Western form of it) has legitimized the placement of false or substitute originals, the hiding of origins behind a text that invites you NOT to seek the impetus that gave it birth. The supplement (translation), which was supposed to serve the original, be added on to it to make up for the lack of the text in another language, instead supplants the original and serves in its stead.

This undecidability between original and translation and this structure of supplementarity, where the supplement has the ability to supplant, make it clear that the dominant discourse on translation has the typical features of the metaphysical logocentrism that is the object of Jacques Derrida's deconstructive interventions. Original/translation is one of those hierarchical dichotomies that metaphysical discourse has recourse to, but that closer scrutiny reveals to be impure. The translation can supplant the original because the difference between them is adulterated, at times imperceptible; by the same token, an original can pretend to be a translation (pseudotranslation). In deconstructing this binary, we recognize that what is original or primary is translation, in a sense that is not limited to interlingual translation (just as Derrida expands the notion of writing in deconstructing the speech/writing binary). Thus Derrida suggests, in a possibly relevant lecture on translation, that if he is to speak in an intelligible and transparent way, as a good guest, he would have to "speak a single language, namely that of the addressee, here of the host [*hôte*], a language especially designed for whoever must and can understand it, a language that is shared, like the very language of the other. . . . A language that is, in a word, translatable." The speech, his original contribution to the discourse on translation, is already shaped by translation, by the possibility and necessity of translatability. The words are like the word *relevant* that he is discussing, which "carries in its body an on-going process of translation."[19] The words come pretranslated. Moreover this undecidability, which leads us to the primacy of a kind of generalized translation, is the condition of possibility of writing and translation, as well as the condition of their impossibility: no original is entirely original without translation, and no translation is perfectly equivalent to its original. In other words (translating intralingually to other terms), as Derrida avows in that same lecture, "I don't believe anything can ever be untranslatable—or, moreover, translatable."[20]

The theoretical grounding of the conditions of possibility of pseudotranslation and its links to a particular Western conception of translation (which I have only sketched here) have not been adequately addressed either in the literature on forgeries or in studies of pseudotranslation (even though translation studies in general has thoroughly critiqued this conception of translation). Following Toury's lead, the many case studies that make up the bulk of the literature on pseudotranslation have tended to focus on the pragmatic functions pseudotranslations perform in the target language culture and literature. Pseudotranslations borrow the power translations have had to serve as a site for innovation. The history of translation offers a plethora of examples of the use of translations to introduce innovations and to justify deviations from reigning norms, whether it is the introduction of new genres and techniques (like Vasily Zhukovsky's introduction of the elegy, ballad, and Byronic tale genres to Russian poetry through influential translations) or controversial ideas (English Renaissance women translators offering alternative models of gender dynamics by translating fiction from the Continent).[21] Toury, whose work developed Itamar Evan-Zohar's polysystems theory for translation studies, suggested that pseudotranslations often pursued the same goals, and dozens of case studies have borne this out.[22] Polysystems theory conceives of literature as a system of systems with hierarchies of norms and values and attempts to account for the dynamics of literary developments. Translation would be one system within the polysystem of literature. The theory owes an important debt to Russian Formalist and Czech structuralist theories. Studies of pseudotranslations often examine how the marking of a text as a translation enables innovative interventions into the literary system. The stamp of foreign approval, or the excuse of foreign mores, lowers the barriers of reigning norms in the receiving culture to allow a space for innovative expressions. Insofar as literary forgeries also frequently aim to introduce innovative creative techniques and perspectives (an aspect the literature on forgeries has addressed), pseudotranslation here again offers a tested means for their propagation. The fact that the institution of translation significantly enables the innovative aspect of Macpherson's texts against the backdrop of contemporary poetic practices to be received and accepted is something forgery studies has not analyzed.

How else is translation like mystification or forgery? What the reigning concept of translation (which allows for the supplanting of the original) and the practices associated with it hide, what they *mystify*, is first translation *process* (all the interpretive choices, decisions, hesitations, and willful substitutions), second, translation *context* (the translator's intentions, power differences, publication norms), and third, the very *difference* that makes translation necessary (incommensurability of languages, cultures, chronological distance). As Beebee notes, dominant translation practices suppress what happens in translation's "black box," whatever stands between the original text and the translated text and determines their relationship. The translated text offers a fiction of equivalence, and we come to it ready to suspend disbelief and buy into that fiction.[23] In translating the Czech declaration "Mám tě rád," the translator writes "I love you" rather than "He says he loves you," performing a mimesis of the original text that mimics fully formed and comparable communication and removes the translator as intermediary, making her invisible (following Beebee's citation of Naoki Sakai's Japanese example).[24] The one thing not permitted to the translator is to write as oneself, to reveal the interpreter behind the curtain. Rather, as the early theorist Peter Daniel Huet advised, "a translator must therefore become like Proteus: he must be able to transform himself into all manner of wondrous things, he must be able to absorb and combine all styles within himself and be more changeable than a chameleon."[25] Are these not precisely the qualities also of the effective literary forger? Translator and forger both must ventriloquize the voices of others.

It would certainly be hard to imagine a thoroughgoing reform of translation practice that would begin to make visible the translator, translation process, and context in an extensive way, and that is not really the point of such criticisms. Imagine the opening of *Anna Karenina* mediated by a marginally hostile translator: "The narrator, with his positivistic inclination toward grand generalizations, declares all happy families to be alike, while he will presumably, in the course of the next thousand pages, go on to demonstrate in minute pseudoscientific psychological analysis the second half of his postulate, that every unhappy family is unhappy in its own way." Horror! Who wants to go there? But let us consider again the footnote, that much maligned textual addition, violator of the economic law of translation, that offers a small opening, a peek into the black box, and disturbs the veil of false originality and the intention of the translation to fully stand in for the original.[26] Its opponents are the defenders of an orthodoxy that makes pseudotranslation both possible and problematic.

Just how problematic pseudotranslation is in this paradigm can be illustrated by Emily Apter's treatment of it in an essay titled "Translation with No Original: Scandals of Textual Reproduction." Her framing questions ask whether "a literary technology of reproduction that has sublated its origin [that is, pseudotranslation] [can] still be considered a translation? Or should it be considered the premier illustration of translational ontology, insofar as it reveals the extent to which *all translations* are unreliable transmitters of the original, a regime, that is, of extreme untruth?"[27] In concluding her analysis of two examples, she declares that

> the revelation of translational false coin leaves the reader aware of the dimension of epistemological scam or faked-up alterity inherent in *all translation*. . . . The implied ethics of translation presupposes a contract holding between reader and translator whereby the former assumes the good faith effort of the latter to deliver an authentic copy of the original. In breaching that contract, Louÿs and Rexroth exposed the ways in which all translators are to some extent counterfeit artists, experts at forgeries of voice and style.[28]

In Apter's reading, the existence of pseudotranslations reveals that ALL translation is an epistemological scam marred by ethical complicity in an ontological regime of untruth! Translators are nothing but forgers. But Apter is not out to dismiss translation or marginalize it and relegate it to the realm of the dark arts. This most scandalous reading of pseudotranslation is strategic for Apter, whose real agenda is, much like mine, aimed at a change in how we conceive of translation, a shift in paradigms that offers a different configuration for translation ethics as well. This is a moment where translation theory can also learn from the theoretical studies and rehabilitation work conducted in the study of forgeries.

Both Apter and Beebee offer alternative ways of viewing translation, through Walter Benjamin's notion of the afterlife of a text. Apter offers a notion of translation as textual cloning, to draw attention to "the conditions of textual reproducibility," while Beebee emphasizes rewriting and the extension performed on a text by translation.[29] Insofar as these perspectives eliminate or at least marginalize any discussion of "equivalence" between original and translation (I myself would declare it taboo) and emphasize the change inherent to translation, they offer little ground to a scandalous reading of pseudotranslation and its implications for translation as a whole (although Apter's metaphor of cloning seems to keep some form of equivalency in the picture). Beebee offers a model reading of a set of pseudotranslations that were received as scandalous—the fictions of B. Wongar, presumably an Australian Aboriginal who turned out in fact to be a Serbian refugee who had lived among the Aboriginals. Rather than inquiring about Sreten Bozić's ethnicity and the ethics of his mimicry, Beebee examines the quality of his fictional representation, and in particular the representation of Aboriginal language and cultural difference by means of pseudotranslation.[30] Treating pseudotranslation and translation as forms of creative writing results in different questions being posed and different conclusions being drawn.

Theoretical treatments of mystification and the rehabilitation of literary forgers have relied on a similar strategy, legitimizing forgery as a form of creative writing. As noted in chapter 1, Nick Groom suggests that literature legitimizes its inventions by using forgery to mark a limit to invention beyond which lies illegitimate invention. Thus forgery helps to constitute literature as a legitimate practice by serving as its illegitimate other. K. K. Ruthven performs the Derridean deconstruction of this binary opposition (genuine literature / forgery), arguing that spuriousness is the common ground of literature and forgery and literature cannot free itself from the spurious.[31] Literature and literary forgery, then, have a common ground and are as undecidable as original and translation. Groom discusses forgers as practitioners of poesis in its most basic sense.[32] In their readings, forgery as a making is returned to the realm of creative writing, where it waits for translation to fully rejoin it.

Embracing the creative side of translation may mean submitting ourselves to the risk of accusations of pseudotranslation, mystification, forgery, but if we recognize those as creative writing as well, it deprives such accusations of any bite. What if we said, "Yes, translation is a form of mystification, of forgery, that is, of creative writing"? We could explore again the Protean side of the translator, indicated by Huet, the mimicry and ventriloquism involved in, to use the neoclassicist topos, making the writer speak in a new language to a new audience. We might harness the potent mystifying power of translation, its poetic license to supplant the original text. How might we, for carefully chosen purposes, use the creative mimesis of translation to allow a translation to say more in a cross-cultural dialogue than the original text could say in its culture? Or to say something new in a new cultural context? This is a power that translators have often used, translating "controversial, dangerous, or somehow 'unsuitable' texts as a form of oblique speech" to address their own cultural context.[33] Our creativity and our careful, contextual ethical decision making are our only limits.

I would argue, if we want to really understand translation, literature, creative writing, that pseudotranslation and mystification offer an opportunity to change perspective and see certain aspects far better. Translation studies certainly should further explore the phenomenon of pseudotranslation and engage the rich literature on mystification and forgery in the process, and students of forgery should pay more attention to what translation studies can elucidate about the enabling conditions and functions of pseudotranslation as a device.

The Czech Manuscripts

Translation plays a crucial role in making the texts of the Czech manuscripts accessible to the Czech reading public, such as it was at the end of the second decade of the nineteenth century. Hanka was able to publish an edition of the Queen's Court Manuscript just over a year after he "discovered" it, in late 1818 (though the publication was dated 1819). The Old Czech text with its old orthography and obsolete grammatical forms would have been unreadable to all but a handful of the most educated; in fact, few Czechs at the time were literate even in the newly reconstituted modern Czech literary language. Hanka included his translation into modern Czech and that of his friend Svoboda into modern German, the language in which the majority were educated. These translations were the means by which most readers became familiar with the Czech manuscripts.

A page from the 1819 edition of the Queen's Court Manuscript is reproduced in figure 3.1. The poem "The Rose" begins at the top of the page, with the Old Czech text on the left and the modern Czech on the right. The textual apparatus, paratextual materials (including Hanka's introduction), and publishing conventions all tell us, implicitly and explicitly, that the original is on the left and the translation is on the right. (The German translation fol-

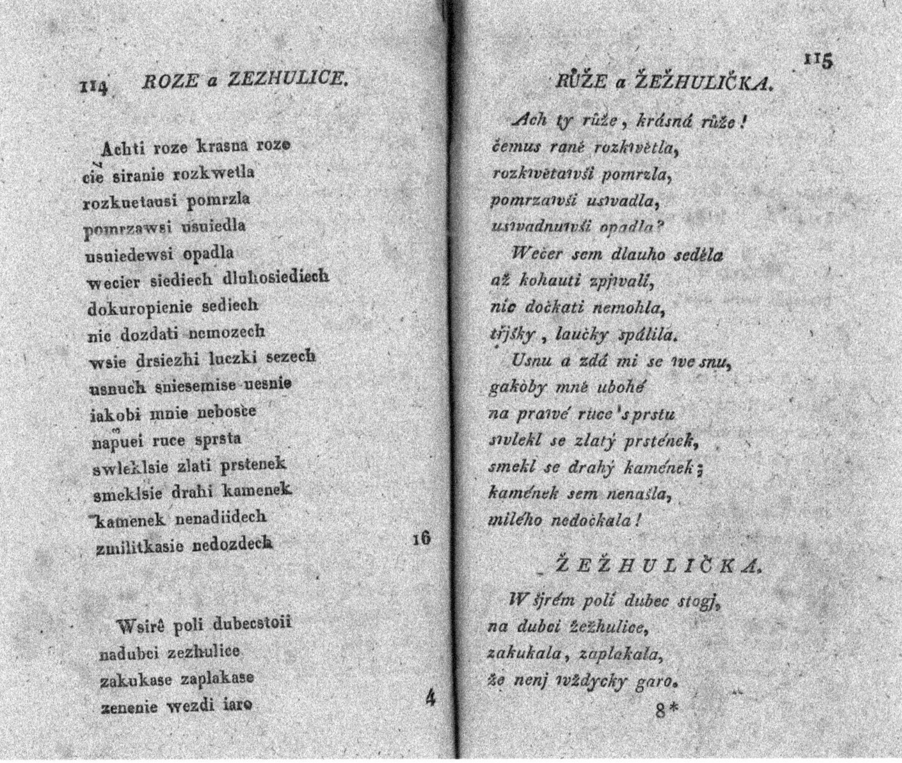

114 *ROZE a ZEZHULICE.*

Achti roze krasna roze
cie siranie rozkwetla
rozkuetausi pomrzla
pomrzawsi usuiedla
usuiedewsi opadla
wecier siediech dluhosiediech
dokuropienie sediech
nic dozdati nemozech
wsie drsiezhi luczki sezech
usnuch sniesemise uesnie
iakobi mnie neboсe
napuei ruce sprsta
swleklsie zlati prstenek
smeklsie drahi kamenek
kamenek nenadiidech
zmilitkasie nedozdech 16

Wsirê poli dubecstoii
nadubci zezhulice
zakukase zaplakase
zenenie wezdi iaro 4

115

RŮŽE a ŽEŽHULIČKA.

Ach ty růže, krásná růže!
čemus rané rozkwětla,
rozkwětawši pomrzla,
pomrzawši uswadla,
uswadnuwši opadla?
Wečer sem dlauho seděla
až kohauti zpjwali,
nic dočkati nemohla,
třjšky, laučky spálila.
Usnu a zdá mi se we snu,
gakòby mně ubohé
na prawé ruce 's prstu
swlekl se zlatý prstének,
smekl se drahý kamének;
kamének sem nenašla,
milého nedočkala!

ŽEŽHULIČKA.

W šjrém polí dubec stogj,
na dubci žežhulice,
zakukala, zaplakala,
že nenj wždycky garo.

8*

FIGURE 3.1. Two pages from the first edition of the Queen's Court Manuscript containing the poem "The Rose."

lowed in the back of the volume.) But is that really the case here? While critics have made conflicting cases for who authored particular poems in the manuscripts, with Hanka usually ascribed the lyric poems and the epics ascribed variously to Linda, Hanka, or Svoboda, the general consensus is that Hanka is responsible for the final Old Czech form of all of the poems. If that is the case, then the Old Czech texts may themselves be the product of translation, whether in whole or in part, from other, presumably modern Czech, texts. Where, then, is the translation on this page from the first edition, and where is the original? It could be the reverse of what we are told. The original could be the modern Czech text on the right (with its frequent antiquated terms and forms) and the Old Czech text its translation. Or, perhaps, the original text, in whatever linguistic form it took, is not here at all and what we have is a direct translation of it into Old Czech, on the left, and an indirect (second-degree, pivot, or relay) translation of that first translation, a back translation into modern Czech, on the right. In either case, what we think we are seeing is not at all what we are actually seeing. The original is absent or disguised. On the left, we have a pseudo-original (a product of translation) and, on the right, a pseudotranslation (that may be the closest text we have to the original form of composition).

Such a form of publication is itself a kind of mystification, one that relies on our conventions for presenting originals and translations to conceal the more complicated origins of the texts on the page. In a very real sense, then, this first edition of the manuscript was the first of the "cover" mystifications (most of which appeared in the late 1820s) serving to legitimize the Old Czech of the manuscript (see the discussion of these later in this chapter). Within our Western conceptualization of translation, the translation is secondary, derived from an original text that it serves and imperfectly renders. In comparing these two texts on the page, as readers we direct our questions to the text on the right: Is "až kohouti spívali" (until the cocks crowed) a good rendering of "dokuropenie sediech" (sat until cock song)? Or, does the added punctuation accurately render the implied intonation and syntactical construction of the original? And so on. If we ask anything about the text on the left, it is: What does the text mean? Or, how to read that odd combination of letters, questions that are answered by the text on the right. We do not direct questions or skepticism to the text on the left—as an original text, within the paradigm of translation, it is source, not product; model, not imitation; authoritative, not open to revision. The fact that readers came to know the manuscript through a published bilingual translated edition, which made it accessible and readable in spite of its archaic orthography, grammar, and vocabulary, directed scrutiny away from the Old Czech text of the manuscript. The publication form uses the institutions of translation to establish the authority of the pseudo-original text. Certainly the manuscripts belong in a discussion of the phenomenon of pseudotranslation.

But are we correct in suggesting that the Old Czech text of the manuscripts, and not just the Queen's Court but also the Green Mountain Manuscript, is a product of translation? Karel Krejčí challenged the prevailing assumption that the Old Czech text was a product of translation, arguing that the esthetic qualities of the text rely heavily on the qualities of the Old Czech language: on sound repetitions that derive from the grammar and morphological forms of Old Czech (for example, heavy repetition of the "*u*" sound) and would not have appeared in a modern Czech precursor, on the tastefully done compound adjectives, on the aesthetic qualities of the personal and place names in old forms in the text, and on the short adjective epithets attached to the names of characters. He concluded, "From the fact that the Old Czech forms constitute an inseparable layer of the aesthetic object, it follows that the poems were not translated from new Czech into Old Czech but were written directly in a language that the author created for his purposes; in their details, of course, the language forms could have been corrected in order to raise the probability of an ancient origin."[34] There is much in this formulation that is useful and that we shall return to, once we have assembled a variety of evidence that the Old Czech text is, nonetheless, a product of translation in a number of ways. To begin our counterargument, it is worth examining an underlying assumption that seems to be at work here: that translation cannot involve the creation of new aesthetic qualities that were not in the original. Krejčí denies that the Old Czech text could have been a product of translation from a modern Czech text because it has features that the modern Czech source text could not have had. Such a denial presumes that translation cannot add anything new, requires that it remain subordinate to the original by transmitting only those qualities present in the original. This forbids translation the status of a creative act. Such a perspective is part and parcel of the reigning conception of translation, which makes translations subordinate and inferior to their originals, and it is an assumption that pseudotranslations take advantage of to hide their creative innovations. After all, why should Hanka not have sought, in translating into Old Czech from draft modern Czech versions of the lyric and epic poems that would make up the manuscripts, to continue the creative process, aimed ultimately at re-creating the imagined idealized forms of the lost tradition of original Czech poetry? Hanka was explicit about what he saw as the greater aesthetic qualities offered by Old Czech in his introduction to the first edition, where he laments the losses brought by translation (back?) into modern Czech:

> My modernized rendering does not and cannot achieve the profundity and beauty of the original reading, for among other things I have had to change particularly the dual number and antiquated simple past tenses (narrative or historical preterit, and also present passive participles . . .), which give the language an unequaled precision, vigor, and liveliness, into regular plurals, and partly into the compound past tense, partly into the future tense.[35]

The fact, then, that some of the finer aesthetic qualities of the Old Czech text could only exist in Old Czech, does not rule out the possibility that those qualities were sought and added in the creative process of translation into that language.

In this second period of the Czech Revival (1806–30), in fact, translation was an essential creative method.[36] As Vladimír Macura has shown, translation was a fundamental principle of culture creation for the Czechs in this period, which he terms its *překladovost*, or "translationality." Translation was a site of active cultural competition and a tool for the expansion and cultivation of the reviving Czech language. Translations were frequently either presented as or taken for original works.[37] Hidden translation underlies a number of important works of the period, including Josef Jungmann's Czech language and literature textbook *Slovesnost* (Literature, 1820), which compiled material from Karl Heinrich Ludwig Pölitz, Johann August Eberhard, Georg von Reinbeck, and Christian August Clodius, or his influential article on classicality in Czech literature ("O klasičnosti literatury vůbec a zvláště české," 1827), half of which is taken from the introduction to Pölitz's *Das Gesammtgebiet der deutschen Sprache* (1825).[38] The so-called first work of Czech philosophy, Antonín Marek's *Logika nebo Umnice* (1820), is more a first successful introduction of philosophical terminology into modern Czech than a new work of philosophy, as it translates (shortening and at times adapting) Johann Gottfried Christian Kiesewetter's *Grundriss einer allgemeiner Logik nach Kantischen Grundsätzen* (1806).[39] The names of the translated authors and the source works are not given, nor are the texts marked as translations (although Jungmann at least signals in his article that he will be "making use . . . of what one of the better German writers said about [classicality]").[40] We will soon see that similar practices of hidden translation and a fundamental formation on the model of translation also mark the manuscripts, which rank high among the most influential literary works of the period.

That translation was a fundamental shaping force in the poems of the manuscripts, even in places where there is no question of a hidden translation behind the text, was shown in 1935 by Roman Jakobson for the epic poems in the ten-syllable deseterac form. As discussed in chapter 2, this verse form in the manuscripts does not resemble native Czech ten-syllable verse in the shape of its meter but takes a form that strongly suggests an orientation toward imitation of the South Slavic epic line. Native Czech ten-syllable verse, and the South Slavic deseterac in its native environment along with it, shows a higher incidence of metrical stress on the ninth syllable than on the seventh, marking the end of the line clearly for metrical form (Foley's "right justification"). But the different nature of word stress between Czech (with stress fixed on the first syllable) and BCS changes this relationship when a composition in Czech follows the word patterns of the South Slavic epics. In Hanka's translation of Karadžić's epic about Tsar Lazar, by Jakobson's calculation a word boundary falls before the seventh syllable in 60 percent of the lines, but before the ninth syllable in only 33 percent of the lines. This is in a translation proper. In the manuscripts, in epic poems that are not in themselves translations, nonetheless the same inverted relationship, in a less extreme form, presides: for "Jaroslav," word boundaries fall before the seventh and ninth syllables 75 percent and 69 percent of the time, respectively; for "Oldřich," 79 percent and 76 percent; for "Libuše," 67 percent and 60 percent. Jakobson argues that this is a sign that the authors of the epic poems in the manuscripts were oriented toward the imitation of the South Slavic form.[41] An implicit translation shapes the fundamental form of these original verses.

For the lyric poems of the manuscripts, as was shown long ago, a more direct form of translation is often involved. The most blatant example of hidden translation is the poem "The Rose," which is almost entirely composed of lines translated from two Russian songs from Mikhail Chulkov's first volume of *Sobranie raznykh pesen* (1770).[42] There need not have been an intermediary first translation into modern Czech in this case if Hanka was the translator—the most likely scenario as we shall see.

Ach, ty róže, krásná róže,
čemu si raně rozkvetla,
rozkvetavši pomrzla,
pomrzavši usvědla,
usvědevši opadla?
Večer sěděch, dlúho sěděch,
do kuropěnie sěděch;
nic doždati nemožech,
vsě dřezhy, lúčky sežech.
Usnuch, snieše mi sě ve sně,
jako by mně nebošce
na pravéj ruce s prsta
svlekl sě zlatý prstének,
smekl sě drahý kamének.
Kamének nenadjidech,
zmilitka sě nedoždech.

Chulkov, no. 145
Ax ty sad li ty moj sadočik,
Sad ty zelenoe vinogrod'e
K čemu ty rano razcvetaeš',
Razcvetavši sad zasyxaeš',
Zemlju list'em ustilaeš'?
. . .
Ja večer, večer, moloden'ka
Dolgo večera prosidela,
Ja do samova do razsvetu,
Vsju lučinušku pripalila,
. . .
Vse tebja, moj drug, dožidalas'.
No. 143
Mne malo spalos', mnogo videlos'.
Ne xoroš ta mne son prividelsja,
Už kaby u menja u mladešinki,
Na pravoj ruke na mizinčike,
Raspajalsja moj zolot persten',
Vykatalsja dorogoj kamen'.[43]

There is minimal adaptation here, changing the garden to a rose, extending the poetic picture of its demise, and the final two lines drawing the tragic conclusion (though this too is partly borrowed from no. 145). Otherwise, we have a largely successful (and quite literal at times) verse translation into Old Czech from the Russian originals. Other lyric songs from the Queen's Court

Manuscript, along with the opening of the separate "Song to Vyšehrad," also adapt and translate parts of songs, generally more loosely, from this source—and in fact, largely from the same section of this source (likely source songs include numbers 136, 142, 143, 145, 148, 172, and 187).[44]

Jan Máchal was first to link this form of creative adaptation and the sources used for it to Hanka. Chulkov's songbook is in the collection of the National Museum Library (where Hanka worked as librarian) along with an 1810 songbook published in Moscow, the *Noveishii i polnyi obshchenarodnyi pesennik*, both with markings linking them to Hanka, and both served as sources not only for songs in the forged manuscripts but also, tellingly, for many of the "original" songs Hanka composed and published after 1816.[45] His own songs often begin with a fairly close translation from a source song in these songbooks and continue with a free improvisation; others are entirely paraphrases or adaptations.[46] The coincidence of methods of composition and sources remains one of the strongest pieces of evidence that Hanka is the author of the lyric songs of the manuscripts.

In addition to this practice of hidden translation (which was not at all outside the norms of his context), Hanka also published translations of Serbian and Russian folk songs marked as such, as noted in chapter 2. An examination of his *Prostonárodní srbská muza, do Čech převedená* (Serbian folk muse, led over into Bohemia; 1817) will help to establish Hanka's methods as a translator, which will be useful to a further examination of the manuscripts. Jiří Levý, the outstanding theorist and historian of Czech translation, called Hanka "one of the first translators . . . of the Czech school [of literal translation]."[47] This new method of literalism puts him in harmony with the latest German romantic practices and recommendations. Friedrich Schleiermacher argued in 1813 that an "indispensable requirement" of true translation was "a disposition of the language that not only departs from the quotidian but lets one perceive that it was not left to develop freely but rather was bent to a foreign likeness."[48] That is, the source language should be allowed to carefully shape the target language. He further suggests that literal translation is the obvious way to achieve this, but cautions repeatedly that this is a dangerous method, with a fine line between successful transfusion of a foreign character into the target language and abuse of the target language. Let us examine Hanka's method, which may cross that line into abuse at times.[49]

The most obvious means of foreignizing is the adoption of lexical items from the source language (which included two Russian poems in this volume alongside the Serbian ones) into the target language. Specific foreign terms are allowed to go untranslated, only minimally adapted to Czech grammar through declension. Hanka does this very frequently with nouns and rarely

Table 3.1 Hanka's unmarked borrowings of terms

HANKA'S TEXT IN TRANSLATIONS	MÁCHAL'S NOTES [WITH MY GLOSSES][1]
Car, Caryce	[Car, Carica, (that is, Tsar, Tsaritsa) unglossed by Hanka or Máchal]
Vůkol se mile potůčky blyštěli v *struhách*	Vokrug mily ručejočki blistali v strugach [*sic*, should be "v strujach"] ["The sweet brooks around glistened in streams." Hanka adapts the Russian final term here instead of translating to "v proudech." But the Czech term *strouha* means something like "ditch" or "gutter," which destroys the image.]
Skryl se *svět* s oči	Skrylsja svět (tj. světlo) iz glaz [Hanka's translation says, "The *world* (svět) disappeared from his eyes," rather than the *light* (světlo).]
Není minuty ni *času*	Nět minuty, ni časa (tj. hodiny) ["There's not a minute or an hour," except *čas* means "time," not "hour," in Czech.]

[1] Václav Hanka, *Hankovy písně a Prostonárodní srbská muza, do Čech převedená*, ed. Jan Máchal, Novočeská knihovna, č. 3 (Prague: Nákl. České akademie císaře Františka Josefa pro vědy, slovesnost a uměni, 1918), 235, 252 (258), 253 (258), 254 (258). These are Máchal's transliterations from the Russian.

with adjectives, marking these lexical borrowings with glosses in footnotes. Examples, with their glosses, include the following: *v . . . monastyru* (*klášteře*, monastery), *čiši* (*koflík*, cup), *do luha* (*luh—háj*, grove), *kštice* (*dlouhé vlasy*, long hair), *brvy* (*obočí*, brows), *svilu* (*hedvábí*, silk), *prozračné* (*prohledací*, transparent).[50] These largely concern terms and names that add local color to the translation. Sometimes, but rarely, Hanka does not footnote terms he leaves untranslated. Máchal in his edition glosses some of these himself in notes; others, he marks as mistranslations (see table 3.1).

In the last three examples, there is incompatibility between the meaning of the borrowed Russian word and an existing Czech word. These look like mistranslations, but we might also consider them as examples of what Macura termed *phonological translation*, a technique common in the Czech Revival for translation from Slavic sources, but also used for sources that promised a transfer of cultural capital through the close language relationship that such a method implied. It involves minimally adapting the foreign word to Czech grammar, morphology, and orthography. Macura notes that this technique could be "performed entirely consistently" word by word, "or just partially, in a few places in the text and thus in a manner merely suggestive (and consequently of course significant)."[51] Hanka's use of this technique is limited, but very significant.

When we move from nouns and adjectives to verbs, the same techniques of borrowing and phonological translation are much less well tolerated by critics of the translation. Literalism here causes more problems of understanding, a more radical decentering of the target language. Hanka's literalism here, his refusal to translate certain words, is more challenging. He is not afraid even

Table 3.2 Hanka's borrowing of foreign verbs and verbal forms

HANKA'S TRANSLATIONS	MÁCHAL'S NOTES WHERE FOUND[2]
Těžké jsou mně rány osvojili	doslova podle srb.: těžke su me rane osvojili (tj. přemohly)
a pro jeho zdraví družečka prosila i pro své neštěstí jemu rozkázala	pro jevo zdorov'je družka razprosila, pro svoje neščastje jemu razkazala (tj. po jeho zdraví se ptala a o svém neštěstí mu vyprávěla)
Celovalis', milovalis' ptáci hledíc libovalis'	
Vzdálí Echo rozléhalos', a srdéčko radovalos'	

[2] Hanka, 255, 258, 254.

to let the grammar of the source alter the target language (see table 3.2 for examples).

In the first example, marked as "literal" by Máchal, Hanka not only translates the verb phonologically (thus rendering in Czech "my heavy wounds overcame me" as something like "my heavy wounds adopted me / adapted to me"), he also keeps the helping verb, which is unnecessary in the modern Czech past tense. By keeping the Russian verbs and prepositions in the second example, Hanka turns "she asked about his health and told him of her misfortune" into something like "she asked him for his health and ordered him for her misfortune." In the final two examples from Russian, Hanka translates the verb phonologically (for example, *ljubovat'sja* > *libovat se*) or *gives the impression of* phonological translation (*rozléhalos'* is translated from *razdavalos'*, NOT *razlagalos'*, and *radovalos'* from *vosxiščalos'*, NOT *radovalos'*) but lets the reflexive particle follow the grammar of the original language (writing it connected to the verb rather than separately as required by Czech grammar).[52] Finally, we should note that the Russian translations are entirely of a type with the Serbian ones with regard to the technique of literalism. If anything, the resulting semantic problems may be greater with the Russian songs (Máchal, who appealed to Hanka's imperfect knowledge of Serbian to explain some of the "errors," argued that the Russian songs were better translated).

I would argue that what we see in Hanka's literalism is something subtly different from Schleiermacher and the Germans' approach to a literalism that foreignizes the target language. It is also different from the cultural appropriation that Macura associates with the Czech Revival practice of phonological translation as an aspect of a general translationality. As I have argued elsewhere, Hanka's strange translation practice is formed in the context of the period's ideology of the Slavic language.[53] For Hanka, there is essentially no difference between Russian, Serbian, and Czech—all are dialects of a common Slavic language; in that sense, there is no need to translate. Hanka resists translating

Russian and Serbian words that he can instead simply "lead in" to Czech, restoring to Czech a broader Slavic lexical base. It is thus not foreignizing, like the German practice, which is connected to a philosophical conception of identity building and *Bildung* through an experience of the foreign (and which also may be linked back to Macpherson's literalizing pseudotranslation).[54] Nor is it appropriative, because Russian culture and Serbian culture are not foreign cultures that can be appropriated, but native cultures, a part of the Czech self-identity that has been forgotten and that Hanka is restoring. Just as there is no need to translate, then, neither is there a particular need to distinguish between the Russian and Serbian muses. Note Hanka's title: *Srbská muza, do Čech převedená*. The inclusion of Russian songs in the collection is not indicated, and the fact that this is a translation is only suggested in a playfully ambiguous manner. He uses a Czech word that does not mean "translate" exactly, but is close to one that does (a *převod* can be a translation, though this is not its most common sense), while in both Russian and Serbian the verbal participle in this form *does* mean translated (while its primary Czech meaning is, as I have rendered it, "led in," particularly when the destination is not the Czech language, but the Czech lands). Even the title thus suggests that Hanka is both translating and not translating. Although his motivation and ideological foundation is different from the German romantics, his treatment of the language of translation is similar. Levý called the idea that the target language should transmit the character of the source language "the most dangerous thesis of romantic translation theory." "The romantics asked a near impossibility from translation: the preservation of the individuality of the very language material, the exchange of which is the very essence of translation practice."[55] Hanka, too, refuses the basic work of translation, the exchange of language material, and, in that sense, he *is* guilty of mistranslation, or of the general failure of translation that Levý argued was common to the romantics.[56]

I would suggest that at least some of the so-called mistakes Hanka makes here are deliberate, a part of Hanka's performance of a common and ancient Slavic folk idiom. The manuscripts offered another opportunity for a similar performance in which we will find analogous techniques at play. While the performance in the instance of his translation of Serbian folk songs, as explicit translation, was not perceived as masterful by critics, the reception of the manuscripts and the originality and authenticity ascribed to them suggest that similar techniques there, further refined, resulted in a performance we should recognize as masterful.

The hidden translations from Russian in the lyric songs of the manuscripts do not exhibit the same kind of problems of comprehension deriving from phonological translation that the translations in the Serbian muse volume do.

In that, they are closer to the hidden translations behind Hanka's original songs, which were very well received at the time, some even entering into oral circulation.[57] Nonetheless, one can find problematic instances of literalism. In "The Rose," Hanka's mix of literal and adaptive translation in the opening lines leads to a grammatical problem. In the lines "čemu si raně rozkvetla, / rozkvetavši pomrzla," (why did you bloom early / having bloomed, froze), which translate "K čemu ty rano razcvetaeš′, / Razcvetavši sad zasyxaeš′" (Why do you bloom early, / Having bloomed, garden, dry up), Hanka, rather than "leading in" the Russian verb (as he might have in the Serbian muse volume), translates it properly into Czech (the root *cvet* becoming *kvet*). But in changing from present to past tense in the first line, Hanka also changes to a perfective rather than imperfective form of the verb, which is then followed by the participle of the imperfective form in the next line. This alteration of verb aspect in the Old Czech (not found in the Russian) is at best grammatically awkward, if not an outright error, which is multiplied to three instances as Hanka improvises in extending the poetic image in the following lines.[58]

That example appears to be a mistake, rather than a deliberate bending of the target language to the (hidden) source. While Hanka's use of Russian songbooks as sources for his hidden translations in the manuscripts' lyrics are a well-established bit of evidence for his authorship of those songs, his practice of phonological translation as a means of performance of Slavic identity has not been examined in relation to his possible authorship, or collaboration in the authorship, of the epic poems. One has to be careful of drawing too definitive of conclusions on the basis of such evidence, however, because the technique of phonological translation was not unique to Hanka in the period, and the borrowing of terms from Slavic languages in particular had been modeled by the "father" of Hanka's generation, Jungmann, in his translations. (In fact, Jungmann borrowed needed new terms from Slavic languages even when translating from non-Slavic languages.)

Here it is worth noting Dolanský's thesis and evidence regarding the authorship of the epic "Záboj." Josef Linda cited about forty-five lines from that poem in his 1823 play *Jaroslav Šternberg v boji proti Tatarům* (Jaroslav Sternberg in battle against the Tartars). The cited lines use modern Czech grammatical forms and frequently differ both from the Old Czech of the manuscript and from Hanka's modern Czech translation. Given Linda's vague assertion, in the preface, of authorship of all of the material in the play (often read as an attempt to claim an authorial hand in the manuscripts without actually asserting that directly), Dolanský suggests that the lines as cited in the play may represent the original text of the epic, authored by Linda, before it was translated into Old Czech by Hanka, who later also retranslated that back to modern Czech.[59] Some of the features of phonological translation examined below are already present in "Linda's original" text (Dolanský documents how much Linda's poetic vocabulary in general owes to Ossian and the *Igor Tale*), and others appear in the Old Czech text and Hanka's translation but not in "Linda's."[60] This suggests how difficult it may be to distinguish between Linda's and Hanka's authorial contributions, when they seem to have shared so many techniques and tendencies.

We already examined, in chapter 2, examples of terms in formulaic phrases borrowed from Russian and Serbian that we might now reconsider as examples of phonological translation. These include terms like *jarý* (wild; from the wild bull formula) where the term did exist in Old Czech, but in a different sense (spring). It includes terms that did not exist in Old Czech but were recognizable either from related forms or context, like *sloveso* (word; related to Old and modern Czech *slovo*) and *komoň* (horse). This second term, borrowed from the Old East Slavic, is recognizable in context because it is part of the formulaic phrase *rúčí komoň* (swift steed), which appears in a form more fully translated into Old Czech, *ručie koně*, twice previously in the same epic ("Čestmír") and in multiple places elsewhere in the manuscripts. It also includes cases where even the grammatical adaptation to the target language typical of phonological translation is refused (similar to Hanka's treatment of the reflexive verb particle in his translations), as in the term *oteň* ("father's," in the formulaic phrase *s otňa zlata stola*, from her father's golden throne), which uses both the short/nominal adjective form that was rare in Old Czech and much more common in the Russian source and a different manner of forming the possessive than that in use in Old Czech. Another notable instance is the adjective *ladny* in the phrase *po Strezibor ot Sázavy ladny* (for Strezibor from lovely Sázava) in the calling of the assembly in "Libuše's Judgment." Dolanský notes that the adjective is a variant in BCS of the adjective for cold, a typically formulaic description of a river (as exemplified earlier in the same poem in introducing the younger of the sons in the dispute: "Staglav chraber na Radbuze chladně," Staglav the brave on the cold Radbuza).[61] But *ladný* in both Old and modern Czech has a different sense, meaning "graceful" or "beautiful." It is unclear whether the authors here misunderstood the South Slavic adjective as being the same as the Czech adjective or whether they understood it perfectly well (it is only used in this instance, in a formulaically correct description of a river) but only translated it phonologically, introducing interference with the Czech sense of the term.

To these examples one could add many more, moving beyond the realm of formulaic phrases. There has been extensive discussion of the many Russianisms in the manuscripts, of which Miroslav Komárek considers the following as most indisputable (no solid evidence of related Old Czech forms having ever been presented): *bodrost* (cheerfulness; from Russ. *bodrost'*), *plzný* (useful; from Russ. *poleznyj*), and *nevzmožno* (impossible; from Russ. *nevozmožno*), each of which shows the characteristic minimal adaptation to Czech morphology and grammar typical of phonological translation.[62] A less strict interpretation of Russianisms that allowed for the Russian inflection of possibly existing Old Czech forms might include in the list *vrah* (enemy, murderer; compare Russ. *vrag*, enemy), *lútý* (fierce; compare Russ. *ljutyj*), and *vterý* (second, versus standard Old Czech *druhý*; compare Russ. *vtoroj*). I have not seen a similarly systematic discussion of Serbianisms in the manuscripts, though Dolanský's book offers a lot of possibilities, among them *vládyka* (lord; compare Serb. *vladika*, bishop) and the use of *junoše* and *jun* (young man) to name young warriors, like the *junak*, the hero of South Slavic epic.[63] The vocabulary of the epic songs in the manuscripts is shaped in numerous instances by phonological translation from Russian and Serbian sources.

So is the grammar. Among the linguistic evidence for the inauthenticity of the manuscripts, the grammatical evidence is weightier than that of particular words, as it demonstrates highly improbable *systematic* deviation from language norms. High in the list of such deviations are the following: (1) a very high frequency of short or nominal adjective forms in the attributive function (for example, *črn les* instead of *črný*) in comparison with other Old Czech documents; (2) a predominance of adverbs ending in *-o* rather than *-e*, while *-e* predominated in Old Czech and *-o* endings increased only during the documented history of Czech; and (3) the overwhelming predominance of *i* used as a copulative conjunction, instead of *a* as in Old Czech and modern Czech.[64] While these features have also mostly been discussed as grammatical Russianisms, they can equally be seen as Serbianisms.[65] I would venture that the coincidence of such features in the relevant Russian and Serbian epic texts may have helped to determine the authors' use of them in reconstructing an equivalent ancient Czech oral idiom. The Russian and Serbian lexemes and grammatical forms that are infused into the pseudo Old Czech of the manuscripts are a result of a technique of nontranslation that alters the target language. This is a performance of Slavic commonality, and the "mistakes" here are systematic and seemingly intentional.

We should return here to Krejčí's argument about translation and the centrality of the Old Czech texts. His formulation of his conclusion is important when he writes that the poems were "written directly in a language that the author created for his purposes." Notice that he does not say that they were written in Old Czech, because the language of the manuscripts differs in some important ways from genuine Old Czech. In fact, in their frequent use of short adjectives as well as compound adjectives—two moments of key aesthetic functionality of the texts for Krejčí—the manuscripts differ significantly from Old Czech, and both of these are driven by hidden translation. Krejčí himself notes that most of the compound adjectives in the text are not attested in Old Czech, but represent imitations of Homer's use of such adjectives in his ancient Greek.[66] Thus, hidden translations from ancient Greek, BCS, and Russian help to shape an aesthetically pleasing false Old Czech for use in the manuscripts.[67] But this is a macaronic language derived from hidden translation that differs from Hanka's in his own translations (if perhaps not in his "original" songs) only in the high quality and taste of its execution. I am willing to accede to Krejčí's argument that the manuscripts were composed in "a language that the author created for his purposes" and not insist that there was a translation from modern Czech to Old Czech (though we shall get to some evidence for this as well shortly); however, it is clear that one cannot separate hidden or implicit translation, and the practice of phonological translation in particular, from this creative process of composition into an artificial language.

That the distortion of the Old Czech language may have been intentional and related to reigning translation practices is attested to by Hanka's own translation of the manuscripts back into modern Czech. While he could not make use of the archaic forms of the past tense, as he notes in his introduction, he did, nonetheless, include forms of the dual number beyond that typical for modern Czech (for example, *krásnýma rtoma*, red lips). There is a significant degree of coincidence with the Old Czech text in his use of archaic verb constructions, word forms, phraseology, and stylistic features.[68] These features bend the modern Czech translation in the direction of the Old Czech text (or, perhaps, if this translation is a hidden original of sorts, anticipate a fuller translation into Old Czech). Other features in the modern Czech version represent the preservation of the results of phonological translation from Russian and Serbian (or, again, possibly the first manifestation of such translation). Like the Old Czech text, the modern Czech text includes many short or nominal adjective forms.[69] Similarly, the use of *i* as a copulative conjunction predominates, with only 9 of 264 instances being changed to *a* in the modern Czech text (and 21 additional instances being simply eliminated). Adverbs in *-o*, however, are in the vast majority of cases translated to adverbs in *-e*.[70] This is the exception to the general tendency. Of the lexical Russianisms and possible Serbianisms discussed earlier, the majority are unaltered in the modern Czech text, even the obscure *komoň* (horse). *Sloveso* (word) is translated once as *slovo* and left once as *sloveso*. A few forms that would have presented greater difficulty for comprehension are changed. *Oteň* (father's) is rendered with modern

Czech possessive forms; *plzný* becomes *užitečný*, *vterý* is consistently changed to *druhý*, and *lútý* is modernized to *lítý*. Interestingly, the single instance of *jun* (in the genitive plural, *junóv*) is rendered as *junků*, underlining even more firmly the link to the BCS *junak*. The marked similarity in the foreignization of the language between the Old Czech text and Hanka's translation suggests quite convincingly that this alteration of the language was deliberate and purposeful in both cases, no matter which text came first.

The manuscript authors' practice of phonological translation from Russian and Serbian with its effects of foreignizing the language of the text, a technique similar to that deployed in many pseudotranslations, greatly resembles Hanka's techniques of translation and composition. It is a romantic literalist technique, even if the motivation and ideological underpinning here is different from the German practice, emphasizing not cultural appropriation and foreignization, but recovery of a broader Slavic identity from the past. *This principled distortion of the Old Czech language in the text is in conflict with the need to produce a believable Old Czech text*, a conflict that was probably only latent at first, but certainly became manifest when Dobrovský rejected the Green Mountain Manuscript, and particularly after he went public with his objections and philological evidence in 1824.

I would like to return here one more time to Krejčí's helpful formulation: "From the fact that the Old Czech forms constitute an inseparable layer of the aesthetic object, it follows that the poems were not translated from new Czech into Old Czech but were written directly in a language that the author created for his purposes; in their details, of course, the language forms could have been corrected in order to raise the probability of an ancient origin."[71] The transition here to the process of correction of the text is now worthy of our attention. But there is not a neat line one can draw between the process of the composition of the text of the manuscripts in a language of the author's creation and the correction of the text to the norms of Old Czech. There is evidence of correction happening over a longer period of time—initially probably by Hanka's likely "scribe" František Horčička under Hanka's direction, and later by Hanka himself in a variety of modes. This process of correction includes both the pursuit of greater conformity with standard Old Czech and further attempts to alter that standard in the direction of the Slavicized language of the manuscripts. Corrections were made in the process of creating the physical manuscripts, before they were "discovered" and put into circulation; further corrections were made to the manuscripts after they had already been seen and entered the collection of the National Museum; additional corrections were made when the text was transcribed for publication; and, finally, other manuscripts and texts appeared that gave corroborating evidence of some of the incorrect forms in the manuscripts.

The evidence we have for corrections to the manuscripts themselves and to tendentious transcription of the manuscripts by Hanka applies only to the Queen's Court Manuscript, not the much shorter Green Mountain Manuscript. The Queen's Court Manuscript is remarkable not only for the large number of erasures and corrections in the text, in comparison to other manuscripts, but also for the unusual tendency for the corrections to replace newer language forms with older language forms; most medieval scribes tend to correct older language forms to the standards and norms of their own language.[72] There are two kinds of corrections to distinguish here: those involving adding different letters in the same ink as the other writing in the manuscript, sometimes with a scraping of the manuscript to remove letters and replace them, and those involving primarily writing over the manuscript in a different ink, sometimes with scraping also involved. The first sort were most probably done while the manuscript was still first being prepared and the same writer still could use the same ink; the second could have been done later, even much later.

Corrections of the first sort include a large number of changes in the writing of the manuscript to fix spelling errors, omitted letters, and similar orthographical problems, but also corrections from newer grammatical endings to older and from newer phonological forms to older.[73] The latter include a number of changes of masculine animate endings in the accusative case from a vowel ending to an older zero ending in the poem "Čestmír and Vlaslav": "Kruvoj vezí Vojmíra" to "Vojmír" (l. 59); "Neklana kněze" to "Neklan kněz" (l. 63), and so on.[74] In "Jaroslav," the newer "od boha" (from God) is altered to "ot boha" (l. 206), and "klidno" is changed to the form that would have preceded the historical Czech vowel shift, "kludno" (l. 185).[75] What do such corrections suggest? They could be the results of the interference of the scribe's own modern Czech when copying the text to the manuscript, thus introducing errors that had to be corrected. But they could also be part of an ongoing process of translating the original text (in whatever language form it took) into a more correct representation of Old Czech.

These changes do not address the systematic deflection of the language of the manuscript toward Russian or Serbian language norms or the borrowing of lexemes, with a couple of minor exceptions. Ignác B. Mašek addresses two changes in conjunctions, one from *a* to *i* and one from *i* to *a*.[76] These offset and in any case do not begin to address the scores of cases of *i* used in place of the expected *a*. The other case is interesting: the Russianism *bodrost* (cheerfulness), which occurs a single time, has been corrected to *bedrost* by scraping away part of the *o*.[77] The result looks phonologically more Czech, but *bedrost* was no more a word in Old Czech than *bodrost*. It is unclear when this scraping occurred—it could have been a later attempt to alter an obvious Russianism. In any case, most editions read *bodrost* here ("Ludiše and Lubor," l. 33).

The corrections in a different color ink have been assigned to Hanka on the basis of his testimony in the process of his court case against the editors of *Tagesbote* for libel, for an anonymous article that named him the author of the manuscript and also discussed the corrections in the manuscript. Hanka admitted to going over some of the faded letters in pen to make them more easily readable.[78] He did not admit, although it is clear, that sometimes the new ink emendations involved changes in the text. For example, in an archaizing change parallel to the accusative case changes made in the original ink, Hanka changed "krahujce zlobného" (evil sparrow hawk) to the older form "krahujec zlobivý" ("Zbyhoň," l. 44).[79] And in "Jaroslav" (l. 210), the adjective "rozhoralé" has been changed to "rozharalé," a possible older form.[80] Jan Gebauer noted a number of these kinds of changes, though, that also spoiled correct archaic forms.[81] Here again, the changes do not address the systematic deformation of the Old Czech language. In fact, one such change adds an additional adverb ending in *-o*, changing *mudra / u* to *mudro* ("Ludiše and Lubor," l. 39).[82]

Additional corrections were made by Hanka in transcribing the text from the manuscript for publication. Some of these merely involved following his own later corrections in the manuscript ("krahujec zlobivý"). Others involved fixing the meter of poetic lines by adding and subtracting syllables (including several cases of adding or omitting the conjunction *i* at the beginning of lines).[83] None address grammatical or lexical Slavicisms.

From the foregoing discussion it is clear that the extended and multipronged process of correcting the Old Czech language of the manuscript, which may in part reflect a correction of the translation from modern Czech forms in some original text, was never directed at correcting the systematic errors that derived from an implicit phonological translation from Slavic texts.

What, then, about the additional manuscripts, the "cover" falsifications, that appeared later, giving further evidence of the language forms, ideas, and cultural values of the manuscripts? Rather than correcting the purposeful errors against the norms of Old Czech, these additional texts aimed to establish the Slavicized language of the manuscripts as the norm, or at least an alternative norm, of Old Czech. The "Song to Vyšehrad" belongs not to the group of cover falsifications, but properly alongside the Queen's Court and Green Mountain Manuscripts. It was the first manuscript fragment discovered, in 1816 by Linda, Hanka's roommate and friend, in the binding of a book he had been using as a footrest. The thirty-one-line fragment of a love lyric was initially accepted by Dobrovský, who dated it to the thirteenth century; but with the appearance of the Green Mountain Manuscript, he reconsidered it and declared it also false and Hanka as its author. As a result, it was treated with greater reservation than the more important Queen's Court Manuscript, and it was among the first to be publicly recognized as a falsification, in 1858, by scholars who still defended the primary manuscripts. Like the Queen's Court Manuscript, it had later erasures and corrections that would come to be attributed to Hanka.[84] It also resembles that manuscript in its language forms and further confirms the programmatic Slavic orientation in the language. In the short text we find multiple instances of nominal adjective forms (*Vyšegrade tvrd*, Vyšegrad firm, l. 2; *pochladeček mil*, sweet shade, l. 14) and adverbs in *-o* (*veselo*, happily, l. 16; *mutno*, sadly, l. 17; *pozdno*, late, l. 24). Conjunctions are few, but in line 3 we probably expect *a* rather than *i* to join *směle i hrdě*.[85]

Of the later cover falsifications, the first and perhaps most important was a set of Czech glosses added to the National Museum Library's copy of the *Mater verborum*, a popular medieval Latin dictionary that explained Latin, along with some Greek and Hebrew, words. Czech glosses, alongside Latin and German ones, were discovered in the manuscript in 1826 by the linguist Eberhard Gottlieb Graff in the presence of Hanka. The Old Czech vocabulary represented in the glosses gave a picture of the religion, worldview, and close linguistic ties of the Czechs to other Slavs, a picture that supported the manuscripts. Dobrovský, who was advanced in age, accepted their authenticity, but doubts were raised by his protégé, the Slovenian Kopitar, who in correspondence with Dobrovský in 1828 suggested that the number of glosses had increased since the moment of their discovery. In 1877, Antonín Baum and Adolf Patera published their conclusions, based on Patera's paleographic study of the glosses from eleven years earlier, that the majority of the glosses were false (950, versus 339 authentic ones) and had been added over a number of years in paint, versus the ink of the original glosses, sometimes also with erasures and corrections.[86] The glosses include a large number of terms that would be controversial in the manuscripts; of interest to us here are those that represent again the minimal phonological translation or outright borrowing of Russian and Serbian terms. These, with the Latin words they gloss, are as follows (with the page from the listing in Baum and Patera's study in parentheses): *bodr*: *promus*, *promptus* (the adjective from which *bodrost* is formed; 491); *jarý*: *uehemens* (495); *jun*: *puber* (496); *junoše*: *adolescens* (496); *komoň*: *equus*, along with *koň*: *equus* (496); *ladný*: *nitens*, *serenum* (497); *lěpota*: *pulcritudo* (498); *liutý*: *ferox* (498); *plzný*: *frugalis* (503); *vrah*: *diabolus* (512). It is notable that *vrah* is here with its Serbian sense, rather than the Russian sense of "enemy" as it is used in the manuscripts. Further, the terms *ladný* glosses are perhaps evidence that

Hanka *did* misunderstand the sense of the Serbian adjective he had borrowed for formulaic use, which meant "cold."

The other later falsification worth examining here is a manuscript with the Latin text of a fragment of the Gospel of St. John with an interlineal Old Czech translation, found by Hanka in a book binding in 1828. The language forms suggested it belonged to the early eleventh century. Dobrovský initially accepted it, but within a month changed his mind and made Hanka swear not to have it published in the journal of the Czech National Museum, as had been planned. Hanka published it soon after Dobrovský passed, and opinions were divided, with growing private reservations in the second half of the century until Alois Vojtěch Šembera and Antonín Vašek both publicly declared it false in 1878 and 1879. The letters of the translation were later determined to have been painted, rather than written.[87] Vašek cited the nominal adjectives as evidence against both of the main manuscripts and the Gospel text, which included the following in his listing: "dav mnog, dniu slavnu, syn člověč, zrno žitno, v život věčen, dnem slavnem, samégo boga věrna (and perhaps even more in addition)."[88] A glance at the text, in comparison with the Olomouc gospel from 1421, also shows a markedly more frequent use of *i* as a conjunction, with twenty-three instances in cases when the Olomouc gospel uses *a*.[89] There are almost no adverbs in the text, but there are a number of Russianisms, listed as follows along with the corresponding place in the Olomouc gospel (with pages from Josef Jireček's publication in parentheses): *ne-vsegda* / *nevždycky* (not always, 16); *lubí* / *miluje* (loves, 18); *dlžno vzvýšiti* / *mosí povýšen býti* (must be lifted up, 20); *pascě* (compare Russ. *pasxa*) / *velikonoci* (Easter or Passover, 22); *plti* (compare Russ. *plot'*) / *tělesenstvie* (flesh, 24); *drugý* / *jiný* (another, 24).

The cover falsifications, then, can also be seen as a part of a strategy to correct the errors introduced into the Old Czech of the manuscripts, not, as in the actual corrections in the manuscripts themselves, by making them conform better to the norms of Old Czech, but instead by further instantiating the Slavicized language forms that purposefully deformed Old Czech, turning errors into laws. This alteration of the norms of Old Czech can be seen to be the result of an implicit orientation toward the phonological translation of Russian and South Slavic texts, part of a language strategy that aimed to reconstruct the oldest forms of Czech in a way that conformed to the motivating ideology of a shared Slavic past and fundamental national identity. Such phonological translation shares techniques with practices of pseudotranslation, particularly in the foreignization of the target language (although the ideology behind the Czech practice would deny in principle that the source languages are foreign or that the alteration of Old Czech amounts to its foreignization). We cannot really know what form the original versions of the poetry of the manuscripts took, but it seems likely to have been at least a mix of Old and modern Czech, which underwent a further (but limited!) process of translation into Old Czech, both before and after it was inscribed in the physical manuscripts. The Old Czech text of the manuscripts, then, can be profitably examined as a kind of pseudo-original, being itself the result of techniques shaped by implicit translation, phonological translation, and pseudotranslation. And the modern Czech translation by Hanka can be placed beside Macpherson's versions of his Gaelic originals, with its bending of modern Czech toward both the Old Czech text and the same Russian and Serbian sources that formed it.

CHAPTER 4

Faith, Ritual, and the Manuscripts

The unique status the manuscripts achieved as part of the Czech national myth, taking on the status of sacred texts and cult objects, was discussed in the introduction, where credit for this development was given to the mythological interpretations of the manuscripts by nationalist scholars. But for that interpretation to take hold and be accepted by a broader public, in order for the cult of the manuscripts to develop by the 1860s, people needed to come into contact with the manuscripts and that interpretation in ways that convinced them of their authenticity and the truths that underwrote. This chapter explores a number of ritual and commemoration practices, as well as some other forms of contact with the manuscripts, that brought people in touch with the manuscripts and helped to instill in many a deeply personal faith in their authenticity and a cultlike attachment to them.

Did the manuscripts also achieve this status in part due to the lack of a clear religious affiliation for the Czech national movement? Did the manuscripts serve as an alternate form of national religion? Czech nationalism is strikingly different from that of many of its neighbors, where religion plays a prominent role as a marker of national identity (Catholic Poles and Croats, Orthodox Serbs and Russians). Czech-language culture had at times thrived in, at times greatly suffered in, periods of religious dissent and conflict, from the early Protestant Hussite movement and wars to the Thirty Years' War and defeat at White Mountain in 1620, with the subsequent Counter-Reformation.

Joseph II's Patent of Toleration (1781) allowed the Protestant side of Czech culture to reemerge alongside the Catholic side, a development that many credit for helping to stimulate the beginning of the Czech national movement.[1] But in many ways that history made religion and religious symbols dangerous for the national movement, as they threatened to once again divide rather than unite the national collective. The manuscripts, with their image of the pagan Czechs resisting outside domination and religious influence, may have offered a neutral ground for common identification, without actually requiring Czech patriots to drop their religious affiliations. As we will see, faith in the manuscripts and its ritual cultivation and manifestation seems to partake of that playful character of Czech Revival culture described by Vladimír Macura, where play always operates with a "fuzzy border between the serious and the unserious."[2]

The status of the manuscripts as cult objects and their central place in the national faith is most clearly seen in the moment when this faith was massively challenged by a group of professors in the new Czech university that emerged from the splitting of Charles-Ferdinand University in Prague into German and Czech faculties. The coordinated scholarly amassing of evidence, begun in 1886 with Tomáš Garrigue Masaryk and the historical linguist Jan Gebauer in the lead, led to the recognition that the manuscripts were indeed forgeries, at first in scholarly circles and eventually more broadly as well. In memoir accounts and later reflections on the so-called manuscript wars, the participants in the debates and those who were affected by them repeatedly compare belief in the authenticity of the manuscripts to religious faith.

In his memoirs, the historian Josef Šusta recalls his encounter with the historical arguments against the manuscripts as a young student just out of *gymnázium* (secondary school) in the early 1890s. He compares his change in perspective on the manuscripts to a loss of religious faith:

> I did not entirely understand that keen critical study [Jaroslav Goll's], not having sufficient knowledge of the sources used in it, but it was my first contact with the atmosphere in which I would shortly be so deeply anchored [that is, at the university]. Faith in the manuscripts, so important a pillar of my views to that point on the ancient national past, fell away from me all at once, so to speak, and just as in saying farewell to one's childish religious faith, it passed almost without painful upheaval, but rather like something obvious.[3]

Šusta's easy loss of faith stands in stark contrast with those who continued to defend the manuscripts, and even with some of those who would lead the campaign against them, like Gebauer, who clearly struggled with the painful implications of the linguistic evidence. He had been regularly publishing articles in defense of the manuscripts, but there is a telling long pause from 1882 through 1884 before his first article in 1885 that called the Queen's Court Manuscript into question.[4] His daughter Marie recalled this period in her memoirs:

> The six years that separate Antonín Vašek's polemics against the manuscripts from Jan Gebauer's polemics were for Daddy a period of great suffering, a period of painful, necessary transformation. . . . Those years were a crisis, as Daddy himself later named the time, a long drawn-out crisis from which there was no recovery back to the old, beautiful faith. . . . Daddy later described in letters what he went through when, instead of defending those supposed witnesses to the thousand-year development of the culture of our nation, he found only more and more proof that it had all been deception and delusion! Those were shocks for him and terrible blows, sharp as when a knife cuts through flesh."[5]

Šusta's easier loss of faith could be attributed to his age and the critical flexibility of early adulthood, but perhaps also to the atmosphere in which it had formed, in a period when the manuscripts were already under serious question. He recalls writing a drama, "Záboj," as a gymnasium student, based on the epic "Záboj, Slavoj, and Luděk" in the Queen's Court Manuscript, and what led to it:

> In school we were required to study it industriously in lessons on Old Czech language, and professor Paleček only made a cautious remark on the battle that the question of its authenticity had just unleashed. Articles in "Osvěta" [the journal of the defenders] strengthened us in our faith in that monument and the five-act drama "Záboj" grew up under my pen in a few short weeks so laudably soaring [*tak chvalně rozletělým*] that the eloquent tirades with which the drama abounded didn't even have the necessary punctuation.[6]

In his formative years, Šusta experiences both the inculcation of faith in the manuscripts and the campaign against them, leading to the quick loss of his new and still fragile faith.

Others had been faithful for longer. Jan Herben, in a volume of reflections by participants in the manuscript battles from the perspective of twenty-five years later, asked how the manuscripts' defenders could have ignored the obvious evidence amassed by Gebauer, Masaryk, Goll, and others and defended them so ardently. He saw the answer in their status as part of a national dogma: "It would be nothing if people had merely defended [the manuscripts], but instead they strangled their opponents with patriotic ropes. There is but one explanation: a national dogma was at stake and dogmas are not tested, one simply believes in them."[7] Gebauer later referred to the defenders as "rukopisověrci" (manuscript-believers), suggesting a kind of religious cult.[8] And Goll, in his attempt to sympathize and understand the vehemence of the defenders from the distance of twenty-five years, nonetheless likened them to religious fanatics burning heretics at the stake: "[Today] we can more easily understand the pain and perhaps even the wrongful anger of the defenders, from whom we took a piece of their national faith. We can explain to ourselves why it even came to fanatical cruelty here; heretics were always burned, so long as there were plenty of believers."[9] In fact, of course, no one was burned, but the pressure put on these scholars by the Czech community defending the manuscripts was intense. The publisher of the journal *Athenaeum*, in which the attack was launched, pulled out in 1887, and Masaryk had to gather funds to continue publication. Gebauer's daughter had to endure ridicule from a Czech teacher at school, and he had great difficulties publishing his scholarly work for almost a decade.[10] The untimely deaths of Antonín Vašek and Alois Vojtěch Šembera, whose publications in the late 1870s provided key evidence of forgery that would be consolidated by Masaryk's allies, were blamed on the intense pressure put on them by the patriotic community. Šembera's son consequently became an enemy of the Czech national movement.[11]

How did the manuscripts come to occupy such an entrenched position? How did faith in the manuscripts come to be so essential a sign of one's status as a Czech patriot that any expression of doubt resulted in one being labeled as a national traitor, an opponent of the Czech cause? "Víra se vžije," says Herben, in a phrase hard to render in English: faith takes hold, gets lived into place.[12] How did belief in these manuscripts become so intrinsic a part of Czech national patriotic life? I will show that the association between belief or faith in the authenticity of the manuscripts and Czech patriotism was established very early and that the roles played by the manuscripts in some quasi-religious rituals of Czech patriotic national life, including rituals of conversion, rebaptism and renaming, and eventually confessions of faith, along with less religiously marked commemorations of the discovery of the Queen's Court Manuscript made these manuscripts an almost inseparable part of Czech national self-identification for a great many.[13]

A connection between patriotism and belief in the manuscripts is first asserted in the polemics over the authenticity of the Green Mountain Manuscript in 1824, when Dobrovský was first forced to go public with his suspicions. For Dobrovský, the association between patriotism and belief was entirely negative. Angered by what he saw as a betrayal by his former students in his Slavic seminar and convinced that they had forged the Green Mountain Manuscript, Dobrovský is insistent that no one be fooled by it. The opening sentence of his article, titled "Literarischer Betrug" (Literary fraud), brings great rhetorical force and the weight of extensive research against too ardent patriotism that would lead to blind belief:

> The notion that somebody could be so bold as to present an obviously forged scrawl containing the Judgment of Libuše in Czech verse—if not to deceive the educated world, then at least to fool a few gullible, warm-blooded patriots [*leichtgläubige wärmere Patrioten*], who would love nothing more than to boast of an ancient relic in their language—almost defies comprehension. And in a century, no less, in which we mock the privilege Alexander [the Great] granted to the Slavs; laugh at the treaty, recorded in stone, between the Slavs and the Marcomanni; are abashed at the Arcani scientiae Czechicae; dismiss as blatant flattery the prophesy of Libuše, rendered in Latin hexameter by Marignola; regard Doctor Johann Smera's letter to [Kievan prince] Vladimir as waggish fantasy; declare the ancient Polish chronicle of Nakor, discovered around 1574 in a walled tomb, a fable; in which we have branded the Russian Joachim and the Hungarian notary Belas as changelings; and, more recently, unmasked the false Christian who sought to pass himself as the son of Boleslav.[14]

The translation here breaks out as a second sentence the extensive clause inserted into the first in Dobrovský's convoluted original, which lists historical sources and legends that had been criticized or shown false by research conducted by Dobrovský's teacher Gelasius Dobner or by Dobrovský himself.[15] Twice further in his short article he connects easy belief or gullibility to over-ardent patriotism.

In his reply, Václav Alois Svoboda, a poet and first translator of both manuscripts into German as well as a friend of Dobrovský's suspects, Hanka and Josef Linda, turns Dobrovský's negative association into a positive one. Svoboda claims the honor of warm or ardent patriotism against Dobrovský's cold logic, which he also exposes as not logical in its argumentation, but merely the expression of a different preformed belief:

> He finds his earlier stated conviction strengthened by a single look at the manuscript.[16] But his vehemence, his skirting of all thorough argumentation, the fact that he further constantly speaks only in platitudes of all too devout, gullible wishes of all too ardent patriots [*allzufrommen, leichtgläubigen Wünschen allzuwarmer Patrioten*]—(and is it then an honor not to be one? to coldly and heartlessly pick at the glory of the ancestors?), finally the frequent contradictions and variations in his opinions and hypotheses make his conviction suspicious to us.[17]

In claiming the ardent patriotism here, Svoboda continues to associate it with belief in the authenticity of the manuscripts, with both figured positively. Doubts, which are also treated as mere beliefs, are cold and negative. Svoboda later addresses Dobrovský's skepticism regarding the historical accuracy of the events depicted in the manuscript:

> The ordered court of Libuše further seems perhaps to displease him. We have to absolutely avow that we do not share Mr. D's opinion on the cultural level of our ancestors. We cannot think ourselves so outrageously rough, so entirely uneducated, as this critic paints us. We are conditioned to think so not only by our patriotism, of which we are in no way ashamed, but also by the idea of Humanity.[18]

Here too the ability to believe, rather than doubt, is figured positively and in connection not merely with a narrow patriotism but with a broader humanism. Even though Svoboda takes on Dobrovský's arguments and engages him in a scholarly discussion of evidence, the rhetoric cited here suggests that one's convictions about the authenticity or inauthenticity of the manuscripts is beyond any argumentation, is a result of an intuitive insight (Dobrovský's own passionate rhetoric seems to support Svoboda's interpretation). This appeal to the irrational is very romantic in a certain way. It is also very familiar from the debates over the authenticity of the East Slavic *Slovo o polku Igoreve* (Igor tale) in which proponents from both sides often begin from the "obvious" conclusions formed in intuition and go on to collect evidence in support of that irrational insight.[19] In any case, I would suggest that we see here very early on the formation of a kind of paradigm for the reception of the manuscripts among self-proclaimed Czech patriots that makes belief in the manuscripts a natural part of one's national convictions. In the years following this exchange, among Czech patriotic circles, Dobrovský had few followers in his skepticism.[20]

Narratives of Conversion

Who were these self-proclaimed Czech patriots, then, that might embrace the manuscripts? In the first few decades of the nineteenth century, they were a very small but distinct group that, if a nation consists in its self-identified members, constituted the active core of the Czech nation amid a mass population of nationally indifferent Czech and German speakers. Czech national patriotic society (that is, those who identified as part of the Czech nation and participated in the national movement) in this period has been described by contemporaries as a kind of peculiar religious order, or, more negatively, as a "sect of Czech zealots" or a "club" (according to Dobrovský, as cited by Macura)—more recently, some have suggested it resembled a kind of lodge of Freemasons (Dobrovský and others were members) or other secret society.[21] Here we see new social forms (nationhood) operating through analogy with other social forms, with religious forms prominent among them. In the main metaphor of the day, the Czech nation was conceived of as sleeping, and those who had awakened (to their Czech national identity) were *buditelé*—awakeners, charged with the task of awakening the entire nation. One was not simply born into the Czech nation, though one be born into a Czech-speaking family. Through the German-language education they all received, many were encouraged to consider themselves members of the German nation. Being Czech frequently involved a process or moment of self-realization and an act of self-declaration. And this transformation of self-identification became ritualized in the Czech national community with typical forms for encouraging it: an older patriot mentoring a younger one, awakened mothers raising patriotic sons. The activity of awakening was a primary sign of one's belonging to Czech society. In his biography of the composer Bedřich Smetana, Zdeněk Nejedlý describes the typical activity of a member of the newly forming and active Czech patriotic society of the 1830s: one reads the Czech press and "entices and converts to the faith others, not yet awakened."[22] Here again we see the religious analogy, with becoming Czech likened to religious conversion. There was a decidedly evangelical aspect to the recruitment of new adherents to the Czech cause, as Josef Bojislav Pichl recalled in his memoirs: "It was the endeavor and responsibility of every conscious patriot to spread love of country and the Czech language, and there was always a great delight among us when someone was won over by one of us. 'The twelve apostles spread Christ's faith so that now its adepts number over 100 million,' the too-soon-departed Josef Wagenknecht once said. 'There are more of us and our cause is as just and holy.'"[23] Pichl also recalled expeditions of members of Czech patriotic society around 1830 in Prague: "The target of their visits would often be well-known so-called nests of renegades [*odrodilců*, that is, "natural" Czechs who did not identify as such], which were either to be brought into the faith or disbanded."[24]

I should note here that Macura, the great Czech semiotician and student of the Czech National Revival, has also discussed the ritual aspect of becoming Czech, but on the model of an initiation rite into a secret society.[25] I do not disagree, but rather wish to emphasize another model, that of religious conversion, which fits better with aspects of the practices and experiences of certain patriots and with the general quasi-religious aspect of ritual practices surrounding the manuscripts. The rite of passage of conversion through reading in particular has venerable precedent in the conversion narrative of St. Augustine, which also cites its own precedent in the story of a monk, as related to him by Ponticianus, who was converted reading the *Life of St. Anthony*, and in the conversion of St. Antony himself, who was present at a reading of the Gospel and was converted. Augustine had been struggling with a lack of will to fully embrace Christianity, but confronted by these examples of others and led into great inner turmoil, as he relates in the eighth chapter of his *Confessions*, he suddenly heard a child's voice saying, "Take up and read!" He randomly opened St. Paul's epistle to the Romans and read a passage from the thirteenth chapter that resolved his turmoil and confirmed his will.[26] Becoming Czech through reading, then, as opposed to being mentored and brought in or raised by a patriotic mother, seems to best respond to an underlying model of religious conversion. The monk and writer Josef Vojtěch Sedláček invoked St. Paul's conversion in narrating his own story of Czech awakening through reading:

> One day when asking at the Plzeň post office for German newspapers and magazines, I spotted by chance Hromadka's Viennese Czech News. Driven by curiosity, I reached for the supplement to that Newspaper, containing poetic and other literary works that J. Jungmann, D. Kinský, P. Šafařík, V. Hanka, V. Al. Svoboda, J. L. Ziegler, M. Sychra, F. Hek, M. Patrčka, F. Turinský and others submitted to that publication back then. I read and was astonished! That supplement contained among other pieces a poem so fluidly and delectably written, and at the same time so high-flown and touching that Sedláček had hardly been accustomed to reading in German or other languages. It was, he said, *as if scales [belmo] fell from his eyes*; he felt himself suddenly enchanted and transported to the days of his childhood, when his ears heard the sounds of his mother tongue with delight.[27]

Sedláček recalls, in the detail of scales falling from his eyes, the completion of Saul's conversion with Ananias's laying on of hands prior to his baptism from Acts 9:18.

Conversion presents a number of difficulties for analyzing it as a rite or ritual, given that it is supposed to be a spontaneous and unrepeatable event. The anthropologist Peter G. Stromberg considered the conversion event as such inaccessible to analysis, whereas the conversion narrative, which can "be compared to a ritual in which the drama of the conflict of supernatural forces is reenacted," offered a more proper place for analysis.[28] He expressed skepticism toward the transformation that is supposed to have occurred in the conversion event and instead suggested that "if the conversion has some efficacy in transforming identity, that efficacy should be sought first of all in the narrative" and in its ritual repetition, which enables gradual change.[29] The author of Sedláček's biographical sketch, Antonín Rybička, notes that "Sedláček himself often narrated these facts to his friends and students with no small enthusiasm."[30] It must have been a common question among Czech patriots to ask, how did you become a Czech? And the stories appear to have been traded widely through the community. Macura observed that the mentor and mentee pairs were long remembered in patriotic circles: who brought in whom.[31]

These narratives of transformation (whether on the model of conversion or initiation), ritualized within the patriotic community, later became a topos in the memoirs, obituaries, and biographies of awakeners. Rybička, in his collection of biographical sketches of early Czech awakeners, *Přední křisitelé národa českého* (Foremost revivers of the Czech nation, 1883–84), consistently includes an account of how the subject became nationally conscious; other sources are less consistent. Not in every case does this appear as a kind of eureka moment of awakening or religious conversion. As one might imagine, in most cases there were many factors that influenced the realization that one is, or one has decided to become, Czech. That is, in most cases one imagines that there was a longer process of input and reinforcement that gradually leads to a decision or realization that may or may not be experienced as momentary. Sometimes the mentor who encouraged the process figures largely in the narrative. Dobrovský is considered to have been won over to Slavic studies and the Czech cause by his teacher Václav Fortunát Durych.[32] At other times, the future patriot's reading and personal experiences have a more important role. The "father of the Czech nation" and author of its first history, František Palacký, relates in his memoir the result of two experiences in his youth: "I caught fire entirely with genuine patriotic ardor, which has not since gone cold with me, nor, God grant, will it ever go cold."[33] What were the two experiences? First, while passing through the Slovak town of Trenčin on his way to his secondary school studies in Prešpurk (Bratislava), he was asked by his host to explain, as a Moravian, some passages in some news articles in Czech and was ashamed to find he understood them no better than his host. He dedicated himself to learning his mother tongue as a result. And second, not long after, he read Josef Jungmann's dialogues, "On the Czech Language," with their program for the revival of Czech-language culture. These were the texts that ultimately lit the patriotic fire just mentioned.[34] Palacký, a protestant, notably does not use any religious analogy in relation to this in his account.

Such transformations or conversions may be common to other subject nations in this time period. While I was working on this topic, a colleague discovered a similar, almost mystical event in the life of the Ukrainian writer Panteleimon Kulish.[35] In his memoir about Nikolai Kostomarov, Kulish recounts how he and Kostomarov became Ukrainian patriots: "Nikolasha, like all of us wards of Russian schools, at first disdained Ukrainian [*xoxlatčina*] and thought with the language of Pushkin. But a remarkable event happened to both of us, in two distant points in Malorossija. A collection of Ukrainian songs by Maksimovich (1827) fell into his hands in Kharkiv, and I, in Novgorod-Seversk, also by chance came to own the Ukrainian *dumy* [epic ballads] and songs by that same Maksimovich (1834). We both in a single day [*v odin den'*] went from Great-Russian nationalists to Ukrainian nationalists."[36] How mystical the event was depends on how one reads the phrase "v odin den'"—was it on the same day or in a single day for each of them? I do not know how common an experience this may have been among Ukrainian patriots (this event likely occurred in the late 1830s), but the ritual narration of such transformations does not seem to have become a practice in the beleaguered Ukrainian national movement.

For the Czechs who were part of patriotic society in the first half of the nineteenth century, these transformations were pursued in awakening activities and relived in their frequent ritualized narration in Czech society. The cultural compulsion to discover and elevate such moments, however hard to find they be, even has transferred into historical and biographical scholarship. For example, in reading the memoirs of the poet Jan Kollár, one has the sense of a death by a thousand cuts (or a rebirth to a new Czech life through similar suffering). Kollár himself does not single out a moment of transformation or a single most important influence or experience among the many that clearly made him into a Czechoslav patriot. (Kollár's patriotism was never merely Czech; himself a Slovak, he followed the broader Slavic line of Czech patriotism common at the time.) This has not stopped his biographers from seeking such a key moment, whether in his university studies in romantic Jena (1817–19) or elsewhere.[37] Indeed, it seems natural that the author of the epic sonnet cycle *Slavy dcera* (Daughter of glory), a Slavic divine comedy with a Slavic heaven, purgatory, and hell, should have at some point converted to this Slavic national religion. Two authors have claimed to see this moment of conversion/awakening in Kollár's brief visit in Prague on his way home from Jena in March 1819, and both have connected it, at least in part, to the first publication of the Queen's Court Manuscript, which became available in the last quarter of 1818.

Ferdinand Menčík suggests that Kollár noticed the brighter, more optimistic atmosphere in Prague, in contrast with two years earlier, resulting from the discovery of the important manuscript, and that the memory of the discovery of the manuscript led him to encourage his compatriots, in his epic *Slavy dcera*, not to despair but to pursue their national cause.[38] Vladimír Forst, also drawing on Kollár's letters from the time, suggests his meeting with Jungmann in Prague and acquaintance with the manuscript led him to a new dedication to national work.[39] This is speculative to a large degree—there is little specific evidence in the memoir or letters. One piece of indirect evidence, not cited fully by these authors, is the following passage from his Prague visit in his memoir:

> What a difference there was between when I first and now for the second time saw Prague! Back then I was still as innocent as Adam in paradise, now I have eaten of the tree of nationality a fruit bitter and causing spiritual pain; it seemed to me that Prague was the petrified history of the Czech nation. At Vyšehrad some rubble was showing from a pagan temple: having poked loose a fragment from it, I carried it with me wrapped in paper and keep it to this very day.[40]

Kollár is, as always, interesting. A protestant like Palacký (they were acquainted from the Bratislava lyceum), he does not avoid religious reference, but rather than a conversion (or an awakening), he figures his new awareness of nationality as a biblical fall from innocence to knowledge—still a religious figure, but one that is darker and more troubling, necessitating a search for (national) salvation. How Menčík gets from this passage to the more optimistic atmosphere in Prague is unclear to me! But I do see the Queen's Court Manuscript implied in this passage, precisely in the fetish object that Kollár selects as a Prague souvenir, a piece of the stone history of the Czech nation. There never was a pagan temple at Vyšehrad, where the first fortifications appeared in the tenth century (that is, after the ruling Czech princes had been Christianized), nor, likely, was there at the older site of Hradčany, where Prince Bořivoj I built the first fortifications after being baptized in 883. That Kollár sees the rubble at Vyšehrad as the ruins of a pagan temple is a vision that is strongly influenced by the Old Czech legends (in which Libuše had her seat there), made newly relevant by the two pagan-period epics in the Queen's Court Manuscript. There is a strong desire to hold on to this pagan period, imagined as purely Czech, untainted by the non-Slav influences that accompanied Christianization. This is the source and origin of Czech national identity, newly reimagined in the manuscripts, and Kollár, with his troubling new knowledge of the fallen state of the Czech nation, clings to what he presumably conceives as a piece of it from its pure, unfallen state as to a holy relic.

With Kollár we see our first example of the possible involvement of the forged manuscripts in an oblique rite of passage into Czechness, in the form of awakening or conversion or, in this particular case, figured as loss of innocence.[41] Others have left more explicit evidence of the Queen's Court Manuscript as a text that prompts this transformation. Palacký himself, already burning with patriotic fire, on reading the first publication of the manuscript fresh off the press records his ecstasy in his diary (the first entry for 1819 and thus just a few months before Kollár's passage through Prague) and rededicates himself to his homeland, figured here as a mother: "At the start of this year, with inexpressible joy I read, along with dear Šafařík, the Queen's Court Manuscript for the first time. You have come into your glory, o my Homeland! Once again you have raised your reverend head, and the nations look to you with wonder! . . . To you, benevolent mother, be rededicated my life and my breath!"[42] Here, the transformation already in the past, the text provokes a rededication in rhetoric with religious overtones. The effect of the first edition on Josef Vlastimil Kamarýt and his friend František Ladislav Čelakovský was evoked in their correspondence by the former on the publication of Hanka's second edition in 1829: "For me, I love the first publication more, because in its simplicity it is closer to its origins; and also it calls to mind when we first got acquainted with the Queen's Court Manuscript; when we pranced about with the verses of Záboj and Lumír in the Krumlov alleys in Budějovice, as you well remember; all of that is like forget-me-nots woven into that first wreath given to us."[43] Kamarýt here references a formative experience, though not necessarily a singularly formative transformation.

For others, the manuscripts *are* associated with the decisive moment of transformation. Pichl, whose memoirs cited earlier described the apostolic mission of Czech patriots to convert the lapsed, narrates his own initiation into the Czech cause as well. He recalls the welcome he was given to the Prague Old Town *gymnázium* (in the late 1820s) by the teacher František Jan Svoboda, who encouraged his pride in Czech history, including the fact that the Czechs had defended Christian Europe from the Tartar hordes (a fact in evidence primarily from the Queen's Court Manuscript epic "Jaroslav"). "Whoever knew prof. Svoboda personally, and especially those who had the fortune to be his student, knows how he could speak heart to heart. . . . I was touched deeply in my heart and carried away in my thoughts; that moment gave my outlook and endeavors a new direction and I became a conscious Czech."[44] Not only does Svoboda give evidence from the manuscript, but Pichl himself figures Svoboda as one of the bardic heroes of the manuscripts, implicitly citing Slavoj's praise of Záboj's singing: "Hark you, Záboj, you sing heart to heart / A song from the midst of sorrow like Lumír / Who moved with words and singing / Vyšehrad and all the homeland."[45] Pichl is similarly moved by the "heart to heart" words of Svoboda. And while Pichl does not figure his turn toward conscious Czechness as a religious conversion, the struggle in the epic "Záboj" includes resistance to cultural hegemony that involves religious conversion from paganism to Christianity. As Záboj sings, just before the praise from Slavoj just cited,

> So came a foreign one
> By force to the village
> And ordered us in foreign words.
> And as is done in foreign lands,
> From morn to night,
> So children and women
> Had to do here.
> And we are to have but one companion
> For the whole path from Vesna to Morana.[46]
> They drove the sparrowhawks from the groves,
> And the same gods as in foreign lands
> Were to be honored here
> And offered sacrifices.
> And it was not permitted to beat
> Foreheads before the gods
> Nor to feed them at dusk.
> There where our father gave food to the gods,
> Where he went to praise them,
> They felled all the trees,
> Overturned all the idols.[47]

While Pichl does not himself figure his initiation as a conversion, he invokes the epic from the manuscripts that thematizes religious identity as a part of Czech identity and the resistance to conversion to foreign faiths. The claiming of his own Czech identity, then, can still be read as a symbolic return to the Czech faith as a reconversion. Pichl's interest in the manuscripts and ancient Czech history, including its religious aspect, is also reflected in one of his first book purchases: Josef Linda's *Záře nad pohanstvem* (Dawn over paganism).[48]

The Jireček brothers, Hermenegild and Josef, connected their transformation directly to the reading of the manuscripts, which they discovered as secondary school students (likely in the late 1830s to early 1840s):

> The *gymnázium* library had a tiny collection of Czech books, which the teachers of the younger grades loaned to students almost illicitly. From that library we two, my brother and I, obtained the Queen's Court Manuscript, and that little "booklet" [*knížečuška*] determined our national consciousness. Ever since we read Záboj and Jaroslav, we have felt

> deep in our hearts that we are Czechs. I will not even mention the enthusiasm that was awakened by the poetic beauties of individual songs.[49]

Josef Jireček would go on, as a specialist in literature and the son-in-law of Šafařík, to be one of the most important defenders of the authenticity of the manuscripts in the later nineteenth century. For him, and for many like him, the manuscripts were an essential part of the Czech national myth with which they so strongly identified and even a part of their ritualized rite of passage in becoming Czech.

The ritualized stories told in the Czech community also included cases of cross-national conversion, where a "natural" German is converted to being Czech. Such was the case of Karl Agnel Schneidr, who in 1817 at the age of fifty-one, after many years of contact with Czech patriots, finally joined the Czech community and began to write his poetry in Czech rather than German.[50] Others might not convert fully, but at least be won over as a fellow traveler to the Czech cause. The Queen's Court Manuscript transformed Moritz Hartmann from an enemy to a friend, at least for a while in the view of the Czech community. As Václav Nebeský wrote in 1852, "One of our most tenacious enemies, M. Hartmann, enticed by the powerful magic contained in these ancient songs, skillfully translated a number of them into German."[51] But the translation might never have been a sign of such a transformation. Lena Dorn suggests Hartmann's Czech interests were motivated politically, by his anti-monarchist stance, and that when Czech politics took on a more anti-German coloring after 1848, he clearly repudiated that approach.[52] In his memoirs, published less than a decade after Nebeský's expressed delight at his conversion, Hartmann in fact cites the publication of the manuscript as the beginning of this negative turn in Czech nationalism.[53]

In several cases, then, the manuscripts have been documented (truly or falsely) as texts that brought new patriots into the Czech community. Naturally, not every case that may have occurred is documented, but some important, if far from neutral, cultural observers from the period made remarks that suggest this effect may have been far more widespread. Nebeský recalled the excitement and hope in the national movement in the period around the time of the discovery of the Queen's Court Manuscripts and the effect that the discovery had:

> The pomp [*sláva*] with which it was greeted everywhere drew the nation's attention to the language, and our youthful endeavors, and the refined delights and fresh originality of the discovered poems, inclined many hearts to the language in whose sounds they were garbed; yes, many who had been cast down by our poverty and lost hope in the rise

> and success of patriotic endeavors were revived by them and clung more warmly to their nationality.[54]

Jakub Malý credited the founding of the National Museum along with the discovery of the manuscripts for the positive turn that the national movement took in the third decade of the nineteenth century:

> Both old manuscripts presented an image of the pure Slavic culture of our ancient period, and no Czech heart unalienated from its homeland remained unmoved, and each felt uplifted by a lofty national pride. Those were enchanting sounds, but familiar to us; it was a voice from afar, but nonetheless near to our sensibility—"here was sung heart to heart." Those resemblances between ancient and contemporary times that appear for any time differences, that eternal task of the Czech to fend off foreign attacks, defend their nationality against deadly foreign elements, be forever on guard against "German neighbors," these all created a kind of solidarity of the most ancient and current national endeavors; an awakened nationalist recognized as his holy responsibility continuing the battle begun by his ancestors, the defense of national individuality under the same slogan.[55]

The revivifying effect Nebeský and Malý both ascribe to the manuscripts suggests that their role in the spread of the Czech national movement at the time was significant.

It is important to emphasize that the conversions based on the reading of the manuscripts documented here all precede the enshrinement of the manuscripts as sacred documents of the national mythology in the second half of the century. These are not conversions based on established sacred texts. The analogy with conversion belonged more broadly to the Czech movement in this early period, and the role of conversion text was also played by the work of contemporary poets and authors—Kollár's poems and Jungmann's programmatic texts are cited just as frequently. By the 1840s, the Czech community was growing quickly and resembled a club or secret society less and less, including in the aspect of initiation or conversion, which was mostly replaced by the inculcation of Czech identity in patriotic families and by teachers in schools, which made a later conversion unnecessary. It is also noteworthy that the explicit comparisons to conversion are usually made by the cited authors not in reference to their own entry into the Czech patriotic community, but rather regarding the community's efforts to bring in others—the exception in the above examples being the monk Sedláček. The ritualized retelling of narratives of initiation into the community most resembles a quasi-religious ritual of narrating conversion stories when the transformation in the tale derives from reading (following the model of St. Augustine), when the narrative appeals to the theme of religious identity and conversion in the manuscripts, or, finally, when what is being narrated is the evangelical activity of bringing others into the national community. Those who were brought in by the manuscripts or heard of others so converted may have been more ready to believe in the authenticity of the manuscripts and later accept their sacralization in the national mythology.

Rechristening or Rebaptism

While the rite of passage of conversion or initiation can be narrated in ritualized forms in response to the question of how you became Czech, it leaves no external sign of its completion. When confronting a new acquaintance, how could one know whether that person had experienced this transformation, whether the individual belonged to Czech patriotic society? At times, it could be dangerous to ask. Many Czech patriots chose to mark this rite of passage with a sign, a marker indicating their belonging to the Czech nation, by rechristening themselves with a patriotic name. The practice became fashionable in the second decade of the century and, like the initiation and conversion narratives, largely disappeared as Czech society became more self-evident in the 1840s. The source of the fashion is known: we have an account of a large group of people taking such names together in a kind of ceremony or ritual of rebaptism around the year 1810 that became a model for later patriots in taking their names.[56] Rybička, in his biographical sketch of the life of the Catholic priest Josef Ziegler, describes the event:

> Once a few friends and good acquaintances were gathered at his home ardently discussing things concerning our literature and nationality. Making use of the occasion, Ziegler spoke earnestly and pithily about these things, indicating how every folly that glories in foreign ways is detrimental in no small way to national feelings and consciousness, and how precisely our ancestors acted more resolutely and nationally insofar as they gloried in native and patriotic customs, dress and names: Vratislavs, Bořivojs, Soběslavs, Libušes, Boženas, Ludmilas, and so forth. And he encouraged his friends present, each one of them, for the more successful revival of patriotic feeling, to also foster the use and spread of national names in place of the foreign and unknown names favored among us so far. As Ziegler himself had already taken the second Czech name "Liboslav" to follow his baptismal name, he now persuaded his present

> guests to act similarly, with which they complied and were later known as Jaroslavs, Zdirads, Sudipravs, Sudimírs, Mírovits, Silorads, Hostivits, Lidurads, Dobromilas, Boženas, Vlastas, and so on. This event later received no small praise and such participation that every Czech writer and patriot added another Czech name to his baptismal one.[57]

In a footnote, Rybička lists all of the "novokřtěnci"—the newly or rebaptized, or perhaps Anabaptists.[58] As he did with the narratives of conversion, Rybička here faithfully transmits a legend from Czech patriotic society in the period regarding the founding of this patriotic name tradition in a kind of rite of rebaptism and renaming. I should note that Ziegler and his friends were not actually the first to take such names, but Ziegler does appear to be responsible for the institutionalization and ritualization of the practice. To take one prior example, the writer Antonín Puchmajer, a member of the first generation of Czech awakeners, took the name Jaroslav as a patriotic name, in honor of the Šternberk noble family (and thus the name of the same Jaroslav who is the hero of the epic poem by that name in the Queen's Court Manuscript, leading the Czech defeat of the Tartars—and in that sense, his patriotic name belongs retroactively to the manuscript).

Alois Jirásek evokes this legendary rebaptism in a scene from his novel *F. L. Věk: Obraz z dob našeho národního probuzení* (F. L. Věk: A portrait from the period of our national awakening). The title character, Věk (a fictional counterpart to the Czech composer František Vladislav Hek), visits Ziegler in 1811, and Ziegler tells him of how the poet Matěj Polák has recently been won over to Czech poetry (from German) and changed his name to reflect that—he is now Milota Zdirad Polák. Ziegler encourages Věk:

> "You should also let yourself be rechristened. There's already a bunch of us Anabaptists [*novokřtěnců*]; they accepted it here at my place when I suggested it. I am Liboslav, Polák is Milota, father Král is Mírovit; Patrčka too, he is Silorad [that is, Force-joy, in a false etymology], he loves physics as you know. Silorad . . . and you . . . what about you . . ."
>
> "I'm not a writer, father."
>
> "That doesn't matter. The doctor from Ústí Koráb also doesn't write and he accepted patriotic baptism. He's Lékoslav [that is, Medislav]. What matters is that everyone already with his name publicly declares he's a patriot, to show his way of thinking. Why all these Fridolinas, Edmunds, and Richards in the romantic fashion? We have our own vigorous names. It was better when they used to only use domestic names. So just show the world that we're Czech, we're here, and that will also encourage many who are hesitating."

"Yes, fellow patriot, yes," Věk agreed enthusiastically. "I'll be rebaptized."

"I've already thought of one for you. You're a musician, you love harmony [lad], so let your name be Ladislav. . . . You're accepted into the brotherhood."[59]

Jirásek combines in this literary depiction what we have presented as competing analytical metaphors, depicting rebaptism as initiation into a brotherhood or fraternal society.

Most often the rechristening involved the taking of a second name, following the fashion of the times for triple names, in which the patriotic name followed the baptismal name: Terezie *Vlasta* Heková, Magdalena *Dobromila* Rettigová, Jakub *Budislav* Malý, Josef *Vlastimil* Kamarýt, Michal *Silorad* Patrčka, Josef *Krasoslav* Chmelenský, Jan Alois *Sudiprav* Rettig, Václav *Vladivoj* Tomek. Sometimes the patriotic name entirely displaced the given name, as for Božena (Barbora) Němcová, and other parts of the name could change as well: Antonie Reissová used the name Bohuslava Rajská. Vladimír Macura has analyzed the fascinating semiotic qualities of these names: women's names most often appealed to the highest religious or moral values (Božena, Dobromila), while men's names were more varied and could indicate patriotism (Vlastimil), a relationship to art and aesthetics (Krasoslav, Ladislav—this one representing a folk etymology for an existing name, as seen in the Jirásek excerpt above), one's profession (Sudiprav—law, Silorad—physics, Lékoslav—medicine), or the image of the warrior hero (Vladivoj).[60] The taking of a patriotic name has, then, certain overdetermined, ritualized forms, in addition to the ritual aspect of taking a name.

While some of these patriotic names had prior use, many of them were artificial and newly formed to conform to the symbolic naming practice of representing one's profession or values (Sudiprav, Silorad, Budislav—a real awakener's name). The manuscripts appear as this practice is gaining momentum in Czech patriotic society and offer not only a host of good old Czech names, some very old (Beneš, Lutobor, Svatoslav, Ratibor, Věstoň, Zdeslav), but also a number of newly formed names that sometimes used the same derivational forms as the new names of Czech patriots (Bolemír, Záboj, Lumír, Kruvoj).[61] Moreover, the key patriotic values reflected in the highly symbolic names chosen—moral and religious piety, love of country, and especially the attributes of the warrior hero—are values that the manuscripts also modeled for Czech patriots. So while the manuscripts cannot be credited with inspiring this naming practice, they certainly strongly reinforced it.

Patriotic names were frequently used in Czech society as a kind of nickname, in place of the given name. They also had wide use as pseudonyms for writers publishing their work, sometimes with just the patriotic name and family name, sometimes as a second name as in the examples above. Family names could also be transformed, which could involve changing the orthography of the name (Schneidr—Šnajdr, Rettig—Retík, Kamareith—Kamarýt) or translating a name (Fejérpataky—Bělopotocký, Benedikti—Blahoslav).[62] Some writers also used a geographical name marking their place of birth or professional activity; so, for example, Václav Alois Svoboda, Hanka's friend and ally, sometimes signed as Václav Svoboda Navarovský, indicating the village where he was born. The use of nicknames was widespread and the use of pseudonyms in publication very common; there is a notable freedom and creativity in the naming practices of this second generation of Czech awakeners, which is consonant with the ironic performance of identity explored in chapter 1. But few can match the many guises under which Jan Evangelista Purkyně published and signed—his list of pseudonyms literally goes from A to Z and includes Russian forms of his name (Ivan, Ivan Josipovič); geographical names (Libochovický, Libochovský); some parodic patriotic names (Sumslavus, Maloslav [Littleslav]); classical figures and gods (Anaxagoras, Ovidius Naso, Pallas Athéně); a palindrome name (Babimor Romibab); and other hilarious joking guises (Honza ze Vsi [Johnny from the village], Prof. Dr. Punčoška [Stocking]).[63]

A transformation from a German writer with a German name to a Czech writer might require multiple transformations; Karl Agnel Schneidr became, at age fifty-one, Karel Sudimír Šnajdr. Sometimes the altered names and patriotic names became part of the figure's identity, particularly if they used the name consistently, so that we know these historical figures by their transformed patriotic names (Božena Němcová). We may not even remember there was a transformation, that the national poet, Mácha, for example, was given the name Ignác, but Czechified it as Hynek and added Karel to form the name we now know him by: Karel Hynek Mácha.[64] Other experimental transformations were dropped, so we now write Jan Alois Sudiprav Rettig and not Retík. And patriotic names that were used infrequently or by figures on the margins of patriotic society for whatever reason have not remained attached to those figures—Václav Alois Svoboda occasionally signed his work as Vládyboř, and Pavel Josef Šafařík signed as Jozef Jarmil on an isolated occasion.[65]

Šafařík, as a Slovak protestant who never lived or studied in Prague, was clearly on the outside of the Czech patriotic society in Prague and in eastern Bohemia around Ziegler, where the practice of rechristening was most common, as was his friend Kollár, who seems never to have used any patriotic name or nickname. But another protestant educated at the lyceum in Bratislava, František Palacký, came to live and work in Prague and became a prominent figure in Czech patriotic society, yet he too never used a patriotic name or nickname. This raises another possibility, that for some protestant figures the patriotic play with rechristening initiated by a Catholic priest was perhaps too uncomfortable, too close to heresy to trifle with. The fuzzy border between serious and nonserious play at rebaptism might have been more comfortably transgressed by those more distant from such religious practices, in the Catholic church.

Notably, the suspects in the forging of the manuscripts are also exceptional in their relation to the naming practices of Czech society. Hanka, Linda, and Svoboda all made use of a geographic name in signing some of their work, marking the village of their birth: Hořeňovský / Hořiněvský, Mitrovský, Navarovský. Svoboda's use of a patriotic name was limited, and Hanka and Linda did not use one at all (Linda's pseudonym Pravdomil Solkyneštěkavec appears parodic). None of them used such a name as a nickname in Czech society, though Hanka and Svoboda did make use of alternate forms of their first names. Hanka's moved in the direction of the Russian name Viacheslav: Váceslav; he sometimes signed work as Váceslav Váceslavič, using the Russian patronymic. Svoboda's inclined toward the German Wenzel: Věnceslav; he signed his publications in German as Wenzel or Wenceslaw.[66] Jungmann used neither a patriotic name nor a geographical one, but his younger followers nicknamed him "Bat'uška" (Russian: father), and his son was named Josef Josefovič, also using the Russian patronymic. Hanka and Jungmann's Russophilia shapes their (limited) patriotic play with their names.

The manuscripts, which were not yet widely treated as sacred texts, reinforced the practice of patriotic naming and also became a potential source of patriotic names, though this was less common than we might expect, perhaps because most of the names in the manuscripts did not lend themselves to the kind of transparent symbolic reading possible for the names that prevailed in the patriotic practice. In listing those who took their patriotic names from the manuscripts, we have to exclude those who took the name Jaroslav, as it is impossible to determine that the manuscripts in particular were the source for this common name that was in use as a patriotic name already before the manuscripts appeared. Our potential list would then include at least the following figures: Václav *Bolemír* Nebeský, Antonín *Bolemír* Marek, Karel *Slavoj* Amerling, and Václav *Záboj* Mařík.[67] In some of these cases, an explicit connection to the manuscripts as inspiration for the naming is difficult to pin down. Mařík is a marginal figure, a Czech teacher who spent his professional life in Croatian lands, far from Czech patriotic society, and likely went there already with his patriotic name. He did later make a free translation into Croatian of an article on the manuscripts by the Jireček brothers in 1858.[68] Karel Slavoj Amerling, as he is known today, never signed himself as such. Slavoj, a name like

Záboj that could only have come from the manuscripts, was widely used as his nickname in patriotic society, but he signed using it or a translated form of his last name, Strnad, with a geographical name: Karel Strnad, Slavoj Klatovský, Strnad Klatovský. The Queen's Court Manuscript was among the texts that his teacher at the gymnasium, J. M. Toupalík, used to awaken his interest in Czech literature.[69] He also published an article in 1848 titled "Věštby vítězové—Záboj a Slavoj" (Prophets of Vítěz—Záboj a Slavoj) in the journal for teachers, *Posel z Budče* (Courier from Budeč).[70]

Bolemír as a patriotic name could have been formed using the naming conventions of patriotic society as easily as taking it from an entirely marginal figure in the manuscripts (Lubor's first victim in the bloody knightly tournament narrated in the epic "Ludiše and Lubor"). While Nebeský was familiar with the Queen's Court Manuscript in Josef Wenzig's German translation before he became consciously Czech, that transformation is typically credited to Kollár's poetry, rather than the manuscript, and to his entry into Prague patriotic society. When he published his first poems in Czech in 1838, signing them as Václ. Bolemír Nebeský, the prevailing mood and outlook of the poems, with their "quiet pain" (*tichý bol*) and "modern world-weariness" (*světobol*), was likely sufficient explanation for his patriotic name.[71] For Antonín Marek, it is unclear how much use he made of the patriotic name Bolemír or what may have inspired its use at least as a pseudonym for some publications along with a geographical name: Bolemír Izborský.[72] Certainly, it did not become enough a part of his identity to be included in how he is remembered today.

If names from the manuscripts did not gain wide use as patriotic names in the 1820s to 1840s while such names were in fashion, they did enjoy much wider use later, beginning in the 1860s, when the manuscripts themselves achieved the status of sacred text and when changes in Austrian policy giving the right of association allowed for the formation of hundreds of patriotic groups of different varieties, from choral societies and theater groups to Sokol gymnastics clubs and libraries, many of which were named for heroes from the manuscripts, but also for Hanka.[73]

Rituals of Commemoration

According to his own account, it was on September 16, 1817, St. Ludmila's Day, in the vault in the tower of St. John the Baptist Church, in the dust among a collection of arrows from Jan Žižka's time, that Hanka discovered a tiny but extremely valuable manuscript fragment, later named for the place of its discovery, Dvůr Králové, the Rukopis královédvorský, or Queen's Court Manuscript. The testimony of eyewitnesses to the discovery, collected over forty years later for Hanka's libel lawsuit (to which we shall return shortly), differs as to whether the manuscript was found behind a cabinet in a hollow in the wall or in the cabinet among the arrows, some of which were fletched with parchment from similar manuscripts (as Hanka claimed), or fell out of an old hymn book that had been lying on top of the cabinet, or whether it mysteriously appeared in Hanka's hands, the witness is not sure from where.[74] "At first glance," Hanka wrote, "they appeared to be Latin prayers, but what joy moved my heart when I saw they were in Czech, and how that joy grew as the further I read, the more excellence and attractiveness I found! Such a pity only 12 small pages and two narrow strips remained of it! It is written on parchment in small script; Mr. Dobrovský determined by the script that it was copied between 1290 and 1310, but composed, certain pieces in particular, much earlier. Even more lamentable is the irretrievable loss of the remainder."[75] It is indeed small, but it was believed to contain the oldest known examples of a lively Czech poetic tradition, and it would transform the way the Czechs thought of the deep past of their nation.

The fortieth anniversary of this discovery was commemorated in 1857 with an event that can be said to represent *the first Czech mass national festival*, at least the first that was not a funeral (Karel Havlíček's funeral in 1856 was a notable assembly with national implications as well). How was this important, but not very long-lived, tradition invented? How was it celebrated? And what made the manuscript an appropriate symbol for national commemoration? How did the tradition disappear or lose its national significance? And finally, were there any religious aspects to this form of ritual behavior involving the manuscripts, which peaked in the period when they were venerated as sacred national texts?[76]

The first anniversary of the discovery of the Queen's Court Manuscript was an event only for the discoverer himself, Hanka, but he marked it with some commemorative words and a significant publication. The first edition of the manuscript was published, by Hanka, late in 1818. It opens with a brief introduction by Hanka, titled "Připomenutj." The title gave me pause when I was translating it for my own edition of the manuscripts. I rendered it as "reminder," but thought it a strange title—was this a reminder of the fact that he, Hanka, found the manuscript? Or the manuscript as a reminder of the glories of the Czech past? What is his introduction a reminder of? But if one pays attention to the date at the end of the text, another translation—commemoration—suggests itself. He signs off the introduction: "In Prague, the 16th of September, 1818," dating the text to the precise one-year anniversary of the discovery, a date he gives in the second paragraph of the text.[77] Hanka here is making us witness to his own commemoration, marked by this momentous publication, of his discovery of the manuscript, and perhaps offering it as a model to others, suggesting that the discovery of this manuscript is an event worthy of commemoration, of *připomenutí*.

It would be many years before anyone other than Hanka and perhaps his friends commemorated the discovery. A more public tradition arose in Dvůr Králové in the mid-1840s among local university students, returned from Prague, who filled their summer holidays by arranging dance parties (*besedy*) in the town. The idea of celebrating the local discovery of the Queen's Court Manuscript in one of these parties came, according to his own later semifictionalized account, from Jan Č. Brdička, who had purchased a new edition of the manuscripts and realized their local and national significance.[78] The first rather ad hoc celebration, then, happened on September 16, 1845 (that is, on the twenty-eighth anniversary of the discovery), as one of these parties. According to the anonymous account sent to the literary newspaper *Květy*, Brdička composed the introductory address, which was read by Marinka Scheiblowá, as well as some novel verses to the song that would become the Czech anthem "Kde domov můj?" ("Where Is My home?," a song at this point only ten years out from its composition, but already on the way to becoming a central national song), which were sung, along with some other Czech songs, in between dances.[79] Two poems from the manuscript, "Kytička" (The nosegay) and "Beneš Hermanův" (Beneš, son of Herman), were also declaimed, the latter by Brdička. The anonymous contributor of the description of the event wished for more such celebrations and implicitly offered the event as a model for other such events: "If only our gentlemen students would celebrate also in the coming years the epoch-making (*swětodějinný* [*sic!*]) discovery of the Queen's Court Manuscript!"[80]

The thirtieth anniversary was marked on September 22, 1847, more deliberately and festively by the same groups in Dvůr Králové.[81] The celebration, which occupied a single evening, remained a local affair but is interesting, as Jitka Ludvová has noted, for the way that "the manuscript themes entered into particularly intensive contact with other patriotic and nationalist symbols and became an inseparable part of a broad complex of figures, themes, images, and stories."[82] At a moment, then, when the Czech national movement was becoming a mass movement, the Queen's Court Manuscript was joining with a complex of other national symbols in a ritual marking of a nationally significant event. That evening, the hall was decorated with a large banner reading "30th anniversary of the discovery of the Queen's Court Manuscript 1817 by Václav Hanka" in between two dahlia wreaths, beneath which there was a picture drawn by a local, Bedřich Landrok, of two angels holding a page of parchment with the beginning of the epic "Čestmír and Vlaslav." Brdička opened the celebration with a short speech, followed by a recitation of the manuscript songs "The Rose" and "The Lark" by K. Stuchlík, with accompaniment by Landrok. P. K. Haas declaimed the manuscript ballad "Zbyhoň," which was followed by humorous verse read by H. Haas. Another song was followed by the distribution of the memorial booklet by Brdička, who had it published in Prague at his own expense, from which all the gathered sang "Kde domov můj?" "with heartfelt harmony." Songs and dances alternated, along with a cheer of "Glory to the discoverer of the Queen's Court Manuscript!"[83]

Brdička's small memorial booklet, *A Wreath Woven for the Thirtieth Commemoration of the Discovery of the Queen's Court Manuscript, Celebrated the 16th of September, 1847 in Dvůr Králové*, served as a commemorative volume.[84] As we will see, fundraising and commemorative publications became requisite for national commemorations later. The volume included a fictionalized description of the planning and celebration (Brdička appears as the character Lubomír) and a small selection of poems. These included one dedicated to the manuscript's discoverer (Hanka) from the thankful townsmen (*královdvořané*); one by Hanka's friend Tichoslav Sklenčka, whom he had been visiting that fateful day and who, by many accounts, was present at the discovery; two that are modern variations on lyrics from the manuscript; and one that consists in several local variant stanzas modeled on the eventual national anthem, like this one: "Kde domov můj, kde domov můj! / V Dvoře—v němž se choval poklad, / Slávy Čechův skvělý základ / Na obzoru duševním, / K slasti bratřím pokrevním: / Sou památky předkův mojich, / V tomto Dvoře domov můj!" (Where is my home, where is my home! In the Court in which a treasure lay, the splendid foundation of the Czechs' glory in the field of the spirit, for the delight of our blood brothers are the memorials of my ancestors, in that Court is my home!).[85] Such verses certainly mark the elevation of the manuscript into a national symbol.

Let me make a brief aside on the variations on songs from the manuscript authored by Brdička: they suggest another similarity to the Ossianic poems of Macpherson, which unleashed a rash of imitation poetry across Europe as inspired readers sat down to compose their own Ossianic verses.[86] His version of "The Nosegay" follows closely the form and syntax of the original to relate a love scene with Jeník and Bělinka, in which, rather than Bělinka falling into the water trying to catch a bouquet as in the original, a bouquet instead falls out of her dress and she teases Jeník to exchange signs of his love for the story of her gathering of the bouquet. In the original, the unnamed speaker addresses the bouquet, promising symbols of her devotion to the one who had set it afloat. The second song, "Touha" (Longing), echoes "Opuštěna"

(Forsaken), but turns that poem of loss into one of homecoming.[87] Michal Charypar, in an article dedicated to the influence of the manuscript lyrics on new Czech poetry in the first half of the nineteenth century, notes a number of instances in which poets directly echoed songs from the Queen's Court Manuscript. Josef Opočenský, for example, published a poem titled "Kytice a jinoch" (The nosegay and the youth), which narrates how the bouquet in the manuscript poem came to be floating down the stream, but the verse forms and syntax echo instead the poem "The Rose," thus mixing sources from the manuscript.[88] Charypar notes that "The Nosegay" was one of the most inspirational of the manuscript texts for modern Czech poetry.[89] He examines a handful of imitations of other songs as well as texts that attempted the synthesis of all the songs or their recombination in a larger work, but the overall number of such echoes is surprisingly small, especially in comparison to the flood of Ossianic poetry.[90]

The wider world only became aware of and began to participate in the anniversary celebrations in Dvůr Králové starting with the fortieth anniversary in 1857, but, since this was the era of absolutism and the police of interior minister Alexander Bach, this greater visibility would have its consequences. The results for the Czechs of the revolutionary uprisings in 1848 were mixed. The initial uprising in Vienna in March quickly led to government overturn and the promise of constitutional reform, but the interests of Czech and German liberals diverged rapidly. The Slavic Congress convened in Prague was seen as a rival to the Frankfurt parliament, and the clashes between radical students and the army in Prague in June were suppressed by General Alfred Candidus Ferdinand, Prince of Windisch-Grätz, in just five days, which also prevented the Bohemian Diet from convening and contributing on behalf of the Czechs to the advancing reform proposals. Some genuine and lasting reform did take place, including the freeing of the serfs, but when the young Francis Joseph I took the throne in December, the hopes for a constitutional order were quickly dashed. Further, the police uncovered the so-called May Conspiracy among Czech radical democrats in early May 1849 and sentenced the leaders, like Josef Václav Frič, to exemplary severe punishments. The Czechs had gained a liberal political voice and experienced briefly some democratic processes, but in the punitive period of absolutism that followed, they lost their free press (Karel Havlíček was exiled following his persistent efforts to maintain it in December 1951), and Bach's police suppressed political and cultural activities through networks of informants and censorship.[91]

The fortieth anniversary celebration in 1857 was possible in part because the age of the manuscript suggested its commemoration was not about current national politics. That year, the celebration outgrew its *beseda* (dance party) origins, and the young women and students as organizers gave way to the town dignitaries and invited guests. The high point of the celebration was the unveiling of a statue of Záboj, hero of the oldest pagan epic poem of the manuscript, in the fountain in the main town square of Dvůr Králové. The statue had been commissioned by the town brewers, at a cost of twelve thousand *zlatých*, from the local sculptor František Wagner, with the assistance of his younger brother, Antonín Pavel Wagner (who would later decorate the National Theater with sculptures of Záboj and Lumír, a figure from the same epic).[92] The event was originally planned for September 16 but was delayed to September 29 due to a minor dispute between the brewers and the sculptors. The organizers wrote to Hanka to invite him to the celebration, but the invitation was declined. Nonetheless, to everyone's delight, Hanka arrived the evening before the celebration and, as the most prominent person present, took a central place in the ceremonies, including reading a poem he had composed for the occasion—this surprise arrival was, intended or not, a fine piece of stagecraft.[93] Men's choirs from Jaroměř and Hradec Králové, there for the event, serenaded him in his hotel that evening.[94] (For this same anniversary, Hanka received a very fine gift: an album of handwritten verse by the leading poets of the younger generation, including Jan Neruda, Vítěslav Hálek, Josef Václav Frič, Gustav Pflegr Moravský, and others.)[95]

The celebration opened the following morning at eight with loud music throughout the town, welcoming the many out-of-town guests who were arriving. Mass was then celebrated at nine in the St. John the Baptist Church, with the music led by the composer Josef Krejčí (later the director of the Prague conservatory), who came from Prague with a choir for the occasion. This included performances of the oldest Czech hymns, "Hospodine pomiluj ny" (Lord have mercy on us) and "Svatý Václave, vevodo České země" (St. Václav, prince of the Czech lands). After a welcome for the honored guests at the home of the brewer's leader *pan* Kubský, a procession was led by the subregional governor, town mayor, and town council to the main square and the veiled monument. As the square filled with people, Krejčí led his choir in a cantata and the Dvůr Králové school director, Landrok, gave a lengthy speech on the meaning of the occasion, noting that the monument was "more of national than town" significance.[96] At that point, the veil was lifted and Landrok led the crowd in three cheers of "Slava!" (Hurrah/glory), first for the ancestors who composed the manuscript, second for Hanka the discoverer, and third for the local sculptors. Antonín Tkadlec, a local teacher, then declaimed the poem "Záboj" in a modern Czech translation. This was followed by readings of various poems from the manuscript by visiting dignitaries and locals in the many languages into which it had already been translated. Hanka read in Old

Czech and Polish, a visiting professor of Italian from Prague, Felice Francesconi, read in Italian, French, and English, and others read in Croatian, Slovenian, and German, thereby making manifest the European significance of and response to the manuscript. Krejčí again led his choir in a cantata he had composed for the occasion, and Hanka's new poem was distributed to the entire crowd present—a lovely souvenir. Again, the national anthem was sung, followed by performances by the visiting choirs. The crowd then disbursed to the local pubs, where "many a toast was made," and later reconvened for the evening ball at seven, in a hall decorated with many banners, including the main one depicting Záboj above a bust of Hanka.[97]

Reflecting on the occasion ten years later, Antonín Víták would conclude, "We can boldly state that the celebration unveiling the statue to Záboj was, in the period of Bach's government [no less], the first national celebration."[98] And although it pales in comparison to the celebration that would occur ten years later, on the fiftieth anniversary, I think we can agree that a tradition here was being established for a celebration that aspired to national significance, both in its scope and in its symbolism.[99] As Karel Šima reminds us, these kinds of national festivals were a ritual activity that required careful planning and goals to bring together different "collective identities [to] intersect and mutually overlap, transform and form completely new ones. Celebrations became one of the means by which romantic nationalism gradually gained hegemony in European societies."[100]

For the Prague chief of police, when he learned of the event several months later, it was precisely a concern about the possibility of establishing such a nationalist Czech tradition that led him to try to do something about it. Anton von Päumann was well known for his careful surveillance of Czech emancipatory efforts, so when Vienna authorities took notice of a small note in the *Neue Preussische Zeitung* on December 31, 1857, commenting on the celebration and the anti-German sentiments the manuscript presented, in harmony with Hanka's own anti-Germanism, he quickly responded to their inquiry.[101] He noted in his report to the minister of police already on January 6 that the tendentious manuscript was being taught in the schools and that the potential doubts about its authenticity were being forgotten, so that it was becoming more and more a national symbol. He noted Hanka's activities in 1848 and warned that, as there had already been a similar celebration ten years earlier, in 1847, there was a danger of similar nationalist demonstrations every ten years.[102] Hanka had been particularly active in the revolutionary year, serving the new Slovanská Lípa (Slavic Linden) cultural and political organization as president, while it existed, helping to plan the Slavic Congress in Prague, running for the planned Czech parliament, and bravely defending the National

Museum from military attack as a part of the Svornost (Concord) regiment.[103] By March, Päumann had already conceived of a plan: he had one of his officers draft an article casting doubts on the Queen's Court Manuscript, without naming Hanka as the forger, and asked that the ministry arrange to get it placed in a highly visible foreign newspaper, like the *Augsburger Allgemeine Zeitung*.[104]

The time was ripe for such an attack. That same January of 1858 a commission of the National Museum had subjected two of the cover falsifications, the "Love Song of King Václav" and "Song to Vyšehrad," to chemical tests and had found them to be modern falsifications. The tests confirmed the prior philological and paleographic analysis of the young Viennese Bohemist Julius Feifalik, who also expressed his doubts about the Queen's Court Manuscript and promised to subject it to a similar investigation.[105] Police minister Johann Franz Kempen von Fichtenstamm, however, declined to pursue Päumann's plan, as his own internal analysis suggested that such an approach would only politicize the issue, which Czech scholars already seemed to be addressing on their own.[106] When a museum commission decided in July NOT to subject the Queen's Court Manuscript to similar testing due to a lack of credible evidence against it, though, Päumann forged ahead even without Vienna's approval.

During October 5–29, 1858, a series of anonymous articles under the title "Handschriftliche Lügen und palaeographische Wahrheiten" (Manuscript lies and paleographic truths) appeared in the Prague newspaper *Tagesbote aus Böhmen*. They began innocently enough with an example of literary forgery from Scotland, Macpherson's Ossianic poetry, but quickly moved to the newly revealed Czech manuscript forgeries and the doubt they cast on the Queen's Court Manuscript. They finished by naming Hanka the likely leader of "the Old Czech school of writing." Hanka's reply on November 4 was printed, but also subjected to ironic commentary by the editor, so that, under pressure from Czech leaders, Hanka sued the editor, David Kuh, for libel on November 11 (Palacký suggested that Hanka's reticence derived from the fact that he was perhaps flattered by the suggestion he had written the manuscript).[107] Hanka framed his suit as one that would provide evidence that he had discovered the manuscript over forty years earlier in the church tower vault and therefore he did not fabricate it; Judge Theodor Rišlánek accepted the case in this form. The suit, then, did not solicit expert testimony or examine the evidence for or against forgery, but rather gathered evidence from eyewitness testimony and documents related to Hanka's discovery in 1817.[108]

While the courts quietly conducted their investigation and collected witness testimony and documentary evidence over the following months, a more public trial of the philological and historical evidence was happening in the press as Feifalik and Max Büdinger published studies that cast serious doubts on the medieval provenance of the Queen's Court Manuscript, eliciting replies from Palacký, the Jireček brothers, and Nebeský, among others. Václav Vladivoj Tomek also investigated the origins of the manuscript containing "Libuše's Judgment" and provided evidence of its discovery at the castle Zelená Hora u Nepomuku.[109] The fact that the *Tagesbote* publisher, Kuh, was Jewish brought out some unfortunate anti-Semitic rhetoric in some of the Czech nationalist defenses of Hanka.[110]

The trial would be the first under a new press law from 1852, and with the scandalous accusation at stake, it was much anticipated and closely followed at home and abroad.[111] The hearing was held August 25, 1859. It involved the presentation of the carefully gathered eyewitness testimony that had been collected from the few still surviving witnesses to that day of discovery as well as documentary evidence, including a critical record of the transfer of ownership of the manuscript from the town of Dvůr Králové to Hanka in late 1818, a document that implied, legally, that the manuscript had been the possession of the town before it became Hanka's.[112] Based on this evidence, Hanka had proved his case and the court came to its logical conclusion, convicting Kuh and sentencing him to the loss of his one hundred gulden bail, two months in jail, and payment of court costs.[113] This was a significant victory for Hanka and Czech national activists and a legal vindication of the Queen's Court Manuscript.

Kuh immediately appealed, but the appeals court in Prague upheld the conviction and the full sentence on September 26, 1859, which should have been the end of Kuh's legal recourse. However, Kuh made an unusual appeal to the emperor for clemency, and, as a result, his case was taken up by the Viennese high court in an entirely extralegal manner. On reviewing the materials from the two previous trials, that court, on April 12, 1860, vacated Kuh's prison term and the payment of court costs in his sentence.[114] This unusual government interference in the case raised Czech suspicions, though these could only be confirmed many years later.[115]

Päumann had used Kuh for his provocation, and it likely suited the police to have the conviction upheld but the punishment negated as a way to protect their provocateurs while shielding their own involvement from public scrutiny.[116] For the Czechs, though, the high-profile case confirmed for many the authenticity of the manuscripts along with Hanka's innocence, and the shadowy government interference only bolstered their resolve to defend what they saw as their legitimate national patrimony against false slander and attempts to divide them in their national aspirations.

The opportunity for a public demonstration in support of Hanka would not wait long. After a brief illness, Hanka passed away on January 11, 1861. In his massive funeral celebration, the commemorative traditions developing in Dvůr Králové joined productively with another rising tradition of national commemoration at the funerals of major Czech nationalist figures. In the interpretation of Marek Nekula, Hanka's funeral is a breakthrough moment in the establishment of rituals of national mourning, developing and expanding the ritual of the funerals of Josef Jungmann and Karel Havlíček Borovský.[117] Given the tremendous public manifestation at Hanka's funeral, it is little wonder that the ailing Božena Němcová desired to follow his model and be buried beside him at Vyšehrad, which she was just under a year later.[118]

The funeral was planned by the board of the National Museum, where Hanka had served as librarian. The body was laid in state in the museum courtyard, with the museum itself draped in black banners. Following the singing of Czech songs by the Hlahol society over the casket, the funeral procession led from the museum through the crowded streets of Prague to Vyšehrad. The procession was led by a riflemen's brigade, followed by school students, choirs, the clergy, then the deceased with his honors, representatives of the museum, the heads of royal offices, the university rector, the royal academic society and professors, the board and council of the capital city of Prague, a deputation from Dvůr Králové, a deputation from the Estates Theater, writers and artists, university students, and riflemen. In the center was the deceased, in a coffin decorated with laurels (a tradition Němcová had helped to establish at Havlíček's funeral) and with his Russian medal of the knightly order of St. Vladimir. The tips of the bier cover were carried by Palacký, Tomek, Josef Wenzig, Prince Rudolph of Thurn and Taxis, František Ladislav Rieger, and Frič—in other words, the highest representatives of Czech patriotic society. The coffin was followed by a copy of the multilingual Polyglot edition of the manuscripts carried on a plush pillow and surrounded by a wreath of laurel.[119] As the procession made its way, the observers in the streets joined in, creating, as Nekula notes, a symbolic living chain that linked Slavic Vyšehrad back to the center of Prague.[120] At Vyšehrad, following the singing of a Czech dirge, the body was placed in the ground.[121] The national newspaper *Národní listy* estimated the crowd at forty thousand, while the German-language *Bohemia* gave ten to twelve thousand as its count. For the Czech press, the event gave concrete evidence of the "multitude and zeal" of the Czech national body.[122] The national significance of the funeral was also indicated by the accounts of ceremonies and requiem masses in other towns across the Bohemian territory published in the journal *Lumír* (note the name!). Ludvová notes that the songs and poems of the manuscripts were brought to even greater public awareness as they were declaimed and sung in dozens of towns as a part of these memorial ceremonies.[123]

Before the coffin was buried, attendees competed for leaves of laurel from the coffin as memorials of the service. In addition, copies of a poem by Jiljí Vratislav Jahn were distributed, and one could buy small busts of Hanka by the sculptor Tomáš Seidan and even copper coins with a likeness of Hanka (this followed traditions from church burial rituals).[124] A memorial book titled *Funeral March* was also published, which included some of Hanka's songs set to music alongside the national anthem. Proceeds from the sale of the book were dedicated to the erection of his monumental gravestone, and money began to flow in for the same through a collection begun by the Matice Foundation and donations sent to the national newspaper.[125] At the same time, in Dvůr Králové it was decided to erect Hanka a more living monument, one that would contribute to the cultivation and development of the Czech language, to which he had devoted his life. A collection was begun, then, to raise money for the building of Hanka's Theater—note that this precedes the similar patriotic collections for the National Theater at the funerals of other patriots, which ritualized the practice established at Hanka's funeral.[126]

The momentum generated by the large fortieth anniversary commemoration and Hanka's funeral continued with the celebrations of the forty-fifth anniversary of the finding of the manuscript in 1862. A plaque was placed on Hanka's birth house in Hořiněves, with the usual accompaniment of songs and the presence of a couple thousand, including the Prague political elite, and a two-day celebration took place in Dvůr Králové, including a ball and a requiem mass for Hanka.[127] The monument on Hanka's grave was erected in 1863 (figure 4.1), and planning soon began for a large fiftieth anniversary celebration. This included (ultimately unrealized) plans for a small collection of musical compositions on themes from the manuscripts, an initiative that may have given Wenzig (who, we recall, participated centrally in Hanka's funeral) the impulse to begin work on what would become the libretto for Smetana's opera *Libuše*.[128]

The fiftieth anniversary year, 1867, did not begin well at all for Czech nationalists. Defeat in the Prussian war once again forced the Austrian court to compromise and enable political reform, but the prime beneficiaries were the Hungarians. The Ausgleich that established a dual Austrian and Hungarian monarchy left the Czech hopes for self-governance destroyed. The Czech policy of loyalty to the crown with the aim of reestablishing the Bohemian state's rights had proved less effective than the resolute Hungarian boycott. Czech protest took various forms, including a boycott of the Reichsrat, a del-

FIGURE 4.1. The monument on Václav Hanka's grave, Vyšehrad cemetery. The inscription reads, "Nations do not expire so long as their language lives." Photo by Ludek—Own work, CC BY-SA 3.0, https://commons.wikimedia.org/w/index.php?curid=854710.

egation that visited the Russian ethnographic exhibition in St. Petersburg and secured an audience with Tsar Aleksandr II, and demonstrations at the return of the Bohemian crown to Prague from Vienna.[129] The lavish three-day fiftieth anniversary celebration of the discovery of the manuscript, on September 28–30, also took on a heightened emotional and political coloring.

Czech national society had become far more visible since the end of Bach's absolutist era following the Austrian defeat in the Sardinian and French war in 1859—as noted earlier, the right of association allowed hundreds of patriotic groups to form, including choral societies (four hundred in the course of ten years), amateur theater groups, and Sokol gymnastic associations. Many of these took their group names from the epic heroes of the manuscripts: Lumír, Záboj, Slavoj, and Jaroslav.[130] These groups, each under their own

FIGURE 4.2. Mayor Bedřich Tinus speaking near the statue of Záboj in Dvůr Králové during the celebrations of the fiftieth anniversary of the discovery of the manuscript. Illustration by Emil Zillich, *Světozor* 1, no. 15 (1867): 148.

banners, formed a very visible part of the celebrations, with at least thirty choirs providing musical accompaniment to the festivities. And, of course, the manuscripts served as the cause and visible center of the celebration, with a Polyglot edition carried around on a silk pillow in a wreath of laurel and decorated with Slavic ribbons—a fetish object—as the celebration proceeded first to the Záboj statue on the main square (figure 4.2), then on to the church where the Queen's Court Manuscript was found, and finally to the Hanka gardens for the centerpiece of the celebration: the unveiling of a bust of Hanka (by Antonín Pavel Wagner) and the ceremonial laying of the cornerstone of the future Hanka Theater in the gardens purchased by the town for that purpose—a ceremony that again prefigured the massive event around the laying of the cornerstone of the National Theater the following year.[131]

This time, too, the Prague political and cultural elite turned out for the celebration, with Palacký and Rieger joined by Jan Evangelista Purkyně, Karel Sladkovský, and Karel Sabina as central participants, along with representatives of prominent patriotic associations from Prague and other towns around the country, and thousands of other visitors from towns near and far, including "even some from the banks of the Neva and Volga."[132] The town was entirely decorated in banners in the national and Slavic colors, with patriotic slogans. The celebratory processions were marked by the ringing of bells and firing of mortars.[133] Music again played a prominent role, although a notable absence in the reports for this celebration is any explicit mention of the singing of the national anthem; it may nonetheless have been a part of the periodic outbreaks of patriotic song that punctuated the program. Instead, the reports emphasize the performance of a number of pieces of music specially composed for the occasion, and in the evening concert on the first day, recitation of the poem "Jaroslav" and performance of three songs from the manuscript were accompanied by a more ambitious musical program that included opera arias and overtures by Richard Wagner, Giacomo Meyerbeer, and Gaetano Donizetti alongside work by Czech composers and Slavic folk songs.[134]

While the second day was largely rained out, Palacký, Rieger, and Sladkovský did witness the testimony of the local church sexton Jan Šáfr entered in the court regarding the discovery of the manuscript, to which he had been an eyewitness as a fourteen-year-old boy, belated testimony for Hanka's lawsuit as it were.[135] The third day was marked by a requiem mass for Hanka, an evening ball, and a charity banquet for the poor, as a bookend to the first day's exclusive afternoon banquet with toasts from the most prominent visitors.[136] Fundraising for Hanka's Theater was conducted by the local women, who organized a popular bazaar in which they sold photos of the town, of the Záboj statue, and of the church tower along with a commemorative history of the town by Antonín Víták, which was also given out to prominent guests during the ceremonies. The demand for print editions of the manuscripts could not be met by the meager supply the Prague booksellers had provided.[137]

The height of the celebration, for the anonymous author of the commemorative volume published shortly after the event, was the speech by Sladkovský at the church tower on the morning of the first day, which evoked an ecstatic response from the gathered public: "In the eyes of the assembled thousands glimmered copious tears of the greatest enthusiasm, at the same time painful and joyful. When the speaker finished, there was no end to the cries of 'Sláva!,' comrade embraced comrade and the entire assembly was as if electrified, as if enraptured."[138] What had so electrified the audience? An object lesson in Czech patriotism and heroic self-defense based on the epic "Záboj, Slavoj, and Luděk" from the manuscript. The speech clearly shows how effective the manuscript could be as a model for contemporary Czech behavior and for the formation of national mythology. The epic recounts the liberation of Czech tribes from subjugation to a foreign power, most likely Charlemagne, who has forced them to convert to Christianity and suppressed their pagan gods and customs. With a song, the heroic Záboj enflames the hearts of his compatriots to train and then fight against the foreign domination. Záboj and Slavoj lead the attack on the king's army under the traitor Luděk, who serves as the local overlord, and the battle ends in a rout. Sladkovský opened his speech citing Záboj's song, sung in a moment of grief at their subjugation, linking the current Czech situation to the one a thousand years earlier: "'Men of brotherly hearts / And flashing eyes! / I sing you a song from the utter depths. / It comes from my heart, / From a heart most deeply / Engulfed in grief.'" Throughout the speech Sladkovský continually returns to the relevance of the epic as a model for how they should respond to their current plight. To take just one moment, in which he again cites Záboj's song:

> With pride we name ourselves the sons of those fathers whose heroics the poems of the Queen's Court Manuscript sing, and who did not allow foreigners to "order [them] in foreign words" in their homeland. As sons of those fathers, to whom they bequeathed this land, we all certainly feel the holy obligation to defend as bravely as our forefathers our national independence and autonomy against any kind of unauthorized foreign influence. The song of the Queen's Court Manuscript is for us a sublime model of the most sacrificial love of the homeland, love of freedom and national independence.[139]

This political rhetoric makes it clear that the discovery of the manuscript was not merely a pretext, an otherwise neutral event that was used as an occasion for national celebration and protest under the influence of Czech political circumstances. Rather, the manuscript itself provided inspiration and a rich symbolic ground for national entrepreneurs to manifest their patriotic feelings. And such rhetoric was not unique to the commemorations of the discovery of the manuscript. Jaroslava Janáčková has shown that the manuscripts were frequently actualized and cited during this time in public speeches and meetings of town councils "for the formation of civic morals."[140]

If the manuscripts could model good nationalist values and civic morals, the celebrations of the discovery of the Queen's Court Manuscript could also bring together a new formation of the national community. Just as the funerals of Czech nationalists borrowed from church funerals (memorial busts and coins), so did the festivities in Dvůr Králové make use of practices from church festivals, including the ringing of bells and firing of mortars and celebrations of requiem masses. Šima notes how the fiftieth anniversary celebration brought together symbols of local and national significance and further invested them with sacred significance, resulting in a new national symbolic complex.[141]

The fiftieth anniversary in 1867 was the height of the commemorations of the manuscript's discovery as national celebration. Its reverberations continued for some time: Hanka's Theater was opened in 1874 (it now stands on Václav Hanka Square, probably the only one so named in the country), and collections for the National Theater continued apace. While the town of Dvůr

Králové prepared a sixtieth anniversary celebration, the report in *Národní listy* evidenced clear disappointment in its humbler realization and the lack of visiting participants, for which economic conditions and other unnamed obstacles were cited.[142] Dvůr Králové was losing its place as a prominent stage for national celebration, and the manuscripts were coming under ever more troubling scrutiny. Palacký's large funeral had taken place in Prague the year prior. And, having waited for a decade not to trouble Palacký with the finding, Antonín Baum and Adolf Patera published an article not long before the celebration, exposing another of the cover falsifications—three-fourths of the Czech glosses in the medieval Latin dictionary *Mater verborum*, many of which gave corroborating evidence of certain linguistic peculiarities and the level of early cultural advancement found in the manuscript, were shown to be false modern insertions.[143] Certainly, these are among the obstacles to the sixtieth anniversary celebration.

By the time of the seventieth anniversary, the manuscript wars had broken out. Tomáš Garrigue Masaryk and his colleagues at the university launched their campaign to expose the falsity of the manuscripts in his journal *Athenaeum* in the February 1886 issue. By July 1887, with 60 articles having been published in *Athenaeum* alone, and over 130 in total in all journals and newspapers, Masaryk was ready to declare victory: "The scientific side of the debate over the *RKZ* is definitively settled. The recognition that the Manuscripts are forged will have a salutary effect in the sciences and through the sciences, and also in many practical questions of our public life. . . . If we have a look at the overall outcome, we can sincerely rejoice, because truth is beginning to triumph, and truth never harmed anyone in the final analysis. It is not for the first time, nor for the last, that truth triumphed among us!"[144] The pages of *Národní listy*, which the editor Julius Grégr used as a tribune to lead the defense of the manuscripts, carried only one small notice of plans to commemorate the anniversary, consisting of a theater presentation by the amateur theater group Hanka in Dvůr Králové, beginning at seven thirty in the evening on September 18.[145] No report of the event, which returned the celebrations to something resembling their more humble beginnings in the 1840s, followed.[146]

While debates over the manuscripts would continue for several decades, with evidence for and against authenticity being investigated and weighed more carefully, the majority of the scholarly community quickly accepted that they were a product of the early Czech Revival. The wartime one hundredth anniversary passed in 1917 without any larger public events, then, but was marked by commemorative articles in a variety of newspapers and journals.[147] With Hanka now seen more as a forger than a heroic discoverer of the national past, the basis for broad national celebrations was no longer there.

Among the broader public, though, there have always remained some who do not accept the scholarly arguments and evidence that the manuscripts are false. The Czechoslovak Manuscript Society (Československá společnost rukopisná) was founded in 1932 to keep the debates going and defend their authenticity, activities that it continues to this day.[148] And in Dvůr Králové, local patriots seem loath to give up the circumstance that, for a while, put them into the center of Czech national activity. As a point of local pride, then, the manuscripts are still defended there—my young tour guide who took me in 2018 into the church tower vault where the manuscript was found cited a few pieces of evidence from the manuscripts' defenders regarding their authenticity to dismiss the "myth" of their forgery.

In the intervening years, the monuments put into place in national commemorations in the town suffered from the decline in faith in the manuscripts. Hanka's bust was removed during Masaryk's presidency to make way for a planned statue of the president (a nice symbol of Masaryk's victory over Hanka), and the Záboj statue was removed to the town's periphery in 1950; however, it was returned in 2005 and was joined by another monument, *Rukopisy* by Jaroslav Černý, near the Václav Hanka Square in 2006 (figure 4.3).[149]

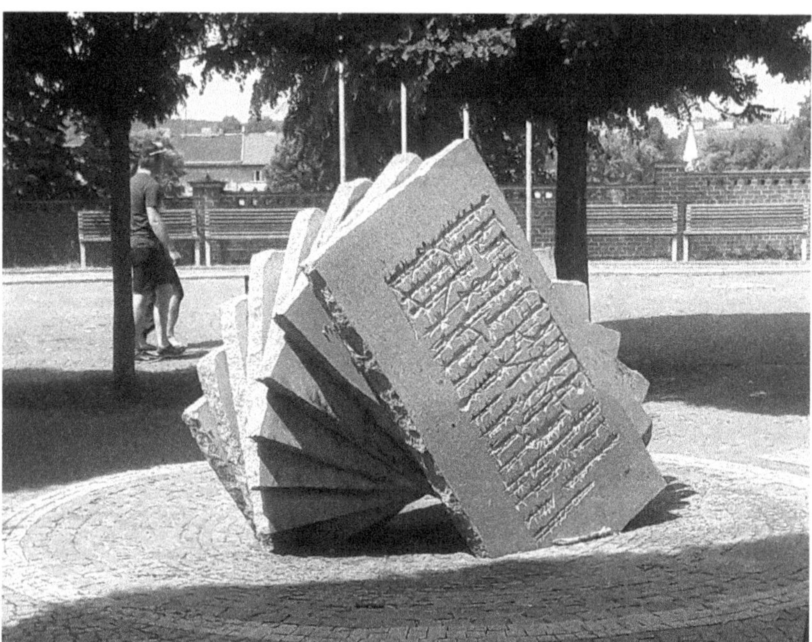

FIGURE 4.3. *Manuscripts* (Rukopisy) by Jaroslav Černý. Author photo.

The periodic celebrations of the discovery of the manuscripts with their sacralizing and fetishizing of the texts created personal bonds to the manuscripts connected to experiences of national community building. Similar bonds were forged in Hanka's libel suit and the memorials for Hanka celebrated around the country upon his demise. Contact with the manuscripts in school reading and dramatic productions made them integral in many others' formative experiences as Czech patriots. By the final third of the century, then, the interpretation of the manuscripts that made them the foundation of the national mythology met with a public that had a variety of experiences of contact with the manuscripts and public demonstrations of their significance that supported such an interpretation. Belief in the authenticity of the manuscripts was, for many, an integral part of being Czech. That other Czechs might not agree, might even deliberately attack their authenticity, angered and appalled.

Ritual Defenses, Confessions of Faith

Articles and books defending the authenticity of the manuscripts were a regular phenomenon in their reception from the time of Svoboda's early reply to Dobrovský's criticisms in 1824. In the first half of the century, when there were few who doubted the Green Mountain Manuscript and almost none who doubted the Queen's Court Manuscript, the defenses were not so much replies to articles by skeptics as attempts to inoculate the manuscripts from doubt so they could serve as a support for the developing national myth, which at that point was still a "minority" myth (see the discussion in the introduction).[150] These defenses were largely written by qualified experts and published in scholarly journals and were not great in quantity. Toward the end of this period, though, such defenses already began to take on a certain ritualized character, deploying and repeating the same commonplace arsenal of citations and proofs to validate the manuscripts' mythic status.[151] Following Hanka's libel lawsuit and the scholarly arguments by Feifalik and Büdinger in the late 1850s and early 1860s, the production of defenses was stimulated by the doubts expressed both in expert publications and in the broader press. At this point, the national myth, with the manuscripts as its support, was well established and the defenses operated within it in an established ritualized form, so that the defenses themselves were seen through the mythic lens as a reflection of the constant need of the Czech nation to defend itself and its faith against outside aggression.[152] The defense of the manuscripts becomes, by mythical extension, equivalent to the defense of the entire distinct Czech national existence. While in earlier periods the defenses of the manuscripts often helped to advance scholarly methods and knowledge, in this period, due to their crystallized, ritualized form, they no longer do, and it is the skeptics that bring new methods and advance knowledge of the manuscripts.[153] Such defenses nonetheless remained relatively small in number and were still mostly produced by qualified experts.

With the publication of Šembera's and Vašek's arguments in the late 1870s, though, the situation changed fundamentally, as the question of the manuscripts' authenticity could no longer be so easily framed as a Czech defense against the outside. The internalization of the dispute raised the stakes for the national myth. Now defenses began to be produced in much larger numbers and not just by experts, and they appeared in all levels of the press. In Šembera's case, the responses in the press even preceded the publication of his critical argument.[154] Czech nationalist intellectuals of all types rose to the defense of their sacred manuscripts, making use of the ritualized form such defenses had taken. For the majority, their defense was their only published statement on the manuscripts.[155] This included prominent writers (Sofie Podlipská, Jan Neruda, Eliška Krásnohorská), prominent intellectuals from other spheres (Primus Sobotka, Jan Matouš Černý, Vincenc Brandl), a slew of secondary school teachers, some teaching Czech language and literature (like Vašek) but many not, along with many others less prominent.[156] Some of the more prominent defenders were not qualified as experts, but took up the cause in the absence of new defenses from more qualified experts, like the lawyer and politician Julius Grégr, who led the defenses as editor of the journal *Národní listy*, or Oldřich V. Seykora, a journalist and secondary school teacher who published a series of feuilletons in the *Čech* journal, both of whom later published their essays in book form.[157]

Mojmír Otruba followed up his study of how the manuscripts became integrated into the national mythology (see the introduction) with a structuralist study of the defenses published between 1878 and 1900, in the period of the "internal" Czech national dispute, and their semantics, raising the question as well of what social ritual the publication of these defenses constituted. He argues that they all appear as variants on an invariant, ritualized argument form. He closely examines the rhetorical strategies of the defenses, which, insofar as they address the scholarly argument at all, tend to draw on the same evidence (in ritualized form) and indict the scholarly qualifications and moral qualities of the skeptics and place them outside the bounds of the national collective. On the semantic level, these defenses primarily create opposing value categories, *NÁROD* (nation) and *OPONENT*, where the nation category collects all positive values (including morality and science) and the opponents represent the destruction of all these collective values, and thus the nation.

The basic argument of all these defenses is that *OPONENT škodí NÁROD* (the opponent harms the nation).[158] The defenses thus demarcate clear lines of national belonging and exclusion based on belief in the authenticity of the manuscripts.

Otruba sees this as a kind of rhetorical game that is asymmetrical, with a predetermined outcome, and finds analogies in ritual acts of purification, like the Catholic rite of excommunication.[159] Certainly, this is what the texts are doing rhetorically in casting the doubters out of the national collective with its faith in the manuscripts. But the social ritual that the authors of defenses are participating in when producing such texts seems to me to have a different significance. While Otruba's analysis is of essential value and key to my reading of the functioning of the manuscripts as sacred texts, I disagree with his conclusion about the ritual that the defenses represent. Rites of communal purification or excommunication are typically dependent on and carried out by communal or church authorities. But the striking thing about the defenses of the manuscripts in this period is how widespread they were, how democratic in participation. It was not sufficient for the national scholarly authorities to have defended the manuscripts and to have already cast their doubters out of the national collective. Rather, it seems that it was incumbent on all patriots to make a kind of public statement in defense of the manuscripts. For me, the ritual is more one of inclusion than exclusion. I would suggest that we see the ritual not in what the documents do rhetorically (casting out the opponents), but in what the authors are doing by making such a statement—the speech act as the ritual act—following an authoritative rhetorical pattern. The ritual the authors are participating in resembles making a public statement or confession of faith, marking themselves as members of the community of believers.

Making such a statement seems to have been incumbent on those who saw themselves as faithful members of the national community. This community does indeed appear at times similar to a protestant sect (Dobrovský's accusation), with their evangelical practice of recruiting new members, their earlier practice of adult rebaptism (recalling the radical Anabaptist reformation) and renaming, and now their later impulse to publicly confess their faith in their own sacred texts. What is the significance of this religious cast to the rituals of Czech national society? It does appear that in a number of significant ways the manuscripts and their accompanying myth of the ancient Czech national origins with a pagan religious identity of its own did function as a kind of national religion in place of institutionalized religions that may have divided, rather than united, the Czech collective. Even as Czech patriots made such religious analogies and used religious language and ritual forms to describe and perform their Czech national identity, though, they did so in a kind of serious play, and it is doubtful any of them would have claimed a real religious affiliation with the nation and its myth. Rather, the Czech national myth offered them a common site for belief and affiliation that could resemble religious belief, and sometimes this became all too serious, as perhaps for protestant patriots who did not join in to rechristen themselves with patriotic names or for the national heretics who dared to doubt the authenticity of the manuscripts, challenging their authority as sacred texts.

These doubters also founded their national identity on the manuscripts, as Dalibor Dobiáš has observed in reading their memoirs, but based on a remythologization that made the loss of faith in the manuscripts into the birth of a new, modern national identity that opposed faith in lies to a truth revealed by skeptical investigation.[160] This can be seen, ironically, as just another myth that still kept the manuscripts and one's stance on them at the center of the question of national identity and propelled debates on the "meaning of Czech history" for a long time to come.

Conclusion

The high tensions and high stakes of the late nineteenth-century debates on the authenticity of the manuscripts are, thankfully, a thing of the past. Occasionally, someone from close to the academic mainstream will step out to challenge the accepted conclusion that the manuscripts are forgeries from the early nineteenth century, and this is as it should be, as a part of the self-critical reexamination of evidence that ensures that the reigning scholarly perspective remains on solid ground. The Czech Manuscript Society, while not offering any new evidence, at least tries to keep alive doubts and maintain the fiction that the debate is still ongoing. But in fact, qualified experts largely ignore its provocations and do not engage it in debate, because this is less productive than many other questions they can research around the manuscripts. The two unequal sides, then, coexist in relatively harmonious disagreement.

The occasion of the two hundredth anniversary of the discovery of the Queen's Court Manuscript in 2017 made this visible on the national stage and allowed the town of Dvůr Králové to once again participate in a larger, more national commemoration of Hanka's "discovery." The National Museum marked the event with the exhibit *The Masaryk Phenomenon* from September 15 to October 1, and Czech Radio, Stanice Vltava, broadcast on the evening of the fifteenth a discussion of Hanka with scholarly experts. Even the castle at Zelená Hora, where the second major manuscript was found and which had not played any part in prior commemorations, mounted an exhibit. In Dvůr Králové there were a variety of events throughout the month of September and into October, organized by the town's Slavoj Library, the town museum, and Hankův dům (Hanka's House, as the theater is now called). This included a visit by the Jára Cimrman Theater for a production of *České nebe* (Czech heavens); a two-day exhibit of the original of the Queen's Court Manuscript (billed as its return home); concerts on September 16 and 23, the latter including additional festivities like a period market; and lectures on September 18, 19, and 25 (these all by members of the Czech Manuscript Society). The town library produced a facsimile edition of the Queen's Court Manuscript (see figure I.1, in the introduction), and the Czech Manuscript Society released its book, *RKZ dodnes nepoznané* (The manuscripts, unknown to this day).[1]

The tension between the local and national commemorations, with discussions of Hanka as a forger and celebrations of Masaryk juxtaposed to lectures by the Manuscript Society and the manuscript's return "home" (as if it really had been rotting in that tower vault), is manifest as well in the fact that the local highlight in Dvůr Králové may well have been the visit of the celebrated Cimrman Theater, which has made mystification into a very popular Czech art form. Jára Cimrman is a character created by Ladislav Smoljak and Zdeněk Svěrák, an unrecognized Czech genius supposedly responsible for major technological inventions and an actor in key historical events. In a 2005 Czech Television public poll to determine the "Greatest Czech," Cimrman was leading the polling until, embarrassed, Czech Television disqualified him as a fictional character. The play *Czech Heavens* directly addresses the issue of the forged manuscripts, as Cimrman is supposed to have belonged to the camp of those who denied their authenticity. The play opens with a seminar dedicated to Cimrman's life and work. The play *Czech Heavens* is, it turns out, one of his works, which was also found as a manuscript in a sugar refinery. Svěrák presents a paper, "Manuscript Forgeries," in which he assesses Cimrman's relationship to the manuscripts, concluding, "We understand to a certain extent the good intentions of the falsifiers. And we are even capable of understanding that that kind of work was enjoyable. But to make up events that never happened and figures that never lived, and for years to mystify the entire nation, that really, but really sickens us."[2] Such a line from one of the inventors of Cimrman positively crackles with hilarious dramatic irony. The second part presents Cimrman's play itself, in which a panel of great historical Czechs (St. Václav, Jan Amos Komenský, Jan Hus, Karel Havlíček Borovský, grandfather Čech, and Božena Němcová's granny) decides on the fate of other historical characters, whether they will be admitted to the Czech heavens or have to remain in purgatory. The turn comes for Hanka and Linda, and the commission is initially confused as to their gender (Hanka and Linda can be women's first names), but when this is sorted out, the time comes to vote. Komenský argues, "Did they help the nation? They helped. I would accept them into heaven." Hus replies, "Did they deceive the nation? They deceived. I would not accept them into heaven." The vote is taken, and with two for, three against, and one abstention, Hanka and Linda are consigned back to purgatory.[3]

Given the prominence afforded to the Czech Manuscript Society's defense of the manuscripts in the commemorations in Dvůr Králové, the play must have sounded a jarring counter note, with its playful treatment of the "discoverer" as a certain falsifier. I wish I had been in the audience to feel the conflicting play of emotions in the reactions of the public. The organizers were certainly brave to be willing to subject their local pride to a bit of fun, but perhaps this was a cost they were willing to bear for the opportunity to bring such a prominent theater to the town and allow the local celebrations to briefly regain a modicum of popular attention, which they had in spades in their period of glory as the site of major nineteenth-century national commemorations.

The playful treatment of mystification in *Czech Heavens* also illustrates the greater distance from the debates on authenticity and reflects a new trend, identified by Catherine Servant, in recent literary works inspired by the manuscripts. Now Hanka and Linda are as likely to be characters as the heroes of the epic poems, and the drama is provided by the political and social debates around the manuscripts rather than the epic battles depicted in them.[4] This is the case as well with the debut novel by the now rather prominent novelist Miloš Urban published in 1998, *Poslední tečka za Rukopisy* (A final full stop after the manuscripts; the title implies something like "the last word on the manuscripts"). The novel was published under the pseudonym Josef Urban, which offered a mystifying misdirection regarding authorship given the prominence of a number of Urbans among the members of the Czech Manuscript Society.[5]

The novel itself is a parody of Miroslav Ivanov's investigative work on the manuscripts: it presents itself as a kind of nonfictional literary detective story belonging to the genre of "literatura faktu" (literature of fact, or nonfiction). As in Ivanov's work, the narrator, Josef Urban, is a persona of the author as intrepid researcher, sorting through the available evidence and controversies.[6] In this case, though, Urban is a rather misogynist narrator who plays up his vices and uses a young talented colleague and lover, Marie, who actually figures out most of the secret. But, because he hides from her one of the four letters needed to fully unravel the secret, he is able to exclude her and write a habilitation dissertation on his own, explicitly not thanking her or recognizing her contribution (although the "novel" is dedicated to her), in which he uncovers the feminist conspiracy behind the manuscripts and thus achieves his own promotion. The conspiracy (spoiler alert!) is that in the early nineteenth century, Magdalena Rettigová discovered two talented young women whom she helped to disguise themselves as men in order that they receive the education they deserved and be able to attain the status they could have only as men. They are Hannelore Vierteilová and Linda Janowitzová, who disguised themselves as Václav Hanka and Josef Linda (later, Linda assumed the identity of a young woman who passed away and became Barbora Mandlová, Hanka's wife). The conspiracy involves forging all of the cover falsifications ("Song to Vyšehrad," "Love Song of King Václav," *Mater verborum*, Gospel of St. John, and so on) around the manuscripts, which are themselves revealed in fact to be genuine but to have been doctored to sow doubts about them as well. The women also falsified the Russian and Serbian folk songs that were later uncovered as the purported sources of the lyrical songs of the Queen's Court Manuscript. Sir John Bowring was involved in this aspect, and the art restorer Horčička (a friend of Linda's) helped to make the manuscripts look more fake. The reason the falsifications became more and more obvious is that the conspirators in fact hoped it would be revealed, so their talents could be recognized (hence the later blatant "Libuše's Prophecy" forgery). Božena Němcová was brought into the conspiracy as Rettigová was dying, to continue to pass it along, but she herself died shortly thereafter.[7]

The irony here is thick, with a contemporary woman's talent and achievement being hidden as others are finally, after a long wait, revealed; though in fact, the novel reveals quite clearly Marie's contribution, so the text works both ways. And the ultimate point might be how little has changed since the difficulties of Rettigová and Němcová and their contemporaries as talented women in the Czech world. The novel manages to synthesize two prominent strains of mystification from the early nineteenth-century Czech Revival: the manuscripts and the gender-crossing publication of women's poetry by male writers. What the novel also clearly demonstrates is how good, fun fiction can be made with the convoluted controversies around the manuscripts—it is likely that *Czech Heavens* borrows the confusion about the gender of Hanka and Linda from this novel.

Rather than the "last word" on the manuscripts, this novel offers a productive new way of engaging with them creatively. And of course, there can be no "last word" on the manuscripts. There will always be new disciplines and theoretical perspectives (like translation studies and oral-formulaic theory) that open up new areas for research and create new knowledge on the manuscripts, their sources and models, poetics, and social and political significance. The time may be ripe now for another reassessment of the authorship of the manuscripts, sorting and weighing the evidence gathered over the years for Hanka's, Linda's, and Josef Jungmann's likely contributions to particular poems. We are also now in a far better position to assess the significance of the manuscripts to the Czech national movement, given the high quality and number of studies that have returned them to that context and examined both the positive and negative effects they had.

In the European context, the manuscripts offer important lessons on the distorting effect of nationalism and national movements on the cultural spheres. These movements operated with an artificially homogenizing concept of national culture as an enduring collection of shared practices, behaviors, proclivities, and values unique and specific to each nation, rather than, as any good student of culture in various fields across the social sciences and humanities today would have it, culture as a realm of debate and conflict over values, with constant innovation and borrowing of practices, values, and behaviors from others. In order to create and maintain this fiction of a national culture, nationalist entrepreneurs found it necessary both to invent new ancient traditions and to significantly alter or reinterpret those that they found. This is true of every national cultural movement. The Czechs seem to have come to agreeable terms with themselves as a nation with a penchant for mystification. They were forced, by the manuscripts, to confront the artificial aspect of their national culture long before many other cultures (even if, at the time, they would not have recognized this confrontation as such). There is much to be gained from using the manuscripts to open up other cultures to similar necessary confrontations.

Notes

Highlights and Lowlights in the Life of the Manuscripts (Chronology)

1. Pavla Machalíková, "Rukopisy královédvorský a zelenohorský a výtvarné umění v Čechách, od inovace k novému kánonu," in *Rukopisy královédvorský a zelenohorský v kultuře a umění*, ed. Dalibor Dobiáš (Prague: Academia, 2019), 2:1014–17 (hereafter "RKZ a výtvarné umění"). The painting is reproduced on 1015.

2. Susan Helen Reynolds, "A Scandal in Bohemia: Herder, Goethe, Masaryk, and the 'War of the Manuscripts,'" *Publications of the English Goethe Society* 72 (2002): 61.

3. Reynolds, 58; Marijan Šabić, "Chorvatská recepce Rukopisů královédvorského a zelenohorského," in *Rukopisy královédvorský a zelenohorský v kultuře a umění*, ed. Dalibor Dobiáš (Prague: Academia, 2019), 2:1322.

4. On the polemics, see Dalibor Dobiáš, "Mezi Rukopisem královédvorským a zelenohorským (1817–1829)," in *Rukopisy královédvorský a zelenohorský a česká věda (1817–1885)*, by Dalibor Dobiáš et al. (Prague: Academia, 2014), 44–49. Czech translations of the articles are included in the same volume, on 260–279. An English version of Dobrovský's first article can be found in David L. Cooper, ed., *The Queen's Court and Green Mountain Manuscripts with Other Forgeries of the Czech Revival*, Czech Translations, vol. 6 (Ann Arbor: Michigan Slavic Publications, 2018), 148–50 (hereafter *The Manuscripts*).

5. On this and subsequent compositions by other composers, see Vlasta Reittererová, "Zhudebnění lyrických textů Rukopisu královédvorského," in *Rukopisy královédvorský a zelenohorský v kultuře a umění*, ed. Dalibor Dobiáš (Prague: Academia, 2019), 2:875–931.

6. Chemical methods of the period were not sufficient to distinguish the entire manuscript's age. See Dalibor Dobiáš and Miroslav Novák, "Spor o roli Rukopisu královédvorského a zelenohorského v diskursu národa (1829–1840)," in *Rukopisy královédvorský a zelenohorský a česká věda (1817–1885)*, by Dalibor Dobiáš et al. (Prague: Academia, 2014), 94–96.

7. Key excerpts in Czech can be found in Dalibor Dobiáš et al., *Rukopisy královédvorský a zelenohorský a česká věda (1817–1885)*, Literární řada (Prague: Academia, 2014), 329–47. English excerpts in Cooper, *The Manuscripts*, 161–77.

8. Michal Fránek, "Ve stínu česko-německého antagonismu (Rukopisy královédvorský a zelenohorský v letech 1853–1866)," in *Rukopisy královédvorský a zelenohorský a česká věda (1817–1885)*, by Dalibor Dobiáš et al. (Prague: Academia, 2014), 156–57 (hereafter "Ve stínu antagonismu").

9. See Machalíková, "RKZ a výtvarné umění," 1025, 1042.

10. Fránek, "Ve stínu antagonismu," 160, 162–69.

11. Martin Hrdina and Kateřina Piorecká, "Věřit a vědět (Rukopisy královédvorský a zelenohorský v letech 1867–1885)," in *Rukopisy královédvorský a zelenohorský a česká věda (1817–1885)*, by Dalibor Dobiáš et al. (Prague: Academia, 2014), 220–27.

12. Hrdina and Piorecká, 227–35.

13. Michal Fránek and Jiří Kopecký, "Rukopisy královédvorský a zelenohorský a česká opera," in *Rukopisy královédvorský a zelenohorský v kultuře a umění*, ed. Dalibor Dobiáš (Prague: Academia, 2019), 2:962–75 (hereafter "RKZ a česká opera").

14. Here again, while the methods used were up-to-date and even innovative, they were not likely capable of distinguishing a genuine old manuscript from a good fake. Miroslav Novák and Dalibor Dobiáš, "Chemické a mikroskopické zkoumání rukopisu královédvorského v letech 1886–1889 a jeho reflexe tehdejší českou společností," in *Rukopisy královédvorský a zelenohorský v kultuře a umění*, ed. Dalibor Dobiáš (Prague: Academia, 2019), 1:260–61, 266–67, 279.

15. Machalíková, "RKZ a výtvarné umění," 1036–41.

16. Václav Petrbok, "'Tohle bláznivé studium jednoho zfalšovaného dokumentu': Rukopisy a čitanky středných škol v Čechách v letech 1820–1918," in *Rukopisy královédvorský a zelenohorský v kultuře a umění*, ed. Dalibor Dobiáš (Prague: Academia, 2019), 1:217–23.

17. Miroslav Ivanov, *Tajemství RKZ* (Prague: Mladá Fronta, 1969), 489–91.

18. Josef Smolík, "Zlaté mince s domnělým opisem Pegnaze," *Rozpravy České akademie věd a umění*, tř. 3, č. 35 (1906): 3–20.

19. Dalibor Dobiáš, ed., *Rukopis královédvorský; Rukopis zelenohorský*, Česká knižnice (Brno: Host, 2010), 266 (hereafter *RKZ*).

20. Milan Ducháček, "'Pravda není to, co jest, ale to, co býti má': Noetika Františka Mareše a ideové zdroje obnovení sporu o Rukopisy královédvorský a zelenohorský v době první republiky," in *Rukopisy královédvorský a zelenohorský v kultuře a umění*, ed. Dalibor Dobiáš (Prague: Academia, 2019), 1:285–88.

21. Dobiáš, *RKZ*, 268.

22. Dobiáš, 272–73; Ivanov, *Tajemství RKZ*, 566–631.

23. Fránek and Kopecký, "RKZ a česká opera," 935, 1001–5.

Introduction

1. For a more detailed analysis of the dialogues and a discussion of Jungmann's program, see David L. Cooper, *Creating the Nation: Identity and Aesthetics in Early Nineteenth-Century Russia and Bohemia* (DeKalb: Northern Illinois University Press, 2010), 73–84.

2. Unless otherwise indicated, all translations here and in subsequent chapters are mine. Josef Jungmann, *Boj o obrození národa; Výbor z díla*, Svět a my, sv. 9 (Prague: F. Kosek, 1948), 36.

3. Josef Hrabák, *Studie o českém verši*, Učebnice vysokých škol (Prague: Státní pedagogické nakl., 1959), 183–204; Ladislav Cejp, "Jungmannův překlad Ztraceného ráje," in *Překlady*, by Josef Jungmann (Prague: Státní nakl. krásné literatury, hudby a umění, 1958), 1:360–430.

4. Antonín Rybička, *Přední křisitelé národa českého: Boje a usilování o právo jazyka českého začátkem přítomného století* (Prague: Tiskem a nákl. knihtiskárny F. Šimáčka, 1883), 2:377–80.

5. Lubomír Sršeň, "Příspěvky k poznání osobnosti Václava Hanky," *Sborník Národního muzea*, řada A—Historie, 63, no. 1–3 (2009): 7.

6. G. N. Moiseeva and Miloslav Krbec, *Iozef Dobrovskii i Rossiia: Pamiatniki russkoi kul'tury XI–XVIII vekov v izuchenii cheshskogo slavista* (Leningrad: Nauka, Leningradskoe otdelenie, 1990), 212–13.

7. Julius Dolanský, *Neznámý jihoslovanský pramen Rukopisů královédvorského a zelenohorského* (Prague: Academia, 1968), 15–17 (hereafter *Neznámý pramen*).

8. Jan Máchal, "Úvod," in *Hankovy písně a Prostonárodní srbská muza, do Čech převedená*, ed. Jan Máchal, Novočeská knihovna, č. 3 (Prague: Nákl. České akademie císaře Františka Josefa pro vědy, slovesnost a uměni, 1918), xix–xx.

9. Vladimír Forst, Jiří Opelík, and Luboš Merhaut, eds., *Lexikon české literatury: Osobnosti, díla, instituce*, vyd. 1 (Prague: Academia, 1985), 2:58.

10. Dalibor Dobiáš, ed., *Rukopis královédvorský; Rukopis zelenohorský*, Česká knižnice (Brno: Host, 2010), 213–14 (hereafter *RKZ*).

11. Donald Rayfield, "Forgiving Forgery," *Modern Language Review* 107, no. 4 (October 2012): xxxi.

12. Benedict Anderson, *Imagined Communities: Reflections on the Origin and Spread of Nationalism* (London: Verso, 1991); Ernest Gellner, *Nations and Nationalism*, New Perspectives on the Past (Oxford: Blackwell, 1983); Miroslav Hroch, *Social Preconditions of National Revival in Europe: A Comparative Analysis of the Social Composition of Patriotic Groups among the Smaller European Nations* (Cambridge: Cambridge University Press, 1985); Tara Zahra, "Imagined Noncommunities: National Indifference as a Category of Analysis," *Slavic Review* 69, no. 1 (2010): 93–119; Cooper, *Creating the Nation*.

13. Dalibor Dobiáš, "Pevnost na troskách dávné zbořeniny: K dvěma staletím recepce Rukopisů královédvorského a zelenohorského," in *Rukopisy královédvorský a zelenohorský v kultuře a umění*, ed. Dalibor Dobiáš (Prague: Academia, 2019), 1:19, 25.

14. Milan Otáhal's extensive survey of the manuscripts controversy can be seen as a late, representative example of such an attempt to explain away the manuscripts. While offering a detailed overview, it is marred by its moralistic perspective and by a number of outright errors. Milan Otáhal, "The Manuscript Controversy in the Czech National Revival," *Cross Currents* 5 (1986): 247–77.

15. Dalibor Dobiáš et al., *Rukopisy královédvorský a zelenohorský a česká věda (1817–1885)*, Literární řada (Prague: Academia, 2014), 598–99, 590–93 (hereafter *RKZ a česká věda*).

16. The manuscript is often referred to by the abbreviation RK. I follow the translation of the name into English by its second English translator, Albert Henry Wratislaw, which has gained some currency, even if one often does not translate the names of towns (though here in adjectival form) and even though "The Manuscript of Queen's Estate" might be a more accurate rendering. See Zdeněk Beran, "RKZ anglicky—Víc než jen překlad," review of *The Queen's Court and Green Mountain Manuscripts*," ed. and trans. David L. Cooper, *Česká literatura* 68, no. 1 (2020): 94.

17. Jaroslav Kašpar, "Rukopis královédvorský a zelenohorský—Paleografický přepis," in *Rukopisy královédvorský a zelenohorský: Dnešní stav poznání*, ed. Mojmír Otruba, Sborník Národního muzea v Praze, řada C—Literární historie, sv. 13–14 (Prague: Academia, 1969), 275.

18. Václav Nebeský, "Kralodvorský Rukopis," *Časopis českého musea* 26, no. 3 (1852): 149.

19. Václav Hanka, "Připomenutj," in *Rukopis Králodworský: Sebránj lyricko-epických národnjch zpěwů, wěrně w půwodnjm starém gazyku, též w obnoweném pro snadněgšj wyrozuměnj s připogenjm německého přeloženj* (Prague: Bohumila Haze a Joz. Krause, 1819), iii. English translation in David L. Cooper, ed., *The Queen's Court and Green Mountain Manuscripts with Other Forgeries of the Czech Revival*, Czech Translations, vol. 6 (Ann Arbor: Michigan Slavic Publications, 2018), 142–44 (hereafter *The Manuscripts*).

20. This manuscript is often abbreviated as RZ; together the two main manuscripts are often abbreviated RKZ. Czechs also often refer to them simply as the Rukopisy. My use of "manuscripts" should be read as referring primarily to the two main manuscripts, sometimes by extension to include the "Song to Vyšehrad."

21. Kašpar, "Paleografický přepis," 315.

22. Cooper, *The Manuscripts*, 149.

23. Today the manuscript is part of the museum's collections.

24. Dobiáš et al., *RKZ a česká věda*, 593.

25. Dobiáš, "Pevnost na troskách," 37n57. Pavla Machalíková, "Rukopisy královédvorský a zelenohorský a výtvarné umění v Čechách, od inovace k novému kánonu," in *Rukopisy královédvorský a zelenohorský v kultuře a umění*, ed. Dalibor Dobiáš (Prague: Academia, 2019), 2:1014–17 (hereafter "RKZ a výtvarné umění"). The painting is reproduced on 1015.

26. Josef Hanuš, "Český Macpherson: Příspěvek k rozboru literární činnosti Josefa Lindy a k provenienci RK a RZ," *Listy filologické* 27, no. 2 (1900): 109–34; nos. 3–4, 241–91; no. 5, 337–56; no. 6, 437–57. Ivanov showed that precisely Hanka had the necessary sources to compose the epic "Oldřich and Boleslav." Miroslav Ivanov, *Tajemství RKZ* (Prague: Mladá Fronta, 1969), 409–11. Dolanský argued that the epics closer to South Slavic models were more likely largely Hanka's work, while the more Ossianic epics, "Čestmír and Vlaslav" and "Záboj, Slavoj, and Luděk," and the ballad "The Stag" bore Linda's authorial stamp. Dolanský, *Neznámý pramen*, 204–9.

27. Karel Krejčí, "Některé nedořešené otázky kolem RKZ," in *Literatury a žánry v evropské dimenzi: Nejen česká literatura v zorném poli komparistiky* (Prague: Slovanský ústav AV ČR, 2014), 444 (the article was first published in 1974). Ivanov, *Tajemství RKZ*, 203–7. Mojmír Otruba, "Rukopisy královédvorský a zelenohorský," in *Lexikon české literatury: Osobnosti, díla, instituce*, ed. Jiří Opelík (Prague: Academia, 2000), 3:1331.

28. Just a few months earlier, in his introduction to the first edition of the Queen's Court Manuscript, Hanka had foreseen such a discovery: "Did not King *Václav*, the father of Otokar († 1253), himself sing? in Czech?—and perhaps some of his songs the Germans have translated for themselves, desiring to preserve them in that way." Hanka, "Připomenutj," iv. Cooper, *The Manuscripts*, 143.

29. Dobiáš et al., *RKZ a česká věda*, 601–3.

30. Dobiáš et al., 603–6.

31. Dobiáš et al., 607.

32. Dobiáš et al., 607–11.

33. The words are Hanka's from his text accompanying the publication. Cooper, *The Manuscripts*, 191. It is hard not to read some symbolism into the name of the manuscript where the parchment was found. The discovery of old parchments with epic poetry in the binding of newer books is not at all implausible, as the headlines a couple of months after this introduction was drafted reminded us. As Alison Flood wrote in

the *Guardian*, "Dr. Tamar Atkin from Queen Mary University of London was researching the use of books during the 16th century when she came across the fragment from the hitherto lost Siège d'Orange in the binding of a book published in 1528. Parchment and paper were expensive at the time, and unwanted manuscripts and books were frequently recycled." Alison Flood, "Fragment of Lost 12th-Century Epic Poem Found in Another Book's Binding," *Guardian*, November 18, 2021, sec. Books, https://www.theguardian.com/books/2021/nov/18/fragment-of-lost-12th-century-epic-poem-found-in-another-books-binding.

34. Dobiáš et al., *RKZ a česká věda*, 611–13.

35. Vladimír Macura, *Znamení zrodu: České obrození jako kulturní typ*, Nové, rozšířené vydání (Prague: H & H, 1995), 114.

36. Karel Titz, "Studie o RK," *Listy filologické* 62, no. 2–3 (1935): 127n2. Palkovič recalled the incident in his 1832 article on the Green Mountain Manuscript. Rožnay claimed he had been allowed to copy the beginning of the poem out of a book he had seen at someone's home in Prešpurk (Bratislava), but he was not allowed to say who the owner was. Palkovič quickly added the information to his lectures, but he later removed it when he grew suspicious. Rožnay admitted the ruse when he returned from his studies in Tübingen to take up a position as a preacher. Jiří Palkovič, "Libušin soud," *Tatranka* 1, no. 1 (1832): 68–69.

37. Iva Krejčová, "O pramennou hodnotu Rukopisů královédvorského a zelenohorského (1840–1853)," in *Rukopisy královédvorský a zelenohorský a česká věda (1817–1885)*, by Dalibor Dobiáš et al. (Prague: Academia, 2014), 102–110.

38. See Michal Charypar, "Motiv, syžet, poetika: Písně Rukopisu královédvorského a jejich vliv na novočeskou poezii do příchodu Májovců," in *Rukopisy královédvorský a zelenohorský v kultuře a umění*, ed. Dalibor Dobiáš (Prague: Academia, 2019), 1:446–49; John Neubauer, "Introduction: Folklore and National Awakening," in *The Making and Remaking of Literary Institutions*, vol. 3 of *History of the Literary Cultures of East-Central Europe, Junctures and Disjunctures in the 19th and 20th Centuries*, ed. Marcel Cornis-Pope and John Neubauer (Philadelphia: John Benjamins, 2007), 269–85. Charypar, in "Motiv, syžet, poetika," notes that the sexual and scatological Czech folkloric material is finally in the process of publication (449n9).

39. Macura, *Znamení zrodu*, 113. Again, as the headlines reminded a couple of months after this introduction was drafted, multiple male authors hiding behind a female pseudonym is still a productive form of mystification. This time it was the million-euro Spanish literature Planeta Prize being awarded to top crime fiction author Carmen Mola that brought the three male authors out from behind their pseudonym to collect their prize. Nicholas Casey, "Behind a Top Female Name in Spanish Crime Fiction: Three Men," *New York Times*, October 29, 2021, sec. World, https://www.nytimes.com/2021/10/29/world/europe/spanish-writer-carmen-mola-true-identity.html.

40. Macura, *Znamení zrodu*, 111–12, 115. One of the admiring poets was Josef Krasoslav Chmelenský, another friend of Čelakovský's, who wrote her some admiring verses and then joined the game by replying with a sonnet on her behalf. Forst, Opelík, and Merhaut, *Lexikon české literatury*, 2:411.

41. John Bowring, *Cheskian Anthology: Being a History of the Poetical Literature of Bohemia, with Translated Specimens* (London: R. Hunter, 1832).

42. Macura, *Znamení zrodu*, 112. For example, Čelakovský included some of the folk song imitations of his friend Josef Vlastimil Kamarýt. Forst, Opelík, and Merhaut, *Lexikon české literatury*, 2:639.

43. Bowring, *Cheskian Anthology*, 253.

44. Macura, *Znamení zrodu*, 112.

45. Macura, 112–13.

46. First called the Wallersteinsche Judenchronik. For full details, see Iveta Cermanová, "Ramschakova kronika—Židovské falzum z doby Rukopisů," in *Rukopisy královédvorský a zelenohorský v kultuře a umění*, ed. Dalibor Dobiáš (Prague: Academia, 2019), 2:1127–52.

47. Dobiáš, "Pevnost na troskách," 43. Beyond Czech-language scholarship, the manuscripts are also finding their place in discussions elsewhere of nineteenth-century practices of forgery and mystification. See János M. Bak, Patrick J. Geary, and Gábor Klaniczay, eds., *Manufacturing a Past for the Present: Forgery and Authenticity in Medievalist Texts and Objects in Nineteenth-Century Europe*, National Cultivation of Culture, vol. 7 (Leiden: Brill, 2015).

48. Gábor Klaniczay, "The Myth of Scythian Origin and the Cult of Attila in the Nineteenth Century," in *Multiple Antiquities—Multiple Modernities: Ancient Histories in Nineteenth Century European Cultures*, ed. Gábor Klaniczay, Michael Werner, and Ottó Gecser (Frankfurt: Campus Verlag, 2011), 203.

49. Julia Abramson, *Learning from Lying: Paradoxes of the Literary Mystification* (Newark: University of Delaware Press, 2005).

50. Dobiáš, "Pevnost na troskách," 13. To be sure, both are later works, and Mácha was not really enshrined as the national poet until the second half of the century, but both are also much more reader-friendly works. For a full listing of the publications of the manuscripts, see Dobiáš et al., *RKZ a česká věda*, 590–94.

51. Dobiáš, "Pevnost na troskách," 30. On the history of their incorporation into school readers, see Václav Petrbok, "'Tohle bláznivé studium jednoho zfalšovaného dokumentu': Rukopisy a čitanky středných škol v Čechách v letech 1820–1918," in *Rukopisy královédvorský a zelenohorský v kultuře a umění*, ed. Dalibor Dobiáš (Prague: Academia, 2019), 1:183–238. A table with their school reader publication information can be found on 229–38.

52. Dobiáš, "Pevnost na troskách," 30.

53. Mojmír Otruba, "Poezie, mýtus a hodnota (Konkretizace a estetické hodnocení Rukopisu královédvorského)," *Česká literatura* 16, no. 4 (1968): 357–92.

54. Alan Dundes, introduction to *Sacred Narrative: Readings in the Theory of Myth*, ed. Alan Dundes (Berkeley: University of California Press, 1984), 1.

55. Joseph Georg Meinert, "Über die Königinhofer Handschrift," *Archiv für Geographie, Historie, Staats- und Kriegskunst* 10, no. 1 (1819): 2. Translation in Cooper, *The Manuscripts*, 145–47.

56. Joep Leerssen, "Ossian and the Rise of Literary Historicism," in *The Reception of Ossian in Europe*, ed. Howard Gaskill (London: Thoemmes, 2004), 109–25. Note that Meinert was the student of, and immediate successor to as professor of aesthetics at Prague University, August Gottlieb Meissner, one of the most important propagators of Ossianism in the Czech lands. Tomáš Hlobil, "Ossianism in the Bohemian Lands," *Modern Language Review* 101 (2006): 789–97.

57. Leerssen, "Ossian and Literary Historicism," 124.

58. William Bascom defines myth, as opposed to the other prose forms of folklore—legend and folktale—by its time setting and by the belief in the truthfulness of the tale (by its tellers and audience). William Bascom, "The Forms of Folklore: Prose Narratives," in *Sacred Narrative: Readings in the Theory of Myth*, ed. Alan Dundes (Berkeley: University of California Press, 1984), 5–29.

59. Otruba, "Poezie, mýtus a hodnota."

60. On the composition of songs based on the manuscripts, see Vlasta Reittererová, "Zhudebnění lyrických textů Rukopisu královédvorského," in *Rukopisy královédvorský a zelenohorský v kultuře a umění*, ed. Dalibor Dobiáš (Prague: Academia, 2019), 2:875–931.

61. Macura, *Znamení zrodu*, appendix of illustrations, nos. 18 and 19.

62. On the visual arts, see Machalíková, "RKZ a výtvarné umění." On opera, see Michal Fránek and Jiří Kopecký, "Rukopisy královédvorský a zelenohorský a česká opera," in *Rukopisy královédvorský a zelenohorský v kultuře a umění*, ed. Dalibor Dobiáš (Prague: Academia, 2019), 2:933–1006.

63. Jan Hájek and Milan Hlavačka note 1848 as the key year in the shift to the third phase of the national movement. Jan Hájek and Milan Hlavačka, "The Birth of the Modern Czech Nation (1792–1848)," in *A History of the Czech Lands*, by Jaroslav Pánek and Oldřich Tůma, 2nd ed. (Prague: Karolinum Press, 2018), 328.

64. Otruba, "Poezie, mýtus a hodnota," 380, 383.

65. Otruba, 381–87.

66. Milan Hlavačka, "Czechs during the Revolution and Neo-Absolutism (1848–1860)," in *A History of the Czech Lands*, by Jaroslav Pánek and Oldřich Tůma, 2nd ed. (Prague: Karolinum Press, 2018), 345–62.

67. Pavel Cibulka, Jan Hájek, and Martin Kučera, "The Definition of Czech National Society during the Period of Liberalism and Nationalism (1860–1914)," in *A History of the Czech Lands*, by Jaroslav Pánek and Oldřich Tůma, 2nd ed. (Prague: Karolinum Press, 2018), 365, 372.

68. Hájek and Hlavačka, "Modern Czech Nation," 339–40.

69. Cibulka, Hájek, and Kučera, "Czech National Society," 371–73.

70. Cibulka, Hájek, and Kučera, 374.

71. Otruba, "Poezie, mýtus a hodnota," 386–87.

72. Jan Herben, *Deset let proti proudu, 1886–1896: Zpomínky a zkušenosti českého novináře* ([Prague]: Nákl. vlastním, 1898), 88.

73. Jan Herben, *Boj o podvržené rukopisy: Zpomínky po 25ti letech*, Knihovnička "Času," č. 58 (Prague: Pokrok, 1911), 25.

74. Again, the closest analogue may be with the Ossianic poetry and the roles it played for Gaelic-speaking Scots, who never doubted the authenticity of the material and for whom belief in the authenticity took on a spiritual aspect. "Spirituality was . . . as closely connected to the defense of *Ossian* as it was to the creation of the myth; creativity and affirmation went together. For many, indeed, *Ossian* was primarily a question of personal belief that seems to have transcended, or ignored, hard evidence. People believed in *Ossian* as if they were dealing with biblical texts, and [Presbyterian] ministers led and nurtured that belief." But this Ossianic myth did not result in the kind of confrontation we find in the late nineteenth century in the Czech lands, even if sharper questions about the authenticity of the poetry began to be posed around 1870 by Scottish scholars. Donald E. Meek, "The Sublime Gael: The Impact of

Macpherson's *Ossian* on Literary Creativity and Cultural Perception in Gaelic Scotland," in *The Reception of Ossian in Europe*, ed. Howard Gaskill (London: Thoemmes, 2004), 52, 42.

75. Dobiáš, *RKZ*.

76. Dobiáš et al., *RKZ a česká věda*.

77. Antonín Vašek, *Filologický důkaz, že Rukopis Kralodvorský a Zelenohorský, též zlomek Evangelia sv. Jana jsou podvržená díla Vácslava Hanky* (Brno: Nákladem spisovatelovým, 1879), iii. English translation in Cooper, *The Manuscripts*, 178.

78. Dalibor Dobiáš, ed., *Rukopisy královédvorský a zelenohorský v kultuře a umění*, 2 vols. (Prague: Academia, 2019).

79. Mojmír Otruba, ed., *Rukopisy královédvorský a zelenohorský: Dnešní stav poznání*, Sborník Národního muzea v Praze, řada C—Literární historie, sv. 13–14 (Prague: Academia, 1969).

80. Julius Enders, *Rukopis Zelenohorský a Královédvorský: Vznik, styl a básnická hodnota staročeské orální poesie* (Prague: Neklan, 1993).

81. The members of the Czech Manuscript Society, which defends the authenticity of the manuscripts or at least attempts to keep the controversy over their authenticity alive, concluded their volume released for the recent two hundredth anniversary of the discovery of the Queen's Court Manuscript with a desire that someone would pay more serious attention to Enders's findings. I do, but they will not be happy with my conclusions. Karel Nesměrák et al., *RKZ dodnes nepoznané* (Prague: Česká společnost rukopisná, 2017), 149.

1. Forgery as a Romantic Form of Authorship

1. See the overview of the reception of the manuscripts in the edition by Dalibor Dobiáš. Dalibor Dobiáš, ed., *Rukopis královédvorský; Rukopis zelenohorský*, Česká knižnice (Brno: Host, 2010), esp. 263, 267 (hereafter *RKZ*).

2. The renewal of interest in Macpherson followed the work of Fiona J. Stafford and Howard Gaskill. Nick Groom led the way in the reevaluation of Chatterton. Fiona J. Stafford, *The Sublime Savage: A Study of James Macpherson and the Poems of Ossian* (Edinburgh: Edinburgh University Press, 1988); Howard Gaskill, "'Ossian' Macpherson: Towards a Rehabilitation," *Comparative Criticism* 8 (1986): 113–46; Howard Gaskill, *Ossian Revisited* (Edinburgh: Edinburgh University Press, 1991); Fiona J. Stafford and Howard Gaskill, *From Gaelic to Romantic: Ossianic Translations*, Textxet: Studies in Comparative Literature, vol. 15 (Amsterdam: Rodopi, 1998); Howard Gaskill, *The Reception of Ossian in Europe*, The Athlone Critical Traditions Series: The Reception of British Authors in Europe (London: Thoemmes, 2004); Nick Groom, "Thomas Chatterton Was a Forger," *Yearbook of English Studies* 28 (1998): 276–91; Nick Groom, *Thomas Chatterton and Romantic Culture* (New York: St. Martin's Press, 1999).

3. On Hanka's marginalization in the context of the history of Czech romanticism, see Dalibor Tureček, "Časopis 'Deutsches Museum' Friedricha Schlegela a česká obrozenská literatura," in *Mezi texty a metodami: Národní a univerzální v české literatuře 19. století*, ed. Dalibor Tureček and Zuzana Urválková (Olomouc: Perliplum, 2006), 125–27. There are exceptions, such as Felix Vodička's work on Linda's 1818 novel *Záře nad pohanstvem* (Dawn over paganism, 1948), which treats its important place in the working out of a modern Czech prose idiom. But Linda's innovations in prose are not

treated in relation to his part in the influential poetry of the manuscripts, so that legitimate authorial innovation and forgery are kept separate. Jaromír Loužil's compelling reading of the confrontation of the Christian and pagan worlds in Linda's novel (1978) makes the novel a kind of atonement on Linda's part for the sin of participating in the forgeries. Here genuine authorial creativity is motivated by guilt for illicit authorial activity, which at least maintains a relationship between the two spheres. Felix Vodička, *Počátky krásné prózy novočeské: Příspěvek k literárním dějinám doby Jungmannovy* (Prague: Melantrich, 1948); Jaromír Loužil, "Bernard Bolzano a Rukopisy: Josef Linda," *Česká literatura* 26, no. 3 (1978): 220–34.

4. Dobiáš, *RKZ*, 190, 264–65.

5. There remains as well, of course, the problem that the participation of the putative authors, aside from Hanka, remains more or less uncertain.

6. William K. Wimsatt and Monroe C. Beardsley, *The Verbal Icon: Studies in the Meaning of Poetry* (Lexington: University of Kentucky Press, 1989), 3–18.

7. Nick Groom, *The Forger's Shadow: How Forgery Changed the Course of Literature* (London: Picador, 2002), 61.

8. Scott Carpenter, *Aesthetics of Fraudulence in Nineteenth-Century France: Frauds, Hoaxes, and Counterfeits* (Farnham, England: Ashgate, 2009), 5.

9. There is no agreement on terms in the literature, and scholars deploy or advocate for terms that depend on their own emphases or the particular cases they analyze. K. K. Ruthven inclines somewhat idiosyncratically toward *the spurious* as a general term, but ultimately suggests that there is no way through the chaos of both synchronic and diachronic diversity in usage to a satisfactory general term (K. K. Ruthven, *Faking Literature* [Cambridge: Cambridge University Press, 2001], 34–39). In a recent article, Groom uses *fakelit* as a general term, under which he distinguishes between *counterfeit*, *forgery*, *plagiarism*, and *hoax* (Nick Groom, "Romanticism and Forgery," *Literature Compass* 4, no. 6 [2007]: 1633–36). *Mystification*, which seems to have become the general term of choice among Russian and Czech scholars, has not found much of a place in the English-language discussions, with the notable exception of Abramson, who analyzes French practices (Julia Abramson, *Learning from Lying: Paradoxes of the Literary Mystification* [Newark: University of Delaware Press, 2005]). One of the appeals of *forgery* is the double sense of the term in English, pointing at the same time to falsification and to making (that is, *poesis*) and thus the culture-creative aspect of certain falsifications.

10. A. A. Zalizniak, *"Slovo o polku Igoreve": Vzgliad lingvista*, Studia philologica, malaia seriia (Moscow: Iazyki slavianskoi kul'tury, 2004), 12, 30. Zalizniak analyzes the strategies of both of these skeptics. Keenan, even as he absolves Josef Dobrovský of the guilt of forging *Slovo*, appeals to his mental illness as a part of the complex of causes for his complicity: "What Dobrovský did do, seen in context, was to write a few harmless passages in imitation of the *Zadonshchina* and other texts that he had recently read, and in the style of other early Slavic heroic narratives that he knew well. . . . Given the manner in which the text seems to have evolved, and taking into account the agency of Malinovskii and perhaps others, it is entirely possible that the text we have represents no single intent of Dobrovský's, but is the product of a series of separate acts, some of them irrational, not all of them his, over which he ultimately had little control." Edward J. Keenan, *Josef Dobrovský and the Origins of the Igor' Tale*, Harvard Series in Ukrainian Studies (Cambridge, MA: Harvard Ukrainian Research Institute and the

Davis Center for Russian and Eurasian Studies, 2003; distributed by Harvard University Press), 424–25.

11. Susan Stewart, *Crimes of Writing: Problems in the Containment of Representation* (New York: Oxford University Press, 1991), 31.

12. Stewart, 41.

13. Stewart, 37.

14. Psalmanazar had already had a career as an impostor, traveling on fake passports since age sixteen and presenting himself in Germany and the Netherlands as a Japanese pagan. There Innes detected his hoax and threatened him with exposure in order to secure his cooperation in a staged baptism designed to impress the bishop of London. The two conspirators traveled to London together in 1703, and Psalmanazar successfully won over the public there. He published his forged history of Formosa the following year, at the age of twenty. Stewart, 33–34.

15. Groom, "Romanticism and Forgery," 1642.

16. Fiona J. Stafford, "Introduction: The Ossianic Poems of James Macpherson," in *The Poems of Ossian and Related Works*, by James Macpherson, ed. Howard Gaskill (Edinburgh: Edinburgh University Press, 1996), xii–xiv.

17. The internal evidence of the poems, with their celebration of the Šternberk and Lobkovic houses, does suggest at least some attempt to appeal to those noble families that were playing an important role in the National Revival.

18. Joep Leerssen, "Ossian and the Rise of Literary Historicism," in *The Reception of Ossian in Europe*, ed. Howard Gaskill (London: Thoemmes, 2004), 124. See discussion in the introduction, under "The Significance of the Manuscripts." Iva Krejčová provides a more detailed exploration of the significance of the epic genre in the period and how that discourse shaped the reception of the manuscripts. Iva Krejčová, "Mezi hrdinstvím a heroikomikou: Tematizace Rukopisů královédvorského a zelenohorského v česky psané básnické epice první poloviny 19. století," in *Rukopisy královédvorský a zelenohorský v kultuře a umění*, ed. Dalibor Dobiáš (Prague: Academia, 2019), 1:403–8.

19. The demands on Macpherson derived from similar reasoning, that there must have been a Scottish epic, at an early stage in the development of this historical conception. Ruthven, *Faking Literature*, 9. Leerssen shows how effective Macpherson's production of this epic material was in the consolidation of this understanding of European literary traditions. Leerssen, "Literary Historicism."

20. František Palacký, "An- und aussichten der böhmischen Sprache und Literatur vor 50 Jahren," in *Gedenkblätter: Auswahl von Denkschriften, Aufsätzen und Briefen aus den letzten fünfzig Jahren* (Prague: Verlag von F. Tempsky, 1874), 23–24. "Auch den Čechen erzählte ihre Geschichte von alten Helden- und Minnegesängen: aber die Zeit schien uns davon nichts aufbewahrt zu haben; den die gereimten Legenden . . . die Romane des vierzehnten Jahrhunderts, hatten keine nationale Bedeutung. . . . Schon glaubte man alles unwiederbringlich verloren, als dem Herrn Hanka das Glück zu Theil ward . . . , zu Königinhof in Böhmen Ueberbleibsel eines schönen böhmischen Codex zu entdecken. . . . Nur sechs grössere Heldengesänge, und acht kleinere köstliche Lieder vergönnte uns das Schicksal: doch lasset uns auch dafür dem Genius der Čechen dankbar sein!" The editor, Jernej Kopitar, declined to print the article, citing the problems likely to ensue from its politically questionable stance.

21. Ruthven also draws the analogy between Indo-European linguistics' efforts to reconstruct the origins of language and the drive toward origin that motivated so many forgeries, in a chapter titled "Fantasies of Originality." He notes, in a passage worth quoting, that the problem with the quest was its projection of a unitary language as source: "A desire for 'the' origin is symptomatic of a monism that seeks to subordinate diversities to a prior singularity from which they are deemed to have derived. A famous example is that Indo-European *Ursprache* which nineteenth-century philologists tried to reconstruct in response to Sir William Jones' conjecture in 1786 that Sanskrit, Greek and Latin had evolved from a no longer existent common source. What questers find when they reach the limits of their enquiries, however, is never a singularity. Instead, it is one of those hybridities or creolisations that lead Jean-Loup Amselle to argue in his *Mestizo Logics* (1990) 'that mixture is originary.'" Ruthven, *Faking Literature*, 132.

22. Vatroslav Jagić is credited with debunking the myth of Old Czech epic. Vatroslav Jagić, "Gradja za slovinsku narodnu poeziju," *Rad JAZU* 37 (1876): 33–137. See Jaroslav Vlček, *Dějiny české literatury*, Dějiny literatur (Prague: Státní nakl. krásné literatury, hudby a umění, 1960); and Dobiáš, *RKZ*, 247. Roman Jakobson, on the other hand, demonstrated the existence of remnants of Common Slavic epic verse forms in Czech oral poetry. Roman Jakobson, "Slavic Epic Verse: Studies in Comparative Metrics," in *Selected Writings* (The Hague: Mouton, 1966), 4:414–63.

23. Roman Jakobson, "In Memory of V. V. Hanka," in *Language in Literature*, ed. Krystyna Pomorska and Stephen Rudy (Cambridge, MA: Belknap Press of Harvard University Press, 1987), 401. The original article, in Russian, was published as "Pamiati V. V. Ganki," *Tsentral'naia Evropa* 4 (1931).

24. Andrew Taylor discusses the marginality of the Roland manuscript and the problematic way it has been taken as representative of French national tradition. Andrew Taylor, *Textual Situations: Three Medieval Manuscripts and Their Readers*, Material Texts (Philadelphia: University of Pennsylvania Press, 2002), chap. 2.

25. David L. Cooper, "Competing Languages of Czech Nation-Building: Jan Kollár and the Melodiousness of Czech," *Slavic Review* 67, no. 2 (2008): 301–20.

26. Vladimír Macura, *Znamení zrodu: České obrození jako kulturní typ*, Nové, rozšířené vydání (Prague: H & H, 1995), 133–38; Rado L. Lencek, "Kopitar's Slavic Version of the Greek Dialects Theme," in *Zbirnyk na poshanu profesora doktora Iuriia Shevel'ova = Symbolae in honorem Georgii Y. Shevelov*, ed. William E. Harkins, Olexa Horbatsch, and Jakob P. Hursky (Munich: Logos, 1971), 244–56.

27. Martin Procházka, "Obrozený Ossian: Macphersonův model a produkce dějinnosti v české romantické kultuře," *Česká literatura* 41, no. 1 (1993): 25–47; Tureček, "Časopis"; Iva Krejčová, "Rukopis královédvorský a ohlas písně o nibelunzích," *Česká literatura* 58, no. 4 (2010): 425–43.

28. Homer, *The Odyssey of Homer*, trans. Richmond Lattimore, Perennial Classics (New York: Perennial, 1999), 11.363–69.

29. Laura M. Slatkin, "Composition by Theme and the *Mētis* of the *Odyssey*," in *Reading the Odyssey: Selected Interpretive Essays*, ed. Seth L. Schein (Princeton, NJ: Princeton University Press, 1996), 230.

30. Slatkin, 230–33.

31. Ruthven, *Faking Literature*, 63–73.

32. Groom, *The Forger's Shadow*, 2.

33. Ruthven, *Faking Literature*, 121.

34. Margaret Russett, *Fictions and Fakes: Forging Romantic Authenticity, 1760–1845*, Cambridge Studies in Romanticism (Cambridge: Cambridge University Press, 2006), 61–62.

35. Ruthven, *Faking Literature*, 121–45.

36. Russett, *Fictions and Fakes*, 5.

37. Melissa Frazier, *Romantic Encounters: Writers, Readers, and the "Library for Reading"* (Stanford, CA: Stanford University Press, 2007), 48.

38. Frazier, 5–6.

39. Macura, *Znamení zrodu*; Vladimír Macura, "Rukopisy aneb O mystifi kování českém," in *Češi a němci: Dějiny, kultura, politika*, ed. Walter Koschmal, Marek Nekula, and Joachim Rogall (Prague: Paseka, 2001), 409–14.

40. I argue this position in David L. Cooper, *Creating the Nation: Identity and Aesthetics in Early Nineteenth-Century Russia and Bohemia* (DeKalb: Northern Illinois University Press, 2010), 255–56.

41. Ruthven, *Faking Literature*, 86.

42. Nicholas Hudson, "'Oral Tradition': The Evolution of an Eighteenth-Century Concept," in *Tradition in Transition: Women Writers, Marginal Texts, and the Eighteenth-Century Canon*, ed. Alvaro S. J. Ribeiro and James G. Basker (Oxford: Clarendon Press, 1996), 161–76.

43. James Macpherson, "A Dissertation concerning the Antiquity, &c. of the Poems of Ossian the Son of Fingal," in *The Poems of Ossian and Related Works*, by James Macpherson, ed. Howard Gaskill (Edinburgh: Edinburgh University Press, 1996), 48–50; James Mulholland, "James Macpherson's Ossian Poems, Oral Traditions, and the Invention of Voice," *Oral Tradition* 24, no. 2 (2009): 393–414. The end of the "Songs of Selma" offers a pathos-ridden example of Ossian's projection of his voice into future times: "Roll on, ye dark-brown years, for ye bring no joy on your course. Let the tomb open to Ossian, for his strength has failed. The sons of song are gone to rest: my voice remains, like a blast, that roars, lonely, on a sea-surrounded rock, after the winds are laid. The dark moss whistles there, and the distant mariner sees the waving trees." James Macpherson, *The Poems of Ossian and Related Works*, ed. Howard Gaskill (Edinburgh: Edinburgh University Press, 1996), 170.

44. Martin Procházka noted the difference in methods of historical mediation, from the Ossianic poems' reliance on voice to the Czech manuscripts' material documents, which results in a "problematic relationship of writing and voice" in the Czech poems. Procházka, "Obrozený Ossian," 38–39.

45. Dobiáš, *RKZ*, 278. See the analysis in chapter 2.

46. Hanka, in his introduction to the first edition of the Queen's Court Manuscript, raises the question of authorship and asks if Záviš z Falkněstejna (executed in 1290) might not have written the poems. Václav Hanka, "Připomenutj," in *Rukopis Králodworský: Sebránj lyricko-epických národnjch zpěwů, wěrně w půwodnjm starém gazyku, též w obnoweném pro snadněgšj wyrozuměnj s připogenjm německého přeloženj* (Prague: Bohumila Haze a Joz. Krause, 1819), ii–iii; English translation in David L. Cooper, ed., *The Queen's Court and Green Mountain Manuscripts with Other Forgeries of the Czech Revival*, Czech Translations, vol. 6 (Ann Arbor: Michigan Slavic Publications, 2018), 143. The period concept of the *Heldenlied* (heroic song) did not preclude the existence of a sin-

gle author (Edward R. Haymes, "The Germanic *Heldenlied* and the Poetic *Edda*: Speculations on Preliterary History," *Oral Tradition* 19, no. 1 [2004]: 43–62). But by midcentury, when the first real questions were raised about the Queen's Court Manuscript, study of folk songs had advanced, including the role of the oral tradition in shaping the songs. I am suggesting here that the manuscripts themselves project a different authority than one embodied in a single author.

47. In the use of storm similes for battle, the manuscripts most resemble that strange Old East Slavic "epic" *Slovo o polku Igoreve*, which, as Boris Gasparov has shown, incorporates epic material into a narrative that functions on the level of myth. B. Gasparov, *Poetika "Slova o polku Igoreve"* (Moscow: Agraf, 2000).

48. Dobiáš, *RKZ*, 241; Vlček, *Dějiny české literatury*, 483.

49. Vlček, *Dějiny české literatury*, 485.

50. For example, a stricter notion of authenticity already was becoming visible in the 1830s. Dalibor Dobiáš and Miroslav Novák, "Spor o roli Rukopisu královédvorského a zelenohorského v diskursu národa (1829–1840)," in *Rukopisy královédvorský a zelenohorský a česká věda (1817–1885)*, by Dalibor Dobiáš et al. (Prague: Academia, 2014), 87.

51. Vlček, *Dějiny české literatury*, 481.

52. Dobiáš, *RKZ*, 228.

53. Groom, "Romanticism and Forgery," 1627–28; Howard Gaskill, "Introduction: 'Genuine Poetry . . . like Gold,'" in *The Reception of Ossian in Europe*, ed. Howard Gaskill (London: Thoemmes, 2004), 1–3, 9–10.

54. Dafydd Moore, "The Reception of *The Poems of Ossian* in England and Scotland," in *The Reception of Ossian in Europe*, ed. Howard Gaskill (London: Thoemmes, 2004), 29.

55. Donald E. Meek, "The Sublime Gael: The Impact of Macpherson's *Ossian* on Literary Creativity and Cultural Perception in Gaelic Scotland," in *The Reception of Ossian in Europe*, ed. Howard Gaskill (London: Thoemmes, 2004), 42.

2. Successful Forgeries

1. Julius Dolanský, *Neznámý jihoslovanský pramen Rukopisů královédvorského a zelenohorského* (Prague: Academia, 1968), 15–17 (hereafter *Neznámý pramen*).

2. Jan Máchal, "Úvod," in *Hankovy písně a Prostonárodní srbská muza, do Čech převedená*, ed. Jan Máchal, Novočeská knihovna, č. 3 (Prague: Nákl. České akademie císaře Františka Josefa pro vědy, slovesnost a uměni, 1918), xix–xx. See David L. Cooper, *Creating the Nation: Identity and Aesthetics in Early Nineteenth-Century Russia and Bohemia* (DeKalb: Northern Illinois University Press, 2010), 96–97, for a full translation of the short article and analysis.

3. Vuk Stefanović Karadžić, *Songs of the Serbian People: From the Collections of Vuk Karadžić*, ed. Milne Holton and Vasa D. Mihailovich, Pitt Series in Russian and East European Studies (Pittsburgh: University of Pittsburgh Press, 1997), 4.

4. Dolanský, *Neznámý pramen*, 22–23. The small volume also included two Russian songs.

5. These ranged from 40 to 201 lines in length in Hanka's translation. See Dalibor Tureček, "Hankova verze jihoslovanské hrdinské epiky," *Bohemica litteraria* 18, no. 1 (2015): 40–55, on how Hanka's translation represented Serbian song. On Hanka's

translation methods, see David L. Cooper, "Autor-překladatel-padělatel: Translace a mystifikace v Hankově Prostonárodní srbské múze a Puškinových Písních západních Slovanů," in *Historické fikce a mystifikace v české kultuře 19. století: Sborník příspěvků z 33. ročníku symposia k problematice 19. století, Plzeň, 21. února 2013*, ed. Martin Hrdina and Kateřina Piorecká (Prague: Academia, 2014), 59–69.

6. Karadžić, *Songs*, 11.

7. Only "Beneš Son of Herman" and "Ludiše and Lubor" make no use of the ten-syllable line. The two epics set in the pagan period in the Queen's Court Manuscript, "Čestmír and Vlaslav" and "Záboj, Slavoj, and Luděk," make partial use of the ten-syllable line.

8. Kirsha Danilov's collection of byliny were known among the Czechs from its 1804 edition (Mojmír Otruba and Marie Řepková, "Literárněvědná kritika RKZ," in *Rukopisy královédvorský a zelenohorský: Dnešní stav poznání*, ed. Mojmír Otruba, Sborník Národního muzea v Praze, řada C—Literární historie, sv. 13–14 [Prague: Academia, 1969], 122). On Macpherson's adaptive translation of the traditional material, and what was actually derived from the traditional forms, see Fiona J. Stafford, *The Sublime Savage: A Study of James Macpherson and the Poems of Ossian* (Edinburgh: Edinburgh University Press, 1988), 90–93. See also Howard Gaskill, "'Ossian' Macpherson: Towards a Rehabilitation," *Comparative Criticism* 8 (1986): 113–46.

9. Robert Mann in *Lances Sing* attempts to make the case for the oral formulaic nature of the *Igor Tale* (Robert Mann, *Lances Sing: A Study of the Igor Tale* [Columbus, OH: Slavica Publishers, 1990]). See B. Gasparov, *Poetika "Slova o polku Igoreve"* (Moscow: Agraf, 2000), on the myth-epic form of the tale and its relation to oral traditions, esp. 473–78. Hanka published his translation of the tale in 1821 and, in his translation of a passage of Nikolai Karamzin's history about Prince Igor, adds, when Karamzin calls the *Igor Tale* the only work of its kind for Russians, that the Queen's Court Manuscript was the same for Czechs, definitively linking the two texts. Václav Hanka, "Igor Swatoslawič (Wýpiska dle Karamzjna)," *Krok* 1, no. 1 (1821): 82; Václav Hanka, *Igor Swatoslawič: Hrdinsky zpiew o taženj proti Polowcům. Werně w půwodnjm gazyku, s připogenjm Českého a Německého přeloženj* (Prague: U Haze, Krausse, Endersa, 1821).

10. Albert Bates Lord, "Avdo Međedović, Guslar," in *Slavic Folklore: A Symposium*, ed. Albert Bates Lord (Philadelphia: American Folklore Society, 1956), 122–32.

11. Albert Bates Lord, *The Singer of Tales* (Cambridge, MA: Harvard University Press, 1960), 13.

12. For a detailed account of the development of this theory, see John Miles Foley, *The Theory of Oral Composition: History and Methodology* (Bloomington: Indiana University Press, 1988), chaps. 1–3. Parry and Lord preferred to record the Muslim singers because they were capable of singing songs of lengths approaching Homeric epic size. Foley explains that these singers had developed a highly ornamental style to provide lengthy entertainment over the thirty days of Ramadan celebrations and due to the greater leisure that had been available to them as the ruling class under the Ottoman Empire (John Miles Foley, *Traditional Oral Epic: The Odyssey, Beowulf, and the Serbo-Croatian Return Song* [Berkeley: University of California Press, 1990], 40). And yet the much shorter songs of the Christian singers, like those collected by Karadžić, belong to the same language and tradition, making use of the same story patterns and a shared traditional phraseology (John Miles Foley, *Immanent Art: From*

Structure to Meaning in Traditional Oral Epic [Bloomington: Indiana University Press, 1991], 97).

13. Jaroslav Mezník, "Recenze," review of *Rukopis Zelenohorský a Královédvorský: Vznik, styl a básnická hodnota staročeské orální poesie*, by Julius Enders, *Český časopis historický* 92, no. 2 (1994): 355–56; Mojmír Otruba, "Pravé kontra nepravé rukopisy—a co dál," *Literární noviny* 3, no. 33 (1992): 4. Note that no review appeared in the journal *Česká literatura*.

14. Mojmír Otruba, ed., *Rukopisy královédvorský a zelenohorský: Dnešní stav poznání*, Sbornik Národního muzea v Praze, řada C—Literární historie, sv. 13–14 (Prague: Academia, 1969); "Seznam prací PhDr. Julia Enderse," Česká společnost rukopisná, accessed September 6, 2019, http://rukopisy-rkz.cz/rkz/urban/r/enders/soupis2.htm. Enders published a second linguistic study of the manuscripts that same year, and had published a new edition of the manuscripts, edited from the perspective of the manuscripts' authenticity, in 1991.

15. Julius Enders, *Rukopis Zelenohorský a Královédvorský: Vznik, styl a básnická hodnota staročeské orální poesie* (Prague: Neklan, 1993), 178.

16. Lord, *The Singer of Tales*, 30.

17. Foley, *Traditional Oral Epic*, 65. Foley notes that the complexity of the hexameter line shapes the relatively high degree of formulaic diction in Homeric epic, where a greater thrift was necessary (128). See also his discussion in Foley, *Immanent Art*, 139–50.

18. Lord gives two examples that fill the four-syllable portion of the South Slavic epic line: "Any name of a city with a dative of three syllables can be used instead of Prilip [u Prilipu]: *u Stambolu, u Travniku, u Kladuši*. Instead of *a u kuli*, 'in the tower,' one can say *a u dvoru*, 'in the castle,' or *a u kući*, 'in the house.'" Lord, *The Singer of Tales*, 35.

19. Foley, *Traditional Oral Epic*, 124.

20. Lord, *The Singer of Tales*, 47.

21. Lord, 34.

22. Lord, 53.

23. See Foley, *Traditional Oral Epic*, 162–63.

24. Lord, *The Singer of Tales*, 47. A "small" sample from a rich source base for Lord—note that for the Czech manuscripts we will be examining just 576 ten-syllable lines in five poems that total 955 lines. Lord's use of a sample passage to assess the formulaic density of the poetry was not his innovation, but follows Parry's example using 25 lines from the openings of the *Odyssey* and the *Iliad*. Foley, *Theory*, 29.

25. Foley, *Immanent Art*, 16.

26. Foley, 16.

27. "Seznam prací PhDr. Julia Enderse."

28. Enders, *Rukopis Zelenohorský a Královédvorský*, 126–27. An online version of this book by Enders is available here: http://www.rukopisy-rkz.cz/rkz/enders/erozbor/erozbor.htm.

29. Enders, *Rukopis Zelenohorský a Královédvorský*, 183–87.

30. Enders, 187.

31. Enders, 107.

32. Enders, 178.

33. Enders, 178.

34. Foley, *Traditional Oral Epic*, 3–4, 162–63.

35. Enders, *Rukopis Zelenohorský a Královédvorský*, 179. Note that Lord in his sample analysis examines just fourteen lines, but against a corpus of twelve thousand lines to determine their formulaic status. Lord, *The Singer of Tales*, 45–47.

36. See Enders, *Rukopis Zelenohorský a Královédvorský*, 181, for this admission.

37. Enders, 190–91.

38. Enders, 110–12.

39. Foley observes in *Traditional Oral Epic* that the verse does seem to exhibit, as often noted, a trochaic tendency but that the shaping of the verse is not through bisyllabic feet but through these underlying principles, which leave the seventh syllable entirely flexible, as is seen in the singers' practices (87). Note that the ictus can be fulfilled in this verse by dynamic stress or by an appropriate combination of vowel quantity and rising/falling intonation (177n36).

40. These word size counts include the binding of proclitics (like prepositions, conjunctions, and the negative particle) to the following word as a unit.

41. Foley, *Traditional Oral Epic*, 85–106, 173.

42. Foley, 176. The stable syllable count and caesura, which are also necessary, are noted on 182 in note 46.

43. Lord, *The Singer of Tales*, 65.

44. Foley, *Traditional Oral Epic*, 165–97.

45. Foley, 197.

46. Foley, 161, 198. Terracing is explained further when the first example of it is examined.

47. Foley also offers such traditional rules for Homeric epic and Old English epic.

48. Foley, 200.

49. See the details of Foley's readings, 178–96.

50. In a study published in 1871, Josef Truhlář proposed just such emendations, in both directions, to the poem "Záboj," and was thus able to raise the total number of ten-syllable verses in that epic to 91 out of 255. (Dalibor Dobiáš et al., *Rukopisy královédvorský a zelenohorský a česká věda (1817–1885)*, Literární řada [Prague: Academia, 2014], 768 [hereafter *RKZ a česká věda*]).

51. Václav Flajšhans counts thirteen instances in sixty lines, which would amount to 21.7 percent (Viktorin Vojtěch and Václav Flajšhans, eds., *Rukopisy královédvorský a zelenohorský* [Prague: Česká grafická unie, 1930], 4 [hereafter *RKZ*]).

52. In "Jaroslav" there are also some anomalous lines that best divide into 3 + 7 (l. 114) or 7 + 3 (ll. 149, 281). Dolanský also counted 55 of 289 lines that did not have the deseterac caesura in that epic (Dolanský, *Neznámý pramen*, 127).

53. Again, I am counting here not isolated lines or pairs of lines with ten-syllable counts, but only runs of at least three lines.

54. Dobiáš et al., *RKZ a česká věda*, 468. This volume includes a reprint of a section of *Die Echtheit* in its anthology, translated into Czech by Petr Píša.

55. Dobiáš et al., 767.

56. Dobiáš et al., 503, 508–9. (Goll's article is also reprinted in this volume.) Goll finds 24 verses in "Libuše's Judgement" with a caesura after the sixth syllable (19.8 percent, compared to my 9 verses for 7.4 percent). What accounts for the discrepancy? There are a surprising number of lines with word breaks after both the fourth and sixth syllable (two-syllable words filling syllables 5–6): in the first 30 lines

there are already 17 such lines. If one takes the caesura after the fourth syllable as normative and after the sixth as deviant (as I have done, in comparison with the deseterac), all of these lines would fit the norm. If, as Goll suggests, we have variation between two caesuras, then depending on the particular syntax of the line, one might see the caesura in either place. Thus Goll finds, in the course of 121 lines, an additional fifteen examples of caesura following the sixth syllable, all lines that I have counted for correct caesura after the fourth.

57. In fact, aside from Jakobson's 1935 article "K časovým otázkám," I have found almost no treatment of the ten-syllable epic line from major Czech scholars of verse. Jakobson identifies two relevant cases for the question of whether the failure to maintain a strict caesura after the fourth syllable is evidence against the manuscripts' medieval provenance: a medieval tradition of Czech ten-syllable verse without a fixed caesura, exemplified by the poem "Ot božieho těla" (From God's body), that approximated the contemporary Latin decasyllable, and folk song "deseterac" with a strict caesura in the proper place, with Czech and Polish examples recorded in the fifteenth century and current folk song traditions in Slovakia and eastern Moravia (Roman Jakobson, "K časovým otázkám nauky o českém verši," *Slovo a slovesnost* 1 [1935]: 48). He takes the caesura evidence, on that basis, as inconclusive. Again, if one takes seriously the connection between genre and form for traditional oral epic (a problem that was just beginning to be formulated as part of oral-formulaic theory at this time), then none of this evidence is at all relevant (although the folk song verse is striking, the examples come from lyric songs that include lines of other lengths as well).

58. See, for example, Karel Horálek, *Počátky novočeského verše* (Prague: Nákladem Karlovy University, 1956), esp. 98–99; Karel Horálek, *Studie o slovenské lidové poezii* (Prague: Státní pedagogické nakl., 1962), 307–8. Because the songs in the manuscripts were neither syllabotonic nor quantitative, they could be used by both sides to further their arguments. Iva Krejčová has examined how a pair of mock epics by members of the older generation (committed to Dobrovský's syllabotonic prosodic reform) deploy the manuscripts in these polemics. The works concerned are Vojtěch Nejedlý's unpublished "Bohyně" (1819) and Šebestián Hněvkovský's revised "Děvín" (1829). Iva Krejčová, "Mezi hrdinstvím a heroikomikou: Tematizace Rukopisů královédvorského a zelenohorského v česky psané básnické epice první poloviny 19. století," in *Rukopisy královédvorský a zelenohorský v kultuře a umění*, ed. Dalibor Dobiáš (Prague: Academia, 2019), 1:411–20.

59. With regard to the verse shape and caesura for this translation, just 6.5 percent of the lines do not have a word boundary after the fourth syllable (13 of 201 lines). These can be divided into 5 + 5 (4 instances), 6 + 4 (7 instances), 3 + 7 (1 instance), and 3 + 6 (l. 158, a hyposyllabic line).

60. Jakobson, "K časovým otázkám," 48–49.

61. References to the Old Czech text, by poem and line number, refer to the 2010 edition by Dalibor Dobiáš (Dalibor Dobiáš, ed., *Rukopis královédvorský; Rukopis zelenohorský*, Česká knižnice [Brno: Host, 2010] [hereafter *RKZ*]). The same text is reprinted in David L. Cooper, ed., *The Queen's Court and Green Mountain Manuscripts with Other Forgeries of the Czech Revival*, Czech Translations, vol. 6 (Ann Arbor: Michigan Slavic Publications, 2018) (hereafter *The Manuscripts*), with facing English translation from which the translations here are adapted.

62. In line 285, this large five-syllable patronymic is likely the cause for the anomalous 7 + 3 division of the line, "mečem Kublajevica zachvati" (struck down Kublai's son with his sword).

63. Dolanský, *Neznámý pramen*, 137.

64. Vojtěch and Flajšhans, *RKZ*, 7. One can find roughly fifteen examples of *oj* followed by the vocative in Karadžić's publications from 1814 and 1815 in speech taglines, like "Njoj govori srpski knez Lazare," "Oj Boga mi, gospo Anićelija!," and "Oj, čuješ li, srpski car-Stjepane." Vuk Stefanović Karadžić, *Srpske narodne pjesme: Skupio ih i na svijet izdao Vuk Stef. Karadžić* (Vienna: U štampariji Jermenskoga manastira, 1845), vol. 2.

65. Robert Austerlitz defined a terrace as "a complex of two lines in which the latter portion of the first line is identical with the former portion of the following line" (Robert Austerlitz, *Ob-Ugric Metrics: The Metrical Structure of Ostyak and Vogul Folk-Poetry*, FF Communications, edited for the Folklore Fellows, vol. 70, no. 174 [Helsinki: Suomalainen Tiedeakatemia, 1958], 65). This figure of repetition is quite common in Slavic oral epic poetry, and Austerlitz's term has been adopted by many researchers.

66. See Foley, *Immanent Art*, 121, on the function of terracing.

67. After accusing Enders of not paying attention to meter and genre in analyzing formulas, I want to be clear that I am not merely repeating that mistake here. I have accounted for meter and the possibility of formulaic language within the meter and concluded that we are not dealing here with a genuine oral-formulaic tradition. I am analyzing not formulas, but quasi-formulas that imitate oral-formulaic diction in metrical situations that, even when they occur in ten-syllable lines, differ systematically from the deseterac line and are not themselves responding to an implicit system or grammar of traditional rules. I will always mark the moments when I go outside the ten-syllable line that is the center of my comparison to the deseterac tradition.

68. In fact, the second half of line 10 also has its own independent repetition (with grammatical adjustment), at line 19 in the song.

69. Dolanský suggests that the adjective *chladný* for the river is most likely borrowed from the BCS tradition, where it is a frequent epithet applied to rivers or water, whereas the Czech folk song examples he cites prefer the synonymous adjective *studený*. Dolanský, *Neznámý pramen*, 56.

70. Dolanský, 61–62. For English versions, see Karadžić, *Songs*, 286–87, 303–4.

71. Dolanský, *Neznámý pramen*, 59–60.

72. Dolanský, 11, 19, 7. Dolanský's volume, like his two others on sources for the Czech manuscripts, offers hundreds of examples of parallels to this source that are entirely unconvincing, making for frustrating reading. This passage represents one of just five or six from the entire book full of examples that seem to offer credible evidence, enough to make a case that Kačić Miošić's volume is a probable source for the forged manuscripts, but a case that has been entirely watered down in a flood of weak parallels and strained argumentation.

73. Dolanský further observes that the adjective in the phrase *ot Sázavy ladny* (from lovely Sazava) is likely also a variant form of the BCS adjective for "cold" used earlier, *chladný*, which Hanka (or another author) misunderstood to be equivalent to the Czech adjective *ladný* (graceful). The description of a river as cold is traditional, while a graceful river is a literary innovation (Dolanský, 56–57). Compare this passage from "Lov Markov s Turcima" in Karadzic's 1814 volume of songs: "A Jarko ga ogrejalo sunce /

Kod malena sela Dubrovice / Na Dunavu lepoj vodi ladnoj." Karadžić, *Srpske narodne pjesme*, 2:491.

74. Cooper, *The Manuscripts*, 157.

75. Lev Aleksandrovich Dmitriev and Dmitrii Sergeevich Likhachev, eds., "Slovo o polku Igoreve," in *"Izbornik" (Sbornik proizvedenii literatury Drevnei Rusi)* (Moscow: Khudozh. lit., 1969), 200 (emphasis mine).

76. Vladimir Nabokov, trans., *The Song of Igor's Campaign: An Epic of the Twelfth Century* (New York: Vintage Books, 1960), 40 (emphasis mine).

77. These forms—*kamo, tamo, semo*—existed in Old Czech as well (in contemporary Czech: *kam, tam, sem*), so here it is a question not of borrowing but of the suggestive echo of an antiquated form that further links the manuscripts to other Slavic traditions.

78. See Enders, *Rukopis Zelenohorský a Královédvorský*, 126–27, for a full list. I included 139 combinations in my own analysis, leaving out only a few that seemed unlikely to repeat.

79. Totals in this analysis will be greater than the 139 adjective-noun combinations, as they include repetitions as well.

80. See numerous examples of the focusing function of the second colon in Foley's analyses, in Foley, *Traditional Oral Epic*, 178–96.

81. Lord, *The Singer of Tales*, 46 (Lord's translation, author's emphasis).

82. See Enders's list of formulas (which also includes combinations that occur only in the ballads and lyric poems) for comparison (Enders, *Rukopis Zelenohorský a Královédvorský*, 183–87). I follow Foley in recognizing identity across morphological variation as a part of the multiformity of traditional phrasing. Of these nine, all are discussed or mentioned below, except *šero jutro* (gray morn), *četné voje* (numerous armies), *lútá buřa* (wild storm), and *(pře-)silná paže* (mighty arms). Enders's list, which he compiled using a computerized concordance, enabled me to add an additional handful of examples, here and below, to those I had found by hand marking and counting. With my partners in the associated digital project, we then double-checked with our own analysis of the lemmatized text of the manuscripts (to eliminate morphological variation), using Natural Language Toolkit (NLTK) collocation searching to find significant repeated combinations, and found two more, added below.

83. Other examples include *lútí Tataři* (fierce Tartars), *bystra kopie* (swift spears), *trapná žízn* (painful thirst), *jelení skok* (a deer's leap), *roda stara* (old family line), *rodná bratry* (full brothers), *rodná sestra* (full sister), *dediny otné* (father's estate), *Otava kriva* (crooked Otava), *žírna vlast* (fertile homeland), *otňo zlato siedlo* (father's gold seat), *Dobroslavský chlmec* (Dobroslav's fastness), *Kamen most* (stone bridge), *slavný sněm* (great assembly), and *ostrý meč* (sharp sword).

84. These are *jasno slunce* (bright sun), *plachý zvěř* (timid animal), *zapolena zraky* (enflamed eyes), and *modrý vrch* (blue mountain).

85. These are *(vele-)slavný kněz* (glorious prince), *lúté boje* (fierce battles), *dobří ludie* (good people), *teplá krev* (warm blood), *lepotvorná / lepá dcera* (fair daughter), *šíra lesa* (wide forest), *tvrdý hrad* (firm castle), *temná noc* (dark night), and *(pře-)lútá săč* (cruel slaughter). Note that in several of these an intensifier is added to the epithet in one of the repetitions. Unlike Lord, who is able to compare a fourteen-line sample to a corpus of twelve thousand lines, we are able, by adding the remainder of the manuscripts

to the ten-syllable portions, to add to those 3,093 words just 3,674 additional words for comparison.

86. As noted earlier, fixed epithets are an aspect of traditional oral phraseology that extends beyond epic. In our further analysis of the functioning of the formulaic aspect of these phrases, we will continue to limit ourselves to the ten-syllable-line epics.

87. Dobiáš notes a set of contrasting elements that also link these two epics: dark and light, closed (secret) space versus open space, height and depth. Dobiáš, *RKZ*, 294.

88. "Il'ia Muromets i Kalin-Tsar'," Russkie byliny, accessed September 9, 2019, http://www.byliny.ru/content/text/ilya-muromets-i-kalin. A. F. Gilferding was the second collector of Russian oral epics, who collected over 300 songs. T. G. Riabinin was considered one of the finest singers. Translation from James Bailey and T. G. Ivanova, eds., *An Anthology of Russian Folk Epics*, Folklores and Folk Cultures of Eastern Europe (Armonk, NY: M. E. Sharpe, 1998), 68. Flajšhans suggests the "brash head" formula comes from a commonplace in the byliny collection by Danilov (Vojtěch and Flajšhans, *RKZ*, 7).

89. Vojtěch and Flajšhans, *RKZ*, 29.

90. Dmitriev and Likhachev, "Slovo o polku Igoreve," 198.

91. Nabokov, *Igor's Campaign*, 33.

92. Some readers will have noticed that this is also a ten-syllable line. It joins only one other such line in this passage, immediately following it, and so was not counted among the ten-syllable lines for my analysis (which counted only runs of three or more lines).

93. We could also compare the formula for mounting horses in the Russian byliny, which in the version of the singer Riabinin repeats as "ony seli na dobryx konej, poexali." Note that the formulaic adjective for the warhorse in the bylina is "good" rather than "swift." See Patricia M. Arant, *Compositional Techniques of the Russian Oral Epic, the Bylina*, Harvard Dissertations in Folklore and Oral Tradition (New York: Garland, 1990), 49.

94. Iva Krejčová, "Literární obraz slavné minulosti v rané recepci Rukopisu královédvorského a zelenohorského: Konstituování mýtu národní literatury," in *České literární romantično: Synopticko-pulzační model kulturního jevu*, ed. Dalibor Tureček (Brno: Host, 2012), 165–66.

95. The comparison to foxes is also made in the poem "Záboj." Another frequent comparison is to stags, a prey animal but one with some formidable defenses.

96. See Vojtěch and Flajšhans, *RKZ*, 23, which cites byliny 46 and 47 from the Danilov collection and notes the *Igor Tale* source.

97. It is joined by *krutá krutost* (cruel cruelty) in a non-ten-syllable part of "Záboj" (l. 205).

98. Antonín Vašek, *Filologický důkaz, že Rukopis Kralodvorský a Zelenohorský, též zlomek Evangelia sv. Jana jsou podvržená díla Vácslava Hanky* (Brno: Nákladem spisovatelovým, 1879), 62. See Cooper, *The Manuscripts*, 186, for the English translation. The first phrase comes from "Libuše's Judgment," l. 60.

99. Václav Hanka, "Připomenutj," in *Rukopis Králodworský: Sebránj lyricko-epických národnjch zpěwů, wěrně w půwodnjm starém gazyku, též w obnoweném pro snadněgšj wyrozuměnj s připogenjm německého přeloženj* (Prague: Bohumila Haze a Joz. Krause, 1819), iii; Cooper, *The Manuscripts*, 142.

100. Miroslav Komárek, "Jazykovědná problematika RKZ," in *Rukopisy královédvorský a zelenohorský: Dnešní stav poznání*, ed. Mojmír Otruba, Sbornik Národního muzea v Praze, řada C—Literární historie, sv. 13–14 (Prague: Academia, 1969), 226–27.

101. "Oldřich": *šedošero jutro* (gray-dark morn, l. 14; repeats as *šero jutro* at line 38). "Jaroslav": *jarobujná sila* (vigorous strength, l. 71; the adjective repeats with a different noun in "Ludiše and Lubor"), *hlasonosná obět* (resounding sacrifice, l. 229; Flajšans identifies this as a Latin Christian commonplace, *hostiam vociferationis* [Vojtěch and Flajšhans, *RKZ*, 22]), and *dřevce sėhodlúhé* (fathom-long lances, l. 286). "Čestmír": *drva vysokorostlá* (trees grown-tall, l. 90), *blahodějné jutro* (gladsome morning, l. 116), *dcera lepotvorná* (comely daughter, l. 117; repeats as *lepá dcera* at line 60), and *tur jarohlavý* (wild-headed bull, l. 186). "Záboj": *les dlúhopustý* (long-desolate forest, l. 8). "Libuše": *voda strebropěna* (silver-foamed waters, l. 2), *zlatopieska glína* (golden-grained clay, l. 6), *Otava kriva zlatonosna* (Otava, crooked and gold-laden, l. 12), *Brdy vletorečné* (Brdy, Vltava-washed, l. 38), *Mžě strebronosná* (silver-laden Mže, l. 40), *desky pravdodatné* (law-giving tablets, l. 51), *plamen pravdozvěsten* (truth-speaking flame, l. 53), *svatocudná voda* (holy-judging water, l. 54), and *věkožizní bozi* (ageless gods, l. 60).

102. This last half-translates a South Slavic fixed epithet, "ljuta zmaja." See Dolanský's multiple examples (Dolanský, *Neznámý pramen*, 67).

103. Dmitriev and Likhachev, "Slovo o polku Igoreve," 196. As Dolanský notes, the first of these phrases also repeats a commonplace from South Slavic epics, "tiho govoriti" (Dolanský, *Neznámý pramen*, 77, 92).

104. These epithets have also been considered in the question of authorship of the epic poems. Miroslav Ivanov cited a number of identical epithets in Josef Linda's novel *Záře nad pohanstvem* (Dawn over paganism, 1818), which was submitted to the censor in 1816 before the "discovery" of the Queen's Court Manuscript. These include some we have examined, for example, *temná noc* (dark night), *hustá tma* (thick darkness), *lítý boj* (fierce battle), *široká prsa* (broad breast), and *šedivé jitro* (gray dawn). The majority appear in "Záboj," "Čestmír," and "Jelen," which Dolanský had concluded on other evidence belonged to Linda. Miroslav Ivanov, *Tajemství RKZ* (Prague: Mladá Fronta, 1969); Dolanský, *Neznámý pramen*, 170–71, 208–9.

105. Lord, *The Singer of Tales*, 34.

106. Again, see Dolanský, *Neznámý pramen*, 77, 92.

107. Václav Hanka, *Hankovy písně a Prostonárodní srbská muza, do Čech převedená*, ed. Jan Máchal, Novočeská knihovna, č. 3 (Prague: Nákl. České akademie císaře Františka Josefa pro vědy, slovesnost a uměni, 1918), 237. See Vojtěch and Flajšhans, *RKZ*, 63.

108. Or, as for Flajšhans, this is another piece of evidence that the two manuscripts have the same author, and that author is Hanka.

109. See the analysis below of the motif of single combat in the *battle* theme for an example that does amount to quasi-formulaic repetition.

110. This repeated epithet-noun phrase was not treated above because it occurs in "Čestmír" in a twelve-syllable line (that divides two sections of ten-syllable lines), and thus not at all in the corpus analyzed for quasi-formulas but only in the comparative material.

111. Dmitriev and Likhachev, "Slovo o polku Igoreve," 206–8; Nabokov, *Igor's Campaign*, 59.

112. Vašek, *Filologický důkaz*, 62. For the English, see Cooper, *The Manuscripts*, 186.

113. John Miles Foley, *The Wedding of Mustajbey's Son Bećirbey as Performed by Halil Bajgorić*, FF Communications, no. 283 (Helsinki: Suomalainen Tiedeakatemia, 2004), 195. See the dozens of lines in Karadžić's two collections from 1814 and 1815 of the form: "Kad u jutru jutro osvanulo." Karadžić, *Srpske narodne pjesme*, 2:46, 119, 195, 249, 289, etc.

114. Dolanský, *Neznámý pramen*, 96.

115. Foley, *The Wedding*, 195.

116. In contrast, the interjection *aj* serves primarily as an emotional interjection in the manuscripts. There are a few cases, however, where *aj* also seems to mark a transition ("Záboj," l. 76) or where *ajta* does not ("Záboj," l. 73).

117. Dolanský, *Neznámý pramen*, 138. There are at least fifteen instances of phrases involving jumping to feet in the epic songs published by Karadžić in 1814 and 1815. Karadžić, *Srpske narodne pjesme*, 2:27, 32, 33, 49, 68, 79, 128, etc.

118. Foley, *Immanent Art*, 83–87.

119. Foley, 85.

120. The same could be demonstrated for the opening lines of "Libuše's Judgment" for the Green Mountain Manuscript.

121. Repetition of prepositions is rare in the South Slavic deseterac form, but more common in the longer Bugarštica form and definitely common in the longer Russian byliny line, so this also has Slavic oral formulaic epic antecedents.

122. Hanka, *Igor Swatoslawič*, xi–xii.

123. For Dobrovský, it was not the form of the Green Mountain Manuscript that awoke his doubts but the content and extreme apparent age. As we have seen, in poetic form it comported very well with the Queen's Court Manuscript. Dobiáš et al., *RKZ a česká věda*, 251.

124. Dobiáš et al., 261, 262.

125. Dobiáš et al., 310, 311–313.

126. Dobiáš et al., 373, 374.

127. Dobiáš et al., 474, 478–85.

128. Michal Charypar points to the wide debates on the folkloric aspect of the manuscripts within the context of the pervasive folklorism in the period (Michal Charypar, "Motiv, syžet, poetika: Písně Rukopisu královédvorského a jejich vliv na novočeskou poezii do příchodu Májovců," in *Rukopisy královédvorský a zelenohorský v kultuře a umění*, ed. Dalibor Dobiáš [Prague: Academia, 2019], 1:445–47). He also suggests that the composition (particularly of the lyric songs) as intertexts of Slavic folkloric texts was an explicit and hidden strategy of the authors, who calculated that the sources would later be discovered and the resemblances would tend to confirm the authenticity of the manuscript poems (452).

129. My graduate research assistant, Demetry Ogoltsev, contributed significantly to the project in all aspects. A full account of the project, its methodology, and results will soon be available in an article: David L. Cooper, Demetry Ogoltsev, and Michal Ondrejcek, "TTR and Entropy as Measures to Characterize a Forgery of Oral-Formulaic Epics," forthcoming in *Oral Tradition* 36, no. 2 (2023). This section summarizes the main points and findings.

130. Vaira Vikis-Freibergs and Imants Freibergs, "Formulaic Analysis of the Computer-Accessible Corpus of Latvian Sun-Songs," *Computers and the Humanities* 12 (1978): 329–39; Dmitry Nikolayev, "A New Algorithm for Extracting Formulas from

Poetic Texts and the Formulaic Density of Russian Bylinas," *Oral Tradition* 30, no. 1 (2016): 111–36.

131. David E. Bynum, *The Dæmon in the Wood: A Study of Oral Narrative Patterns*, Publications of the Milman Parry Collection: Monograph Series, no. 1 (Cambridge, MA: Center for Study of Oral Literature, Harvard University, 1978), 6–11. See also Albert Bates Lord, "Perspectives on Recent Work on the Oral Traditional Formula," *Oral Tradition* 1, no. 3 (1986): 491–93.

132. Vikis-Freibergs and Freibergs, "Formulaic Analysis," 332; Nikolayev, "New Algorithm," 112.

133. Again, for additional data and a full account of our methodology and results, see our forthcoming article in *Oral Tradition*: Cooper, Ogoltsev, and Ondrejcek, "TTR and Entropy."

134. We used the NLTK-provided collocation tools (https://www.nltk.org/_modules/nltk/collocations.html) and, following the methodological suggestions of Christopher D. Manning and Hinrich Schütze, used a high minimum likelihood ratio of 10.83 and a minimum of two occurrences for our collocations. Christopher D. Manning and Hinrich Schütze, *Foundations of Statistical Natural Language Processing*, 2nd printing, with corrections (Cambridge, MA: MIT Press, 2000), 172–75, 610.

135. Lord, *The Singer of Tales*, 68.

136. Foley, *Traditional Oral Epic*, 281.

137. Foley, 284.

138. Foley, 311–12.

139. Foley, 327.

140. It repeats in lines 22, 64, 82, 96, 104, 130, and 136. The initial verb varies slightly in a few cases: "Vzezně," "Vzezní," and "Zevzni." This instance of formulaic language was not discussed above because it does not occur in the ten-syllable epics.

141. We should note that "Beneš" is not a ten-syllable epic, but this passage from "Čestmír" comes from one of the longest sections of that epic that is in the decasyllable form and that encompasses almost the entirety of the final battle sequence or theme.

142. Příruční slovník a databáze lexikálního archivu, s.v. "hora," accessed July 15, 2022, https://psjc.ujc.cas.cz/.

143. Foley, *Traditional Oral Epic*, 327.

144. Homer, *The Iliad*, trans. Richmond Lattimore (Chicago: University of Chicago Press, 1951), 5.136–43.

145. Because the entire European epic tradition derives from Homer via Virgil, one can also point to precedents for the lion simile in other epic texts that the forgers may have seen. Flajšhans cites Torquato Tasso's *Jerusalem Delivered*, book 20, stanza 114, along with a line in "Bitva černopolská" by Hanka's older contemporary Jan Nejedlý (Vojtěch and Flajšhans, *RKZ*, 24). Dolanský points to a lion simile in Mikhail Kheraskov's *Rossiada* (Julius Dolanský, *Ohlas dvou ruských básníků v Rukopisech královédvorském a zelenohorském* [Prague: Univ. Karlova, t. Mír, 1969], 46).

146. Seth L. Schein, *The Mortal Hero: An Introduction to Homer's Iliad* (Berkeley: University of California Press, 1984), 80.

147. Thanks to my graduate student Demetry Ogoltsev, whose excellent undergraduate paper on the Russian *Igor Tale* investigated this tradition. See Michael Speidel, "Berserks: A History of Indo-European 'Mad Warriors,'" *Journal of World History* 13, no. 2 (2002): 253–90.

148. See Krejčová, "Literární obraz."

149. Homer, *The Iliad*, 21.1–4, 7–11.

150. For example, Vašek, *Filologický důkaz*, 63; English translation in Cooper, *The Manuscripts*, 187.

151. Again, it is worth noting that all but two of the lines from "Čestmír" in this passage are decasyllable, while only a single line from "Záboj" is decasyllable. The "Záboj" single combat continues through line 185.

152. Foley, *Traditional Oral Epic*, 369.

153. Foley, 362.

154. Lord, *The Singer of Tales*, 120.

155. Lord, 122.

156. Lord, 186–97.

157. Julius Dolanský, *Záhada Ossiana v Rukopisech královédvorském a zelenohorském* (Prague: Academia, 1975), 32.

158. Ossian, *The Poems of Ossian*, trans. James Macpherson (Leipzig: Bernhard Tauchnitz, 1847), 143, 269.

159. See Dobiáš, *RKZ*, 173–76, for transcription of the fragments with these line numbers.

160. Dolanský, *Neznámý pramen*, 91.

161. Karadžić, *Songs*, 280. The *raja* were the Christian peasants under Ottoman rule. *Dahijas* were the chiefs of the Janissary.

162. Karadžić, 5–6, 277–79.

163. One sees something similar in the Old English *Genesis A*, which translates biblical stories into Old English heroic verse forms, reconceiving it in heroic terms. See Daniel Weissbort and Ástráður Eysteinsson, eds., *Translation—Theory and Practice: A Historical Reader* (Oxford: Oxford University Press, 2006), 45–46.

164. Dolanský, *Neznámý pramen*, 49.

165. There are close analogues in song 129 from Mikhail Chulkov's Russian songbook, addressing the Don, and from Karadžić's 1814 songbook, addressing the Danube. See Vojtěch and Flajšhans, *RKZ*, 61.

166. Karadžić, *Songs*, 232.

167. Vladimír Procházka, "Rukopisy a právní historie," in *Rukopisy královédvorský a zelenohorský: Dnešní stav poznání*, ed. Mojmír Otruba, Sbornik Národního muzea v Praze, řada C—Literární historie, sv. 13–14 (Prague: Academia, 1969), 184.

168. See the Russian bylina "Dyuk Stepanovich" for an example (Bailey and Ivanova, *Russian Folk Epics*, 253–63). In the repertoire of the singer Riabinin, the variant of the opening assembly theme involving boasting generally sets into motion the main action of the song. See Arant, *Compositional Techniques*, 79.

169. We might note here that part of Howard Gaskill's "rehabilitation" of James Macpherson, to counter Irish claims to ownership of the traditions he was presenting, was the argument that "the Gaelic poets of Scotland were legitimate co-heirs of a common culture" and that Macpherson's reworkings belonged to a tradition that was itself already reworking the shared material earlier. See Gaskill, "'Ossian' Macpherson: Towards a Rehabilitation," 118–21, quotation on 119.

170. Foley, *Immanent Art*, 124–33.

171. See Foley, 103–18.

172. T. G. Masaryk noted the lack of heroes in his criticism of the inauthenticity of the epic songs. See T. G. Masaryk, *Z bojů o rukopisy: Texty z let 1886–1888*, ed. Jiří Brabec, vyd. 1, vol. 19, *Spisy T. G. Masaryka* (Prague: Ústav T. G. Masaryka, 2004), 118.

173. Dolanský discusses the connection of the epic to wedding songs and some possible models in the South Slavic tradition. See Dolanský, *Neznámý pramen*, 177–93.

174. Ossian, *The Poems of Ossian*, 215.

175. Jaroslav Mezník, "Rukopisy z hlediska historie," in *Rukopisy královédvorský a zelenohorský: Dnešní stav poznání*, ed. Mojmír Otruba, Sbornik Národního muzea v Praze, řada C—Literární historie, sv. 13–14 (Prague: Academia, 1969), 169–77.

176. Josef Linda, if he is the author or coauthor of the epics songs as has been so often suggested, does somewhat better by at least providing a false motivation for Jaroslav's absence in his later dramatic work on the topic, *Jaroslav Šternberg v boji proti Tatarům* (Jaroslav Sternberg in battle against the Tartars). The trickster-figure character Zatrán attempts to demoralize the defenders of Olomouc by suggesting that Jaroslav has fled and left the city defenseless (Peter Deutschmann, "Ideál divadelní komunikace: Rukopisy a historická dramata v 19. století," in *Rukopisy královédvorský a zelenohorský v kultuře a umění*, ed. Dalibor Dobiáš [Prague: Academia, 2019], 1:495).

177. Foley, *Immanent Art*, 125n58.

178. We have noted the quasi-formula for the mounting of horses in this chapter, but in general the formulaic language and pattern scenes involving horses are diminished from the South Slavic and Russian oral epic models. Our digital analysis shows the word for "horse" among the few nouns in the fifty most common words in both the corpus of songs from Karadžić's (twenty-eighth) and from Danilov's (thirty-first) collections, while it does not make the list in the manuscripts (appearing only in fifty-third place, much farther down the list of common nouns).

3. Translation, Pseudotranslation, and the Manuscripts

1. David L. Cooper, *Creating the Nation: Identity and Aesthetics in Early Nineteenth-Century Russia and Bohemia* (DeKalb: Northern Illinois University Press, 2010), 89–161; Vladimír Macura, *Znamení zrodu: České obrození jako kulturní typ*, Nové, rozšířené vydání (Prague: H & H, 1995), 61–78.

2. Gideon Toury, *Descriptive Translation Studies and Beyond*, Benjamins Translation Library, vol. 4 (Amsterdam: John Benjamins, 1995). See the overviews and bibliographies in the following sources: Paolo Rambelli, "Pseudotranslation," in *Routledge Encyclopedia of Translation Studies*, ed. Mona Baker and Gabriela Saldanha (New York: Routledge, 2008), 208–11; Tom Toremans and Beatrijs Vanacker, "Introduction: The Emerging Field of Pseudotranslation," *Canadian Review of Comparative Literature / Revue Canadienne de Littérature Comparée* 44, no. 4 (December 2017): 629–36. Şehnaz Tahir Gürçağlar, "Pseudotranslation on the Margin of Fact and Fiction," in *A Companion to Translation Studies*, ed. Sandra Bermann and Catherine Porter (Chichester, West Sussex: Wiley-Blackwell, 2014), 516–27.

3. Some of the most recent work, including that of Şehnaz Tahir Gürçağlar, is beginning to address the theoretical side more successfully.

4. To name some favorites: K. K. Ruthven, *Faking Literature* (Cambridge: Cambridge University Press, 2001); Nick Groom, *The Forger's Shadow: How Forgery Changed the*

Course of Literature (London: Picador, 2002); Julia Abramson, *Learning from Lying: Paradoxes of the Literary Mystification* (Newark: University of Delaware Press, 2005); Margaret Russett, *Fictions and Fakes: Forging Romantic Authenticity, 1760–1845*, Cambridge Studies in Romanticism (Cambridge: Cambridge University Press, 2006).

5. Thomas O. Beebee, *Transmesis: Inside Translation's Black Box* (New York: Palgrave Macmillan, 2012), 11.

6. Quoted in Howard Gaskill, "Introduction: 'Genuine Poetry . . . like Gold,'" in *The Reception of Ossian in Europe*, ed. Howard Gaskill (London: Thoemmes, 2004), 11.

7. Gaskill, 12.

8. Howard Gaskill, "'Ossian' Macpherson: Towards a Rehabilitation," *Comparative Criticism* 8 (1986): 137–38.

9. Fiona J. Stafford, "Introduction: The Ossianic Poems of James Macpherson," in *The Poems of Ossian and Related Works*, by James Macpherson, ed. Howard Gaskill (Edinburgh: Edinburgh University Press, 1996), xii.

10. Howard Gaskill, "What Did James Macpherson Really Leave on Display at His Publisher's Shop in 1762?," *Scottish Gaelic Studies* 16 (1990): 67–89.

11. Gaskill, 76–78.

12. Gaskill, "'Ossian' Macpherson: Towards a Rehabilitation," 134.

13. Stafford, "Introduction," viii.

14. Stafford, xiv–xv.

15. Martin Procházka offered a contrastive reading of the kind of cultural translation involved in Macpherson's project and in the manuscripts. I here emphasize continuities. Martin Procházka, "Romantic Revivals: Cultural Translations, Universalism, and Nationalism," in *Cultural Learning, Language Learning: Selected Papers from the Second British Studies Conference, Prague 18–20 October 1996*, ed. Susan Bassnett and Martin Procházka (Prague: British Council, 1997), 75–90.

16. Julia Abramson and Scott Carpenter examine the Mérimée mystification, its techniques and goals, in the context of the widespread practice of such fakery in his contemporary France. Lawrence Venuti examines the Louÿs "translation" as an example of how translation challenges our reigning notions of authorship. Abramson, *Learning from Lying*, 101–15; Scott Carpenter, *Aesthetics of Fraudulence in Nineteenth-Century France: Frauds, Hoaxes, and Counterfeits* (Farnham, England: Ashgate, 2009), 19–43; Lawrence Venuti, *The Scandals of Translation: Towards an Ethics of Difference* (London: Routledge, 1998), 34–46.

17. Douglas Robinson, "Pseudotranslation," in *Routledge Encyclopedia of Translation Studies*, ed. Mona Baker and Kirsten Malmkjaer (New York: Routledge, 1998), 185.

18. Robinson, 183.

19. Jacques Derrida, "What Is a 'Relevant' Translation?," in *The Translation Studies Reader*, ed. Lawrence Venuti, 3rd ed. (New York: Routledge, 2012), 366–67.

20. Derrida, 369.

21. Tina Krontiris, *Oppositional Voices: Women as Writers and Translators of Literature in the English Renaissance* (London: Routledge, 1992).

22. See the bibliographies in these articles: Rambelli, "Pseudotranslation"; Toremans and Vanacker, "The Emerging Field of Pseudotranslation." Tahir Gürçağlar and others have begun to move beyond the functions outlined by Toury, including motivations relating to commerce, power, and gender as well as pragmatic goals in literary institutions beyond literary forms, including expanding readership and the promotion

of particular languages. Tahir Gürçağlar, "Pseudotranslation," 519–20; Toremans and Vanacker, "Introduction," 630.

23. As Lawrence Venuti states in his introduction to the essays from the period, "For Derrida, the relevant translation is mystifying." Laurence Venuti, "1990s," in *The Translation Studies Reader*, ed. Lawrence Venuti, 3rd ed. (New York: Routledge, 2012), 278.

24. Beebee, *Transmesis*, 9.

25. Cited in Beebee, 8. I acknowledge my debt here to Beebee, a former professor, whose fascinating and sophisticated discussion of black box translation issues included a discussion of pseudotranslation in a way that allowed me to make the connections I have made here.

26. This economic law is an implicit quantitative norm in the reigning normative discourse on translation that insists that translations "stay as close as possible to the equivalence of 'one word *by* one word.'" This measuring by words is logocentric as well, and Derrida recommends footnotes as an important strategy for breaking this law. Derrida, "What Is a 'Relevant' Translation?," 370, 369–71.

27. Emily Apter, "Translation with No Original: Scandals of Textual Reproduction," in *Nation, Language, and the Ethics of Translation*, ed. Sandra Bermann and Michael Wood (Princeton, NJ: Princeton University Press, 2005), 160 (emphasis mine).

28. Apter, 167 (emphasis mine).

29. Apter, 171.

30. Beebee, *Transmesis*, 202–5. Beebee is exceptional as a writer on pseudotranslation with great theoretical insight and interpretational verve.

31. Ruthven, *Faking Literature*, 63–73.

32. Groom, *The Forger's Shadow*, 2.

33. Julie Candler Hayes, *Translation, Subjectivity, and Culture in France and England, 1600–1800* (Stanford, CA: Stanford University Press, 2009), 18. Hayes in her introduction challenges the interpretation that sees neoclassicist translation practice as "ethnocentric" and offers a different way of conceiving of the ethics of translation from Antoine Berman's and Venuti's appropriation of the romantics' critique of their predecessors.

34. Karel Krejčí, "Některé nedořešené otázky kolem RKZ," in *Literatury a žánry v evropské dimenzi: Nejen česká literatura v zorném poli komparistiky* (Prague: Slovanský ústav AV ČR, 2014), 442.

35. Václav Hanka, *Rukopis Králodworský: Sebránj lyricko-epických národnjch zpěwů, wěrně w půwodnjm starém gazyku, též w obnoweném pro snadněgšj wyrozuměnj s připogenjm německého přeloženj* (Prague: Bohumila Haze a Joz. Krause, 1819), vi; David L. Cooper, ed., *The Queen's Court and Green Mountain Manuscripts with Other Forgeries of the Czech Revival*, Czech Translations, vol. 6 (Ann Arbor: Michigan Slavic Publications, 2018), 144 (hereafter *The Manuscripts*).

36. Following the periodization of this monumental history of Czech literature: Jan Mukařovský, ed., *Dějiny česke literatury*, Práce Československé akademie věd (Prague: Nakl. Československé akademie věd, 1959), vol. 2.

37. Macura, *Znamení zrodu*, 61–78. For a brief overview of this larger discussion in English, see Vladimír Macura, "Culture as Translation," in *Translation, History, and Culture*, ed. Susan Bassnett and André Lefevere (New York: Pinter Publishers, 1990), 64–70.

38. See Cooper, *Creating the Nation*, 202, for a discussion of the later article. On *Slovesnost*, see Tomáš Hlobil, "Jungmannova charakteristika metafory a německá

estetika 18. století," in *Mezi časy . . . Kultura a umění v českých zemích kolem roku 1800*, ed. Zdeněk Hojda and Roman Prahl (Prague: Koniasch Latin Press, 2000), 224–32.

39. Vladimír Macura, *Znamení zrodu a české sny*, ed. Kateřina Piorecká and Milena Vojtková, Vybrané spisy Vladimíra Macury 1 (Prague: Academia, 2015), 404.

40. Josef Jungmann, *Boj o obrození národa: Výbor z díla*, svět a my, sv. 9 (Prague: F. Kosek, 1948), 102. See the discussion of this article in Cooper, *Creating the Nation*, 200–206. Macura analyzes Jungmann's scholarly translations for texts in which the original author and source *are* given and finds that Jungmann does not at all suppress the translator's identity, in accordance with the usual practice, but intervenes openly and often polemically in mediating the texts of well-known authors.

41. Roman Jakobson, "K časovým otázkám nauky o českém verši," *Slovo a slovesnost* 1 (1935): 48–49.

42. Čelakovský noted the similarities while compiling his collection of Slavic folk songs already in 1821, but did not know what to make of them. Michal Charypar, "Motiv, syžet, poetika: Písně Rukopisu královédvorského a jejich vliv na novočeskou poezii do příchodu Májovců," in *Rukopisy královédvorský a zelenohorský v kultuře a umění*, ed. Dalibor Dobiáš (Prague: Academia, 2019), 1:450.

43. Mikhail Dmitrievich Chulkov, *Sochineniia Mikhaila Dmitrievicha Chulkova*, vol. 1, *Sobranie raznykh piesen* (St. Petersburg: Izd. Otdieleniia russkago iazyka i slovesnosti Imperatorskoi akademii nauk, 1913), 185–87.

44. For details, see Cooper, *The Manuscripts*, 135–39; Dalibor Dobiáš, ed., *Rukopis královédvorský; Rukopis zelenohorský*, Česká knižnice (Brno: Host, 2010), 297–303 (hereafter *RKZ*).

45. Václav Hanka, *Hankovy písně a Prostonárodní srbská muza, do Čech převedená*, ed. Jan Máchal, Novočeská knihovna, č. 3 (Prague: Nákl. České akademie císaře Františka Josefa pro vědy, slovesnost a uměni, 1918), xxiii–xxxiii.

46. See Cooper, *Creating the Nation*, 89–102, for a fuller discussion of Hanka's songs in their context.

47. Jiří Levý, *České theorie překladu*, Český překlad, sv. 1 (Prague: Státní nakl. krásné literatury, hudby a umění, 1957), 127.

48. Friedrich Schleiermacher, "On the Different Methods of Translating," in *The Translation Studies Reader*, ed. Lawrence Venuti, 3rd ed. (New York: Routledge, 2012), 53.

49. The following argument borrows from a fuller analysis in the context of a comparison to Aleksandr Pushkin's translations in my article, David L. Cooper, "Autor-překladatel-padělatel: Translace a mystifi kace v Hankově Prostonárodní srbské múze a Puškinových Písních západních Slovanů," in *Historické fi kce a mystifi kace v české kultuře 19. století: Sborník příspěvků z 33. ročníku symposia k problematice 19. století, Plzeň, 21. února 2013*, ed. Martin Hrdina and Kateřina Piorecká (Prague: Academia, 2014), 59–69.

50. Hanka, *Hankovy písně*, 242, 243, 245, 246, 247, 249, 253.

51. Macura, *Znamení zrodu*, 76.

52. I do not know that this gesture has been examined before, when Hanka uses the Russian form of writing the reflexive particle to suggest that here, as elsewhere, he is just minimally modifying the original language word (phonological translation), when in fact the original word is not close at all, but the translated word serves as a kind of bridge word between the source language and the target language. Here we have something we might call pseudo-phonological translation used as a technique of bending the target language toward the source language.

53. Cooper, *Creating the Nation*, 100–101. Macura also makes this connection in relation to translations from Slavic languages: "Phonological translation is . . . above all a gesture carrying the sense 'we speak the same language.'" Macura, *Znamení zrodu*, 72.

54. Antoine Berman, *The Experience of the Foreign: Culture and Translation in Romantic Germany*, Intersections (Albany: State University of New York Press, 1992). Gaskill argues that the inspiration for the German literal method of translating owes much to Goethe's and Herder's attempts to translate some of the Gaelic "originals" of Macpherson, which at times went even further than Macpherson himself with his foreignized pseudotranslations. Gaskill, "Introduction: 'Genuine Poetry . . . like Gold,'" 13–14.

55. Levý, *České theorie překladu*, 72.

56. Levý, 73.

57. Hanka, *Hankovy písně*, xliv.

58. Komárek notes the problem and says the key to understanding it is the Russian source text. Miroslav Komárek, "Jazykovědná problematika RKZ," in *Rukopisy královédvorský a zelenohorský: Dnešní stav poznání*, ed. Mojmír Otruba, Sborník Národního muzea v Praze, řada C—Literární historie, sv. 13–14 (Prague: Academia, 1969), 271.

59. Julius Dolanský, "Dvě varianty 'Záboje' z RK," *Česká literatura* 20, no. 4 (1972): 328–45.

60. Linda's text actually uses one nominal adjective where the Old Czech text and Hanka's translation use full forms (*cela lesa*, the whole forest); the term *vrah* (enemy) is present as well. But there are no adverbs ending in *-o*, while the Old Czech and Hanka's text have several in the parallel lines; Linda three times uses the conjunction *a* where Old Czech and Hanka have *i*; and the Old Czech text and Hanka's translation also begin a few more lines with *i*, where Linda goes without a conjunction; finally, the adjective form *lútý*/*lítý* appears just once in Linda's text and several more times in the Old Czech and Hanka's translation, replacing Linda's *dravý* and *krutý*. The Old Czech text and Hanka's translation, then, go significantly farther in altering the norms of Czech, as discussed below.

61. Julius Dolanský, *Neznámý jihoslovanský pramen Rukopisů královédvorského a zelenohorského* (Prague: Academia, 1968), 56–57 (hereafter *Neznámý pramen*).

62. Komárek, "Jazykovědná problematika RKZ," 244.

63. Dolanský, *Neznámý pramen*, 74, 76.

64. Komárek, "Jazykovědná problematika RKZ," 224–29.

65. In fact, word frequency data from our digital analysis of the texts shows that the manuscripts' texts have a far higher ratio of the use of *i* in relation to *a* than in the related BCS and Russian texts. The manuscripts use *i* over ten times more often than *a* (271 to 21). A corpus of most of the epic texts from Karadžić's 1814 and 1815 publications has *i* outnumbering *a* at about 2:1 (669 to 304). A corpus of most of the epic texts from the Kirsha Danilov collection of byliny has a ratio of less than 1.5 to 1 (1321 to 981—these are the two most frequent words in the text altogether). The imitation of these sources exaggerates their characteristics significantly.

66. Krejčí, "Některé nedořešené otázky kolem RKZ," 441. See the examples of compounds in chapter 2. In examining the question of whether "ladný," as discussed by Dolanský, was a mistake or not, Krejčí suggests that the mistake may have been intentional (442n7). I am suggesting that this applies as well to dozens if not hundreds more similar "mistakes."

67. Among the non-Slavic languages that invited phonological translation in the period, ancient Greek ranked high for the cultural capital that the implied close language relationship could confer, in competition with German claims to be the mediators of the Greek inheritance.

68. See Dobiáš, *RKZ*, 200.

69. Dobiáš, 200.

70. Exceptions include the following: *jarno* is translated (oddly) as *urno*; *lúto* in just one of six instances as *líto*, instead of *lítě*; *mutno* > *smutno* once, *smutně* twice; *rózno* > *různo*; *strašivo* > *všestrašlivo* once, *strašlivě* once; *strašno* remains the same once, becomes *strašně* once; *tajno* kept once, replaced by *tamo* once (changing the sense and part of speech but keeping the sound qualities); *usilno* kept once, as *usilně* once; *ticho* always *ticho*, in all four instances; and *žalostivo* kept twice, translated as *žalostivě* seven times. The translations of *jarno* as *urno* and *tajno* as *tamo* can be seen as (possibly deliberate) misreadings of the manuscript by Hanka. Dalibor Dobiáš et al., *Rukopisy královédvorský a zelenohorský a česká věda (1817–1885)*, Literární řada (Prague: Academia, 2014), 577 (hereafter *RKZ a česká věda*).

71. Krejčí, "Některé nedořešené otázky kolem RKZ," 442.

72. For summaries of the evidence, see Miroslav Ivanov, *Tajemství RKZ* (Prague: Mladá Fronta, 1969), 469–76; and Dobiáš et al., *RKZ a česká věda*, 576–86.

73. Ignác B. Mašek provides a list of the changes with discussion, from the period before the manuscript wars. Ignác B. Mašek, "Popis korektur a rasur v Rukopise kralodvorském," *Listy filologické* 3 (1876): 176–201.

74. Dobiáš, *RKZ*. Also in lines 126 and 214 of that poem.

75. Viktorin Vojtěch and Václav Flajšhans, eds., *Rukopisy královédvorský a zelenohorský* (Prague: Česká grafická unie, 1930), 21n206 (hereafter *RKZ*); Dobiáš et al., *RKZ a česká věda*, 582.

76. Mašek, "Popis korektur," 180–81.

77. Zdeněk Fiala, "O rukopisech po stránce paleografické," in *Rukopisy královédvorský a zelenohorský: Dnešní stav poznání*, ed. Mojmír Otruba, Sbornik Národního muzea v Praze, řada C—Literární historie, sv. 13–14 (Prague: Academia, 1969), 72; Vojtěch and Flajšhans, *RKZ*, 34n33, illustration 17a. As the illustration in Flajšhans shows, there is at least a small dot of ink under the upper arch of the *o* to help the erasure turn it from *o* to *e*, but it is unclear from the photo if the color of this tiny dot is the same as the other ink.

78. Ivanov, *Tajemství RKZ*, 471.

79. Ivanov, 473; Vojtěch and Flajšhans, *RKZ*, 48n44.

80. Vojtěch and Flajšhans, *RKZ*, 21n210.

81. See Dobiáš et al., *RKZ a česká věda*, 584.

82. Mašek, "Popis korektur," 193. *Mudro* is translated by Hanka as *mudře*.

83. Dobiáš et al., *RKZ a česká věda*, 577, 579. The later changes are in his 1829 edition.

84. Dobiáš et al., 598–99.

85. The text is not included in the Dobiáš 2010 edition but can be found in my bilingual translated edition. Cooper, *The Manuscripts*, 120–22. (Lines are misnumbered there—please excuse the error.)

86. Dobiáš et al., *RKZ a česká věda*, 603–6. Baum and Patera note the erasures and corrections. Antonín Baum and Adolf Patera, "České glossy a miniatury v 'Mater verborum,'" *Časopis národního musea* 51 (1877): 489.

87. Dobiáš et al., *RKZ a česká věda*, 607–11.

88. Antonín Vašek, *Filologický důkaz, že Rukopis Kralodvorský a Zelenohorský, též zlomek Evangelia sv. Jana jsou podvržená díla Vácslava Hanky* (Brno: Nákladem spisovatelovým, 1879), 15.

89. The text is found in Josef Jireček, *O českém prvotním překladu sv. evangelií a obměnách jeho až do XV. století* (Prague: Kateřina Jeřábková, 1859), 5, 16–26.

4. Faith, Ritual, and the Manuscripts

1. For discussion of the competing interpretations, see Hugh LeCaine Agnew, *Origins of the Czech National Renascence*, Pitt Series in Russian and East European Studies, no. 18 (Pittsburgh: University of Pittsburgh Press, 1993), 6–12.

2. Vladimír Macura, *Znamení zrodu: České obrození jako kulturní typ*, Nové, rozšířené vydání (Prague: H & H, 1995), 106.

3. Josef Šusta, *Léta dětství a jinošství: Vzpomínky I* (Prague: Melantrich, 1947), 195.

4. Dalibor Dobiáš, ed., *Rukopis královédvorský; Rukopis zelenohorský*, Česká knižnice (Brno: Host, 2010), 253 (hereafter *RKZ*); David L. Cooper, ed., *The Queen's Court and Green Mountain Manuscripts with Other Forgeries of the Czech Revival*, Czech Translations, vol. 6 (Ann Arbor: Michigan Slavic Publications, 2018), xix (hereafter *The Manuscripts*).

5. Martin Hrdina and Kateřina Piorecká, "Věřit a vědět (Rukopisy královédvorský a zelenohorský v letech 1867–1885)," in *Rukopisy královédvorský a zelenohorský a česká věda (1817–1885)*, by Dalibor Dobiáš et al. (Prague: Academia, 2014), 242.

6. Šusta, *Vzpomínky*, 170.

7. Jan Herben, *Boj o podvržené rukopisy: Zpomínky po 25ti letech*, Knihovnička "Času," č. 58 (Prague: Pokrok, 1911), 5.

8. Herben, 17.

9. Herben, 25.

10. Dagmar Blümlová, "Václav Tille—Zrod pozitivistického skeptika," in *Čas pádu rukopisů: Studie a materiály*, ed. Dagmar Blümlová and Bohumil Jiroušek (České Budějovice: Jihočeská univerzita, Historický ústav, 2004), 78; Herben, *Boj o podvržené rukopisy*, 25.

11. Dobiáš, *RKZ*, 251.

12. Herben, *Boj o podvržené rukopisy*, 5.

13. Dobiáš reminds us that starting in the late 1850s, as more critical evidence was brought forward and the cover falsifications were being exposed, there were a number of peripheral groups in Czech nationalist society in which the authenticity of the manuscripts was not dogma. Dalibor Dobiáš, "Vzpomínání na Rukopisy: Rukopisy královédvorský a zelenohorský v memoárové literatuře," in *Rukopisy královédvorský a zelenohorský v kultuře a umění*, ed. Dalibor Dobiáš (Prague: Academia, 2019), 1:133.

14. Josef Dobrovský, "Literarischer Betrug," *Archiv für Geschichte, Statistik, Literatur und Kunst* 15, no. 46 (1824): 260. Translation in Cooper, *The Manuscripts*, 148–49.

15. For further details on each of these examples, some of which are still controversial, see the annotations in Dalibor Dobiáš et al., *Rukopisy královédvorský a zelenohorský a česká věda (1817–1885)*, Literární řada (Prague: Academia, 2014), 633–34 (hereafter *RKZ a česká věda*).

16. That Dobrovský had declared the manuscript false without having seen it and never closely examined it was false, but the story had a long life as a legend among the manuscripts' supporters.

17. Václav Alois Svoboda, "Libuše als Gesetzgeberin," in *Literární a prozodická bohemika*, ed. Miroslav Heřman, Spisy a projevy Josefa Dobrovského (Prague: Academia, 1974), 158.

18. Svoboda, 160.

19. A. A. Zalizniak, *"Slovo o polku Igoreve": Vzgliad lingvista*, Studia philologica, malaia seriia (Moscow: Iazyki slavianskoi kul'tury, 2004), 23.

20. Exceptions included the Slovak Juraj Palkovič, Josef Vlastimil Kamarýt, and Josef Jaroslav Langer. Dobiáš, *RKZ*, 231, 236.

21. Jakub Malý, *Výbor drobných spisů Jakuba Malého* (Prague: Nákladem kněhkupectví: I. L. Kober, 1876), 2:414; Macura, *Znamení zrodu*, 119, 140.

22. Zdeněk Nejedlý, *Bedřich Smetana*, 2nd ed., 7 vols., Sebrané spisy Zdeňka Nejedlého (Prague: Orbis, 1950–54), 4:82.

23. Josef Bojislav Pichl, *Vlastenecké vzpomínky*, Pamětí, knihovna literárních vzpomínek a korespondence, vol. 3 (Prague: F. Borový, 1936), 25.

24. Pichl, 85.

25. Macura, *Znamení zrodu*, 140.

26. Augustine, *Confessions*, trans. Henry Chadwick, World's Classics (Oxford: Oxford University Press, 1991), 143–44, 152–53.

27. Antonín Rybička slips here from direct quotation to indirect, but the reference to Acts seems to belong to Sedláček. Antonín Rybička, *Přední křisitelé národa českého: Boje a usilování o právo jazyka českého začátkem přítomného století* (Prague: Tiskem a nákl. knihtiskárny F. Šimáčka, 1883), 2:289–90 (emphasis mine).

28. Peter G. Stromberg, "Ideological Language in the Transformation of Identity," *American Anthropologist* 92 (1990): 54.

29. Stromberg, 43.

30. Rybička, *Přední křisitelé*, 2:289.

31. Macura, *Znamení zrodu*, 140.

32. Arne Novák, *Josef Dobrovský*, Zlatoroh, sbírka illustrovaných monografií, sv. 53 (Prague: Nákl. spolku výtvarných umělců Mánes, 1928), 11.

33. František Palacký, *Františka Palackého: Korrespondence a zápisky*, Sbírka pramenův ku poznání literárního života v Čechách, na Moravě a v Slezsku, skupina 2 (Prague: Nakl. České akademie Císaře Františka Josefa pro vědy, slovesnost a umění, 1898), 1:7.

34. On the dialogues and Jungmann's program, see David L. Cooper, *Creating the Nation: Identity and Aesthetics in Early Nineteenth-Century Russia and Bohemia* (DeKalb: Northern Illinois University Press, 2010), 73–84.

35. Thanks to Valeria Sobol for this reference.

36. Ivan Tkachenko, *P. O. Kulish: Krytyko-biohrafichnyi narys*, Krytyka i teoriia literatury (Kharkiv: Knyhospilka, 1927), 9.

37. The Jena argument is made by Felix Vodička in Jan Mukařovský, ed., *Dějiny česke literatury*, Práce Československé akademie věd (Prague: Nakl. Československé akademie věd, 1959), vol. 2.

38. Ferdinand Menčík and Jaromír Hrubý, *Jan Kollár, pěvec slovanské vzájemnosti*, Matice lidu, roč. 27, čís. 6 (běžné čís. 162) (Prague: Nákladem spolku pro vydávání laciných knih českých, 1893), 58, 65.

39. Vladimír Forst, "Kollárovo Pražské Intermezzo," in *Ján Kollár (1793–1993): Zborník štúdií*, ed. Cyril Kraus (Bratislava: Veda, 1993), 108–20.

40. Jan Kollár, *Cestopis druhý, a Paměti z mladších let života Jana Kollára sepsány od něho samého*, Spisy Jana Kollára, díl 4 (Prague: I. L. Kober, 1863), 281.

41. Dobiáš cites another ambiguous connection in Kollár's memoirs to the initiation function of the Queen's Court Manuscript: Šafařík sent a package to him in Jena with a description of the manuscript and some fragments from the text, to which Jan Benedikti had added a note on the envelope encouraging him to remain faithful and stalwart in his love of his nation, "as if he had doubts" about his nationality. Offended, Kollár replied, "*You* yourself be true to the nation—I always will be!" Benedikti, his friend, here uses the manuscript to encourage his commitment to the national cause. Dobiáš, "Vzpomínání na Rukopisy," 125.

42. Palacký, *Korrespondence*, 1:28–29.

43. František Ladislav Čelakovský, *Korespondence a zápisky*, ed. František Bílý and Jaroslav Šťastný, Sbírka pramenův ku poznání literárního života v Čechách, na Moravě a v Slezsku, Skupina 2: Korespondence a prameny cizojazyčné, č. 14, 24, 27–28 (Prague: Nákl. České akademie věd a umění, 1910), 14, https://archive.org/details/korespondencez02elakuoft/mode/2up.

44. Pichl, *Vlastenecké vzpomínky*, 40–41, 42.

45. Cooper, *The Manuscripts*, 63.

46. That is, from youth to death. Vesna is a goddess personifying spring, Morana a goddess personifying death and winter.

47. Cooper, *The Manuscripts*, 63.

48. Pichl, *Vlastenecké vzpomínky*, 51.

49. Hermenegild Jireček, *Rozpominky z mládí*, Jireček: Volné Rozpravy 6 (Mýto Vysoké: Nákladem autorovým, 1909), 12–13.

50. Macura, *Znamení zrodu*, 120; Vladimír Forst, Jiří Opelík, and Luboš Merhaut, eds., *Lexikon české literatury: Osobnosti, díla, instituce*, vyd. 1 (Prague: Academia, 1985), 4:679–80.

51. Václav Nebeský, "Kralodvorský Rukopis," *Časopis českého musea* 26, no. 3 (1852): 131.

52. Lena Dorn, "Rukopisy královédvorský a zelenohorský v němčině: Otazky pro estetiku překladu," in *Rukopisy královédvorský a zelenohorský v kultuře a umění*, ed. Dalibor Dobiáš (Prague: Academia, 2019), 2:1180.

53. Dobiáš, "Vzpomínání na Rukopisy," 130.

54. Nebeský, "Kralodvorský Rukopis," 134.

55. Jakub Malý, *Naše znovuzrození: Přehled národního života českého za posledního půlstoletí*, Politická bibliotéka česká, díl 1 (Prague: J. Otto, 1880), 20.

56. Joseph Ziegler's influence on Michal Silorad Patrčka, one of those named in the following account, can perhaps be used to date the ceremony to around 1810, when Patrčka met him on his business travels. Forst, Opelík, and Merhaut, *Lexikon české literatury*, 3:820.

57. Rybička, *Přední křisitelé*, 1:172.

58. Rybička, 1:193. The list includes a number of figures known to have taken their patriotic names later, like Čelakovský and Kamarýt, who took patriotic names in 1817, so it should rather be read as a list of those who took such names under Ziegler's influence: "*Celakovský* Fr. Ladislav, *Dostál* Jos. Bořita, *Hek* Frant. Vladislav, *Hekova* Vlasta a Ludmila, *Chmelenský* Jos. Krásoslav, *Kamarýt* Jos. Vlastimil, *Kann* Jos. Polemír, *Kerner*

Jos. Libomir, *Korab* Fr. Lékoslav, *Král* Jos. Mirovit, *Kramerius* Václ. Radomil, *Ludvik* Jos. Myslimír, *Padnur*? Jan Domoslav, *Patrčka* Mich. Silorád, *Polák* Mat. Milota Zdirad, *Pešina* Václ. Čechorod, *Plánek* Jan Vlastislav, *Pospišil* Jan Hostivit, *Presl* Jan Svatopluk, *Presl* Karel Bořivoj, *Rautenkranz* (Rautovský) Jos. Miloslav, *Rettig* Jan Sudiprav, *Rettigová* Magd. Dobromila, *Šneider* Karel Sudimír, *Štěpnička* Fr. Bohumir, *Tomsa* Fr. Bohumil, *Trnka* Fr. Dobromysl, *Vambera* Fr. Lidurád, *Veverka* Jos. Budislav, *Vindyš* Jos. Hajislav, *Ziegler* Jos. Liboslav."

59. Alois Jirásek, *F. L. Věk: Obraz z dob našeho národního probuzení* (Prague: Nakladatelství J. Otto, 1925), 5:22.

60. Macura, *Znamení zrodu*, 142.

61. On the names in the manuscripts, see Miroslav Komárek, "Jazykovědná problematika RKZ," in *Rukopisy královédvorský a zelenohorský: Dnešní stav poznání*, ed. Mojmír Otruba, Sbornik Národního muzea v Praze, řada C—Literární historie, sv. 13–14 (Prague: Academia, 1969), 245–48. Komárek cites the interpretation that several new names likely resulted from the shortening of existing names: Lumír < Lutomír, Lubor < Lutobor, Střebor < Střezibor, Kruvoj < Krutovoj, Vlaslav < Vlastislav. It is worth noting that these shortened names appear in the ten-syllable epic poems, and the shortening greatly helped to facilitate the use of the names in that short epic line (see chapter 2 and the problems with the three-syllable name Libuše) (246).

62. Macura, *Znamení zrodu*, 141.

63. Forst, Opelík, and Merhaut, *Lexikon české literatury*, 3:1174, 1177. Here is the full list of pseudonyms in alphabetical order: Abrahám Šestivous; Aesopus Gibbonus; Amos Immewahr; Anaxagoras; Anaxagoras j.; Auch ein Schriftsteller; Babimor Romibab; Bárta Jednota; Bárta Neklej; Bedřich Lesklý; Bos Minor; Cantor physiognomicus; Clocher de Notredame; Čeští sněmovníci; Danois; David; Dr. Durdík Svatopluk; Dr. Pantaleon; Dvořák Hubený; Esopus Gibbius; Fabian Ponocný; Falstaffe; E. Prták; Fr. Polívka, městský kuchař; Franta Nemluvňátko; Franta Zajíček; Honza ze Vsi; I. Ipse; Ivan . . . ; J. E. Libochovický; J. E. P. Libochovický; J. Vtipse Ipse; Jakub Senfkórleen; Jan Dlažba; Jan Ev. Libochovický; Jan Ev. P. Libochovický; Jan Herold; Jan Kaporalský; Jan Libochovický; Jan Nestavovský; Jan P. Libochovský; Jan Prkený Doktor Medicinal; Jan Totus; Jan z Boudy; Jan z Prahy; Jan Zahradník; Januš Nápověda; Jeden od N. L.; Jeden z Českých asimilantů; Jeden z hostí; Jeremiáš Slovíčko; J. U. D. Appl; Kašpar Witzbold, hejtman; Kašpar Zvěřina; Kavalír Kukáč; Lazar Žebrák; Libochovský; Lord Byron; Maloslav "á"; Martialis Pražák; Martin Molnar; Matěj Sumslavus; Mikloš Cikán; Moses Kilka; Nemzeti Lap; Ondřej Frak; Ovidius Naso; Ovidius Valach; P. Libochovický; Pallas Athéně; Pantaleon; Paracelsus; Petr Služebný; Podali Hexametr s Pentametrem; Posthum; Posthumus; Prof. Dr. Punčoška; Próteus Humanus; Quisquid ubi; Rejpal Křešínský; Rusticus Čekálek; Šero veniens; Thomas Cantus; Tlampač kr. Tlumač zde; V. Tomášek; Versifex fortis; Vinař Vodňanský; Vojta Cidlinský; Vratislav z Mitrovic; Zefrin Šmid; along with some that were merely initials: A. A. Z.; ěs; J. J. E. P.; J. Fr. R . . . ; J. N.; J. P.; J.P-ně; P*** (dub.); pě; P-ě; Th . . . ; V/H. J. N.; 1. 5. ano 1. 5.

64. Forst, Opelík, and Merhaut, 3:32.

65. Forst, Opelík, and Merhaut, 4:483, 421. Rybička began his biographical sketch of Svoboda with a justification for including this figure who had been accused of never fully committing to Czech nationality, continuing to write and publish in German and address that public as well as the Czechs. Rybička, *Přední křisitelé*, 2:373.

66. Forst, Opelík, and Merhaut, *Lexikon české literatury*, 2:58, 4:483, 2:1186.

67. Dobiáš, "Vzpomínání na Rukopisy," 125n14; Dobiáš, *RKZ*, 232–33. Forst, Opelík, and Merhaut, *Lexikon české literatury*, 3:96.

68. Marijan Šabić, "Chorvatská recepce Rukopisů královédvorského a zelenohorského," in *Rukopisy královédvorský a zelenohorský v kultuře a umění*, ed. Dalibor Dobiáš (Prague: Academia, 2019), 2:1326.

69. Forst, Opelík, and Merhaut, *Lexikon české literatury*, 1:59.

70. Karel Slavoj Amerling, "Věštby vítězové—Záboj a Slavoj," *Posel z Budče* 1, no. 21, 23, 24, 25 (1848): 340–48, 372–75, 385–91, 405–15.

71. Forst, Opelík, and Merhaut, *Lexikon české literatury*, 3:437; Ferd. Čenský, "Václav Bolemír Nebeský: Studie životopisná a literární," *Osvěta: Listy pro rozhled v umění, vědě a politice* 13, no. 1 (1883): 26.

72. Forst, Opelík, and Merhaut, *Lexikon české literatury*, 3:96.

73. Jitka Ludvová, "Hankovy padělky v české hudbě," *Hudební věda* 27, no. 4 (1990): 308.

74. See Miroslav Ivanov, *Tajemství RKZ* (Prague: Mladá Fronta, 1969), 16–34.

75. Václav Hanka, "Připomenutj," in *Rukopis Králodworský: Sebránj lyricko-epických národnjch zpěwů, wěrně w půwodnjm starém gazyku, též w obnoweném pro snadněgšj wyrozuměnj s připogenjm německého přeloženj* (Prague: Bohumila Haze a Joz. Krause, 1819), iii–iv. Translation in Cooper, *The Manuscripts*, 142.

76. This portion of the chapter and its main argument were drafted before I got a copy of Karel Šima's excellent article, which covers much of the same ground. Some of the conclusions of Šima's insightful analysis will be given, but also some sources that he missed. Karel Šima, "Festivní kultura spojená s Rukopisy: Rukopis královédvorský mezi dynamikou měšťanské společnosti a kultura romantického nacionalismu," in *Rukopisy královédvorský a zelenohorský v kultuře a umění*, ed. Dalibor Dobiáš (Prague: Academia, 2019), 1:91–117.

77. Hanka, "Připomenutj," iv.

78. Jan Č. Brdička, *Věneček uvit třicetileté památce nalezení Rukopisu Kralodvorského: Slaveno 16. září 1847 v Králové Dvoře* (Prague: Knížecí-arcibiskupská knihtiskárna, 1847), 11.

79. Šima raises the question of whether reference to singing the national anthem later in 1857 applies to the Czech anthem or the Austrian one. It could at that time still refer to the Austrian one, but given that a German source refers to a "Volkshymne," it is perhaps more likely the Czech one in that case. Šima, "Festivní kultura," 100n11.

80. Anonymous (v v—), "Z Král. Dvoru (Zkouška. Slavnost nalezení Rukopisu)," *Květy* 12 (1845): 507. Šima notes that *besedy* began in Prague in the early 1840s as an off-season alternative to winter balls, with added elements of recitation, songs, and sometimes comedy. But in the use of the *beseda* for a national celebration, Dvůr Králové moved ahead of Prague. Šima, "Festivní kultura," 94, 116.

81. According to the account published in December in *Pražské noviny*, the *beseda* could not be planned for the sixteenth as that fell during an autumn church fast period. Anonymous (M.), "Z Králové Dvoru (Slavnost nalezení Králodvorského rukopisu)," *Pražské noviny* 23 (1847): 398.

82. Ludvová, "Hankovy padělky v české hudbě," 307.

83. Anonymous (M.), "Slavnost," 398.

84. Šima, "Festivní kultura," 96.

85. Brdička, *Věneček*, 28. Šima observes that these four new stanzas (of which I have cited one) connect local history to national history by focusing on events (many half fictional) of wider significance that took place in or near the town. Šima, "Festivní kultura," 95.

86. Fiona J. Stafford, "Introduction: The Ossianic Poems of James Macpherson," in *The Poems of Ossian and Related Works*, by James Macpherson, ed. Howard Gaskill (Edinburgh: Edinburgh University Press, 1996), xvi.

87. Brdička, *Věneček*, 26–27, 30.

88. Michal Charypar, "Motiv, syžet, poetika: Písně Rukopisu královédvorského a jejich vliv na novočeskou poezii do příchodu Májovců," in *Rukopisy královédvorský a zelenohorský v kultuře a umění*, ed. Dalibor Dobiáš (Prague: Academia, 2019), 1:467.

89. Charypar, 465.

90. Charypar, 463, 466, 467, 478, 479, 480.

91. This overview summarizes from the excellent account in Milan Hlavačka, "Czechs during the Revolution and Neo-Absolutism (1848–1860)," in *A History of the Czech Lands*, by Jaroslav Pánek and Oldřich Tůma, 2nd ed. (Prague: Karolinum Press, 2018), 345–62.

92. Antonín Konst. Víták, *Dějiny kralovského věnného města Dvora Králové nad Labem: K oslavě padesátileté památky nalezení rukopisu Kralodvorskěho* (Prague: Tisk. Dra. F. Skrejšovského, 1867), 131, http://catalog.hathitrust.org/api/volumes/oclc/19945705.html.

93. Víták, 131. Ivanov raised the question of whether this was a staged refusal and triumphant appearance or not. Šima questions whether Hanka really declined the invitation, because he sent his poem to be distributed ahead of time and had a central place in the festivities. In that case, this was excellent stagecraft and another mystification. Ivanov, *Tajemství RKZ*, 336–37; Šima, "Festivní kultura," 99.

94. Anonymous, "Z Králové Dvora," *Lumír* 7, no. 41 (October 8, 1857): 980.

95. Ivanov, *Tajemství RKZ*, 317.

96. Víták, *Dějiny*, 134.

97. Quotation on toasts from Anonymous, "Z Králové Dvora," October 8, 1857, 981. Descriptions of the festivities in Víták, *Dějiny*, 130–37; Anonymous, "V Králové Dvoře," *Lumír* 7, no. 40 (October 1, 1857): 958–59; Anonymous, "Z Králové Dvora," October 8, 1857.

98. Víták, *Dějiny*, 137.

99. Šima agrees that this is the first mass Czech national celebration and remarks that the statue to Záboj was also the first such national monument. Šima, "Festivní kultura," 103.

100. Šima, 91.

101. Michal Fránek, "Ve stínu česko-německého antagonismu (Rukopisy královédvorský a zelenohorský v letech 1853–1866)," in *Rukopisy královédvorský a zelenohorský a česká věda (1817–1885)*, by Dalibor Dobiáš et al. (Prague: Academia, 2014), 157–58 (hereafter "Ve stínu antagonismu").

102. Fr. Roubík, "Účast policie v útoku na Rukopisy roku 1858," in *Od pravěku k dnešku: Sborník prací z dějin československých, k šedesátým narozeninám Josefa Pekaře* (Prague: Historický klub, 1930), 2:436.

103. Vladimír Kopecký, *Plno záhad kolem Hanky* (Zurich: Konfrontace, 1981), 132–33.

104. Roubík, "Účast policie," 437–38.

105. Fránek, "Ve stínu antagonismu," 156–57.

106. Roubík, "Účast policie," 439.

107. Ivanov, *Tajemství RKZ*, 342; Fránek, "Ve stínu antagonismu," 159.

108. Kopecký, *Plno záhad kolem Hanky*, 19.

109. Fránek, "Ve stínu antagonismu," 162–89, 160.

110. Vladimír Kopecký suggests that Päumann chose the newspaper he did in order strategically to set the Czech and Jewish communities against each other. Kopecký, *Plno záhad kolem Hanky*, 160.

111. Roubík, "Účast policie," 446.

112. Kopecký, *Plno záhad kolem Hanky*, 40–41.

113. Kopecký, 60.

114. Kopecký, 63–64.

115. Ivanov, *Tajemství RKZ*, 343–44; Roubík, "Účast policie," 447.

116. Kopecký, *Plno záhad kolem Hanky*, 154.

117. Marek Nekula, *Smrt a zmrtvýchvstání národa: Sen o Slavíně v české literatuře a kultuře* (Prague: Univerzita Karlova v Praze, nakladatelství Karolinum, 2017), 284.

118. Nekula, 286. Nekula argues that Hanka's funeral also led, through the incorporation of the symbolism of the other major forged manuscript, the Green Mountain Manuscript with its epic narration of Libuše's judgment set at Vyšehrad, to the establishment at Vyšehrad of the Slavín cemetery, place of interment of the pantheon of Czech patriots, and to the establishment of the Svatobor Association in 1862, which gave Prague its Slavic face through the erection of monuments to national heroes. Marek Nekula, "Constructing Slavic Prague: The 'Green Mountain Manuscript' and Public Space in Discourse," *Bohemia* 52, no. 1 (2012): 22–36.

119. Nekula, *Smrt*, 274–76; Nekula, "Constructing Slavic Prague," 29–30.

120. Nekula, "Constructing Slavic Prague," 32.

121. Nekula, *Smrt*, 276.

122. Nekula, "Constructing Slavic Prague," 30.

123. Ludvová, "Hankovy padělky v české hudbě," 308.

124. Nekula, *Smrt*, 279.

125. Nekula, "Constructing Slavic Prague," 32–33.

126. Víták, *Dějiny*, 217; Nekula, "Constructing Slavic Prague," 33.

127. Ludvová, "Hankovy padělky v české hudbě," 308; Víták, *Dějiny*, 86.

128. Ludvová, "Hankovy padělky v české hudbě," 312.

129. Agnew, *Origins*, 130–34. See also Pavel Cibulka, Jan Hájek, and Martin Kučera, "The Definition of Czech National Society during the Period of Liberalism and Nationalism (1860–1914)," in *A History of the Czech Lands*, by Jaroslav Pánek and Oldřich Tůma, 2nd ed. (Prague: Karolinum Press, 2018), 365–73.

130. Ludvová, "Hankovy padělky v české hudbě," 308.

131. On the manuscript as a fetish object, see Hrdina and Piorecká, "Věřit a vědět," 205. The course of the celebrations is described in Anonymous (I.S.), "Jubilejní slavnost v Králově Dvoře," *Světozor* 1 (October 4, 1867): 128–29; Anonymous (Eduard Grégr?), *Padesátiletá slavnost objevení Rukopisu Kralodvorského: Odbývaná ve Dvore Kralove* (Prague: Nákladem vlastním, 1867), 14; Ludvová, "Hankovy padělky v české hudbě," 309.

132. Anonymous (Eduard Grégr?), *Padesátiletá slavnost*, 22, 9. One of the participants, Eduard Grégr, brother to Julius Grégr, the editor of *Národní listy*, estimated the crowds at ten thousand. Šima, "Festivní kultura," 110n31.

133. Anonymous (I.S.), "Jubilejní slavnost," 129.

134. Anonymous (Eduard Grégr?), *Padesátiletá slavnost*, 11, 14, 15, 21.

135. Anonymous (Eduard Grégr?), 30–31.

136. Anonymous (Eduard Grégr?), 33–35.

137. Anonymous (Eduard Grégr?), 37.

138. Anonymous (Eduard Grégr?), 14.

139. Anonymous (I.S.), "Jubilejní slavnost," 129. Sladkovský was a popular speaker at many national events at the time. Šima, "Festivní kultura," 106.

140. Jaroslava Janáčková, "Karel Havlíček v Borové," in *Sedm století Havlíčkovy Borové: Sborník k sedmistému výročí první historické zmínky o Havlíčkově Borově* (Havlíčková Borová: MNV a JZD ČSSP, 1989), 42; cited in Dalibor Dobiáš, "Pevnost na troskách dávné zbořeniny: K dvěma staletím recepce Rukopisů královédvorského a zelenohorského," in *Rukopisy královédvorský a zelenohorský v kultuře a umění*, ed. Dalibor Dobiáš (Prague: Academia, 2019), 1:32. I was unfortunately unable to get a copy of Janáčková's study.

141. Šima, "Festivní kultura," 111.

142. Anonymous, "Z Králové Dvora (Oslava šedesátileté památky nalezení rukopisu kralodvorského)," *Národní listy* 17, no. 270 (October 2, 1877): [3]; Ludvová, "Hankovy padělky v české hudbě," 310.

143. Dobiáš et al., *RKZ a česká věda*, 606.

144. T. G. Masaryk, "Poznámky k diskusi o RK a RZ," *Athenaeum* 4, no. 10 (July 15, 1887): 329. English translation in Cooper, *The Manuscripts*, 225–26.

145. Anonymous, "Zprávy spolkové: Ochotnická divadla," *Národní listy* 27, no. 253 (September 15, 1887): [3].

146. Šima missed this source on the plans for the seventieth anniversary. He suggests that this declining trajectory is true of national celebrations in general, which reached their peak in the late 1860s and early 1870s, after which the practice fell into disuse. Dvůr Králové led in both the rise and the fall. Šima, "Festivní kultura," 91–92, 112–13, 117. Šima also gives an account of a relatively large celebration in 1897, of mostly local significance and in which the church symbolism and celebration (St. Vaclav's day) took a more central place. In this, the local significance was not much hurt by the scholarly rejection of the manuscript (114).

147. Miroslav Laiske, "Bibliografie RKZ," in *Rukopisy královédvorský a zelenohorský: Dnešní stav poznání*, ed. Mojmír Otruba, Sbornik Národního muzea v Praze, řada C—Literární historie, sv. 13–14 (Prague: Academia, 1969), 382–83. The Czech Academy planned for a photographic facsimile edition of both manuscripts to be published for the one hundredth anniversary, but it was not realized. Ivanov, *Tajemství RKZ*, 491. For the two hundredth anniversary in 2017, though, the local Slavoj Library in Dvůr Králové did publish such a facsimile edition of the Queen's Court Manuscript (see figure I.1, in the introduction).

148. The society's website, under the title "Rukopisy Královédvorský a Zelenohorský," is available at this address: http://www.rukopisy-rkz.cz/rkz/.

149. Petr Píša, "Druhá část Rukopisu královédvorského a její nálezce Antonín Pfleger Kopidlanský," in *Historické fi kce a mystifi kace v české kultuře 19. století: Sborník příspěvků z 33. ročníku symposia k problematice 19. století, Plzeň, 21. února 2013*, edited by

Martin Hrdina and Kateřina Piorecká (Prague: Academia, 2014), 77–78; Šima, "Festivní kultura," 115.

150. Mojmír Otruba, "Mýtus a ritus: Pokus o sémantickou interpretaci obran pravosti RKZ," *Česká literatura* 18, no. 3–4 (1970): 272.

151. Iva Krejčová, "O pramennou hodnotu Rukopisů královédvorského a zelenohorského (1840–1853)," in *Rukopisy královédvorský a zelenohorský a česká věda (1817–1885)*, by Dalibor Dobiáš et al. (Prague: Academia, 2014), 146.

152. Otruba, "Mýtus a ritus," 272; Fránek, "Ve stínu antagonismu," 170–72.

153. Fránek, "Ve stínu antagonismu," 161, 177.

154. Hrdina and Piorecká, "Věřit a vědět," 221–22. Mojmír Otruba argued that the defenses were thus the primary movers in making the dispute public and political, not the skeptics. But Dalibor Dobiáš notes that Otruba's analysis did not take into account the German-language press, which also made skepticism into a national political argument. Dobiáš, "Vzpomínání na Rukopisy," 127.

155. Otruba, "Mýtus a ritus," 215.

156. Otruba does not list his corpus of defenses. The year-by-year bibliography in the 1969 *Rukopisy královédvorský a zelenohorský: Dnešní stav poznání* volume and the who's who in the dispute list on the website of the Czech Manuscript Society are useful sources for identifying authors of defenses from this period. Some authors listed in the bibliography were not prominent enough to get an entry in the who's who list or other typical sources for bio sketches of nineteenth-century Czechs. Laiske, "Bibliografie RKZ"; Jaroslav Gagan, "KDO Je KDO v RKZ," Rukopisy Královédvorský a Zelenohorský, accessed November 17, 2021, http://www.rukopisy-rkz.cz/rkz/gagan/jag/rukopisy/kdojekdo/kdojekdo_gagan.htm#V.

157. Julius Grégr, *Na obranu Rukopisů královédvorského a zelenohorského*, 2nd ed. (Prague: J. Otto, 1886); Oldřich V. Seykora, *Na obranu Rukopisu královédvorského: České inteligenci na uvaženou podává* (Prague: Cyrilo-Metodějská tiskárna a nakladatelství, 1893).

158. Otruba, "Mýtus a ritus," 231–33.

159. Otruba, 266–68.

160. Dobiáš, "Vzpomínání na Rukopisy," 131.

Conclusion

1. Dana Mentzlová, "Oslavy 200. výročí nálezu Rukopisů královédvorského a zelenohorského | Rukopisy královédvorský a zelenohorský (RKZ)—Padělky nebo staročeské památky?," accessed November 15, 2021, http://rkz.wz.cz/oslavy-200-vyroci-nalezu-rukopisu-kralovedvorskeho-a-zelenohorskeho/.

2. Catherine Servant, "Rukopisy královédvorský a zelenohorský jako faktum a historická fikce: Návraty k Rukopisům v české literatuře druhé poloviny 20. a počátku 21. století," in *Rukopisy královédvorský a zelenohorský v kultuře a umění*, ed. Dalibor Dobiáš (Prague: Academia, 2019), 1:821.

3. Servant, 820–22, 822.

4. Servant, 778.

5. Servant, 796.

6. Servant, 788.

7. Josef Urban [Miloš Urban], *Poslední tečka za Rukopisy (Nová literatura faktu)* (Prague: Argo, 1998).

Bibliography

Abramson, Julia. *Learning from Lying: Paradoxes of the Literary Mystification*. Newark: University of Delaware Press, 2005.

Agnew, Hugh LeCaine. *Origins of the Czech National Renascence*. Pitt Series in Russian and East European Studies, no. 18. Pittsburgh: University of Pittsburgh Press, 1993.

Amerling, Karel Slavoj. "Věštby vítězové—Záboj a Slavoj." *Posel z Budče* 1, no. 21 (1848): 340–48; no. 23, 372–75; no. 24, 385–91; no. 25, 405–15.

Anderson, Benedict. *Imagined Communities: Reflections on the Origin and Spread of Nationalism*. London: Verso, 1991.

Anonymous. "V Králově Dvoře." *Lumír* 7, no. 40 (October 1, 1857): 958–59.

——. "Z Králové Dvora." *Lumír* 7, no. 41 (October 8, 1857): 980–81.

Anonymous. "Z Králové Dvora (Oslava šedesátileté památky nalezení rukopisu kralodvorského)." *Národní listy* 17, no. 270 (October 2, 1877): [3].

——. "Zprávy spolkové: Ochotnická divadla." *Národní listy* 27, no. 253 (September 15, 1887): [3].

Anonymous (Eduard Grégr?). *Padesátiletá slavnost objevení Rukopisu Kralodvorského: Odbývaná ve Dvore Kralove*. Prague: Nákladem vlastním, 1867.

Anonymous (I.S.). "Jubilejní slavnost v Králově Dvoře." *Světozor* 1 (October 4, 1867): 128–30.

Anonymous (M.). "Z Králové Dvoru (Slavnost nalezení Králodvorského rukopisu)." *Pražské noviny* 23 (1847): 398.

Anonymous (v v—). "Z Král. Dvoru (Zkouška. Slavnost nalezení Rukopisu)." *Květy* 12 (1845): 507.

Apter, Emily. "Translation with No Original: Scandals of Textual Reproduction." In *Nation, Language, and the Ethics of Translation*, edited by Sandra Bermann and Michael Wood, 159–74. Princeton, NJ: Princeton University Press, 2005.

Arant, Patricia M. *Compositional Techniques of the Russian Oral Epic, the Bylina*. Harvard Dissertations in Folklore and Oral Tradition. New York: Garland, 1990.

Augustine. *Confessions*. Translated by Henry Chadwick. World's Classics. Oxford: Oxford University Press, 1991.

Austerlitz, Robert. *Ob-Ugric Metrics: The Metrical Structure of Ostyak and Vogul Folk-Poetry*. FF Communications, edited for the Folklore Fellows, vol. 70, no. 174. Helsinki: Suomalainen Tiedeakatemia, 1958.

Bailey, James, and T. G. Ivanova, eds. *An Anthology of Russian Folk Epics*. Folklores and Folk Cultures of Eastern Europe. Armonk, NY: M. E. Sharpe, 1998.

Bak, János M., Patrick J. Geary, and Gábor Klaniczay, eds. *Manufacturing a Past for the Present: Forgery and Authenticity in Medievalist Texts and Objects in Nineteenth-Century Europe*. National Cultivation of Culture, vol. 7. Leiden: Brill, 2015.

Bascom, William. "The Forms of Folklore: Prose Narratives." In *Sacred Narrative: Readings in the Theory of Myth*, edited by Alan Dundes, 5–29. Berkeley: University of California Press, 1984.

Baum, Antonín, and Adolf Patera. "České glossy a miniatury v 'Mater verborum.'" *Časopis národního musea* 51 (1877): 120–49, 372–90, 488–513.

Beebee, Thomas O. *Transmesis: Inside Translation's Black Box*. New York: Palgrave Macmillan, 2012.

Beran, Zdeněk. "RKZ anglicky—Víc než jen překlad." Review of *The Queen's Court and Green Mountain Manuscripts*, edited and translated by David L. Cooper. *Česká literatura* 68, no. 1 (2020): 87–94.

Berman, Antoine. *The Experience of the Foreign: Culture and Translation in Romantic Germany*. Intersections. Albany: State University of New York Press, 1992.

Blümlová, Dagmar. "Václav Tille—Zrod pozitivistického skeptika." In *Čas pádu rukopisů: Studie a materiály*, edited by Dagmar Blümlová and Bohumil Jiroušek, 73–83. České Budějovice: Jihočeská univerzita, Historický ústav, 2004.

Bowring, John. *Cheskian Anthology: Being a History of the Poetical Literature of Bohemia, with Translated Specimens*. London: R. Hunter, 1832.

Brdička, Jan Č. *Věneček uvit třicetileté památce nalezení Rukopisu Kralodvorského: Slaveno 16. září 1847 v Králové Dvoře*. Prague: Knížecí-arcibiskupská knihtiskárna, 1847.

Bynum, David E. *The Dæmon in the Wood: A Study of Oral Narrative Patterns*. Publications of the Milman Parry Collection: Monograph Series, no. 1. Cambridge, MA: Center for Study of Oral Literature, Harvard University, 1978.

Carpenter, Scott. *Aesthetics of Fraudulence in Nineteenth-Century France: Frauds, Hoaxes, and Counterfeits*. Farnham, England: Ashgate, 2009.

Casey, Nicholas. "Behind a Top Female Name in Spanish Crime Fiction: Three Men." *New York Times*, October 29, 2021, sec. World. https://www.nytimes.com/2021/10/29/world/europe/spanish-writer-carmen-mola-true-identity.html.

Cejp, Ladislav. "Jungmannův překlad Ztraceného ráje." In *Překlady*, by Josef Jungmann, 1:360–430. Prague: Státní nakl. krásné literatury, hudby a umění, 1958.

Čelakovský, František Ladislav. *Korespondence a zápisky*. Edited by František Bílý and Jaroslav Šťastný. Sbírka pramenův ku poznání literárního života v Čechách, na Moravě a v Slezsku. Skupina 2: Korespondence a prameny cizojazyčné, č. 14, 24, 27–28. Prague: Nákl. České akademie věd a umění, 1910. https://archive.org/details/korespondencez02elakuoft/mode/2up.

Čenský, Ferd. "Václav Bolemír Nebeský: Studie životopisná a literární." *Osvěta: Listy pro rozhled v umění, vědě a politice* 13, no. 1 (1883): 24–37; no. 2, 128–42; no. 3, 193–211.

Cermanová, Iveta. "Ramschakova kronika—Židovské falzum z doby Rukopisů." In *Rukopisy královédvorský a zelenohorský v kultuře a umění*, edited by Dalibor Dobiáš, 2:1127–52. Prague: Academia, 2019.

Charypar, Michal. "Motiv, syžet, poetika: Písně Rukopisu královédvorského a jejich vliv na novočeskou poezii do příchodu Májovců." In *Rukopisy královédvorský a zelenohorský v kultuře a umění*, edited by Dalibor Dobiáš, 1:445–84. Prague: Academia, 2019.

Chulkov, Mikhail Dmitrievich. *Sochineniia Mikhaila Dmitrievicha Chulkova*. Vol. 1, *Sobranie raznykh piesen*. St. Petersburg: Izd. Otdieleniia russkago iazyka i slovesnosti Imperatorskoi akademii nauk, 1913.

Cibulka, Pavel, Jan Hájek, and Martin Kučera. "The Definition of Czech National Society during the Period of Liberalism and Nationalism (1860–1914)." In *A History of the Czech Lands*, by Jaroslav Pánek and Oldřich Tůma, 365–414. 2nd ed. Prague: Karolinum Press, 2018.

Cooper, David L. "Autor-překladatel-padělatel: Translace a mystifikace v Hankově Prostonárodní srbské múze a Puškinových Písních západních Slovanů." In *Historické fikce a mystifikace v české kultuře 19. století: Sborník příspěvků z 33. ročníku symposia k problematice 19. století, Plzeň, 21. února 2013*, edited by Martin Hrdina and Kateřina Piorecká, 59–69. Prague: Academia, 2014.

———. "Competing Languages of Czech Nation-Building: Jan Kollár and the Melodiousness of Czech." *Slavic Review* 67, no. 2 (2008): 301–20.

———. *Creating the Nation: Identity and Aesthetics in Early Nineteenth-Century Russia and Bohemia*. DeKalb: Northern Illinois University Press, 2010.

———, ed. *The Queen's Court and Green Mountain Manuscripts with Other Forgeries of the Czech Revival*. Czech Translations, vol. 6. Ann Arbor: Michigan Slavic Publications, 2018.

Derrida, Jacques. "What Is a 'Relevant' Translation?" In *The Translation Studies Reader*, edited by Lawrence Venuti, 365–88. 3rd ed. New York: Routledge, 2012.

Deutschmann, Peter. "Ideál divadelní komunikace: Rukopisy a historická dramata v 19. století." In *Rukopisy královédvorský a zelenohorský v kultuře a umění*, edited by Dalibor Dobiáš, 1:485–521. Prague: Academia, 2019.

Dmitriev, Lev Aleksandrovich, and Dmitrii Sergeevich Likhachev, eds. "Slovo o polku Igoreve." In *"Izbornik" (Sbornik proizvedenii literatury Drevnei Rusi)*, 196–213. Moscow: Khudozh. lit., 1969.

Dobiáš, Dalibor. "Mezi Rukopisem královédvorským a zelenohorským (1817–1829)." In *Rukopisy královédvorský a zelenohorský a česká věda (1817–1885)*, by Dalibor Dobiáš, Michal Fránek, Martin Hrdina, Iva Krejčová, and Kateřina Piorecká, 17–62. Prague: Academia, 2014.

———. "Pevnost na troskách dávné zbořeniny: K dvěma staletím recepce Rukopisů královédvorského a zelenohorského." In *Rukopisy královédvorský a zelenohorský v kultuře a umění*, edited by Dalibor Dobiáš, 1:13–51. Prague: Academia, 2019.

———, ed. *Rukopis královédvorský; Rukopis zelenohorský*. Česká knižnice. Brno: Host, 2010.

———, ed. *Rukopisy královédvorský a zelenohorský v kultuře a umění*. 2 vols. Prague: Academia, 2019.

———. "Vzpomínání na Rukopisy: Rukopisy královédvorský a zelenohorský v memoárové literatuře." In *Rukopisy královédvorský a zelenohorský v kultuře a umění*, edited by Dalibor Dobiáš, 1:119–35. Prague: Academia, 2019.

Dobiáš, Dalibor, Michal Fránek, Martin Hrdina, Iva Krejčová, and Kateřina Piorecká. *Rukopisy královédvorský a zelenohorský a česká věda (1817–1885)*. Literární řada. Prague: Academia, 2014.

Dobiáš, Dalibor, and Miroslav Novák. "Spor o roli Rukopisu královédvorského a zelenohorského v diskursu národa (1829–1840)." In *Rukopisy královédvorský a zelenohorský a česká věda (1817–1885)*, by Dalibor Dobiáš, Michal Fránek, Martin Hrdina, Iva Krejčová, and Kateřina Piorecká, 62–96. Prague: Academia, 2014.

Dobrovský, Josef. "Literarischer Betrug." *Archiv für Geschichte, Statistik, Literatur und Kunst* 15, no. 46 (1824): 260.

Dolanský, Julius. "Dvě varianty 'Záboje' z RK." *Česká literatura* 20, no. 4 (1972): 328–45.

——. *Neznámý jihoslovanský pramen Rukopisů královédvorského a zelenohorského*. Prague: Academia, 1968.

——. *Ohlas dvou ruských básníků v Rukopisech královédvorském a zelenohorském*. Prague: Univ. Karlova, t. Mír, 1969.

——. *Záhada Ossiana v Rukopisech královédvorském a zelenohorském*. Prague: Academia, 1975.

Dorn, Lena. "Rukopisy královédvorský a zelenohorský v němčině: Otazky pro estetiku překladu." In *Rukopisy královédvorský a zelenohorský v kultuře a umění*, edited by Dalibor Dobiáš, 2:1153–89. Prague: Academia, 2019.

Ducháček, Milan. "'Pravda není to, co jest, ale to, co býti má': Noetika Františka Mareše a ideové zdroje obnovení sporu o Rukopisy královédvorský a zelenohorský v době první republiky." In *Rukopisy královédvorský a zelenohorský v kultuře a umění*, edited by Dalibor Dobiáš, 1:283–309. Prague: Academia, 2019.

Dundes, Alan. Introduction to *Sacred Narrative: Readings in the Theory of Myth*, edited by Alan Dundes, 1–3. Berkeley: University of California Press, 1984.

Enders, Julius. *Rukopis Zelenohorský a Královédvorský: Vznik, styl a básnická hodnota staročeské orální poesie*. Prague: Neklan, 1993.

Fiala, Zdeněk. "O rukopisech po stránce paleografické." In *Rukopisy královédvorský a zelenohorský: Dnešní stav poznání*, edited by Mojmír Otruba, 49–81. Sbornik Národního muzea v Praze, řada C—Literární historie, sv. 13–14. Prague: Academia, 1969.

Flood, Alison. "Fragment of Lost 12th-Century Epic Poem Found in Another Book's Binding." *Guardian*, November 18, 2021, sec. Books. https://www.theguardian.com/books/2021/nov/18/fragment-of-lost-12th-century-epic-poem-found-in-another-books-binding.

Foley, John Miles. *Immanent Art: From Structure to Meaning in Traditional Oral Epic*. Bloomington: Indiana University Press, 1991.

——. *The Theory of Oral Composition: History and Methodology*. Bloomington: Indiana University Press, 1988.

——. *Traditional Oral Epic: The Odyssey, Beowulf, and the Serbo-Croatian Return Song*. Berkeley: University of California Press, 1990.

——. *The Wedding of Mustajbey's Son Bećirbey as Performed by Halil Bajgorić*. FF Communications, no. 283. Helsinki: Suomalainen Tiedeakatemia, 2004.

Forst, Vladimír. "Kollárovo Pražské Intermezzo." In *Ján Kollár (1793–1993): Zborník štúdií*, edited by Cyril Kraus, 108–20. Bratislava: Veda, 1993.

Forst, Vladimír, Jiří Opelík, and Luboš Merhaut, eds. *Lexikon české literatury: Osobnosti, díla, instituce*. Vyd. 1. 4 vols. Prague: Academia, 1985.

Fránek, Michal. "Ve stínu česko-německého antagonismu (Rukopisy královédvorský a zelenohorský v letech 1853–1866)." In *Rukopisy královédvorský a zelenohorský a česká věda (1817–1885)*, by Dalibor Dobiáš, Michal Fránek, Martin Hrdina, Iva Krejčová, and Kateřina Piorecká, 151–201. Prague: Academia, 2014.

Fránek, Michal, and Jiří Kopecký. "Rukopisy královédvorský a zelenohorský a česká opera." In *Rukopisy královédvorský a zelenohorský v kultuře a umění*, edited by Dalibor Dobiáš, 2:933–1006. Prague: Academia, 2019.

Frazier, Melissa. *Romantic Encounters: Writers, Readers, and the "Library for Reading."* Stanford, CA: Stanford University Press, 2007.

Gagan, Jaroslav. "KDO Je KDO v RKZ." Rukopisy Královédvorský a Zelenohorský. Accessed November 17, 2021. http://www.rukopisy-rkz.cz/rkz/gagan/jag/rukopisy/kdojekdo/kdojekdo_gagan.htm#V.

Gaskill, Howard. "Introduction: 'Genuine Poetry . . . like Gold.'" In *The Reception of Ossian in Europe*, edited by Howard Gaskill, 1–20. London: Thoemmes, 2004.

——. "'Ossian' Macpherson: Towards a Rehabilitation." *Comparative Criticism* 8 (1986): 113–46.

——. *Ossian Revisited*. Edinburgh: Edinburgh University Press, 1991.

——, ed. *The Reception of Ossian in Europe*. The Athlone Critical Traditions Series: The Reception of British Authors in Europe. London: Thoemmes, 2004.

——. "What Did James Macpherson Really Leave on Display at His Publisher's Shop in 1762?" *Scottish Gaelic Studies* 16 (1990): 67–89.

Gasparov, B. *Poetika "Slova o polku Igoreve."* Moscow: Agraf, 2000.

Gellner, Ernest. *Nations and Nationalism*. New Perspectives on the Past. Oxford: Blackwell, 1983.

Grégr, Julius. *Na obranu Rukopisů královédvorského a zelenohorského*. 2nd ed. Prague: J. Otto, 1886.

Groom, Nick. *The Forger's Shadow: How Forgery Changed the Course of Literature*. London: Picador, 2002.

——. "Romanticism and Forgery." *Literature Compass* 4, no. 6 (2007): 1625–49.

——. *Thomas Chatterton and Romantic Culture*. New York: St. Martin's Press, 1999.

——. "Thomas Chatterton Was a Forger." *Yearbook of English Studies* 28 (1998): 276–91.

Hájek, Jan, and Milan Hlavačka. "The Birth of the Modern Czech Nation (1792–1848)." In *A History of the Czech Lands*, by Jaroslav Pánek and Oldřich Tůma, 313–42. 2nd ed. Prague: Karolinum Press, 2018.

Hanka, Václav. *Hankovy písně a Prostonárodní srbská muza, do Čech převedená*. Edited by Jan Máchal. Novočeská knihovna, č. 3. Prague: Nákl. České akademie císaře Františka Josefa pro vědy, slovesnost a uměni, 1918.

——. "Igor Swatoslawič (Wýpiska dle Karamzjna)." *Krok* 1, no. 1 (1821): 81–85.

——. *Igor Swatoslawič: Hrdinsky zpiew o taženj proti Polowcům. Werně w půwodnjm gazyku, s připogenjm Českého a Německého přeloženj*. Prague: U Haze, Krausse, Endersa, 1821.

——. "Připomenutj." In *Rukopis Králodworský: Sebránj lyricko-epických národnjch zpěwů, wěrně w půwodnjm starém gazyku, též w obnoweném pro snadněgšj wyrozuměnj s připogenjm německého přeloženj*, i–iv. Prague: Bohumila Haze a Joz. Krause, 1819.

——. *Rukopis Králodworský: Sebránj lyricko-epických národnjch zpěwů, wěrně w půwodnjm starém gazyku, též w obnoweném pro snadněgšj wyrozuměnj s připogenjm německého přeloženj*. Prague: Bohumila Haze a Joz. Krause, 1819.

Hanuš, Josef. "Český Macpherson: Příspěvek k rozboru literární činnosti Josefa Lindy a k provenienci RK a RZ." *Listy filologické* 27, no. 2 (1900): 109–34; no. 3–4, 241–91; no. 5, 337–56; no. 6, 437–57.

Hayes, Julie Candler. *Translation, Subjectivity, and Culture in France and England, 1600–1800*. Stanford, CA: Stanford University Press, 2009.

Haymes, Edward R. "The Germanic *Heldenlied* and the Poetic *Edda*: Speculations on Preliterary History." *Oral Tradition* 19, no. 1 (2004): 43–62.

Herben, Jan. *Boj o podvržené rukopisy: Zpomínky po 25ti letech*. Knihovnička "Času," č. 58. Prague: Pokrok, 1911.

——. *Deset let proti proudu, 1886–1896: Zpomínky a zkušenosti českého novináře*. [Prague]: Nákl. vlastním, 1898.

Hlavačka, Milan. "Czechs during the Revolution and Neo-Absolutism (1848–1860)." In *A History of the Czech Lands*, by Jaroslav Pánek and Oldřich Tůma, 345–62. 2nd ed. Prague: Karolinum Press, 2018.

Hlobil, Tomáš. "Jungmannova charakteristika metafory a německá estetika 18. století." In *Mezi časy . . . Kultura a umění v českých zemích kolem roku 1800*, edited by Zdeněk Hojda and Roman Prahl, 224–32. Prague: Koniasch Latin Press, 2000.

——. "Ossianism in the Bohemian Lands." *Modern Language Review* 101 (2006): 789–97.

Homer. *The Iliad*. Translated by Richmond Lattimore. Chicago: University of Chicago Press, 1951.

——. *The Odyssey of Homer*. Translated by Richmond Lattimore. Perennial Classics. New York: Perennial, 1999.

Horálek, Karel. *Počátky novočeského verše*. Prague: Nákladem Karlovy University, 1956.

——. *Studie o slovenské lidové poezii*. Prague: Státní pedagogické nakl., 1962.

Hrabák, Josef. *Studie o českém verši*. Učebnice vysokých škol. Prague: Státní pedagogické nakl., 1959.

Hrdina, Martin, and Kateřina Piorecká. "Věřit a vědět (Rukopisy královédvorský a zelenohorský v letech 1867–1885)." In *Rukopisy královédvorský a zelenohorský a česká věda (1817–1885)*, by Dalibor Dobiáš, Michal Fránek, Martin Hrdina, Iva Krejčová, and Kateřina Piorecká, 203–44. Prague: Academia, 2014.

Hroch, Miroslav. *Social Preconditions of National Revival in Europe: A Comparative Analysis of the Social Composition of Patriotic Groups among the Smaller European Nations*. Cambridge: Cambridge University Press, 1985.

Hudson, Nicholas. "'Oral Tradition': The Evolution of an Eighteenth-Century Concept." In *Tradition in Transition: Women Writers, Marginal Texts, and the Eighteenth-Century Canon*, edited by Alvaro S. J. Ribeiro and James G. Basker, 161–76. Oxford: Clarendon Press, 1996.

"Il'ia Muromets i Kalin-Tsar'." Russkie byliny. Accessed September 9, 2019. http://www.byliny.ru/content/text/ilya-muromets-i-kalin.

Ivanov, Miroslav. *Tajemství RKZ*. Prague: Mladá Fronta, 1969.

Jagić, Vatroslav. "Gradja za slovinsku narodnu poeziju." *Rad JAZU* 37 (1876): 33–137.

Jakobson, Roman. "In Memory of V. V. Hanka." In *Language in Literature*, edited by Krystyna Pomorska and Stephen Rudy, 397–405. Cambridge, MA: Belknap Press of Harvard University Press, 1987.

——. "K časovým otázkám nauky o českém verši." *Slovo a slovesnost* 1 (1935): 46–53.

——. "Slavic Epic Verse: Studies in Comparative Metrics." In *Selected Writings*, 4:414–63. The Hague: Mouton, 1966.

Janáčková, Jaroslava. "Karel Havlíček v Borové." In *Sedm století Havlíčkovy Borové: Sborník k sedmistému výročí první historické zmínky o Havlíčkově Borově*, 39–48. Havlíčková Borová: MNV a JZD ČSSP, 1989.

Jirásek, Alois. *F. L. Věk: Obraz z dob našeho národního probuzení*. 5 vols. Prague: Nákladatelství J. Otto, 1925.

Jireček, Hermenegild. *Rozpominky z mládí*. Jireček: Volné Rozpravy 6. Mýto Vysoké: Nákladem autorovým, 1909.

Jireček, Josef. *O českém prvotním překladu sv. evangelií a obměnách jeho až do XV. století*. Prague: Kateřina Jeřábková, 1859.

Jungmann, Josef. *Boj o obrození národa: Výbor z díla*. Svět a my, sv. 9. Prague: F. Kosek, 1948.

Karadžić, Vuk Stefanović. *Songs of the Serbian People: From the Collections of Vuk Karadžić*. Edited by Milne Holton and Vasa D. Mihailovich. Pitt Series in Russian and East European Studies. Pittsburgh: University of Pittsburgh Press, 1997.

——. *Srpske narodne pjesme: Skupio ih i na svijet izdao Vuk Stef. Karadžić*. Vol. 2. Vienna: U štampariji Jermenskoga manastira, 1845.

Kašpar, Jaroslav. "Rukopis královédvorský a zelenohorský—Paleografický přepis." In *Rukopisy královédvorský a zelenohorský: Dnešní stav poznání*, edited by Mojmír Otruba, 275–322. Sbornik Národního muzea v Praze, řada C—Literární historie, sv. 13–14. Prague: Academia, 1969.

Keenan, Edward J. *Josef Dobrovský and the Origins of the "Igor' Tale."* Harvard Series in Ukrainian Studies. Cambridge, MA: Harvard Ukrainian Research Institute and the Davis Center for Russian and Eurasian Studies, 2003. Distributed by Harvard University Press.

Klaniczay, Gábor. "The Myth of Scythian Origin and the Cult of Attila in the Nineteenth Century." In *Multiple Antiquities—Multiple Modernities: Ancient Histories in Nineteenth Century European Cultures*, edited by Gábor Klaniczay, Michael Werner, and Ottó Gecser, 185–212. Frankfurt: Campus Verlag, 2011.

Kollár, Jan. *Cestopis druhý, a Paměti z mladších let života Jana Kollára sepsány od něho samého*. Spisy Jana Kollára, díl 4. Prague: I. L. Kober, 1863.

Komárek, Miroslav. "Jazykovědná problematika RKZ." In *Rukopisy královédvorský a zelenohorský: Dnešní stav poznání*, edited by Mojmír Otruba, 197–273. Sbornik Národního muzea v Praze, řada C—Literární historie, sv. 13–14. Prague: Academia, 1969.

Kopecký, Vladimír. *Plno záhad kolem Hanky*. Zurich: Konfrontace, 1981.

Krejčí, Karel. "Některé nedořešené otázky kolem RKZ." In *Literatury a žánry v evropské dimenzi: Nejen česká literatura v zorném poli komparistiky*, 425–45. Prague: Slovanský ústav AV ČR, 2014.

Krejčová, Iva. "Literární obraz slavné minulosti v rané recepci Rukopisu královédvorského a zelenohorského: Konstituování mýtu národní literatury." In *České literární romantično: Synopticko-pulzační model kulturního jevu*, edited by Dalibor Tureček, 155–92. Brno: Host, 2012.

——. "Mezi hrdinstvím a heroikomikou: Tematizace Rukopisů královédvorského a zelenohorského v česky psané básnické epice první poloviny 19. století." In *Rukopisy královédvorský a zelenohorský v kultuře a umění*, edited by Dalibor Dobiáš, 1:403–44. Prague: Academia, 2019.

——. "O pramennou hodnotu Rukopisů královédvorského a zelenohorského (1840–1853)." In *Rukopisy královédvorský a zelenohorský a česká věda (1817–1885)*, by Dalibor Dobiáš, Michal Fránek, Martin Hrdina, Iva Krejčová, and Kateřina Piorecká, 97–149. Prague: Academia, 2014.

——. "Rukopis královédvorský a ohlas písně o nibelunzích." *Česká literatura* 58, no. 4 (2010): 425–43.

Krontiris, Tina. *Oppositional Voices: Women as Writers and Translators of Literature in the English Renaissance*. London: Routledge, 1992.

Laiske, Miroslav. "Bibliografie RKZ." In *Rukopisy královédvorský a zelenohorský: Dnešní stav poznání*, edited by Mojmír Otruba, 323–408. Sbornik Národního muzea v Praze, řada C—Literární historie, sv. 13–14. Prague: Academia, 1969.

Leerssen, Joep. "Ossian and the Rise of Literary Historicism." In *The Reception of Ossian in Europe*, edited by Howard Gaskill, 109–25. London: Thoemmes, 2004.

Lencek, Rado L. "Kopitar's Slavic Version of the Greek Dialects Theme." In *Zbirnyk na poshanu profesora doktora Iuriia Shevel'ova = Symbolae in honorem Georgii Y. Shevelov*, edited by William E. Harkins, Olexa Horbatsch, and Jakob P. Hursky, 244–56. Munich: Logos, 1971.

Levý, Jiří. *České theorie překladu*. Český překlad, sv. 1. Prague: Státní nakl. krásné literatury, hudby a umění, 1957.

Lord, Albert Bates. "Avdo Međedović, Guslar." In *Slavic Folklore: A Symposium*, edited by Albert Bates Lord, 122–32. Philadelphia: American Folklore Society, 1956.

——. "Perspectives on Recent Work on the Oral Traditional Formula." *Oral Tradition* 1, no. 3 (1986): 467–503.

——. *The Singer of Tales*. Cambridge, MA: Harvard University Press, 1960.

Loužil, Jaromír. "Bernard Bolzano a Rukopisy: Josef Linda." *Česká literatura* 26, no. 3 (1978): 220–34.

Ludvová, Jitka. "Hankovy padělky v české hudbě." *Hudební věda* 27, no. 4 (1990): 299–319.

Máchal, Jan. "Úvod." In *Hankovy písně a Prostonárodní srbská muza, do Čech převedená*, edited by Jan Máchal, ix–xliv. Novočeská knihovna, č. 3. Prague: Nákl. České akademie císaře Františka Josefa pro vědy, slovesnost a umění, 1918.

Machalíková, Pavla. "Rukopisy královédvorský a zelenohorský a výtvarné umění v Čechách, od inovace k novému kánonu." In *Rukopisy královédvorský a zelenohorský v kultuře a umění*, edited by Dalibor Dobiáš, 2:1007–42. Prague: Academia, 2019.

Macpherson, James. "A Dissertation concerning the Antiquity, &c. of the Poems of Ossian the Son of Fingal." In *The Poems of Ossian and Related Works*, by James Macpherson, 43–52. Edited by Howard Gaskill. Edinburgh: Edinburgh University Press, 1996.

——. *The Poems of Ossian and Related Works*. Edited by Howard Gaskill. Edinburgh: Edinburgh University Press, 1996.

Macura, Vladimír. "Culture as Translation." In *Translation, History, and Culture*, edited by Susan Bassnett and André Lefevere, 64–70. New York: Pinter Publishers, 1990.

——. "Rukopisy aneb O mystifi kování českém." In *Češi a němci: Dějiny, kultura, politika*, edited by Walter Koschmal, Marek Nekula, and Joachim Rogall, 409–14. Prague: Paseka, 2001.

——. *Znamení zrodu a české sny*. Edited by Kateřina Piorecká and Milena Vojtková. Vybrané spisy Vladimíra Macury 1. Prague: Academia, 2015.

——. *Znamení zrodu: České obrození jako kulturní typ*. Nové, rozšířené vydání. Prague: H & H, 1995.

Malý, Jakub. *Naše znovuzrození: Přehled národního života českého za posledního půlstoletí*. Politická bibliotéka česká, díl 1. Prague: J. Otto, 1880.

——. *Výbor drobných spisů Jakuba Malého*. Vol. 2. Prague: Nákladem kněhkupectví: I. L. Kober, 1876.

Mann, Robert. *Lances Sing: A Study of the Igor Tale*. Columbus, OH: Slavica Publishers, 1990.

Manning, Christopher D., and Hinrich Schütze. *Foundations of Statistical Natural Language Processing*. 2nd printing, with corrections. Cambridge, MA: MIT Press, 2000.

Masaryk, T. G. "Poznámky k diskusi o RK a RZ." *Athenaeum* 4, no. 10 (July 15, 1887): 327–29.

——. *Z bojů o rukopisy: Texty z let 1886–1888*. Edited by Jiří Brabec. Vyd. 1. Vol. 19, *Spisy T. G. Masaryka*. Prague: Ústav T. G. Masaryka, 2004.

Mašek, Ignác B. "Popis korektur a rasur v Rukopise kralodvorském." *Listy filologické* 3 (1876): 176–201.

Meek, Donald E. "The Sublime Gael: The Impact of Macpherson's *Ossian* on Literary Creativity and Cultural Perception in Gaelic Scotland." In *The Reception of Ossian in Europe*, edited by Howard Gaskill, 40–66. London: Thoemmes, 2004.

Meinert, Joseph Georg. "Über die Königinhofer Handschrift." *Archiv für Geographie, Historie, Staats- und Kriegskunst* 10, no. 1 (1819): 1–4; no. 2, 7–8.

Menčík, Ferdinand, and Jaromír Hrubý. *Jan Kollár, pěvec slovanské vzájemnosti*. Matice lidu, roč. 27, čís. 6 (běžné čís. 162). Prague: Nákladem spolku pro vydávání laciných knih českých, 1893.

Mentzlová, Dana. "Oslavy 200. výročí nálezu Rukopisů královédvorského a zelenohorského | Rukopisy královédvorský a zelenohorský (RKZ)—Padělky nebo staročeské památky?" Accessed November 15, 2021. http://rkz.wz.cz/oslavy-200-vyroci-nalezu-rukopisu-kralovedvorskeho-a-zelenohorskeho/.

Mezník, Jaroslav. "Recenze." Review of *Rukopis Zelenohorský a Královédvorský: Vznik, styl a básnická hodnota staročeské orální poesie*, by Julius Enders. *Český časopis historický* 92, no. 2 (1994): 355–56.

——. "Rukopisy z hlediska historie." In *Rukopisy královédvorský a zelenohorský: Dnešní stav poznání*, edited by Mojmír Otruba, 149–78. Sbornik Národního muzea v Praze, řada C—Literární historie, sv. 13–14. Prague: Academia, 1969.

Moiseeva, G. N., and Miloslav Krbec. *Iozef Dobrovskii i Rossiia: Pamiatniki russkoi kul'tury XI–XVIII vekov v izuchenii cheshskogo slavista*. Leningrad: Nauka, Leningradskoe otdelenie, 1990.

Moore, Dafydd. "The Reception of *The Poems of Ossian* in England and Scotland." In *The Reception of Ossian in Europe*, edited by Howard Gaskill, 21–39. London: Thoemmes, 2004.

Mukařovský, Jan, ed. *Dějiny česke literatury*. 3 vols. Práce Československé akademie věd. Prague: Nakl. Československé akademie věd, 1959–61.

Mulholland, James. "James Macpherson's Ossian Poems, Oral Traditions, and the Invention of Voice." *Oral Tradition* 24, no. 2 (2009): 393–414.

Nabokov, Vladimir, trans. *The Song of Igor's Campaign: An Epic of the Twelfth Century*. New York: Vintage Books, 1960.

Nebeský, Václav. "Kralodvorský Rukopis." *Časopis českého musea* 26, no. 3 (1852): 127–74; no. 4, 129–68.

Nejedlý, Zdeněk. *Bedřich Smetana*. 2nd ed. 7 vols. Sebrané spisy Zdeňka Nejedlého. Prague: Orbis, 1950–54.

Nekula, Marek. "Constructing Slavic Prague: The 'Green Mountain Manuscript' and Public Space in Discourse." *Bohemia* 52, no. 1 (2012): 22–36.

——. *Smrt a zmrtvýchvstání národa: Sen o Slavíně v české literatuře a kultuře*. Prague: Univerzita Karlova v Praze, nakladatelství Karolinum, 2017.

Nesměrák, Karel, Dana Mentzlová, Jiří Urban, and Jakub Žytek. *RKZ dodnes nepoznané*. Prague: Česká společnost rukopisná, 2017.

Neubauer, John. "Introduction: Folklore and National Awakening." In *The Making and Remaking of Literary Institutions*, 269–85. Vol. 3 of *History of the Literary Cultures of East-Central Europe, Junctures and Disjunctures in the 19th and 20th Centuries*, edited by Marcel Cornis-Pope and John Neubauer. Philadelphia: John Benjamins, 2007.

Nikolayev, Dmitry. "A New Algorithm for Extracting Formulas from Poetic Texts and the Formulaic Density of Russian Bylinas." *Oral Tradition* 30, no. 1 (2016): 111–36.

Novák, Arne. *Josef Dobrovský*. Zlatoroh, sbírka illustrovaných monografií, sv. 53. Prague: Nákl. spolku výtvarných umělců Mánes, 1928.

Novák, Miroslav, and Dalibor Dobiáš. "Chemické a mikroskopické zkoumání rukopisu královédvorského v letech 1886–1889 a jeho reflexe tehdejší českou společností." In *Rukopisy královédvorský a zelenohorský v kultuře a umění*, edited by Dalibor Dobiáš, 1:259–81. Prague: Academia, 2019.

Ossian. *The Poems of Ossian*. Translated by James Macpherson. Leipzig: Bernhard Tauchnitz, 1847.

Otáhal, Milan. "The Manuscript Controversy in the Czech National Revival." *Cross Currents* 5 (1986): 247–77.

Otruba, Mojmír. "Mýtus a ritus: Pokus o sémantickou interpretaci obran pravosti RKZ." *Česká literatura* 18, no. 3–4 (1970): 213–77.

——. "Poezie, mýtus a hodnota (Konkretizace a estetické hodnocení Rukopisu královédvorského)." *Česká literatura* 16, no. 4 (1968): 357–92.

——. "Pravé kontra nepravé rukopisy—a co dál." *Literární noviny* 3, no. 33 (1992): 4.

——. "Rukopisy královédvorský a zelenohorský." In *Lexikon české literatury: Osobnosti, díla, instituce*, edited by Vladimír Forst, Jiří Opelík, and Luboš Merhaut. 3:1329–37. Prague: Academia, 2000.

——, ed. *Rukopisy královédvorský a zelenohorský: Dnešní stav poznání*. Sbornik Národního muzea v Praze, řada C—Literární historie, sv. 13–14. Prague: Academia, 1969.

Otruba, Mojmír, and Marie Řepková. "Literárněvědná kritika RKZ." In *Rukopisy královédvorský a zelenohorský: Dnešní stav poznání*, edited by Mojmír Otruba, 83–146. Sbornik Národního muzea v Praze, řada C—Literární historie, sv. 13–14. Prague: Academia, 1969.

Palacký, František. "An- und aussichten der böhmischen Sprache und Literatur vor 50 Jahren." In *Gedenkblätter: Auswahl von Denkschriften, Aufsätzen und Briefen aus den letzten fünfzig Jahren*, 19–47. Prague: Verlag von F. Tempsky, 1874.

——. *Františka Palackého: Korrespondence a zápisky*. 2 vols. Sbírka pramenův ku poznání literárního života v Čechách, na Moravě a v Slezsku. Skupina 2. Prague: Nakl. České akademie Císaře Františka Josefa pro vědy, slovesnost a umění, 1898.

Palkovič, Jiří. "Libušin soud." *Tatranka* 1, no. 1 (1832): 48–69.

Petrbok, Václav. "'Tohle bláznivé studium jednoho zfalšovaného dokumentu': Rukopisy a čitanky středných škol v Čechách v letech 1820–1918." In *Rukopisy královédvorský a zelenohorský v kultuře a umění*, edited by Dalibor Dobiáš, 1:183–238. Prague: Academia, 2019.

Pichl, Josef Bojislav. *Vlastenecké vzpomínky*. Pamětí, knihovna literárních vzpomínek a korespondence, vol. 3. Prague: F. Borový, 1936.

Píša, Petr. "Druhá část Rukopisu královédvorského a její nálezce Antonín Pfleger Kopidlanský." In *Historické fi kce a mystifi kace v české kultuře 19. století: Sborník příspěvků z 33. ročníku symposia k problematice 19. století, Plzeň, 21. února 2013*, edited by Martin Hrdina and Kateřina Piorecká, 70–78. Prague: Academia, 2014.

Procházka, Martin. "Obrozený Ossian: Macphersonův model a produkce dějinnosti v české romantické kultuře." *Česká literatura* 41, no. 1 (1993): 25–47.

——. "Romantic Revivals: Cultural Translations, Universalism, and Nationalism." In *Cultural Learning, Language Learning: Selected Papers from the Second British Studies Conference, Prague 18–20 October 1996*, edited by Susan Bassnett and Martin Procházka, 75–90. Prague: British Council, 1997.

Procházka, Vladimír. "Rukopisy a právní historie." In *Rukopisy královédvorský a zelenohorský: Dnešní stav poznání*, edited by Mojmír Otruba, 179–95. Sbornik Národního muzea v Praze, řada C—Literární historie, sv. 13–14. Prague: Academia, 1969.

Rambelli, Paolo. "Pseudotranslation." In *Routledge Encyclopedia of Translation Studies*, edited by Mona Baker and Gabriela Saldanha, 208–11. New York: Routledge, 2008.

Rayfield, Donald. "Forgiving Forgery." *Modern Language Review* 107, no. 4 (October 2012): xxiv–xli.

Reittererová, Vlasta. "Zhudebnění lyrických textů Rukopisu královédvorského." In *Rukopisy královédvorský a zelenohorský v kultuře a umění*, edited by Dalibor Dobiáš, 2:875–931. Prague: Academia, 2019.

Reynolds, Susan Helen. "A Scandal in Bohemia: Herder, Goethe, Masaryk, and the 'War of the Manuscripts.'" *Publications of the English Goethe Society* 72 (2002): 53–67.

Robinson, Douglas. "Pseudotranslation." In *Routledge Encyclopedia of Translation Studies*, edited by Mona Baker and Kirsten Malmkjaer, 183–85. New York: Routledge, 1998.

Roubík, Fr. "Účast policie v útoku na Rukopisy roku 1858." In *Od pravěku k dnešku: Sborník prací z dějin československých, k šedesátým narozeninám Josefa Pekaře*, 2:435–49. Prague: Historický klub, 1930.

Russett, Margaret. *Fictions and Fakes: Forging Romantic Authenticity, 1760–1845*. Cambridge Studies in Romanticism. Cambridge: Cambridge University Press, 2006.

Ruthven, K. K. *Faking Literature*. Cambridge: Cambridge University Press, 2001.

Rybička, Antonín. *Přední křisitelé národa českého: Boje a usilování o právo jazyka českého začátkem přítomného století*. 2 vols. Prague: Tiskem a nákl. knihtiskárny F. Šimáčka, 1883.

Šabić, Marijan. "Chorvatská recepce Rukopisů královédvorského a zelenohorského." In *Rukopisy královédvorský a zelenohorský v kultuře a umění*, edited by Dalibor Dobiáš, 2:1319–33. Prague: Academia, 2019.

Schein, Seth L. *The Mortal Hero: An Introduction to Homer's Iliad*. Berkeley: University of California Press, 1984.

Schleiermacher, Friedrich. "On the Different Methods of Translating." In *The Translation Studies Reader*, edited by Lawrence Venuti, 43–63. 3rd ed. New York: Routledge, 2012.

Servant, Catherine. "Rukopisy královédvorský a zelenohorský jako faktum a historická fikce: Návraty k Rukopisům v české literatuře druhé poloviny 20. a počátku 21. století." In *Rukopisy královédvorský a zelenohorský v kultuře a umění*, edited by Dalibor Dobiáš, 1:777–822. Prague: Academia, 2019.

Seykora, Oldřich V. *Na obranu Rukopisu královédvorského: České inteligenci na uváženou podává*. Prague: Cyrilo-Metodějská tiskárna a nakladatelství, 1893.

"Seznam prací PhDr. Julia Enderse." Česká společnost rukopisná. Accessed September 6, 2019. http://rukopisy-rkz.cz/rkz/urban/r/enders/soupis2.htm.

Šima, Karel. "Festivní kultura spojená s Rukopisy: Rukopis královédvorský mezi dynamikou měšťanské společnosti a kultura romantického nacionalismu." In *Rukopisy královédvorský a zelenohorský v kultuře a umění*, edited by Dalibor Dobiáš, 1:91–117. Prague: Academia, 2019.

Slatkin, Laura M. "Composition by Theme and the *Mētis* of the *Odyssey*." In *Reading the Odyssey: Selected Interpretive Essays*, edited by Seth L. Schein, 223–37. Princeton, NJ: Princeton University Press, 1996.

Smolík, Josef. "Zlaté mince s domnělým opisem Pegnaze." *Rozpravy České akademie věd a umění*, tř. 3, č. 35 (1906): 3–20.

Speidel, Michael. "Berserks: A History of Indo-European 'Mad Warriors.'" *Journal of World History* 13, no. 2 (2002): 253–90.

Sršeň, Lubomír. "Příspěvky k poznání osobnosti Václava Hanky." *Sborník Národního muzea*, řada A—Historie, 63, no. 1–3 (2009): 1–168.

Stafford, Fiona J. "Introduction: The Ossianic Poems of James Macpherson." In *The Poems of Ossian and Related Works*, by James Macpherson, v–xxi. Edited by Howard Gaskill. Edinburgh: Edinburgh University Press, 1996.

——. *The Sublime Savage: A Study of James Macpherson and the Poems of Ossian*. Edinburgh: Edinburgh University Press, 1988.

Stafford, Fiona J., and Howard Gaskill. *From Gaelic to Romantic: Ossianic Translations*. Textxet: Studies in Comparative Literature, vol. 15. Amsterdam: Rodopi, 1998.

Stewart, Susan. *Crimes of Writing: Problems in the Containment of Representation*. New York: Oxford University Press, 1991.

Stromberg, Peter G. "Ideological Language in the Transformation of Identity." *American Anthropologist* 92 (1990): 42–56.

Šusta, Josef. *Léta dětství a jinošství: Vzpomínky I*. Prague: Melantrich, 1947.

Svoboda, Václav Alois. "Libuše als Gesetzgeberin." In *Literární a prozodická bohemika*, edited by Miroslav Heřman, 152–65. Spisy a projevy Josefa Dobrovského. Prague: Academia, 1974.

Tahir Gürçağlar, Şehnaz. "Pseudotranslation on the Margin of Fact and Fiction." In *A Companion to Translation Studies*, edited by Sandra Bermann and Catherine Porter, 516–27. Chichester, West Sussex: Wiley-Blackwell, 2014.

Taylor, Andrew. *Textual Situations: Three Medieval Manuscripts and Their Readers*. Material Texts. Philadelphia: University of Pennsylvania Press, 2002.

Titz, Karel. "Studie o RK." *Listy filologické* 62, no. 2–3 (1935): 121–29.

Tkachenko, Ivan. *P. O. Kulish: Krytyko-biohrafichnyi narys*. Krytyka i teoriia literatury. Kharkiv: Knyhospilka, 1927.

Toremans, Tom, and Beatrijs Vanacker. "Introduction: The Emerging Field of Pseudotranslation." *Canadian Review of Comparative Literature / Revue Canadienne de Littérature Comparée* 44, no. 4 (December 2017): 629–36.

Toury, Gideon. *Descriptive Translation Studies and Beyond*. Benjamins Translation Library, vol. 4. Amsterdam: John Benjamins, 1995.

Tureček, Dalibor. "Časopis 'Deutsches Museum' Friedricha Schlegela a česká obrozenská literatura." In *Mezi texty a metodami: Národní a univerzální v české literatuře 19. století*, edited by Dalibor Tureček and Zuzana Urválková, 123–41. Olomouc: Perliplum, 2006.

——. "Hankova verze jihoslovanské hrdinské epiky." *Bohemica litteraria* 18, no. 1 (2015): 40–55.

Urban, Josef [Miloš Urban]. *Poslední tečka za Rukopisy (Nová literatura faktu)*. Prague: Argo, 1998.

Vašek, Antonín. *Filologický důkaz, že Rukopis Kralodvorský a Zelenohorský, též zlomek Evangelia sv. Jana jsou podvržená díla Vácslava Hanky*. Brno: Nákladem spisovatelovým, 1879.

Venuti, Lawrence. "1990s." In *The Translation Studies Reader*, edited by Lawrence Venuti, 3rd ed., 271–80. New York: Routledge, 2012.

——. *The Scandals of Translation: Towards an Ethics of Difference*. London: Routledge, 1998.

Vikis-Freibergs, Vaira, and Imants Freibergs. "Formulaic Analysis of the Computer-Accessible Corpus of Latvian Sun-Songs." *Computers and the Humanities* 12 (1978): 329–39.

Víták, Antonín Konst. *Dějiny kralovského věnného města Dvora Králové nad Labem: K oslavě padesátileté památky nalezení rukopisu Kralodvorskěho*. Prague: Tisk. Dra. F. Skrejšovského, 1867. http://catalog.hathitrust.org/api/volumes/oclc/19945705.html.

Vlček, Jaroslav. *Dějiny české literatury*. Dějiny literatur. Prague: Státní nakl. krásné literatury, hudby a umění, 1960.

Vodička, Felix. *Počátky krásné prózy novočeské: Příspěvek k literárním dějinám doby Jungmannovy*. Prague: Melantrich, 1948.

Vojtěch, Viktorin, and Václav Flajšhans, eds. *Rukopisy královédvorský a zelenohorský*. Prague: Česká grafická unie, 1930.

Weissbort, Daniel, and Ástráður Eysteinsson, eds. *Translation—Theory and Practice: A Historical Reader*. Oxford: Oxford University Press, 2006.

Wimsatt, William K., and Monroe C. Beardsley. *The Verbal Icon: Studies in the Meaning of Poetry*. Lexington: University of Kentucky Press, 1989.

Zahra, Tara. "Imagined Noncommunities: National Indifference as a Category of Analysis." *Slavic Review* 69, no. 1 (2010): 93–119.

Zalizniak, A. A. *"Slovo o polku Igoreve": Vzgliad lingvista*. Studia philologica, malaia seriia. Moscow: Iazyki slavianskoi kul'tury, 2004.

Index

Printed in the USA
CPSIA information can be obtained
at www.ICGtesting.com
LVHW052024281023
762307LV00025B/59/J

9 781501 771934